BLACK & DECKER®
OUTDOOR HOME

Vegetable
Gardening

CREATIVE
PUBLISHING
international

Minnetonka, Minnesota

Vegetable Gardening

Your Ultimate Guide

by

Robert J. Dolezal

VEGETABLE GARDENING

Concept: Robert J. Dolezal
Encyclopedia Concept: Barbara K. Dolezal
Managing Editor: Louise Damberg
Photography Editor: John M. Rickard
Designer: Paula Schlosser
Copy Editor: Patricia Connell
Layout Artists: Rik Boyd, Andrea Reider
Photoshop Artists: Hothouse Digital, Christie Santos
Horticulturists: Martha Conaway Claassen, Carrie Heinley,
    Peggy Henry
Photo Stylists: Joyce M. Almstad, Carrie Heinley, Peggy Henry
Research: Shelley Ring Diamond

Copyright© 2000
Creative Publishing international, Inc.
5900 Green Oak Drive
Minnetonka, MN 55343
1-800-328-3895
Printed in U.S.A. by World Color Press
10 9 8 7 6 5 4 3 2 1

President/CEO: David D. Murphy
Vice President/Editorial: Patricia K. Jacobsen
Vice President/Retail Sales & Marketing: Richard M. Miller

Home Improvement/*Gardening*
Executive Editor: Bryan Trandem
Editorial Director: Jerri Farris
Creative Director: Tim Himsel

Created by: Dolezal & Associates,
in partnership with Creative Publishing international, Inc.,
in cooperation with Black & Decker.
● BLACK&DECKER is a trademark of the Black & Decker
Corporation and is used under license.

Library of Congress
Cataloging-in-Publication Data

(Information on file)

ISBN 0–86573–441–0 (hardcover)

PRINCIPAL PHOTOGRAPHER:

John Rickard: Cover, pgs. viii *(bot.)*, 7, 9 *(bot. & top)*, 10, 14, 26–28 *(bot. L.)*, 30–31 *(bot.)*, 32–35, 42, 44 *(R.)*, 45–48, 50 *(mid.)*, 54–58 *(bot.)*, 59–61, 66 *(top)*, 73–74 *(top)*, 77, 79, 85, 87 *(top)*, 89 *(bot.)*, 91–93, 95 *(bot.)*, 96 *(top)*, 98, 100 *(bot.)*, 103 *(L.)*, 105 *(top)*, 108 *(mid.)*, 110 *(mid.)*, 114–115 *(top)*, 116–117 *(top)*, 118, 125, 127 *(bot.)*, 129, 130 *(top)*, 131 *(bot.)*, 132 *(top)*, 133 *(R.)*, 137 *(top & mid.)*, 140, 143 *(steps 4 & 5)*, 146, 148–149, 151–153, 155–157, 165–167 *(top)*, 170 *(step1, 2 & 3)*, 171, 173–175, 178 *(top & bot. L.)*, 179, 181–182, 184–185, 187, 190–191 *bot.*, 194–196, 198, 201 *(step 5)*, 204, 208 *(bot.)*, 210, 212–213 *(top)*, 215–216 *(top & mid.)*, 217 *(top)*, 218, 221, 223 *(bot.)*, 225 *(bot.)*, 228–230 *(step4)*, 231–232, 234, 240 *(bot.)*, 242, 244 *(bot.)*, 245. *(top & R.)*, 246, 248 *(bot. L. & R.)*, 250 *(bot.)*, 251, 254 *(bot.)*, 255 *(top & bot.)*, 257 *(top L. & top R.)*, 259–260, 262–263 *(top)*, 269 *(top)*, 274 *(bot.)*, 278 *(bot.)*, 281–282 *(top)*, 283–284 *(top)*, 285 *(top)*, 286 *(bot.)*, 291 *(top)*, 293, 298–300 *(top)*, 303 *(mid.)*, 308–311, 314–315 *(bot.)*, 316, 319–325, 328–329 *(top)*, 331, –333, 338, 340–341, 343, 346 *(top)*, 348, 351, 355, 357–359, 362–363, 365, 369, 370–371, 373–374, 378 *(top)*, 335, 382, 384–386, 388–390, 392–394, 398–399, & 401–404.

OTHER PHOTOGRAPHY:

Tim Butler: pgs. xvi, 3–4, 11, 38, 44 *(L.)*, 50 *(top, L., & bot.)*, 51, 62, 65, 70, 83 *(bot.)*, 89 *(top)*, 94–95 *(top)*, 102, 112–113, 121, 123, 138, 188, 205, 216 *(bot.)*, 222–223 *(top & mid.)*, 225 *(top & mid.)*, 227, 230 *(steps 1, 2 & 3)*, 239 *(mid.)*, 252, 255 *(mid.)*, 258 *(top)*, 265, 268 *(top)*, 282 *(bot.)*, & 360.
Kyle Chesser: pgs. viii *(top, 3rd & 4th from top)*, ix *(top)*. 2, 8 *(bot.)*, 20, 25, 43, 47 *(top)*, 49, 52–53, 58 *(mid.)*, 63, 65 *(mid.)*, 66 *(bot.)*, 74 *(bot.)*, 75, 84, 87 *(bot.)*, 96 *(bot.)*, 101, 103 *(R.)*, 106, 110 *(bot.)*, 119, 127 *(top)*, 132 *(bot.)*, 133 *(L.)*, 135–137 *(bot.)*, 150–151 *(bot.)*, 154, 164, 170 *(top)*, 172, 186 *(bot.)*, 191 *(top & mid.)*, 193, 199, 206, 207, 213 *(bot.)*, 220, 224, 233, 240 *(mid.)*, 245 *(bot. L.)*, 248 *(top & mid.)*, 254 *(top)*, 256–257 *(bot.)*, 285 *(bot.)*, 290–291 *(bot.)*, 292, 294 *(top)* 296–297, 301–303 *(bot.)*, 304, 305, & 395–396.
Alan Copeland: pg. 272.
Corbis: *Kevin Fleming:* 68, *Raymond Gehman:* 78, *Gary Carter:* 264, *Patrick Johns:* 313 *(top)*, *Richard Hamilton Smith:* 315, *Lee Snider:* 342, *Peter Johnson:* 356, *Hal Horwitz:* 366 *(top)*, *Joel W. Rogers:* 366 *(bot.)*, *Maurice Nimmo:* 367, & *Hubert Stadler:* 372.
Creative Publishing international: pgs. 128, 142, 186 *(top)*, 197, 209, 275, & 279.
Doug Dealey: pgs. viii *(2nd from top)*, 6, 8 *(top)*, 41, 58 *(top)*, 108 *(top)*, 120, 217 *(bot.)*, 277, 284 *(bot.)*, & 287.
Robert Dolezal: pg. 64 *(top)*.
Reed Estabrook: pgs. x, & 266.
David Goldberg: pgs. 109, 115 *(bot.)*, 130 *(bot.)*, & 131 *(top)*.
Saxon Holt: pgs. vii, 12–13, 16, 22–24, 31 *(top)*, 88, 117 *(bot.)*, 161, 219, 274 *(top)*, 317, 329 *(bot.)*, 334, 375, & 378 *(bot.)*.
Horticultural Photography: pgs. 318 & 330.
ImagePoint: pgs. viii *(2nd from top, 2nd from bot. & bot.)*, ix *(2nd top)* 5, 18–19, 28 *(bot. R.)*, 29, 40, 71, 83 *(top)*, 90 *(bot.)*, 100 *(top)*, 105 *(bot.)*, 111, 122, 139, 141, 143 *(steps1, 2 & 3)*, 144, 159–160, 178 *(mid. & bot. R.)*, 180, 183, 192, 200 *(steps 2, 3 & 4)*, 201 *(step 6)*, 202–203, 211, 214, 226, 241, 243, 247, 249, 253, 258 *(bot.)*, 263 *(bot. L. & bot. R.)*, 269 *(mid. & bot.)*, 276, 278 *(top)*, 286 *(top)*, 288–289, 291 *(mid. L., mid. R. & bot. R.)*, 294 *(bot.)*, 295, 300 *(bot.)*, 336, & 349.
Jonathan Nutt–gardenIMAGE: pg. 36.
Pam Pierce: pgs. 236, 238, 239 *(bot.)*, 244 *(top)*, 250 *(top)*, 267, 268 *(bot.)*, 270, 312, 345, 350 & 353.
PhotoDisc Image Stock: pgs. ix *(3rd from top)*, 80, 208 *(top)*, 261, & 280.
Charles Slay: pgs. 21, 167 *(bot.)*, 326–327, 337, 346 *(bot.)*, & 364.

Illustration:

HILDEBRAND DESIGN: pgs. 72, 76, 82, 86, 97, 134, 158, 210, 408–409

The editors acknowedge with gratitude the following for their assistance while preparing this book: Alden Lane Nursery of Livermore California, and Wedekind's Garden Center, Larry Haase, and Ed Zago of Sonoma, California.

Vegetable Gardening
Your Ultimate Guide

CONTENTS

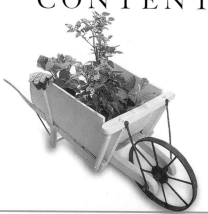

1 Great Vegetable Gardens

Gardens of Grace and Beauty

Page 1

Tour beautiful vegetable gardens, including raised beds, row crops, terraced sites, small space plots, and container gardens—Gardens to Share pg. 10

2 Introduction to Vegetables

The Lure of Gardens and Soil

Page 17

A pastime shared by young and old alike—The Lure of the Soil pg. 20 • A Year in the Garden pg. 25 • A Garden Calendar pg. 30

3 Gardening Basics

Vegetable Gardening Essentials

Page 39

A guide to the basics— Choosing a Garden Site pg. 42 • Great Garden Soil pg. 44 • Soil Preparation and Amendments pg. 49 • Options for Planting pg. 53 • Garden Care Basics pg. 56 • Watering pg. 59 • Other Care Pg. 65

4 Climate & Gardens

Selecting Garden Sites

Page 69

Region and climate—Vegetables and Plant Hardiness pg. 71 • Understanding Climates pg. 75 • Precipitation and Humidity pg. 84 • Effects of Temperature pg. 85 • Microclimate and Regional Differences pg. 88 • Site Location pg. 97

5 Planning Plantings

Preparing to Grow Vegetables

Page 99

Planning—Planning for Garden Care pg. 101 • How Large a Garden pg. 103 • Harvest Timing pg. 108 • Succession and Companion Planting pg. 114 • Choosing a Beautiful Garden pg. 120 • Beyond Style to Space Planning pg. 125 • Varietal Selection pg. 133 • Preparing Soil for Planting pg. 139

6 Planting Your Garden

Planting Seeds or Seedlings

Page 147

Step-by-step—Seeds or Transplants pg. 149 • Planting Weather pg. 159 • A Head Start on the Season pg. 157 • Planting Seeds pg. 166 • Selecting Transplants pg. 173 • Problems with New Plantings pg. 184

7 Caring for a Garden

Tending to Your Vegetables

Page 189

How to care for vegetables—Watering pg. 192 • Fertilizing Vegetables pg. 204 • Cultivating Vegetables pg. 216 • Mulching pg. 220 • Pruning pg. 224 • Staking and Supporting pg. 229

8 Pests & Diseases

Keeping Gardens Healthy

Page 237

Protecting from pests and disease—How Insect Pests Damage Vegetables pg. 239 • Other Significant Pests pg. 252 • The Organic Garden pg. 264 • Beneficial Plants pg. 266 • Plant Diseases pg. 267

9 Harvesting & Preserving

Fresh from the Garden

Page 273

When and how to reap—Harvest pg. 275 • Vegetable Storage pg. 289 • Vegetable Preserving pg. 293

A Vegetable Encyclopedia

Page 307

A guide to most common garden vegetables, with detailed information for planting, care, harvesting and use.

Appendix

Page 407

Useful information, including plant hardiness zones around the world, resources and supplies, plus a glossary of gardening terms and a complete index.

About This Book

Welcome to the involving and satisfying world of home vegetable gardening. It's a world of beauty, involvement, and joy.

Within the pages of this book, a hobby enjoyed by millions around the world will come alive for you—in colorful pictures and descriptive text—as never before.

A few words are in order to help you get the most out of this book. Unlike a novel, *Vegetable Gardening: Your Ultimate Guide* doesn't require a cover-to-cover reading. You may delve into any topic with ease, finding it quickly either in the table of contents or in the complete index at the back of the book. When you arrive at a subject of interest, you'll find a narrative text discussion that will be accompanied by revealing photographs and illustrations. Depending on the topic, it also may feature step-by-step instructions, a secondary discussion, or one or more references to other areas of the book—use them to help round out your knowledge.

If you are a newcomer to vegetable gardening, you may want to read it from front to back—it is arranged in logical order for your needs.

The challenge of providing practical information to gardeners in every climate area led us to include issues that may not apply to you, or to your specific region's needs. Nevertheless, it will give you an overview, an enthusiast's appreciation, and—who knows?—information that might be pertinent to you someday.

For ease of use, no matter where you live, we also included English and metric conversions of all dimensions and weights within the text itself.

We have anticipated that readers will have a variety of skill levels, from amateur to professional horticulturist. Where specific gardening terms are used, we explain them right there on the page, so there is no need to flip back and forth.

A glossary of tools used in the garden, ranging from the common to the more specialized, may be found at the back of the book. There, you also will find an entire encyclopedia of the vegetables themselves, with photographs and complete descriptions of their growth habits and needs, from planting to storage.

Finally, we recognize that some of the best gardening neighbors are over the "electronic" fence, so we have included online research sources as well as more traditional sources.

Last, but certainly not least, we have endeavored to make this book not only a complete, accurate, and easy-to-use reference, but to make it a celebration of this most joyous pastime. We have fashioned it for your use—whether that be gracing your coffee table or a shelf in your garden shed.

ABOUT THE AUTHOR. Robert J. Dolezal is an avid home gardener, writer, photographer, and garden publisher. He brings a broad spectrum of knowledge about vegetable gardening to this work, and has exhaustively researched the forefront of new technological breakthroughs as it affects the home garden.

Mr. Dolezal has been an active participant in the book and magazine publishing profession for over 27 years. His writings and photographs have graced many national and regional magazines, as well as seven books. He lives with his wife and business partner, Barbara, in Livermore, California, USA.

No comprehensive work of this size and scope would be possible without the contribution of many other individuals. All factual content was intensely scrutinized by professional horticulturists, botanists, and biologists from many regions. Editors and other technical personnel reviewed all of the text and photographs to select the very best words and images.

Where no photographs existed to reveal the subject being discussed, professional photographers were assigned to capture them. Horticulturists and stylists assured that proper techniques were demonstrated in all cases, and special care was taken to show every process from the viewpoint of one actually performing the work.

Where photography was unable to show a concept, illustration was commissioned. The result is a unique, visual blending of words, photographs, and illustrations that make the book both lovely and meaningful.

To these contributors—and to many more who made the book possible—our thanks.

It is the goal of every writer and publisher, at minimum, to satisfy the needs and desires of every reader. It was our further objective to excite and intrigue the reader by showing vegetable gardening in its truest light—the best examples, the best thoughts. These pages represent the attainment of our goals.

Vegetable gardening is more than a pastime, it is an avocation. This book is dedicated to those gardeners with a deep love of the land, an abiding respect for nature, and the sense of fulfillment when they nurture, harvest, and share what they have grown.

Vegetable Gardening

Gardens of Grace and Beauty
Great Vegetable Gardens

THEY CATCH THE EYE, great vegetable gardens. Sometimes, with a glance over a neighbor's fence, you see a sideyard filled with tall rows of corn and beans. You're driving down the street and suddenly, around a corner, is a frontyard border filled with mounds of peppers and squash. You check into a hotel, pull open the curtains, and look down to see containers filled with tomatoes and lettuce on a rooftop.

Everywhere across the country there are vegetable gardens. For decades, gardening has ranked at the top of leisure-time activities. Literally millions of us garden.

Statistics do not tell the entire tale, however. After all, there are gardens, and then there are *gardens*. Whether a collection of pots on a patio or deck, an acre planted in neat rows with vegetables, or a precisely planned layout of raised beds and pathways, a well-tended garden reflects the owner's care and pride of craft.

Growing one's own vegetables is a quiet, peaceful pastime. It requires little in the way of expensive equipment, but it does demand attention and time. From the earth, plants grow to yield succulent fruits and fresh-tasting produce. Their flavor and texture remind us that home grown is always better than store bought; their beauty gives us a satisfaction beyond nutrition.

The desire to garden seems born within us. The ways in which each of us responds to the calling is a celebration both of our hobby and our vision. Ever more, these places of refuge and quiet peace are a reflection of our personalities and interests. We explain ourselves by the planting and nurturing of crops.

Let's gain inspiration from some great gardens.

Any space can be right for a vegetable garden. While an ideal garden has special requirements—full sun, fertile soil, and ample space—hundreds of gardens perform adequately despite the lack of one or more desirable traits. For example, container gardeners overcome their site limitations by moving their pots with the sun. Those with hilly locations terrace level beds for planting. Others with hard and rocky soil loosen their plots with compost and amendments that add nutrients and improve drainage.

In the coming pages, we'll share with you all of the ways to prepare a garden. For now, let's load up the barrow with young plants, don the gardening gloves, and pick up the trowel. Here are some great gardens to get the inspiration going.

TERRACED GARDENS. Where there are hillsides, terraces and raised-bed planters can create fertile planting spots. Such gardens add to the land's growing area by leveling the hills with a series of steps walled on the down slope, each filled with earth.

The walls hold the soil in place, preventing erosion during periods of rain. They also allow the gardener to fill the terraces with rich, fertile soil perfectly suited to each vegetable being planted. In addition to their efficiency, such gardens often are among the most attractive and interesting of vegetable gardens as well.

If you live in a home that is situated against a hill, you have the opportunity to create a terraced garden. While building attractive and sturdy walls requires a substantial investment in time and effort, your garden will pay you back with interest.

Row Gardens. These are the classic vegetable gardens. Where space permits, row gardens are the ideal. Crops planted in long lines from north to south take advantage of both morning and afternoon sun, each plant receiving its fair share. Space between rows permits easy access for tasks such as cultivation and irrigation. Row gardens are spacious, attractive, and neat.

To create a row garden, any sod or turf first must be cut and removed. Often, row gardens exist without formal boundaries, but the most attractive ones have borders made up of tidy stone, brick, timber, fencing, or flowers. A border is a practical consideration, too. By establishing a clear, well-defined edge, mowing or sowing of nearby areas becomes easier.

Row gardens have other practical advantages. Because a single crop is planted in each furrow, successions of crops can be planted over time to provide for a sustained harvest. It's easy to imagine such planning in use—think of corn plants of varying heights, young peas next to mature vines, and the like.

Irrigation is made simple as well. A trench beside each row provides an even flow of water to the base of every plant. Use of soaker hoses and special irrigation appliances is minimal. Watering needs also tend to be more consistent than they are with other layouts.

Disease problems are diminished in row gardens as well. The free circulation of air around the plants allows them to dry quickly in the morning sun after irrigation. This limits the potential for fungus and mildew.

Consider a row garden if your space permits and you like the idea of neat and orderly, usually rectangular-shaped layouts. If the area has been used as a garden in the

past, so much the better. If not, spend some time preparing it properly for planting: give it a good tilling, remove all rocks and debris, amend the soil, rake and level it, then plant between the row paths.

If your area is not very spacious, you can stagger your plantings within each row. By offsetting every other plant, you will double your yield over a single planting in a shorter row. Be sure to use vertical space as well by training vine and pod crops to grow up onto supports.

Row gardens likely are the type most of us think about when we contemplate vegetable gardens. They are like mini-farms, both in their appearance and in their reality.

A neat row garden will always gain favorable comment from passers-by, and it will please its owner, too.

SMALL-SPACE GARDENS. Whether by circumstance or choice, small-space gardens—container plantings and scaled-down beds—have become increasingly popular with gardeners across North America.

Many new homes have downscaled lots—sometimes little space at all—so those who would garden in them must adjust their expectations. Even homes with generous land may be owned by gardeners with limited time.

Small space, however, does not have to mean small yield. Because of so-called "French intensive" methods—spacing plantings closely together in soil-enriched beds—gardeners can produce larger harvests than normal from fewer plants.

Choose a small-space garden to complement your residence and your lifestyle. Planting a container herb garden is a good beginning point for those starting out.

Whether you dwell in a city and must garden on a balcony, your home does not permit a large-area garden, or you wish to taste juicy, red-ripe tomatoes picked from a container on your deck, small space gardens are an inviting alternative to commonplace landscape decoration.

RAISED-BED GARDENS. Building planter boxes may seem like an unnecessary exercise when your soil is right at hand, but a quick glance at the photograph above will reveal the special appeal such gardens hold.

A raised-bed garden allows the gardener to overcome problems with native soil by replacing the soil in limited areas; they "raise" the work area, limiting the need for bending and stooping, and they add visual interest and excitement to the landscape.

Planting in raised beds also increases the yield of the garden dramatically because soil conditions then are made ideal and the beds warm earlier in the spring than beds in the ground.

Such gardens were first developed in Europe, where the space for cultivation

always has been at a premium. French, Spanish, Belgian, and Italian gardeners—among others—soon found that planting in such beds reduced the amount of labor required and increased the yield from any given area.

From Europe, raised bed cultivation spread to the entire world. It is positively regarded for its neat and orderly appearance as well as for the outstanding results it provides.

Gardeners who use container beds to grow vegetables can experiment with even more intensive gardening techniques such as microgardening. With such plantings, areas as small as 1 square foot (929 cm^2) are used to sow a few individual plants, usually requiring special care.

Use this technique to grow exotic vegetables or special varietals. When only a small space is used, the extra effort of employing mini-greenhouses, and specialty fertilizers and amendments, is not that labor intensive.

The secrets of raised-bed construction are revealed later in this book [see Constructing Raised Beds, pg. 143]. It's a way to make your garden distinctive and attractive while increasing your volume of produce.

Gardens to Share

The beauty of vegetable gardening is that it appeals to all generations, young and old. If it's true that spending more involved and personal time with children benefits both them and society as a whole, there are few better choices that a parent or other adult can make than to dig, plant seeds, water, hoe, and share thoughts with a child in the pursuit of growing vegetables.

Vegetable gardening is a hobby that everyone can enjoy. At its most strenuous, it provides a healthy workout; most of the time it is a more reflective activity. It is forgiving of physical infirmities and health limitations; it does not require brawn nor even adult-size hands.

It provides an opportunity for knowledge and appreciation of the land to be shared between generations. Ask many gardeners how they started and they will relate fond memories of their relationship with a favorite parent, grandparent, or other relative.

Part of the magic of gardening is seeing things grow, the rest is sharing it with family and friends. Vegetable gardening, at its core, is nurturing and caring—for plants and for others. It engenders a respect for the natural world and the creatures and plants that are a part of it. It allows the gardener to become a player in this creation.

Vegetable gardening is not only an adventure, it's a drama. With every season comes a new world, as plants poke through the soil as though pushed by an unseen hand, and the garden is populated by heroes and villains in the form of beneficial insects and their counterpart pests.

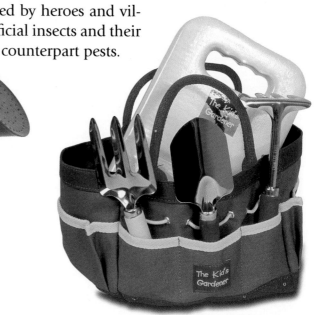

In the pages that follow, the world of gardening will come alive as you discover its heritage and appeal. You will learn how to choose a site for your garden, how to plan your plantings and choose your vegetables, how to plant and care for them, how to defend them from pests and disease, and how to harvest, store, and preserve them.

Included are step-by-step pictures and instructions for nearly every vegetable gardening task.

In the back of the book is a complete vegetable encyclopedia and a glossary of garden tools, plus information about gardening around the world and resources to help you find answers to any gardening questions.

Come and explore the world of vegetable gardening. As you will find, it's a special place, for special people, filled with beauty and great ideas.

The Lure of Gardens
Introducing Vegetables
and Soil

THERE IS SOMETHING SPECIAL about growing your own vegetables. Perhaps it's the lure of a bounty and flavor unmatched by store-bought produce. It may be a sense of competition, a search for the biggest and the best. It might be a simple desire to meet the challenges of planting, care, and harvest. Whatever your reason, as a pastime, hobby, or avocation, growing vegetables is a passion shared with many millions of gardeners. This fraternity of vegetable gardeners shares regard for honest toil, love of the land, the joy of feeling ripe produce in one's hand, and basking in admirers' praise.

Somewhere in our roots, our ancestors divided into two groups; today's vegetable gardeners are descended from those who were gatherers, not nomads and hunters. Our modern civilization stems from decisions made, first by ancient peoples and then by their descendants, to settle down, grow crops, and live in communities. Deep in our collective souls, then, rest the dreams of yesteryear's farmers.

Each year, as spring rolls around, we begin to feel the itch as the days lengthen and the sun warms the earth. We need to don boots and pick up a shovel, to clean up winter's debris and last year's leavings. We suddenly find ourselves on our knees, hands pressed into the rich, dark soil—feeling, testing, smelling. Our eyes seek out the first green shoots of asparagus. Our hands wield hoes and cultivators, removing weeds and lightening the earth.

We neaten up the cold frame, tidy the potting table, and gather our seed packages and transplant stock. In our hearts, we know that we are pushing the season, playing Russian roulette with a late frost, taking a chance. Nevertheless, we press on, taking the risk.

Using a hundred tricks gleaned from our experience, from the advice of friends, and from our reading, we coax new shoots from the ground. We protect tender plants with hot caps and deep mulch and warm the earth with landscape fabric. Another gardening year is under way.

In our mind's eye, we picture neat, orderly rows of head-high corn, bounteous hills of squash and pumpkin, plump-podded peas and beans, perfect heads of cabbage. We smell the just-ripe aroma of garden-grown tomatoes and feel the heft and texture of cucumbers as we place them into a harvest basket. We acknowledge the heartfelt "thank-yous" of our friends as we share our bounty. Then our eyes clear, we raise our elbows from our rake handle, and we return to the work at hand.

There is much to do: turn the soil, spread the compost, finish our planning, purchase our plants. Should the pole beans go here, or there? What can be done to warm that shady spot? Is this the year to install a drip system, pave a path, or raise a bed? We bend our back to our labors and, when day is done, realize how much we love the race as much as we do the finish line.

Vegetable gardening is a pursuit of love. Whether your garden is a windowsill pot or an acre of land, each is nurtured equally with the goal of bringing in a crop while respecting the secret time-honored rituals required to bring forth perfect produce. In these acts are created immutable bonds between the growing plants and the gardeners who tend them.

The Lure of the Soil

Question gardeners about their passion for their hobby and you will receive a multitude of answers. Some like the solitude and peace of the pastime. Others enjoy the community of those who share their hobby. Still others value the accomplishment. Words all invariably use are: "fulfilling," "contentment," "simplicity," "orderly," and "rewarding."

The appeal of growing one's own vegetables is difficult to quantify, measure, or explain. Many times an interest stems from seeds planted in childhood by parents or grandparents, but such is not always the case. There are those whose claim to gardening, it seems, bounded from nowhere—lacking a role model, they simply picked up a hoe or shovel one day and began to clear the earth for a new garden. Whatever the source of inspiration, vegetable gardening is an enduring hobby, one destined to maintain itself throughout a lifetime.

Whether we know it or not, it is the lure of the soil that we're describing—the idea that, through our own hand and effort, soil can be turned from earth into a harvest. Gardeners are drawn to bare ground by a powerful emotion rooted deep in the psyche. Where others see only soil, we picture growing plants filled with flowers and fruit.

Think about it: whenever you are interrupted in your garden, do your eyes tend to stray back to the partially completed planting? You respond, but your mind is elsewhere—among the peas, perhaps, or the radishes. Even though the whole day spans ahead, time seems to be at a premium, for there are many tasks looming.

We also are drawn to the garden because we know it will allow us to become a part of its endless cycle of renewal and growth—sharing in each new leaf, developing tendril, swelling blossom, and ripening fruit. Once engaged, we view each weed or pest as a personal affront, and we thrill at each victory and rescue. Our gardens are extensions of ourselves—each one unique.

Indeed, there are as many different vegetable gardens as gardeners—each a reflection of a personal vision of perfection. Some seek the big prize: the largest pumpkin, the grandest cabbage, the sweetest corn—concocting a special formula of soil and fertilizer, protecting plants from sun scald and hostile weather, supporting prize specimens with special net hammocks, or otherwise babying their gardens. Voracious scouring of all media usually attends this. Whether the objective is a ribbon in a county fair or the admiration of neighbors, the ultimate goal is pride in a job well done.

Other gardeners have a practical bent, wanting a larder full of fresh food, a freezer filled to overflowing, and a pantry loaded with preserves. Their gardens resemble either mini–truck farms or intensive gardens chockablock with stands of berries, legumes, and leafy greens. For them, vegetable gardening is a means to an end, they will tell you, while betraying their intensity and passion with every stroke of a hoe.

Still another group revels in beauty. Their gardens have tidy rows, supports, and beds; are weed free and dressed; and are filled with healthy, well-groomed plants, as well as such vegetable companions as flowers and ornamentals. Herbs may be intricately braided into Italianate geometric patterns, and touches of whimsy may be lent with statuary, sundials, or garden signs.

For others, the garden is a monument to heritage, allowing them to replicate the past and perhaps bond with ancestors. Use of antique tools, time-honored techniques, even plantings of heirloom vegetable varieties are hallmarks of those to whom the garden evokes memories of the past. Many times, such gardens reflect ethnic origins, recall specific kin, and continue traditions within the family.

It does not matter which type of personality you are, for it is the soil that, each spring, beckons each one of us back into the garden.

A Year in the Garden

Those whose lives are not bound to the soil seldom understand the depth of enjoyment attained by those who garden. They see the work but not the progress. They think about the problems, not the rewards. If they have dabbled at it a bit, the situation is made that much the worse. "Gardening is too much trouble," they tell themselves. "I would be better off going to a movie or taking my children to a soccer game."

At the other end of the scale are those who reap enjoyment from nearly every aspect of gardening. They relish times of anticipation. Their reading stands are filled in late winter with seed catalogs and gardening books. In season, they happily give hours to their pastime, clearing schedules of other matters. They plan vacations and family outings around harvests. They are involved in gardening.

These are the extremes, of course. While vegetable gardening requires time and commitment, it needn't overwhelm, nor be consuming. What makes up a year in the garden? Let's look and see.

PLANNING. Before a garden is planted, some research is needed—visiting nurseries and garden centers, talking with fellow gardeners, gathering ideas and materials—to estimate the care the garden will require, incorporate work-saving changes, and overcome problems experienced in prior seasons.

The results of such planning can be a mental exercise or be formalized on paper—a sketch of the garden layout; a notation on a calendar; a turned page in a catalog, magazine, or book; a shopping list; or all of these.

Proper planning reduces unnecessary work, eliminates false starts and rework, saves on costly materials, and, most important, it provides the best result for the effort expended.

Preparation. Preparing to plant may include honing tools, painting lattice, installing raised beds, building a compost bin, or any number of other tasks.

Most important is turning and raking the soil so it is ready to receive seeds and transplants, installing trellises and supports for climbing plants, and fertilizing and amending beds.

While generally a springtime activity, preparation often continues throughout the gardening season as new plantings and ideas are added.

PLANTING. When it comes right down to it, a surprisingly small amount of a vegetable gardener's time is spent planting. Out of months of garden activity, planting actually may take only a few days, yet just that brief time can ensure that young vegetables get off to a good start and avoid early problems from disease. Good planting practices mean that conditions are right—proper soil temperature for the type of plant, choice of the right location, and selection of plants ideally suited to the region.

Planting also means replanting throughout the season. As a vegetable matures and is harvested, space opens for new plantings of the same or other vegetables.

CARE. Most of the time in the garden is spent on nurturing, or attending to the health and well-being of plants: watering, fertilizing, pinching, pruning, cultivating, mulching, and protecting them from pests and diseases.

Many hours are spent just inspecting the plants and their surrounding soil with an eye to taking any corrective actions that may be necessary. Part of this time is spent fingering leaves to see if insects have visited, checking blossoms to make sure they are setting fruit, evaluating foliage color and general plant vigor, picking up handfuls of soil, and testing the ripeness of produce.

This is the time for reflection, correction, and adjustment. Is a planting too dense? Remove the weakest plants or transplant them to other areas of the garden. Does a vine need support? Build a structure for it to climb. Are some vegetables doing poorly? Consider new sites for future seasons while helping them survive. For many, this also is the best time, when the bond between gardener and plantings is formed.

HARVEST. From a few weeks after the garden is planted until late in the season is harvest time. Quick-maturing crops, such as radish and lettuce, are first out of the garden. Next are perennial vegetables, including asparagus, artichoke, and berries. Midseason brings harvests of corn, beans, peas, and summer squash, while autumn yields winter squash, pumpkin, root vegetables, and others that are long to mature.

Proper harvest requires a good observant eye and some understanding of how vegetables ripen. How do you know when a tomato has reached peak ripeness, for instance, or when corn is sweetest and juiciest? Just as important, how do you store and preserve vegetables as the bounty begins to overflow?

Beans and peas can be frozen or dried; cucumbers, carrots, asparagus, and cauliflower may be pickled, while

cabbage can be preserved in the form of sauerkraut. Processing, canning, freezing, and storing of vegetables for the upcoming cold winter months, when those fresh garden tastes are few, will extend the benefits and enjoyment of the home vegetable garden.

POSTSEASON CARE. When the first frost finally hits and there's a smell of rain or snow in the air, it's time for the garden to be cleared of dead foliage and for the soil to be prepared for the coming spring. Neaten the beds by removing all clutter, and add a layer of fresh manure. Layer mulch over perennial vegetable beds to protect them from the elements.

Finally, when the chores are done and the yard is ship-shape, it's time for repairing and thoroughly cleaning garden tools. Remove rust, sharpen blades, repair motors on tillers, and replace all worn or broken parts. Store the tools in a clean, dry place for the winter months.

Vegetable gardening has been compared aptly to boat ownership: there's always something that needs to be done. Fortunately, for true gardeners, there's joy in the doing. Rare is the gardener who feels stressed or depressed after spending the day in the sun and fresh air amidst growing plants.

A Garden Calendar

With millions of gardens and gardeners spread across the continents, it's difficult to generalize about the timing of activities. Those in short-season areas must compress their outdoor gardening efforts into a few short months and, depending on the severity of the winter, may need to start their plantings indoors. Conversely, those in near-tropical regions have the luxury of year-round gardening, sometimes with the benefit of two or more harvests. The order of tasks, however, is the same no matter where you live.

Later in this book, we'll talk about how to recognize some of the special situations that affect vegetable gardens [see Understanding Climates, pg. 75]. For now, let's assume that your garden is one of the many in which a cold winter is followed by a moderately long growing season. Here's how your calendar shapes up:

SPRING. After the last hard frost, followed by lengthening days of sunlight, the gardening season begins. As soon as the soil is workable, turn the manure, compost, and mulch you laid down the previous autumn, mixing them thoroughly into the soil. If you wish, add a bit of fresh compost before digging to boost the amount of available nitrogen and add organic matter to improve the soil's texture. Rake the beds, form mounds and hills as you require, and install plant supports. Repair pathways and edgings as needed.

Purchase seeds at your nursery or garden retailer and

get them started in a cold frame, in a greenhouse, or indoors. Even though the soil is workable and the weather warming, they will need several weeks' head start before conditions are right in the garden for transplanting.

Monitor the soil temperature closely, using the chart provided later in this book [see Soil Temperature for Planting, pg. 162]. Resist the urge to plant in too-cold soil or fungal disease may rot starchy seeds and kill the young seedlings.

Once the soil has warmed sufficiently, plant seedlings and seeds of cool-season vegetables. These are the quick-growing species of leafy greens, many root vegetables, some peas and beans, radishes, carrots, and the cole vegetables—cabbage and its relatives, cauliflower and broccoli. To guard against disease problems later on, choose resistant varieties. Limit pest problems by setting multiple plantings of single vegetables in several different garden locations. Mulch beds heavily with weed-free straw once their plantings have become established.

As hours of sunlight increase and the season progresses, the garden's soil soon will be warm enough to plant warm-season vegetable crops. These include corn, southern peas, drying beans, squash, pumpkin, tomato, and sweet potato. Because these plants need relatively high soil temperatures and substantial warmth throughout their long growing season, start them indoors from seeds or purchase trans-plant stock from your garden retailer if you live in a short-season area.

At about the same time you are planting warm-season vegetables, the first cuttings of young lettuce, radish, and green onions should be ready to harvest. They will be followed in short order by English peas, spinach, rhubarb, asparagus, and the early berries.

Throughout the entire growing season, provide adequate watering, inspect your garden on a daily basis, and fertilize monthly [see Fertilizing Vegetables, pg. 204].

SUMMER. Summer begins with the arrival of the solstice. This solar event marks the longest day of the year and the beginning of many frequent and continuous days of heat. The long daylight hours and heat combine to cause growth spurts in many vegetables, including corn, pumpkin, squash, sunflower, and melons. It is not unusual for foliage to extend an inch (25 mm) or more

a day during this growth period. Many leafy vegetables will begin to bolt at about this time, so replant such slow-bolting varieties for autumn harvests.

Heat also aids flower formation in fruiting vegetables and ensures that they set fruit. If you live in a very warm climate, protect from too-high temperatures or they may become stunted, lose their blossoms, or fail to set fruit. Mulch heavily around low-growing crops to prevent weed growth and to protect them from insect damage.

Stake or cage tomato plants, train pole bean vines up vertical supports, and support heavy fruit such as melon, pumpkin, and squash so they avoid direct contact with the soil. Protect crops from birds and small mammals by erecting net enclosures.

In early summer, harvest peas, beans, late berries, drying onions, garlic, and shallot. In midsummer, harvest peppers, corn, beets, carrots, summer squash, tomatoes, tomatillos, amaranth, parsnips, and salsify. In late summer, harvest peanuts, potatoes, peppers, summer melons, late corn, popcorn, sweet potatoes, drying beans, and southern peas.

Dry peas, beans, corn, and peanuts in a warm, protected location, then package and freeze, or store them in a cool, dry, dark spot.

While the most productive time of the year, summer also requires the most diligence. Throughout this season, water the garden regularly, which may mean more than once a day, and continue to fertilize monthly. Inspect for pest and disease conditions daily and treat at the first signs of damage, such as chewed leaves and stems or developing fungal infections on the undersides of leaves. Harvest all crops at the peak of ripeness and store appropriately.

AUTUMN. As the days grow shorter and the heat of summer passes, plant autumn-harvest crops, including rutabaga, turnip, kale, salsify, beets, and leafy green vegetables. Harvest pumpkin, winter squash, gourds, late potatoes, and winter melon. Tomatoes and cucumbers usually will provide a yield until their vines are killed by frost.

As plants die, remove and compost them so they don't foster disease and insect problems. Remove and store vertical stakes, cages, and trellises after the plants are uprooted.

Once hard frost has killed your annual plants, remove debris from their beds, fertilize the soil with manure or compost, and dig it in before the freeze hardens the soil, taking advantage of those last warm days. Mulch the surface of all areas that need protection from freezing temperatures, including those bearing perennials such as asparagus and cane berries.

As heavy rains or snow begin to fall, the garden has been prepared to rest for winter. Clean, sharpen, and, if necessary, paint and repair all garden equipment and tools. In cold-weather climates, replacing tools at this time of year can be a bargain.

There are many variations to this sequence, depending upon where you live [see Microclimates and Regional Differences, pg. 88]. Adjust the schedule accordingly.

In very cold climates and at high latitudes, the growing season is so short that only a few months of good gardening weather a year are available. Under these conditions, many warm-season vegetables must be coaxed to grow by using special techniques.

In the warm, temperate coastal regions, a vegetable garden may be maintained year-round as autumn and winter are hospitable for the planting of cool-season vegetables.

In some hot climates, such as the desert southwest, the high temperatures of summer may limit the possibilities of cool-season vegetables during that season, but they may be planted in autumn for an early winter harvest, and again in late winter for an early spring harvest.

Throughout modern times, home vegetable gardens have been a mainstay of rural, suburban, and even urban life. They have a long and colorful history, from backyard plots first planted during times of war to community gardens shared by city dwellers. Growing vegetables is a practical demonstration to children (and many times to adults, too) of self-sufficiency—what it is like to take on responsibility, and how honest labor can achieve a goal. The work embodies patience and a host of other virtues.

If you are a prospective vegetable gardener—and this book is your introduction to this world—know that the joy of receiving produce and fruit from nature's hand ranks high among life's great pleasures. In the pages to come, we provide an overview of the basic knowledge required of every vegetable gardener plus step-by-step descriptions and photographs of how to begin participating in the hobby. Vegetable gardening is the ultimate leisure pastime.

We believe we've given you everything to get you hooked forever. You won't be sorry.

Vegetable Gardening

Gardening Basics

Essentials

THERE IS A SECRET about vegetable gardening that we want to share with you first thing: vegetable gardening is easy, fun, and nearly foolproof, despite what you may have been told. Sure, there are lots of details to consider, and tricks that can make a difference in the size of a harvest, but the truth is, anyone can be a successful vegetable gardener. It's a well-known fact to literally millions of gardeners who love fresh vegetables but one seldom recognized by those just starting out. Like any unfamiliar task, it may seem a little intimidating at first.

The world of gardening is filled with many challenges and potential pitfalls—exotic plants that require special growing conditions, the need for soils formulated in laboratories, and care instructions that read like a medieval alchemist's manual—but these generally are not true for vegetables. Nearly all vegetable plantings are bulletproof: give them a little water, a little fertilizer, and good sunlight, and they'll repay your effort with bushels of tasty produce for months on end.

Much of this book is dedicated to providing valuable information and instruction that will help you optimize your vegetable garden. Where we thought you might want additional knowledge, we have provided convenient references and resources. Here and there, we hope this book may even open your eyes to new ideas.

On the whole, though, everything you really need to know about vegetable gardening—the *secrets*—are contained right in this chapter. We call them the gardening basics; you should think of them as the bedrock of your vegetable gardening experience:

- What makes for a good vegetable garden site
- How soil should be prepared for planting
- When you should choose seed over nursery transplants
- What care is required for most common vegetable plants

Having said all this, you would think that the rest of the book would have little to say. While it's true you could pull out this one chapter and garden successfully for many seasons, a day will come when you will want all the other information we have provided.

For example: you encounter problems—pest, disease, or unexpected crop failure—or, alternatively, a successful outcome that you want to repeat. We have included both the gardening basics and the detailed information—like one-stop shopping, we have endeavored to make this book a complete single-source guide to vegetable gardening.

Let's get started by asking the question, "How can I tell if my garden site will be good for vegetables?" The answer depends on the few items found on our checklist.

Choosing a Garden Site

When a gardener sets out to evaluate a site, the foremost considerations are sunlight, ample loose and fertile soil, and abundant water. Other site considerations are discussed in Chapter Five: *Planning Plantings*, but these are the most important.

The most successful gardens are found in locations with full sun throughout the day and season; a well-textured soil enriched with nitrogen, phosphorus, and potassium; and a steady source of water from rainfall or an irrigation system. Nearly any site can be adapted for a vegetable garden, but the very best occur naturally. The most important site consideration is the amount and quality of sunlight it receives.

NEED FOR SUNLIGHT. Sunlight makes plant growth possible. Without light, photosynthesis cannot occur, and plants cannot convert water and nutrients into the simple sugars and starches their cells use for energy. The result is that plants cannot grow much less produce healthy, delicious fruit or greens.

With adequate sunlight, any vegetable plant can thrive. The best garden sites receive sunlight throughout all daylight hours. Ideally, they are not shaded by trees, buildings, or other structures but are located in open fields or yards.

Such conditions, of course, are a luxury in most home gardens. When assessing your site, judge it by the same standards your plants would use: Does it get at least six full hours of sunlight each day? Is the sunlight direct, is it filtered through the leaves of nearby trees, or is it densely shaded by fences or other structures? Can the warming rays of sunlight in the first days of spring raise the soil temperature of the planting beds quickly to the minimum level needed to germinate seeds? Will there be sufficient sunlight when plants mature to ripen their fruits and finish their growth before the first frosts occur?

After you've answered these questions, compare your prospective site to thriving gardens in your neighborhood. Take note of their sun exposure and how the gardener has positioned the plantings within the bed. Then return to your yard and take another look. Many times, the best site for a garden turns out to be entirely different than the first location that was considered.

After all this, what do you do if your only potential garden site happens to be generally sunlight-deficient? How do you overcome the drawbacks of a shady site? One solution may be to locate sun-dependent plants in the limited areas that receive adequate sunlight while reserving the shadier spots for those cool-season vegetables that thrive in limited light. You may consider erecting a light-colored fence in the sunniest margin of the garden to reflect sunlight into shaded areas. There are many options, covered in more detail in Chapter Four: *Climate & Gardens*.

If ample sunlight is the first determinant of a great garden, the quality of the soil is a close second.

Great Garden Soil

The most important aspects of soil—the growing medium that supports your vegetable plants and provides them with the food they need to grow— are texture, makeup, and nutrients, specifically nitrogen, phosphorus, and potassium.

Before we begin our discussion of soil, we'd like to share a tip with you—whatever you do, don't call it "dirt!"

For botanists, horticulturists, and all others who make plants their living, there is no such thing as dirt—just soil. We're all familiar with the phrase "He was just a dirt farmer"; nevertheless, you're sure to get a cluck of the tongue or a wayward glance if you start a conversation at your local nursery or garden retail center with a description of your "dirt." Consider yourself warned.

SOIL TEXTURE. For vegetable gardeners, the principal consideration regarding soil texture is how water will drain—not too fast, not too slow. A soil's ability to drain at a steady rate is the result of its four inorganic components—

gravel, sand, silt, and clay—and its organic components—decayed vegetable matter.

Most gardens, with the simple turn of a spade, will reveal soil that is a mixture of the following elements: some amount of rock, some sand, some silt (fine particles between sand and clay in size), and some sticky clay. Most soils also include naturally occurring organic components.

Problems occur when one or two of these elements predominate: if soil is too rocky, it is difficult to work and drains unevenly; too sandy and the water just pours straight through, never standing where it's needed by the plant roots; too silty and water penetrates too slowly; too claylike and water stands on the soil surface or runs off without wetting the soil beneath. The best garden soils have nearly equal parts of sand, silt, and clay, and very few rocks to impede workability.

These so-called "balanced" soils, or loams, are ideal for vegetable gardening. Because their inorganic components break down on a time scale that is actually longer than a gardener's lifetime, these soils maintain their fine workability for decades.

Later in this chapter we'll provide directions for amending soil to improve texture [see Soil Preparation and Amendment, pg. 49]. First, let's look a bit further into how soil texture may have all the "wrong" components and still be just fine for your garden.

Many of us live in areas of the country where the soil is far from ideal for gardening. For example, in the high mountains, sand and rock is the norm; in the deep South's alluvial flatlands, centuries of flooding have coated the land with deep beds of sticky red clay.

Whatever your area's soil problem, the answer is the same: add compost or other decayed vegetable matter along with ample amounts of the right inorganic amendments. To determine how much of each to add, dig a hole about a foot (30 cm) deep in the garden site. Fill it with water, then measure the time it takes to drain completely. If the hole empties in less than five minutes, the soil is too loose and needs to have more compost and fine inorganic clay and silt added to it. If the water stands for more than 15 minutes, the soil is too dense and needs more compost and sand. It's as simple as that. The complete instructions for conducting such a percolation test are found on the following page.

Conducting a Percolation Test

Adequate percolation—the rate at which soil absorbs moisture—is essential to the health and success of any vegetable garden. Most garden drainage problems are caused by poor soil texture. Determine whether your bed drains too slowly—due to heavy clays and silts—or too quickly—caused by excessively sandy soils. Follow these simple steps:

1 Dig a hole in the area to be tested approximately 2 feet (60 cm) wide and 18 inches (45 cm) deep. Test the soil when it is dry, if necessary, covering the area with plastic for several days prior to conducting the test.

2 Completely fill the hole with water and note the time when it becomes full. With most garden soils, the water will begin to be absorbed immediately. Dense soils will drain slowly while loose ones will empty quickly.

Why is good water percolation important? The answer lies in the critical balance between soil moisture and the air the water traps. Subsurface liquids and gases contain nutrients vital to vegetable growth. Plant roots breathe in oxygen and exhale carbon dioxide. Some—such as the legumes (peas and beans)—even return nitrogen to the soil. They also take in mineral salts and trace nutrients through water.

When too little water is in the soil (much like what happens when soil texture contains too much sand and rock), the plant's roots begin to wither and dry. Within a short time, unless adequate water levels are restored, the plant loses its critical internal water pressure and leaves begin to wither. Steady, frequent irrigation is the only remedy for vegetables planted in too-coarse soils, though it is always wisest to make the soil more hospitable before planting.

At the other end of the spectrum, in fine-textured soils, there is too much water occupying the densely packed spaces between the component grains; the plant fails to absorb enough oxygen to sustain its life and drowns. It's a slow suffocation and a situation for which even the most experienced gardener has limited means of recourse. We'll describe these rescue techniques in Chapter Seven: *Caring for a Garden*.

What should you do if the soil in your garden is really, really bad? For centuries, gardeners in Europe have practiced a technique called "intensive gardening," which is really nothing more than replacing native soil with a good garden mixture of manure, compost, sand, and silt. In some instances, they use raised forms or stone terraces to contain their intensive beds atop the poor native soil—and you can do the same.

Soil texture is just one thing to consider. It's also important that your soil provide a whole host of nutrients for your vegetables. Let's examine some you can add that will keep your plants healthy and bountiful.

3 Time the rate of drainage. Percolation is ideal if the level of water in the hole drops 1–2 inches (25–50 mm) per hour. If your rate is different, amend the soil by adding organic matter until drainage meets this guideline. Very dense clay soils also may require adding garden gypsum.

VEGETABLES AND NUTRIENTS. Every growing green plant needs the three major nutrients—nitrogen, phosphorus, and potassium.

Nitrogen is the most important of these: it is essential for growing foliage, promoting photosynthesis, and resisting diseases above ground.

Phosphorus is the underground equivalent to nitrogen: it promotes root growth, especially the fine "hair" roots that absorb the water and oxygen needed for growth.

Potassium allows the chlorophyll in the leaves and stems to convert nutrients into simple sugars and starches necessary for the plant's health, and it buffers the acid-alkaline balance of the plant.

Healthy, productive vegetable plants need all three of these vital nutrients to prosper, ward off insects and diseases, and grow properly.

In addition to the top three, there are many micronutrients in good garden soil. In fact, most nutritionists believe that the healthful effects of eating organically grown vegetables stem mainly from the presence of these micronutrients in the growing soil. Commercial growers use an inorganic fertilization process to get the major nutrients to their plants, but little effort generally is made to supplement their soils with micronutrient components. In time, commercial fields become depleted of naturally occurring micronutrients—as does the produce grown in them.

Chemical analysis of vegetables grown in rich organic compost compared with those in depleted commercial fields reveals far higher levels of many trace nutrients in the organic produce. Good fertilization practices, as described in Chapter Seven: *Caring for a Garden*, assure that your home-grown produce is every bit as healthful as that from the best organic farms.

In brief, using rich organic compost made from plants grown in your own garden, together with well-rotted animal fertilizers, is one way to provide both the macronutrients and the trace micronutrients your vegetable plants need to thrive and produce healthy harvests.

Now that we've covered the three most important factors that affect plant growth—sunlight, soil, and water, let's turn to techniques for improving garden soil.

Soil Preparation and Amendment

Now that you know how to recognize various garden soils, how to judge their suitability for gardening, and how to improve their textures, let's tackle how to improve garden soil by adding amendments designed to attack specific problems. This information, though a bit beyond "basics," is critical.

The goal for great garden soil is to attain a loose, organics-rich mix of various-size particles that allow air and water to penetrate quickly, hold moisture for long periods, yet drain excess water. The basic prescription for poor soil is to add these organic materials as needed. In fact, many vegetable gardeners believe that as much as half the volume of any planting bed should be made up from compost.

Double Digging

Double digging a garden is an effective way to incorporate soil amendments into a small area. The process thoroughly mixes the amendment material—often compost, fertilizer, or texture-enhancing additives—with the native soil, well down into the root zone. All that usually is required is a stout back and a garden shovel. Follow these easy instructions:

1 Spread amendment across the area to be prepared. For most applications, a layer 2–4 inches (5–10 cm) is adequate.

2 Dig a starter row the length of the bed, 18–24 inches (45–60 cm) deep, about the depth of two shovel heads. Place all excavated soil outside this starter bed rather than atop the amended area to create an open trench.

3 As you dig the second and subsequent rows across the bed, fill the trench with excavated soil and create a new trench parallel to the first. Fill the last trench with soil reserved from the first row dug.

ADDING AMENDMENTS. To amend a planting bed, first spread compost evenly on top of the soil to a depth of 4–8 inches (10–21 cm), then "double dig" it into the soil. Start by digging a trench one shovel head in depth, placing the soil on the ground next to the trench and breaking up any clods larger than 1/2 inch (12 mm) in diameter. Then dig down in the trench a second shovel head in depth, and place that soil on top of the first. Next, dig a second trench parallel to the first one and a shovel width away from it; place the first and second soil diggings into that trench. Repeat this process down the plot until the entire garden has been double dug. (Obsessive gardeners often add another coat of compost and repeat this process at right angles to the first dig, thoroughly mixing the first top coat of compost into the planting bed.) When completed, the bed should be raised as much as a foot (30 cm) higher than it was when you started. You have just added both organic compost and air to the plot, improving the soil and making it ready for planting.

An alternative to the laborious process of double digging is to till the soil with a mechanical tiller. With most standard garden tillers, the rotating tines dig in compost and loosen soil to a depth of about 10 inches (25 cm). This is not as deep as is possible with the double digging method, but the mixing process is very thorough. Tilling is especially effective on previously untreated soil and should be done

when the ground is moist but not sodden. Choose when to till by picking up a handful of soil and squeezing it in your palm—it should crumble apart when you open your hand. If you cannot make a ball, it's too dry; if it doesn't crumble when the pressure is released, it's too wet. When the soil is at the perfect consistency, place all soil amendments atop the ground before tilling.

When using tillers, be sure to follow all the safety precautions recommended by the manufacturer, including wearing protective shoes, clothing, and goggles. Keep children away from the machine during operation.

FINISHING. Whether you have amended your garden soil by double digging or by machine tilling, be sure to rake the plot thoroughly when you're finished, then remove any stones and break up any remaining clods. Raking both smoothes the surface of the plot and levels the ground, which is important to water retention. It is always better to level a garden plot before planting than to resort to later building of terraces and dikes to correct drainage problems.

A final consideration is whether to install drip irrigation lines, irrigation pipe, or soaker hoses along the plot borders. These labor-saving watering aids are inexpensive and greatly reduce the amount of day-to-day care necessary to achieve a great garden. Be sure that supply lines, which often are made of PVC plastic, are buried well below the depth you would normally shovel.

A complete instructional step-by-step is provided later on [see Installing an In-ground Irrigation System, pg. 200].

With sunlight, soil, and water all well considered, let's turn to what is the most exciting part of gardening basics: picking out your vegetable plantings.

Options for Planting

Throughout history, the preferred method of planting vegetables was by seeding them—using either the best seeds from prior years' plantings or acquiring them from a seed grower. Modern agricultural producers now offer a second option—buying transplant stock from a nursery or grower.

Which method to select is a matter of choice and economics. Let's look at each in turn.

GROWING FROM SEED. Many gardeners prefer to grow vegetables from seed because of the range of varietals not commonly available as transplants. They may select seed that is disease or pest resistant, as well as those vegetables that do not produce viable seeds of their own. In addition, if a mini–truck garden comprising extensive plantings is the goal, planting from seed is the only economical alternative.

Growing from seed requires a bit more planning than the simple trip to the nursery required for transplants. Chapter Six: *Planting Your Garden* provides the lead times needed for planting, germination, and growth to transplant size—along with full instructions on how to plant your seeds directly into the garden. With the added responsibility comes a significant benefit—the ability to extend your gardening season.

Because seeding may take place indoors or in cold frames—glass- or plastic-covered boxes set into the garden soil—you may move the planting date six to eight weeks or more ahead of the time it generally would be possible in the outdoor garden.

In general, the benefits of planting from seed are a more extensive selection of vegetables in your garden, better adaptation of plants to their surroundings, and, if seeds are carefully selected, better resistance to diseases. These issues are discussed in more depth in Chapter Six: *Planting Your Garden*.

GROWING FROM TRANSPLANTS. Many gardeners prefer the convenience of planting nursery-grown stock. Horticultural experts have selected the varieties that do best in your area, planted and raised them under optimal conditions, then rushed them to your local nursery or garden retail center just in time for planting. Transplants are an excellent option for gardeners with limited time, though cost

can be a factor if extensive plantings have been planned.

In Chapter Six: *Planting Your Garden*, we provide full instructions for moving nursery starts into the garden, including "hardening"— which helps tender seedlings adapt to potentially harsh outdoor conditions—transplanting, and early care. Read these step-by-step instructions carefully before deciding whether you want to sow seed or opt for transplants.

The major advantage of transplants is ease of selection and speed of planting. Come spring, nursery and garden retail store aisles are filled with trays of the healthiest, most adaptable, and most appealing varieties for your region. This is no small advantage. While seed gardeners may experience germination failure, fungal disease, or other growing disasters, transplants have already made it through the first six to eight weeks of a young vegetable plant's life.

There's something very appealing about raising your vegetables from seed, and there's also something very satisfying about finishing a day's transplanting and finding your beds filled with tender, young vegetable plants. Whether you choose to plant from seed or set in transplants, once the garden is filled with green, care becomes the primary issue.

Garden Care Basics

Full instructions on caring for a vegetable garden are contained in Chapter Seven, but a brief overview of how you can meet your garden's needs may be helpful here. As your garden's caretaker, your responsibilities include inspecting for pests and signs of disease, watering, cultivating, and mulching.

Along with great garden soil and ample sun, care is essential to a healthy, productive, and efficient garden, so let's begin by discussing the process of observing your vegetable garden.

INSPECTING A GARDEN. Regular inspection of your garden is important because it allows you to observe how your plantings are reacting to your care. In addition, it allows you to identify the following conditions:

- Watering problems
- Cultivation problems
- Diseases
- Pest infestations

WATERING CARE. Walk through your garden in the middle and at the end of the day to check on the effectiveness of the watering and other irrigation techniques you are employing. A complete description of proper watering techniques is provided in Chapter Seven, but a short course here may prove helpful.

Closely inspect all plants that appear to be drooping or withered. Follow the instructions for evaluating the soil around each affected plant before taking any type of remedial action—the problem easily could be too much water rather than too little water [see Overwatering, pg. 63].

If the problem is too little water [see Underwatering, pg. 59], follow the instructions for applying water. This should be done immediately in the case of most plants; however, there are exceptions. For example, some succulent and woody plants, such as tomatoes, tend to droop in hot weather. This is unrelated to underwatering, and the plants recover fully by the evening if soil moisture is sufficient.

CULTIVATION CARE. The next condition to notice in your garden is the general state of the planting beds. Are they overgrown with weeds? Has the soil become compacted and dry on the surface? Is the mulch decaying and therefore losing effectiveness as a weed barrier? The answers to these questions all have to do with cultivating [see Other Care, pg. 65].

DISEASE CONDITIONS. Disease in a vegetable garden is a distressing state of affairs. Because most treatable disease conditions tend to be fungal in nature, the earlier they are detected the better. Viral disease infections generally cannot be treated; instead, the affected plants must be segregated immediately and burned to prevent them from infecting neighboring plants. A complete inspection and care regimen for vegetable gardens is covered in Chapter Seven: *Caring for a Garden.*

To detect signs of disease, as you walk through your planting beds turn over leaves near the soil surface. Look particularly for white powdery discoloration, black spots, or other damage. Notice if single leaves are withering on an otherwise healthy plant. Notice stem discoloration and fruit deformities. All may be disease symptoms requiring immediate attention.

PEST INFESTATIONS. As with disease, early detection of plant pests is vital to avoid wholesale chemical warfare or irreversible plant damage. Most responsible gardeners utilize an "integrated pest management" approach that is based on early detection, organic and nontoxic control measures, followed by application of low toxicity controls such as soaps and oils, then limited use of naturally occurring pesticides like rotenone (extracted from the flowers of chrysanthemums) when infestations rage out of control.

To identify a problem, look for tracks and trails of insects on the underside of leaves. Check foliage for bite marks and scoring. Take note of any stems that are discolored or chewed. Look near dark, damp spots for the telltale signs of slugs and snails. If damage is more extensive, look for gopher and mole mounds, rabbit and deer tracks, and other clear signs, such as pecked or half-eaten fruit, of mammal or bird pests.

A full guide to controlling insect and animal pests is provided in Chapter Eight: *Pests & Diseases.* Now that you know how to recognize the problems, let's take a look at the steps that can alleviate them.

Watering

Y ou already know that the nature of the soil in your garden dictates the amount and frequency of watering [see Soil Texture, pg. 44].

As you would expect, the principal irrigation problems are due to underwatering and overwatering. Underwatering can result from soil that drains too quickly, from sporadic or sparse delivery of moisture, or from excessive heat. Overwatering can result from soil that drains too slowly, from too-frequent or too-bountiful irrigation, or from cool growing conditions. Either can be deadly to your vegetable plants. Let's look at each in turn:

UNDERWATERING. Many gardeners believe—incorrectly—that they should water on a schedule. This practice fails to take into account the unique soil and climate conditions in each individual garden. Plants require regular watering—that is, a constant, uninterrupted flow of moisture. Without it, they experience "stress," or loss of critical water pressure in the stems, roots, and leaves, and their roots are exposed to desiccating soil gases and drying air.

Natural precipitation is the best means of irrigation—except in areas subject to acid rain. Water from rain and mist usually is delivered moderately and penetrates the soil well to create a subsurface reservoir for the plant's needs when conditions turn dry. Few areas experience too much rain, but many are subject to drought—an imprecise term to describe periods when plants' water needs are not being met. At such times, the gardener must step in and fill the needs through irrigation.

Despite the drastic appearance of underwatered plants—some lie on the ground as flat as pancakes when they undergo water stress—many species have a remarkable ability to recover

within minutes or hours from the time they again receive water. This is not to say that underwatering should ever be considered an acceptable garden practice. Nearly all vegetable plants that have undergone water stress end up stunted to some degree, mature prematurely, and suffer from poor flowering and fruiting. The message is to react quickly, before foliage shows telltale signs of withering.

IDEAL WATERING. If you do not live in an area that receives frequent rainfall, when should you water, and how much? Try this age-old test for soil moisture: Plunge your hand into the soil near a plant's roots and pick up a handful. Press it together in your fist. Moist, rich garden soil should crumble back into a loosely compacted pile. Do this daily— or even more frequently if conditions are very hot and dry. You soon will get a feel for when the soil a few inches below the surface is becoming dusty and dry.

Whenever soil is dry to the touch, it's time to water. Most garden experts recommend giving plants 1–2 inches (25–50 mm) of water in a single irrigation—as if you had covered your entire garden with a sheet of water to that depth. As the water is absorbed, it fills the porous soil spaces, then slowly is wicked deeper and deeper. Within a dozen minutes, a well-textured soil should have drained all surface moisture.

Pay particular attention when natural precipitation is spotty. If heat becomes extreme, water early in the morning so the surface of the soil and the plant foliage have time to dry before the sun's heat begins to bear down. Watering at this time of day also will prevent leaf damage and potential mildew problems that can be caused by watering atop foliage in the evening. Complete guidelines on watering are found later in this book [see Watering, pg. 192]. You'll also learn what watering tools to use, along with options to consider for installing a permanent irrigation system for your home garden.

A Simple Test for Proper Watering

It's important to know when a garden really needs watering. The easiest way to judge available water in the soil is to visually inspect the planting bed. Use your hand to unearth soil to a depth of 6–8 inches (15–20 cm) beneath the surface, then compare it to the photographs. Water whenever subsurface soil becomes dry.

1 Using your fingers, dig 6–8 inches (15–20 cm) down and remove a handful of soil. Take care to avoid disturbing the roots of any nearby plants.

2 Gently close your hand into a fist and squeeze the soil into a ball. Soil with proper moisture should slowly crumble back apart when you open your hand and the pressure is released. No watering is required.

3 Soil that is too wet will remain in a ball when pressure is released. Allow such soil to dry before irrigating again.

4 Too-dry soil appears dusty and will fail to form a ball at all. Irrigate immediately, applying at least 1 inch (25 mm) of water to the soil surface.

OVERWATERING. Too much water, whether from manual irrigation or a sudden downpour, also can be deadly to plants. Many of the sad and wilted specimens brought in by home gardeners for examination by trained horticulturists are the victims of overwatering. When the plants began to sag, the gardener assumed that it was from dehydration and more water was the cure—a deadly treatment as far as the vegetable was concerned.

As previously explained, dense soil texture is the principal culprit in overwatering. Dense, compacted soil made up of heavy clay resists the natural wicking of water between the soil grains. In desert areas of the United States, soil forms a hardpan layer that is totally impermeable to water—which is why structural engineers line their dams with beds of clay! The most obvious way to avoid overwatering in dense soils is to amend the soil with a loosening agent and abundant organic matter before placing plants in the ground.

If you already have planted and notice standing pools of water, it's a clear tip-off that your plants may be in trouble. What can you do?

Whenever you suspect that poor drainage is a problem in an established garden, cultivate around the outside roots of the plants (remember that the spread of the root system is roughly equivalent to the circumference of the foliage), working in abundant organic compost and mulch. Add a spadeful of garden gypsum ($CaSO_4 \bullet 2H_2O$) every foot or two (30–60 cm) around the plant, and work it in with a hoe or fork. Be sure to incorporate these amendments at least as deep as the plant roots, using the height of the plant as a gauge. In the case of some vegetables, such as all varieties of tomatoes, this will require major excavation since their roots normally extend to as deep as 3 feet

5 Soil with proper texture—a good blend of inorganic minerals and decayed vegetable matter—has excellent water-holding capability. Such soil requires less frequent watering than do either dense or excessively porous soils.

(90 cm). Take care throughout the process to avoid clipping the roots of the plants, but work as close to them as possible.

The objective of this process is to provide the plant with a surrounding bed of good garden soil into which the water may drain and the roots may grow. It's no substitute for good soil in the bed from the beginning, but it can make the difference between ultimate failure and a measure of success.

A different problem occurs when nature decides to overwater. Sustained precipitation or sudden downpours can drown a garden. The only solution in such cases is to get out in the rows with a hoe and dig drainage channels beside the plants to allow for surface runoff. In olden times, almost all gardens were planted in raised rows and hills, partially to anticipate such an eventuality. These so-called "furrow irrigation channels" permit surface water to collect away from the roots.

For more information on watering, check the detailed instructions in Chapter Seven: *Caring for a Garden*. Now let's look at other care, more popularly known as keeping the work to a minimum.

Other Care

There are two other care requirements for your vegetable garden: cultivating and mulching. Neither takes significant time, and both can be accomplished over a span of days, as time permits. They make a measurable difference in your garden's results.

CULTIVATING. The two primary purposes of cultivating vegetable plants are to aerate the soil and eliminate weeds. Aeration will be an ongoing issue for gardeners with dense, claylike soils but seldom an issue for gardeners with well-amended, highly organic, balanced soils. Refer to the section on soil textures for information on how to avoid the need for aerating through cultivation [see Soil Preparation and Amendment, pg. 49].

Even the best soils need cultivation, however, for the elimination of weeds. Cultivation is basically the act of using a hoe, cultivating rake, or garden fork to loosen the soil around each plant. This act of "disturbing" the soil surface enhances water penetration, overturns and cuts any weeds that have become established, and invites the vegetable plant's root system to expand into the loosened soil.

Cultivation should be done around each plant's drip line, the imaginary circle drawn from the outermost foliage straight down to the soil. Dig 3–4 inches (7–10 cm) deep around each plant until all of the surrounding soil is loosened.

Cultivation goes hand in glove with mulching.

MULCHING. Mulching may be the most poorly understood element of vegetable gardening, but the principles are simple: reduce the need for watering; reduce the need for cultivating; and enhance the garden soil.

Mulch is nothing more than organic compost, weed-free straw, or shredded paper placed atop the soil and around the plants to provide a protective barrier. Mulch helps plants retain moisture, protects the soil from receiving the direct effects of strong sunlight and rainfall, and inhibits weed growth. In other words, mulching pays big dividends when it comes to time in the garden.

Nonorganic mulches such as barrier plastic and weed cloth reduce the need for watering and cultivation. Organic compost and straw have the added benefits of providing nitrogen and trace minerals to garden soils as they decompose. They also improve soil texture.

Mastering the basics of vegetable gardening will serve you time and time again. Armed with even this brief knowledge, you are ready to take on almost any kind of vegetable garden challenge.

Remember that vegetable gardening is very forgiving—all your plants need is sunlight, fertilizer, watering, and a little of your time. For centuries, that simple formula has worked to provide a steady stream of nutritious vegetables and produce to home gardeners. Understanding and faithfully applying the basics of vegetable gardening is a sure and simple pathway to quick success year after year.

Within these basic tasks, you'll also find joy. There will come a time when, on a sunny day with your hands resting on a hoe, you'll see before you the very vegetable garden of which you once only dreamed. Winter's fanciful wishes will have materialized in ripening fruit, succulent and savory greens, and neat rows of healthy, thriving crops.

To help you realize your vision, we'll next share information that will help you understand your climate, your region, and the specific garden you wish to plant.

Selecting Garden

Climate & Gardens

Sites

MASTERING THE SKILLS OF GARDENING BASICS is but one part of achieving success with your vegetabe garden; the other is choosing an ideal site to grow vegetables.

Most of us simply accept the impact of location and climate on our vegetable gardens without really understanding the effect of either. Indeed, few of us give more than a moment's thought to gardening considerations except, perhaps, when in the process of moving a household. Despite this subconscious acceptance of location and climate, every gardener has choices that can affect the ease of care. This chapter is devoted to a discussion of the impact location and climate have on the vegetables we grow, the seasons in which we plant, and even the times we harvest.

When it comes to growing vegetables, regional location and climate are only two factors. The elevation at which we live, how the garden site is positioned on the land, the nature of its surroundings, and a host of other considerations—including those we can't predict, such as sudden changes in weather—affect how our gardens grow and the care we must provide them.

For those who are settled into their homes permanently, this review of climate, growing seasons, and site location will be required only once, with the caveat that the site of your vegetable garden can be affected by changing sunlight conditions created by the growth of nearby trees. For others thinking about relocating or who are facing a job transfer to another region altogether, the information presented here will be of current and continuing value when making sense of the gardening conditions in the new location and may even affect the choice of a home.

The material covered here does not relate to vegetables alone. Many facts apply equally well to flower gardening, lawns, trees, and shrubs. Let's get started. In this chapter we'll discuss:

- How garden locales in the country differ, and why

- How climate affects growing seasons

- Why results in one garden may differ from those of nearby neighbors

- What special considerations are required for gardens in extreme high-altitude or far-northerly climates, as well as in the desert southwest, Gulf states, Florida, and Hawaii

- What impact shade, wind, slope, and other environmental factors may have on a garden, and, finally, informed by the above

- How to evaluate garden locations and choose the best site

Vegetables and Plant Hardiness

First, let's begin with where you live. It's common knowledge that, generally, the farther one gets from the equator, the cooler the climate becomes. Equatorial areas are tropical, the middle latitudes are temperate, and the polar regions are marked by extreme cold. It also becomes cooler as the elevation climbs—high mountain tops typically have short summers, while lowland valleys are more temperate. From the perspective of growing-season temperatures, mountain regions resemble "islands" of polar climates in "seas" of warmer lowlands.

Temperature is only one measure of climate, however, along with humidity and precipitation. Consider that the frozen poles are as much deserts as are Death Valley or the Sahara. All receive scant rainfall, and polar air is parched and dry—just bitterly cold rather than searingly hot. One area of Antarctica provides an especially good example of this dynamic: its so-called "dry valleys" are pavements of barren earth and rock, having received no rain or snowfall in decades.

USDA PLANT HARDINESS ZONES. Botanists have endeavored to identify the climate factors that most affect plants. The result of their efforts has been a classification of so-called "growing zones" for the United States, Canada, and Mexico [see the USDA Plant Hardiness Zones on the following page] as well as for Europe and Australia [see Plant Hardiness throughout the World, pg. 408]. These charts reflect knowledge gained over the past 50 years or so of average temperatures in many thousands of geographic locations around the globe.

These charts divide most of the world into 11 plant hardiness zones by grouping those areas that experience similar annual minimum temperatures. For example, zone 1 in the frozen polar regions, with average low temperatures in winter below –50°F (–46°C), encompasses the Arctic and Antarctic, while zone 11 is centered on the equator and features minimum winter temperatures above 40°F (4°C). In the middle of the spectrum, zone 6, which

U.S.D.A. Plant Hardiness Zones
of North America

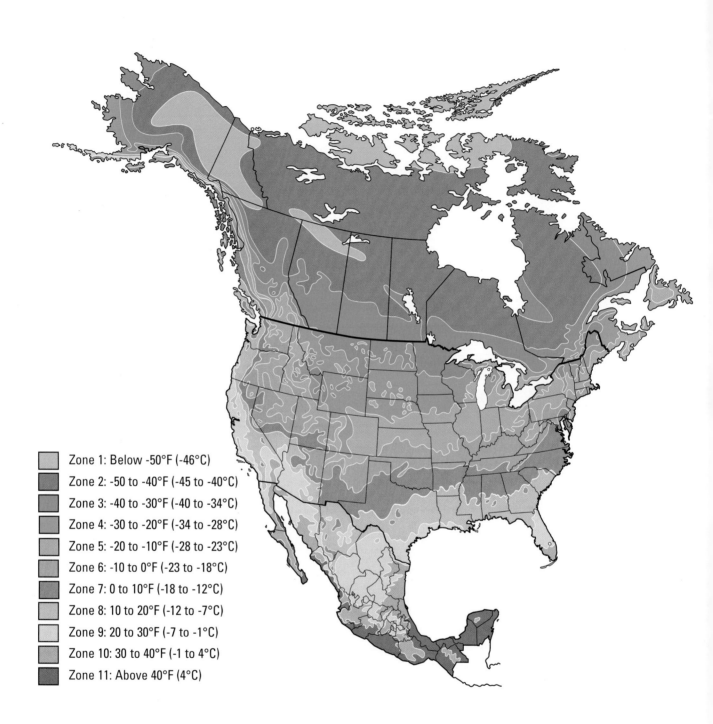

Zone 1: Below -50°F (-46°C)

Zone 2: -50 to -40°F (-45 to -40°C)

Zone 3: -40 to -30°F (-40 to -34°C)

Zone 4: -30 to -20°F (-34 to -28°C)

Zone 5: -20 to -10°F (-28 to -23°C)

Zone 6: -10 to 0°F (-23 to -18°C)

Zone 7: 0 to 10°F (-18 to -12°C)

Zone 8: 10 to 20°F (-12 to -7°C)

Zone 9: 20 to 30°F (-7 to -1°C)

Zone 10: 30 to 40°F (-1 to 4°C)

Zone 11: Above 40°F (4°C)

includes such locations as Vancouver, Canada; Reno, Nevada; Nashville, Tennessee; and Poughkeepsie, New York, experiences maximum low temperatures of –10°F (–23°C). By countless observations made of growing plants in different conditions, botanists have matched each vegetable to its ideal climate zone and come up with adaptations for less-suitable climates.

Finding your plant hardiness zone is easy: identify your locale on the map [see page opposite], or on the map for your region found in the Appendix [see pg. 408]. Note the colored zone, then look in the legend for its number and minimum average winter temperature data. If your geographic area is located on or near the border between two zones, consider your knowledge of local weather conditions to select the zone that best exemplifies your location. This is the most important step in choosing vegetables for planting, followed by the care guidelines set forth in the Vegetable Encyclopedia [see page 307].

OTHER CLIMATE CLASSIFICATIONS. While the plant hardiness zone approach provides a generally useful tool, many gardeners discover practical weaknesses when attempting to apply it to their own personal vegetable gardens.

First, scarcely a winter passes when scores of locations do not set records for new low temperatures—or experience a season so mild that it more closely resembles zones found farther toward the equator.

Second, plant hardiness zones do not take into account seasonal daylight hours, average humidity, and precipitation—which places cool, rainy Kodiak, Alaska, in the same plant hardiness zone as hot, dry Dallas, Texas, humid Washington, D.C., and hot and humid Atlanta, Georgia! Yet, the same trees, shrubs, flowers, and vegetables do not grow equally well—or even during the same planting periods—in all of these varied locations. We'll talk about how to solve this problem later on.

Finally, the plant hardiness zones do not take into account important microclimate conditions prevalent in virtually every area [see Microclimates and Regional Differences, pg. 88]. Microclimates exist because sites are sheltered from or exposed to wind; are situated on warm south-facing slopes or cool northerly exposures; are positioned at the tops or bottoms of hills; or are subject to shade from trees or structures. These "microeffects" can make dramatic differences in results obtained from similar gardens found just a short distance apart—even on opposite sides of the same street.

Given all these imperfections, is the notion of plant hardiness zones useful? Absolutely. They provide general guidelines for gardeners to start considering their sites. Numerous local and regional adaptations also have been developed, some providing additional growing recommendations useful to local vegetable and flower gardeners. Rather than describe all of these other systems, let's focus our attention on recognizing the critical factors that affect your particular vegetable garden. They will help you know what measures to take after selecting a specific site in which to grow your vegetables.

Understanding Climates

U nderstanding your garden's particular climate allows you to recognize the favorable and unfavorable conditions that will direct your plantings and help you make adjustments where needed.

The major climate factors affecting every vegetable garden are:

- Minimum low temperatures

- Hours of sunlight and length of days during the growing season

- Measurable precipitation and humidity during the growth cycle

- Average and maximum temperatures

- Duration of optimal warmth

- Microclimate conditions affecting the garden's site

We'll discuss each of these in turn, along with ways to "fool" Mother Nature if conditions are not ideally suited to vegetable gardening.

MINIMUM TEMPERATURES. Except for plant hardiness zones 10 and 11, which have average minimum winter temperatures of 30°F (–1°C) or higher, the primary influence of low winter temperatures on annual gardening is to establish the times of planting in the spring and cessation at the onset of winter.

The further north a location in the Northern Hemisphere (or south in the Southern Hemisphere), the fewer are the number of days available for gardening. In other words, the periods when both soil and air temperatures are hospitable to vegetable growth become shorter the further northward or southward from the equator.

The period during which a gardener can raise vegetables largely is determined by the date of the last frost in spring and the first frost in autumn or winter. These start and end dates for gardening also define the length of the growing season in each locale throughout the country

Representative Growing Seasons
of North America by U.S.D.A. Plant Hardiness Zone

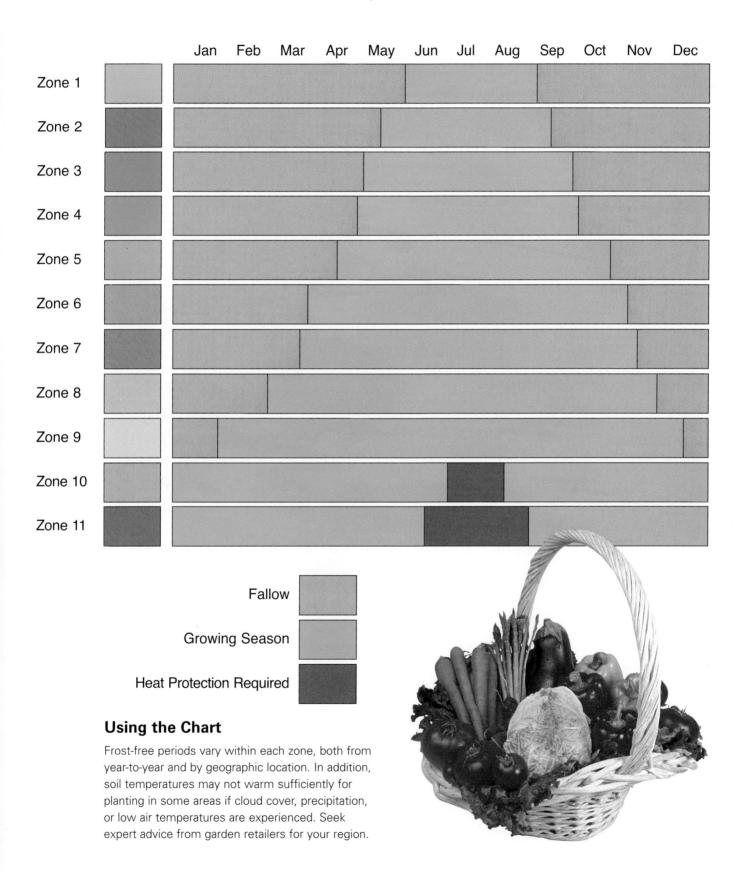

Fallow

Growing Season

Heat Protection Required

Using the Chart

Frost-free periods vary within each zone, both from year-to-year and by geographic location. In addition, soil temperatures may not warm sufficiently for planting in some areas if cloud cover, precipitation, or low air temperatures are experienced. Seek expert advice from garden retailers for your region.

and continent. The chart Representative Growing Seasons, shown on the previous two pages, sets forth the seasonal dates and growing season lengths for a number of major urban areas, as well as for benchmark locations in more rural areas of the United States and Canada. Because these are average dates, your particular locale may have earlier or later first and last freezes due to elevation, unseasonably warm or cool weather, and other factors. Use your local knowledge, together with expert advice, to help tailor the information in these charts to your region and area.

COLD-WINTER CLIMATES. Cold winter temperatures—experienced in autumn in many areas of North America—can kill most annual vegetables as well as any frost-tender perennials. In the extreme-cold, mountainous-terrain climates of the northern United States and most of Canada, temperatures sometimes dip so low as to kill even frost-hardy perennial and root-vegetable species. Areas with these cold-winter temperature extremes effectively halt gardening until spring, when soil temperatures rise to levels that allow seed germination [see Soil Temperature for Planting chart, pg. 162]. To help the gardener know when to plant, all climates

with winters featuring sustained temperatures of less than 20°F (–7°C) are referred to as "cold-winter climates" and are shown on the plant hardiness zone map [see Climate Areas, pg. 81].

Gardeners located in plant hardiness zones 2–4, which experience average minimum winter temperatures colder than –20°F (–29°C), experience short growing seasons and can benefit from season-extension techniques.

Plant hardiness zones 6 and 7, with winter temperatures to –10°F (–23°C), are considered more ideal for vegetable gardening—normal, if you will—and the conventional notion of a cold winter followed by spring planting and fall harvests usually can be followed.

Two other classifications of garden climates exist: the so-called "mild-winter climate" and "reverse-season climate."

MILD-WINTER CLIMATES. Gardens located near temperate ocean coasts in the east and west, as well as those in the far southerly latitudes (or northerly in the Southern Hemisphere) experience so-called "mild-winter climates" [see Climate Areas, pg. 81]. These areas typically are bounded by zones 8–9. They are marked by occasional frosts (or even short-lived periods of hard-freezing conditions), but they typically experience minimum winter temperatures above 20°F (–7°C). Temperatures in these areas are higher because they are buffered by their proximity to relatively warm ocean water. Similar effects may be experienced in other regions near large lakes, especially those in areas that remain ice free in winter.

Along the eastern U.S. seaboard, the warming effect of the Gulf Stream in offshore waters moderates temperatures and climates as far north as Canada. Along the western U.S. coast, the Japanese Current brings cool northern waters south. Both of these currents, and the large thermal mass of the surrounding oceans, regulate the temperatures of overlying onshore air masses. Because of prevailing winds, these moderating effects generally move from west to east.

If your garden is located in one of these areas, plant hardiness zones 8 and 9, you may be able to sustain a vegetable garden year-round.

REVERSE-SEASON CLIMATES. The final category is "reverse-season climates," in which summer temperatures reach extremes too high for most cool-season vegetable crops and winter temperatures seldom dip below 30°F (–1°C) [see Climate Areas, opposite]. These conditions are typical in zones 10–11. Reverse-season climates are most common in the desert southwest of the United States, in Hawaii, and in Florida; in the Mediterranean areas of Europe; and in the northernmost portions of the Southern Hemisphere. Such conditions also are common in the Caribbean and Micronesia, and in many other tropical locations throughout the world.

If your garden is located in plant hardiness zones 10–11, plan on planting a reverse-season garden during the autumn and winter [see Growing Vegetables in Hot Climates, below].

USING CLIMATE INFORMATION. The primary reason for dividing gardening conditions into cold-winter, mild-winter, and reverse-season classifications is simply to help establish planting times that will assure each vegetable sufficient time to germinate, grow, mature, and fruit before extreme temperatures—whether cold or heat—interrupt the growth cycle.

Gardeners can use the chart information, together with the information for each plant in the Vegetable Encyclopedia [see pg. 307], to choose appropriate planting times for their gardens.

WHY CLIMATE ZONES EXIST. Seasonal changes, which we experience as "climate," affect gardeners in a variety of ways. Everyone in a cold-winter climate has noticed how winter sunlight lacks warmth—no matter how clear and sunny the day—compared to the strong, warm

Growing Vegetables in Hot Climates

Gardeners who live in hot desert areas—so-called "reverse-season climates"—should adjust their planting schedules. Cool season crops should be planted in late summer and early autumn to avoid the long days and high temperatures of midsummer. Vegetables may be harvested throughout the autumn—and, in mild climates, all winter long. Whenever a freeze threatens, tender plants should be protected with a covering of breathable fabric and by heavy irrigation. Seeds should be sown early in the spring, as soon as all danger of frost has passed. Crops quick to bolt, such as spinach, lettuce, and cauliflower, may require shading as temperatures climb. They are sensitive both to heat and to sun exposure.

Climate Areas
of the United States of America

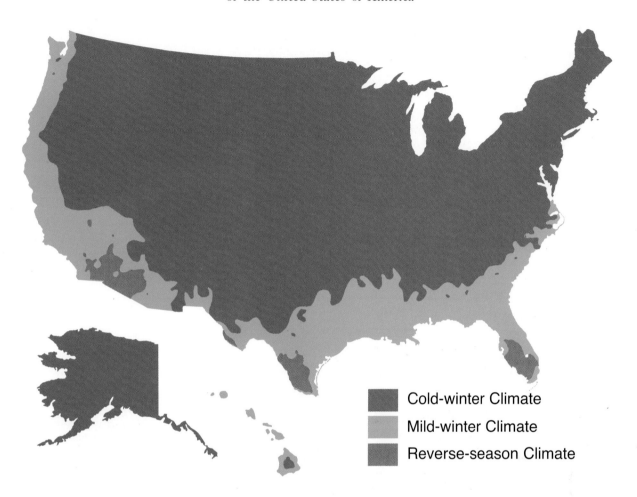

Cold-winter Climate

Mild-winter Climate

Reverse-season Climate

rays of the direct sun in midsummer. Both experiences are caused by the continuously changing angle of sunlight, which strikes the earth's surface obliquely during winter and nearly straight on in summer.

Depending on a garden's location relative to the earth's equator and poles, the angle of sunlight changes from season to season [see Earth and the Sun on the following page]. This is caused by the movement of the earth around the sun as the year progresses. The earth's axis remains fixed as the planet rotates around the sun, with the result being that the sun's energy is concentrated in the Northern hemisphere when it is diffuse in the Southern Hemisphere, or the other way around, while tempersatures in the equatorial regions remain fairly constant.

When it is midwinter in the Northern Hemisphere (at this time the Southern Hemisphere is experiencing its summer), the sun appears to be low in the sky. Shadows are long, and the sunlight lacks warmth. As the sun rises more and more above the equator each spring day (actually, the earth's rotation around the sun and its inclined axis create this effect), it appears to rise in the noonday sky; shadows shorten, the sunlight gains warmth, and air and soil temperatures become more moderate. By June 21 or 22—the summer solstice—the sun stands high in the sky, and our Southern Hemisphere neighbors are in the throes of winter.

Because of how the earth "sits" relative to the sun, seasonal effects become progressively more intense the farther north or south a location is situated from the equator. In other words, the high latitudes generally experience the most severe cold-season winters, with the sun dipping low in the midwinter sky or disappearing altogether in latitudes beyond the Arctic and Antarctic circles. Conversely, those areas closer to the equator have mild-winter climates, with summers that may be too hot for many vegetables to grow, set fruit, or ripen.

Earth and the Sun

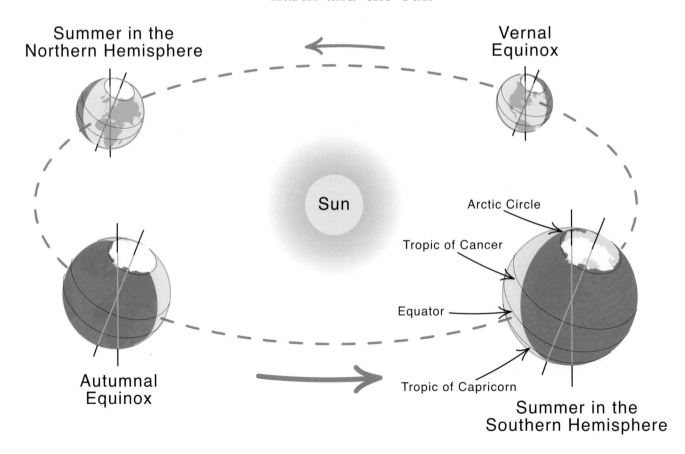

THE PARADOX OF NORTHERLY GARDENS. Amidst the months of cold weather in the northerly latitudes and, for that matter, in the far-southerly latitudes, there is a hidden blessing when it comes to vegetable gardening. While the growing season is short in months, the long, temperate days make gardening, at least in terms of total number of daylight hours, nearly the same as for climates located much nearer the equator [see Representative Growing Seasons, pg. 76].

Vegetables have great respect for the sun. Every sunlit hour is a growing hour for most vegetables—though there are exceptions. For all but these exceptions, adequate hours of sunlight are the key to gardening success.

Consider that year in and year out, farmers in Alaska's remote Matanuska Valley, miles north of Anchorage on the edge of the Arctic Circle, win prize after prize for their mammoth cabbages and pumpkins. Their secret: the nearly 24-hour sunlight experienced during their short, three-month growing season.

The sunlight hours available for planting in Alaska, as well as in most of northerly Canada, almost match those for areas nearer 40° latitude, such as Fargo, North Dakota; Toronto, Ontario; and Kennebunkport, Maine. In fact, Alaskans actually have more total seasonal growing hours than do these locations clustered around the U.S.-Canada border.

Taking into account the growing season in sunlight hours, and not in months, can give any gardener, anywhere, peace of mind—knowing that vegetable plantings are busy growing every minute there is light in the sky.

Precipitation and Humidity

As important as the quantity of sunlight is the presence of sufficient moisture, especially during months of minimum growing temperatures [see Growing Seasons, opposite]. Plants need ample water to grow, ranging from an inch (25 mm) a week to as much as a half-inch (12 mm) a day during critical periods.

PRECIPITATION. Certain areas are blessed with ample rainfall throughout the growing season. The Precipitation map [see Average Annual Precipitation, pg. 86] shows seasonal rainfall totals for many areas of the United States and Canada. These are averages, and as we all know there can be dramatically more or less rainfall during the growing season in any one year.

Locate your garden area on the map. If it averages less than an inch (25 mm) a week throughout the gardening season, plan on irrigating your garden, either with an in-ground system or with hoses or watering cans.

HUMIDITY. Many areas are noted for their high levels of humidity—nothing more than airborne water vapor. The southeastern United States and Hawaii come to mind, as do the more temperate but equally humid midwestern and northeastern areas of the country.

Humidity affects vegetable plant growth by limiting the amount of moisture the plants lose through transpiration—moisture lost by evaporation from their leaves. In short, high humidity helps prevent plant dehydration.

Another reality of humidity, however, is that it provides for dew formation during cool evening and nighttime hours. While this dew supplements water received from nature and other sources, it has a notable downside as well. Excessively moist conditions, especially when coupled with cool nights, are a stimulant to fungal and bacterial disease growth [see Preventing Fungal Disease, pg. 269].

Effects of Temperature

The minimum, average, and maximum temperatures achieved during the growing season, and the total length of time the temperature is optimal, are all important for vegetable growth.

Growing Seasons

Growing seasons for an area often are expressed as the average number of frost-free days between late winter—or spring, in many cold-winter climates—and the first hard freeze of autumn. Local weather forecasters and many agricultural extension agents keep records of such statistics.

A more useful guide may be to measure soil temperatures in your garden. Because soil warms more slowly than air, acceptable planting temperatures may lag days or even weeks behind last-frost dates. Plants do not thrive, and may even die, when planted in soils that are too cold.

The true growing season for a region is the total number of consecutive days that its soil temperatures exceed the levels needed to grow crops.

The stretch should be long enough to ensure that plants have time to germinate, mature, and ripen before killing frosts occur.

MINIMUM TEMPERATURE FOR VEGETABLES. Of greatest concern to the gardener are the minimum temperatures, not only for planting but for growing. Minimum temperatures are unique to each vegetable plant [see Soil Temperature for Planting, pg. 162, and Vegetable Encyclopedia, pg. 307].

The minimum planting temperature assures that the seed of a vegetable plant will germinate and grow, while the minimum growth temperature assures that the plant develops properly up to the flowering stage. Note that the flowering temperature is always at a higher level than the minimum growth temperature, and that still higher temperatures must be reached in order for vegetable flowers to set fruit.

In general, annual vegetables have the following needs:

- Cool-season vegetables—minimum planting temperatures of 40–50°F (5–10°C); minimum growth temperatures of 70–85°F (21–29°C).

- Warm-season vegetables—minimum planting temperatures of 50°F (10°C) and optimal of 60°F (16°C); minimum growth temperatures of 75°F (24°C).

Average Annual Precipitation
Composite Mean Precipitation (January to December) 1950–1997

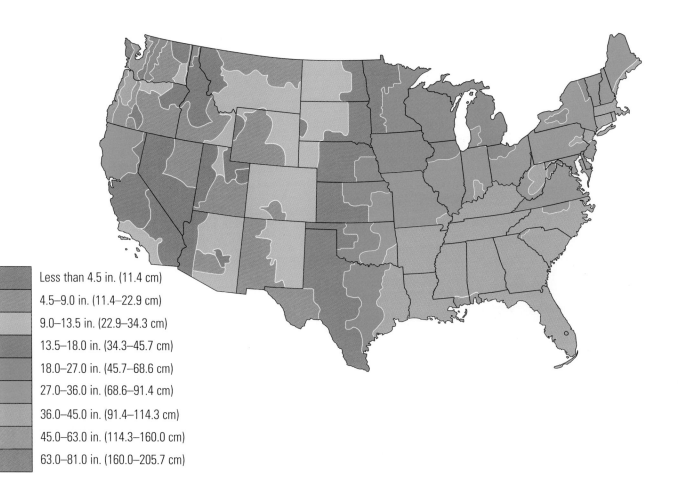

Less than 4.5 in. (11.4 cm)

4.5–9.0 in. (11.4–22.9 cm)

9.0–13.5 in. (22.9–34.3 cm)

13.5–18.0 in. (34.3–45.7 cm)

18.0–27.0 in. (45.7–68.6 cm)

27.0–36.0 in. (68.6–91.4 cm)

36.0–45.0 in. (91.4–114.3 cm)

45.0–63.0 in. (114.3–160.0 cm)

63.0–81.0 in. (160.0–205.7 cm)

AVERAGE GROWING TEMPERATURE. The average temperature is the point at which vegetable plants thrive in typical growing conditions. If your garden location has temperatures that vary far above or below the average for a given vegetable, do not despair. Too-low temperatures may be overcome by raising vegetables in protected locations such as under glass in a cold frame. Too-high temperatures may be moderated with shade structures or shade cloth and ample watering during times of stress.

As important as minimum and maximum temperatures are the number of days of near-optimal temperatures. Before planting, consult the Soil Temperature for Planting chart [see pg. 162] or the Vegetable Encyclopedia [see pg. 307]. Ideally, for most vegetables, at least two-thirds of the

growth time required to reach maturity should be at or above the average growing temperature, while the remaining third should be at temperatures between the minimum and the average.

The key is to match vegetable plantings with the appropriate timing for your climate—planting in spring (in cold-winter climates), in early spring (in mild-winter climates), and in autumn or winter (in reverse-season climates), as your conditions dictate. This assures that, when the plants begin to mature, temperature conditions are optimal to complete their growth cycle or ripen their fruit. In certain climates, successions of plantings may be made and harvested over the course of a long growing season.

MAXIMUM TEMPERATURE FOR VEGETABLES. The maximum temperature is the upward limit that a particular vegetable plant can tolerate. Most cool-season vegetable plants begin to experience difficulty when the thermometer exceeds 86°F (30°C), while warm-season vegetables enjoy heat until it reaches kill temperatures of 110°F (43°C) or higher. Help protect heat-sensitive vegetables from temperature extremes by erecting temporary shade structures made of filtering shade cloth on wooden supports.

Microclimates and Regional Differences

Along with the "big three" factors—climate, precipitation and humidity, and temperature—every gardener needs to understand the effects of microclimates caused by natural and man-made variations from garden to garden, even in the same locale.

Microclimates are the "special situations" that distinguish one gardener's growing conditions from another's, and even from place to place within a garden.

The factors that contribute to a microclimate are:

- Man-made structures
- Nearby landscaping and trees
- Site location
- Prevailing winds
- Local weather conditions and nearby natural features

Let's look at each of these in turn.

MAN-MADE STRUCTURES. Structures affect gardens in a variety of ways. They provide shelter from wind (or direct wind into the garden), reflect or block sunlight, and shelter the garden from precipitation (or allow more moisture in). They also cause other, more subtle effects. When considering your garden site, give some thought to all buildings, fences, arbors, shade structures, patios, and walkways—especially those within 20 feet (6 m) of your planned garden site.

RADIATED HEAT. Any man-made structure, whether a wall or walkway, contains mass. Depending on its materials and their nature and density, the structure may trap or dissipate significant amounts of heat, in much the same way as heat is absorbed by rocks on a beach and radiated into the night sky, often for hours after the sun has gone down.

What is called the "heat-sink" nature of structural mass can benefit your garden, especially if it is located in a cold-winter climate. The presence of nearby warm concrete, rock, brick, and other masonry materials helps soil temperatures rise in the spring and maintain heat in the garden late into autumn. Because dark-colored materials retain heat, use them when building structures nearby.

To minimize heat gain due to mass in warmer climates, use light-colored and insulating materials for garden structures. Good choices include wood painted either white or

off-white, or vinyl, plastic, and lightweight concrete construction materials designed to blend into the environment. You also may want to install overhead shade structures above paths to deflect sun and shade your walkways.

REFLECTED LIGHT AND HEAT. Light-colored surfaces reflect light and heat, while darker colors absorb them. Like radiation, reflection can affect the amount of warmth reaching your garden. For example, a white or light-colored wall facing both the garden and the prevailing sun will reflect light into the garden. Unlike radiation, which continues even after the sun has set, reflection has its primary effect during sunlight hours.

Use reflection to your advantage in cool climates, even those with frequently overcast skies. Substantial light can be reflected into shady garden areas even on a cloudy day, doubling or tripling the heat and energy available for plant growth.

Choose white or other light-colored materials for fences, borders, raised beds, and planters if too little light is a problem; select darker alternatives when too much light is a concern.

Place light-colored structures on the north side of the garden, where their reflected energy will increase light on your vegetables' shady side. Recognize the trade-off, however, since light-colored structures reduce the beneficial effects of radiated heat. Remove such structures or paint them with darker colors if your goal is to reduce the amount of reflected energy.

Avoid excess reflected sunlight in hot climates by planting in locations away from reflecting walls. Such structures may scorch vegetable plants or their fruit; in extreme cases, the combination of direct and reflected sunlight may kill heat-sensitive crops. In cooler climates, vegetables may benefit from being planted near sheltering, reflective structures.

SHADOW AND SHADE. Man-made structures, whether dwellings, outbuildings, or garden structures, cast shadows.

In most climates, garden sites should be chosen for full-sun exposure. Only in the hottest southwestern United States and tropical locations should you consider planting vegetables in shaded spots.

In the Northern Hemisphere, shade increases in the spring and autumn and decreases in summer, when, by mid-June, shadows cast by structures shorten. Avoid placing structures that will shade your garden in spring, when solar heat is most needed to raise soil and surrounding air temperatures. When shade is needed in the hot summer months, a filtering, nonwoven shade fabric, commonly available in garden stores, can shelter plants from excessive sunlight as well as protect them from any inclement weather, including sudden thunder- and hailstorms.

WIND. Upright structures both can block and redirect prevailing wind. On a windy day, note the direction of the air through your garden. How do structures such as garages, fences, and dwellings influence the wind direction and intensity? Is the wind strong enough that you will be forced into constructing protected beds for upright plants such as corn, pole beans, and peas?

Wind effects on a garden can be modified by planting perimeter hedges or landscape trees. Dwarf fruit trees often are ideal for this purpose—just be sure to plant them a minimum of 10 feet (3 m) from the margins of the planting beds.

LANDSCAPE AND TREES. All existing overhead trees, whether deciduous or evergreen, cast shadows on the garden. Their roots, together with nearby shrubs, sap vital nutrients and water from your vegetables and may transfer pests and diseases to your vegetables and garden soil through dropped foliage.

Deciduous trees, which lose their leaves each autumn, offer sunlight to the ground beneath when it is least needed by your vegetable garden. In summer, they cast dense shade over the garden. Toward autumn, their shadows lengthen, increasing the amount of shade at a time when sunlight and heat are most needed for setting and ripening fruit. Evergreen trees behave no better, only they shade their understories year-round.

Avoid problems with trees and shrubs by maintaining enough distance between them and your garden so that the shadows they cast in spring at planting time do not intrude beyond the garden edge. If such is not practical, note the shadowed areas carefully and choose shade-loving, cool-season crops for them. If your heart is set on warm-season crops, light-reflecting structures may benefit the situation [see Reflected Light and Heat, pg. 89].

Site Location

Aside from structures, trees, and surrounding landscape, there are a number of other factors to consider when assessing a site. Take a good look at your prospective, or former, garden. Is the ground on a slope, or is it level? Is it located atop a hill, at its foot, or along a hillside? Which direction does it face, and what are its exposures at different times of the day? How does water run to and from the site? All of these questions and their answers will help you determine a site's potential as a vegetable garden.

SLOPE. If possible, choose a site that is level, or make it level by terracing or installing raised beds. This effort will yield rewards long into the future. Sloped sites invite winds to flow either uphill or downhill, cooling the ground and wreaking havoc on your plantings. In addition, in summer the top of a hill will be cooler than its base (the reverse will be true in winter). If the amount of elevation is significant, the difference between temperatures may be so dramatic that it requires an adjustment of more than one plant hardiness zone [see USDA Plant Hardiness Zones, pg. 72].

Tops and slopes of hills also frequently are drier than the hollows below, which will affect watering requirements of the garden. By creating level terraces on such slopes, irrigation water will flow equally to all parts of the bed and be retained instead of draining away.

WATER CONSERVATION. We've all seen beautifully flat agricultural fields. They often have been graded level with sophisticated laser earth-moving equipment by farmers seeking to reduce the expense of watering their crops. Absolutely level fields receive irrigation water evenly, reducing the amount needed to irrigate the plants. The same principle applies to a vegetable garden.

One easy way to determine your garden's level is by attaching clear plastic sleeves to each end of a hose, filling the hose with water (avoiding any air bubbles), stretching it between two points, allowing the water level to stabilize in the plastic sleeves, and measuring the distance to the ground at each end. Using this simple tool, you can compare and measure absolute level reference points within your garden.

UNEVEN TERRAIN. Because hot air rises and cool air sinks, low spots in a garden will collect cool air, making them unsuitable for many vegetable crops. At the same time, high spots are more exposed to prevailing winds. These factors make leveling all the more important.

DIRECTION AND FACING. Examine your site with a compass in mind. Sites facing south receive extra solar energy, which warms them more quickly in the spring and keeps soil temperatures high in the summer. Conversely, sites facing north receive less of the sun's energy. Add one plant hardiness zone to that typical for your location if your site faces south; deduct one if it faces north.

East-facing sites are benefited by early-morning sun, while west-facing sites are shaded in the morning. Many gardeners believe that early morning sun is especially important, but the truth is, total hours of sun exposure are the critical determinant of plant growth and fruit ripening.

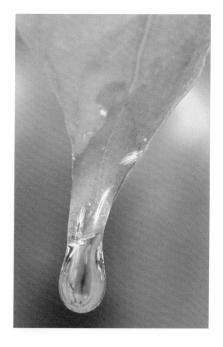

WATER. Placing a garden in former streambeds and hollows, narrow flats between two hills, or other areas where water runoff or pooling is likely to occur may result in erosion. Such areas tend to be boggy, filled with heavy clay or silt, and require abundant soil amendments to achieve workability [see Soil Preparation and Amendment, pg. 49]. Also avoid placing your garden at the top of a hill. Erosion carries soil downhill, so hilltops frequently have poor soil. If you must garden atop a hill, terrace it or add retaining structures to hold the soil in place.

While you may feel that there is little you can do to change the major factors affecting your garden site, there are a number of measures you can take to accommodate or mitigate them. Dealing with a less-than-ideal site is a challenge that is faced by many home gardeners. You will be amazed at how quickly the problems are forgotten when the effort bears results in the form of beautiful and bounteous crops of vegetables.

Part of your challenge, as every gardener's, is getting to know your garden's secrets. You will be spending a good bit of time and effort within its boundaries, and it is not only more enjoyable to know it well, it's also better than wondering or wishing.

In the next chapter, we'll plan the garden. In many ways, it's the most enjoyable part of gardening—all imagination, with a little honest work thrown in to keep us humble.

Heat Zones of the United States
Compiled by the American Horticultural Society

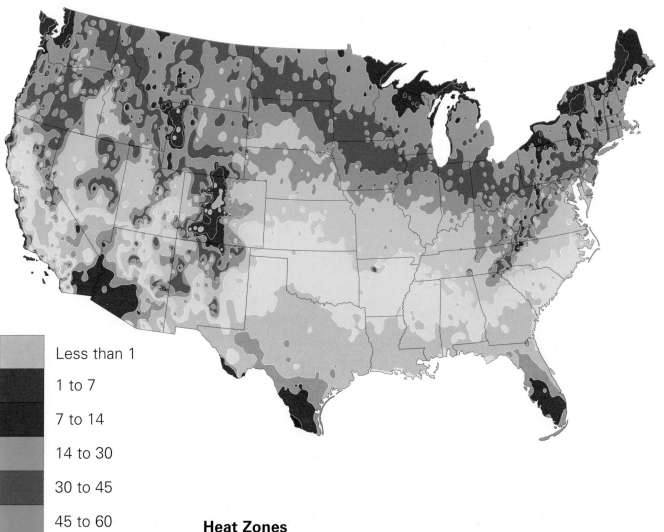

Less than 1

1 to 7

7 to 14

14 to 30

30 to 45

45 to 60

60 to 90

90 to 120

120 to 150

150 to 180

180 to 210

Greater than 210

Heat Zones

The American Horticultural Society Heat Zone map shows the United States, divided into 12 regional areas. Each is based on the annual average number of days between 1974 and 1995 in which its temperature exceeded 86°F (30°C)—the point at which damage begins to occur in cellular plant protein.

Heat Zones are useful for determining whether a specific plant will receive sufficient heat to grow, mature, flower, and fruit, and for judging when protection from excessive sun may be required in very hot climates. Remember, averages oftentimes are misleading. In any given year, the number of hot days may vary up or down by 20 percent or more.

Many garden suppliers now "heat-rate" their plants according to Heat Zone as a convenience to consumers. Use this map, together with the U.S.D.A. Plant Hardiness, Climate Areas, and Average Annual Precipitation maps and the Growing Season chart, to guide your selection, planting, and care of your vegetable plants.

Preparing for the Growing Season

Planning Plantings

THERE ARE AS MANY VISIONS of vegetable gardens as gardeners. Beauty may begin in the eye of the beholder, but it ends in such practical matters as space planning and crop selection. Every home vegetable gardener needs to have a basic understanding of both.

The dynamics are:

- What specific vegetable varieties you want

- How the produce will be used in the family kitchen

- How much will be doled out to friends

- The amount of time, space, and interest you have available to devote to the project

Such planning is required before a garden is established for the first time and annually thereafter at the beginning of each gardening season.

Planning a garden can be approached from any number of different viewpoints. The goal is to satisfy your practical and aesthetic desires, which may include:

- Scaling a vegetable garden to accommodate your lifestyle and interests

- Planting at specific times for strategic harvesting of particular crops

- Maximizing the produce harvested from a small area

- Growing a successive variety of vegetables in the same garden plot during the course of a single growing season

- Creating a beautiful and eye-catching garden

Beginning gardeners may need to think consciously about every element of planning to avoid common pitfalls, or what veterans call "too many zucchinis, too few friends." With increasing knowledge, however, they draw on lessons learned in past seasons to moderate their plant selection, areas of cultivation, and the degree of care needed to achieve the desired results.

Just how does this process take place? Today's good results start with observing and understanding the results of past decisions. Fortunately, the advice of expert gardeners with years of experience is readily available in these pages and at the local garden retailer. Asking questions is an inexpensive, efficient, and reliable alternative to oftentimes costly and time-consuming hands-on experience. Indeed, there probably has never been, as a group, a greater bunch of enthusiasts and advice givers than vegetable gardeners. For every novice planter struggling with an idea, many consultants can be found across the street or over the fence. To them, there are no stupid questions, no ideas unworthy of discussion, no problem not yet encountered.

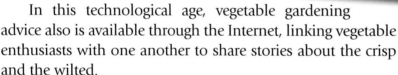

In this technological age, vegetable gardening advice also is available through the Internet, linking vegetable enthusiasts with one another to share stories about the crisp and the wilted.

Another convenient and reliable source of garden advice is the local office of the U.S. Department of Agriculture (USDA), found in the government listings of most telephone books. USDA offices are staffed by knowledgeable workers and usually stock printed bulletins packed with information about local conditions plus tips for planning gardens and planting, growing, and harvesting vegetables. Local USDA staff are especially helpful when difficult or unusual problems arise, or when gardening conditions have been affected by a widespread pest, a disease outbreak, or exceptional weather.

All things being equal, let's first explore some easy and fun ways to plan a vegetable garden for the coming growing season.

Planning for Garden Care

Perhaps the most important consideration in planning a garden is the amount—and consistency—of time you have available for your gardening hobby. Today's world is filled with many distractions, including work, family obligations, recreation, and home maintenance. When a pipe bursts, the boss requires your presence on a Saturday, or the children need to get to their soccer game, gardening often is given secondary priority or no priority at all.

It is a fact of vegetable gardening, however, that plants do not understand these demands on your time. Their needs are simple: ample sunlight; loose, rich, or fertilized soil; and regular watering. Nevertheless, even a weekend's neglect in hot weather at a critical juncture in the growing cycle can permanently stunt a vegetable's ability to form flowers and develop fruit, make the fruit bitter, or put the plant prematurely past its prime. In the worst cases, plants will die altogether and the growing season will be lost for that particular vegetable.

Recreational gardeners burdened with multiple interests and obligations should try as much as possible to make sure their schedules and commitments match the needs of their plantings. Those subject to unplanned demands on their time should consider an in-garden irrigation system of drip lines, clock timers, and soaker hoses. That way, should their gardening time become curtailed, at least the plants will have their watering needs met.

Tending to most of the other needs of a vegetable garden is easier—or at least more predictable. Most fertilizing and nutrition is built into the garden at the time of planting through soil preparation, amending, and fertilizing. A time-strapped gardener should opt for the so-called French-intensive methods, with its deep, double-dug beds loaded with humus, compost, and rich organic matter. Such beds will sustain plants for the entire growing season without needing significant attention other than watering and pest and disease monitoring.

Failure to provide consistent care also will affect the yield of a vegetable garden—usually through loss of plants or fruit to pests and diseases, but sometimes due to insufficient thinning. Fortunately, most routine garden care activities are quick and easy to accomplish, requiring little more than brief walks through the garden to "see how things are growing." A turned leaf here to inspect for insect pests, a pinched sprout there, and most vegetable gardens will fall back into line quickly.

To fully understand the gardener's role in maintenance and upkeep, carefully read the advice given in Chapter Seven: *Caring for a Garden*.

How Large a Garden?

The next garden planning consideration is the size of the area to be devoted to planting. It may be a quick morning's work to replace the potting soil in a container garden but a weekend's intensive labor to till the clay and rocky soil of a quarter acre into a rich and fertile garden plot.

YIELD. The Vegetable Yields chart on the following page is a practical guide to the quantity each vegetable will produce per square yard (square meter) of space in several types of gardens. This will help you decide on the number of plants required for each variety. With this helpful knowledge of the expected bounty—together with a count of the number of hungry mouths expected to consume the produce and an estimate of how much is desired for preserving, canning, and freezing—most gardeners can estimate their yield quickly and plant accordingly. A Planning Worksheet [see page 107] also has been provided for calculations (you may want to photocopy it for future seasons).

SUSTAINED HARVEST. Along with the yield information in the chart, keep in mind that some vegetables produce all their harvest at once while others offer a sustained yield of moderate quantities over a period of months. One good example of the former is the many varieties of hybrid corn. Designed by seed company geneticists for mechanical harvesting on commercial farms, these varietals bloom at the same time, mature their ears all at once, and have an optimum moment of harvest that passes quickly. Any home gardener who has planted a large stand of one or more of these commercial crops must plan ahead; the only practical use for such a bounty is to harvest, blanch, and freeze it all at one time for gradual use within six to eight months of processing. The home gardener who wishes to eat a few ears of

Vegetable Yields

Vegetable	Pounds per Sq. Yd.	Kilograms per M²	Vegetable	Pounds per Sq. Yd.	Kilograms per M²
Artichoke	2.8	1.5	Pepper, Sweet	2.5	1.3
Asparagus	0.5	0.2	Potato	6.9	3.6
Bean, Broad	1.2	0.6	Potato, Sweet	3.3	1.8
Bean, Lima	1.0	0.5	Pumpkin	4.8	2.6
Bean, Snap	1.0	0.5	Radish	1.0	0.6
Beet	5.0	2.7	Rhubarb	0.7	0.4
Broccoli	2.5	1.3	Roquette	4.0	2.1
Brussels Sprouts	3.7	2.0	Rutabaga	6.0	3.1
Cabbage	6.4	3.4	Salsify	2.0	1.0
Cabbage, Chinese	6.5	3.5	Shallot	0.6	0.4
Cantaloupe	5.0	2.7	Spinach	1.8	0.9
Carrot	6.5	3.0	Spinach, New Zealand	1.7	0.9
Cauliflower	2.8	1.5	Squash, Summer	0.5	0.2
Celery	13.2	7.0	Squash, Winter	1.0	0.6
Collards	7.0	3.7	Sunflower, Seed	0.2	0.1
Corn, Popcorn	1.4	0.7	Swiss Chard	2.0	1.0
Corn, Sweet	1.9	1.1	Tomatillo	1.8	0.9
Cucumber	4.0	2.1	Tomato	2.5	1.3
Eggplant	5.6	2.9	Turnip	6.0	3.1
Endive	5.1	2.7	Watermelon	6.0	3.1
Garlic	4.1	2.2			
Greens, Various	5.0	2.7			
Kale	1.6	0.8			
Kohlrabi	5.0	2.7			
Leek	2.4	1.1			
Lettuce	6.0	3.1			
Melon	3.2	1.8			
Mustard	1.5	0.8			
Okra	3.6	1.9			
Onion, Drying	8.5	4.6			
Onion, Green	3.0	1.6			
Parsnip	2.0	1.1			
Pea, English	0.7	0.4			
Pea, Snap	0.7	0.4			
Pea, Southern	0.5	0.2			
Pepper, Hot	2.5	1.3			

corn a few times a week over the course of the summer should instead choose a home garden variety that yields a more measured harvest, or plant several crops in succession as described later in this chapter. However, in either case, more area must be devoted to the corn patch since corn's growing habit requires numerous neighboring stalks to ensure good fertilization and kernel development.

Corn is pollinated by wind, not by insects, and it grows best in communities. It flowers on a feathery stalk atop the plant, which bears multiple male blossoms. Wind carries one plant's individual pollen grains to another's nearby female flowers and silks, which develop atop each immature ear. The flowering ears are found where the foliage joins the stalk. If too few plants are in flower, partial germination results in ears that ripen with missing kernels. Corn should always be planted in blocks of similar varieties to ensure good pollination and to avoid cross-hybridization.

Another example of an all-at-once producer is the determinate tomato varietals. Tomatoes come in two types:

"determinate"—those that form flowers and fruit at the end of the growing stem—and "indeterminate"—plants that flower from fruiting spurs along their stems. Determinate tomatoes bloom, stop growing, then produce their fruit all at once, while indeterminate varietals grow throughout the gardening season, producing a continuing series of flowers and fruit. Luckily, Mother Nature has taken care of any yield problems. Determinate tomatoes are ideal for canning, juicing, and making paste or sauce, while indeterminates are great for eating.

OVERPRODUCTION. When planning the size and therefore the yield of your vegetable garden, you need to be realistic about your own, your family's and your neighbors' forbearance. It is quite one thing to walk across the street to a nodding acquaintance's house with the first lush tomatoes of early summer and quite another to make the same trip with a bushel of over-the-hill parsnips in late autumn. Like such an overenthusiastic gardener, vegetable plants do not know when they've worn out their welcome. The beautiful, eagerly anticipated zucchini blossoms of spring keep right on opening and developing into woody, bat-size squash throughout the summer and autumn until a really good frost finally kills the vine—or a desperate gardener, armed with a sharp spade, brings the overabundant zucchini season to a quick and premature close.

Some moments of thought before the garden was planted might have revealed that a family of two plus a few dear friends could not consume the output of five hills of pumpkins. Conversely, a gardener with a spouse, two grandparents on each side and a bevy of vegetable-loving children with adolescent girl- and boyfriends might avoid recriminating glances around the crowded dining table when an underplanted garden yields a skimpy serving on each plate.

Forewarned is forearmed: those with eyes for 100-foot (30-m) rows of string beans and English peas should also be on the lookout for a massive chest freezer at a nearby garage sale, while those who have large families should poll their members about how much they enjoy lima beans and turnips.

One of the best ways to indulge your enthusiasm for planting and keep a control on the harvest is to go ahead and fill every last patch of soil—with annual flowers. They add color when the garden is still a sea of green, attract bees, and several are edible.

Planning Worksheet

Gardener:_____   Season: _____

Household Members:

_____ _____ _____ _____

Total Servings:_____

Vegetable	Yield/Area	Multiplier	Total Area of Planting
❏ Asparagus	_____	_____	= _____
❏ Bean—Broad	_____	_____	= _____
❏ Bean—Snap	_____	_____	= _____
❏ Beets	_____	_____	= _____
❏ Broccoli	_____	_____	= _____
❏ Cabbage	_____	_____	= _____
❏ Carrot	_____	_____	= _____
❏ Cauliflower	_____	_____	= _____
❏ Chard	_____	_____	= _____
❏ Corn	_____	_____	= _____
❏ Cucumber	_____	_____	= _____
❏ Lettuce	_____	_____	= _____
❏ Melon	_____	_____	= _____
❏ Okra	_____	_____	= _____
❏ Onion—Green	_____	_____	= _____
❏ Onion—Drying	_____	_____	= _____
❏ Parsnip	_____	_____	= _____
❏ Pea—English	_____	_____	= _____
❏ Pea—Black-Eye	_____	_____	= _____
❏ Pepper	_____	_____	= _____
❏ Pumpkin	_____	_____	= _____
❏ Radish	_____	_____	= _____
❏ Spinach	_____	_____	= _____
❏ Squash—Summer	_____	_____	= _____
❏ Squash—Winter	_____	_____	= _____
❏ Tomato	_____	_____	= _____
❏ Turnip	_____	_____	= _____

Harvest Timing

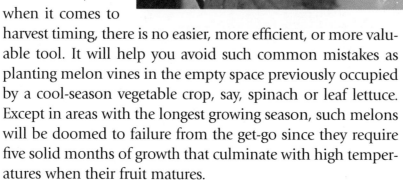

After consideration of space and yield, the next item on every home vegetable gardener's planning list should be timing. The science of plant genetics has given vegetable gardeners a host of options. The accumulated knowledge of many seed companies has been digested and summarized in the Planting Depths, Germination, and Harvest chart [see pg. 168], which reveals how early each variety can be planted in each of the North American climate zones, an estimate of how many weeks (or months) each vegetable takes to reach maturity, flower, and produce fruit, and which ones are single- and which sustained-harvest vegetables. Also included is a scale for adjusting the expected yield for each species and variety.

The chart may appear to be a lot of numbers, but when it comes to harvest timing, there is no easier, more efficient, or more valuable tool. It will help you avoid such common mistakes as planting melon vines in the empty space previously occupied by a cool-season vegetable crop, say, spinach or leaf lettuce. Except in areas with the longest growing season, such melons will be doomed to failure from the get-go since they require five solid months of growth that culminate with high temperatures when their fruit matures.

A bolting spinach and lettuce crop can be replaced safely, however, with quick-maturing and cold-tolerant species such as radishes, carrots, and turnips. Some common harvest-planning plant successions are illustrated in the next section.

HARVEST PLANNING. One of the chief objectives of a home vegetable garden is to provide friends and family with a continuing variety of fresh, tasty vegetables. Attaining this goal may be difficult, however, unless plans for variety in the harvest are made carefully and followed resolutely.

For instance, a dream salad garden might consist of beds of crisp lettuce and other greens, juicy tomatoes and cucumbers, crisp green onions, carrots, and bell peppers—those are, after all, the ingredients of a dream salad. After confronting the information contained in the Planting Depths, Germination, and Harvest chart [see pg. 168] and contemplating the real world of a backyard garden in most growing areas, though, an unsettling realization soon will occur: these vegetables have quite different habits, seasons, and harvest patterns.

Lettuce is usually quick out of the ground and into the salad bowl—between six and eight weeks from planting to harvest. Green onions and carrots typically follow a month or two later, after the lettuce patch has gone to seed, and a month or so after that, the tomatoes, peppers, and cucumbers finally ripen. At least that's the way it would work if all of these seeds were planted on the same day. Fortunately, there is a way around the problem.

First, you can stack the deck a bit in favor of your dream salad by hot framing or starting the tomato, pepper, and cucumber seedlings in a greenhouse while frost is still on the ground (with techniques described in full in Chapter Six: *Planting Your Garden*). Alternatively, you can buy seedlings from your nursery, if time is lacking.

These tender, warm-season vegetables will be transplanted to the garden after six to eight weeks of careful nurturing, after all danger of frost has passed and at about the same time that the cool-season carrot and green onion seeds are sown. Then, about six to eight weeks before the tomatoes and carrots are ready for harvest, you will till the lettuce seedbed and carefully start it on its way—holding back part of the row so that another batch of lettuce can be started three or four weeks later, extending the harvest until the other vegetables ripen.

As long as the summer daylight does not become too strong or daytime hours too long, the second planting of lettuce will cooperate by not bolting. Voilà! The salad is complete, and you sit down with family and friends for a delightful dinner.

Such is the magic of the vegetable gardener's harvest planning. With a little added consideration, taking into account the effect of microclimate variations on growth—planting lettuce, for example, in a somewhat shadier, cooler part of the garden, where the midsummer heat will not send it bolting, while assuring that the tomatoes are in full sun—you will have realized a complete harvest-planning concept.

There is a bit of help to make the job easier, in the form of the Vegetable Succession Planning chart opposite. Keep in mind that in some northern climates the growing season just does not last long enough to permit a full growth cycle. Without a greenhouse in much of midcontinental Canada and throughout the northern tier of the United States, the dream of a coordinated salad planting has to remain just that. A good gardener can fool Mother Nature some of the time—but not by that much!

Vegetable Succession Planning
Example Succession Chart—U.S.D.A. Hardiness Zone 7

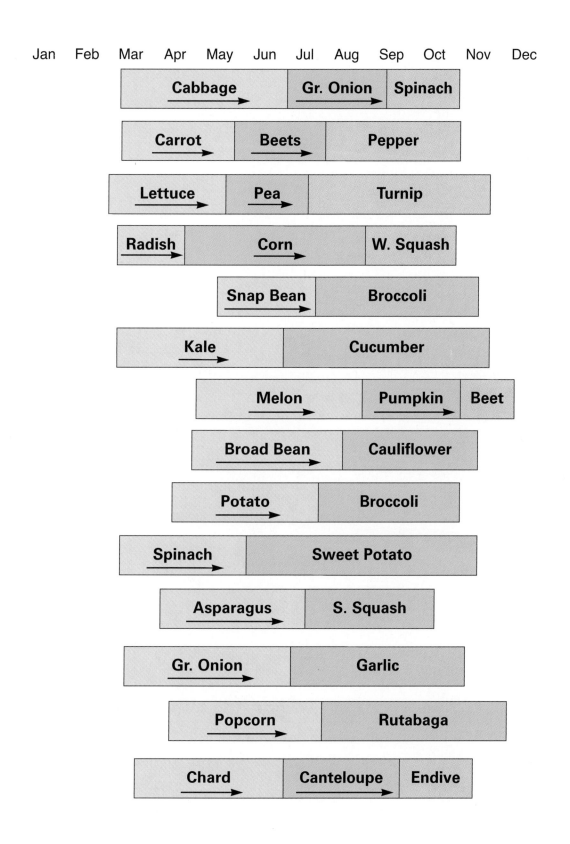

Jan   Feb   Mar   Apr   May   Jun   Jul   Aug   Sep   Oct   Nov   Dec

Cabbage → | Gr. Onion → | Spinach

Carrot → | Beets | Pepper

Lettuce → | Pea → | Turnip

Radish → | Corn → | W. Squash

Snap Bean → | Broccoli

Kale → | Cucumber

Melon → | Pumpkin → | Beet

Broad Bean → | Cauliflower

Potato → | Broccoli

Spinach → | Sweet Potato

Asparagus → | S. Squash

Gr. Onion → | Garlic

Popcorn → | Rutabaga

Chard → | Canteloupe → | Endive

Succession and Companion Plantings

By this point you've been introduced to the preliminaries of garden planning. Control over the garden's yield of vegetables is achieved by envisioning how and how much of the produce will be used in the family kitchen or by friends.

A vegetable garden should provide a continuing and ever-changing bounty of fresh produce to its caretakers. This planning objective requires using gardening techniques wisely, growing more than one crop in succession during the growing season, and planting two or more crops together at the same time or at overlapping times. Home gardeners call the first of these methods "succession planting," while the second is called "companion planting." Both techniques are easy to understand and implement.

SUCCESSION PLANTING. The garden growing season ranges from 120 days (in high mountain regions and the northernmost tier of U.S. states and the Canadian provinces) to 270 or more days (in the temperate coastal regions and balmy South). A quick glance at the Planting Depths, Germination, and Harvest chart [see pg. 168] reveals that many vegetables take the full 120-day season to sprout, mature, and ripen fruit for harvest. Heat-loving species may take even longer than the available season allows, making early-start techniques necessary to bring them to term. The most tender plants (watermelon, cantaloupes, and peanuts) may not grow at all in areas with short growing seasons. Similarly, desert southwest locations will find it impossible to

grow spinach, celery, or other quick-bolting vegetables much after winter's cool temperatures have passed; such cool-season crops usually are planted late in autumn in these "reverse growing" climates.

Other vegetable species—cool-season varieties especially—are characterized by quick growth and early fruiting. These vegetables have short life cycles ranging from eight to ten weeks. Because they are quick to grow and mature, their specialized growth habit can be used to raise a steady stream of vegetables for harvest.

Earlier in this chapter, we discussed plants that fruited for harvesting all at the same time. The determinate varieties of cooking tomatoes, for example, form flowers on the tips of their branches, then the plant stops growing. These flowers develop into bunches of fruit that turn red for picking all at once. If you want to spread out the labor of juicing or canning determinate tomato varieties, plant a stand of several plants one week, then wait two or three weeks and plant a second group, a few more weeks, a third

batch, then a fourth, and so on. Just remember to allow enough time for each planting to mature and ripen before the growing season draws to a close in your region.

At this point, you well might be asking where you will find the space for all of these tomato plants. If you follow these instructions, you quickly will realize that the third round of tomato bushes destined for the garden will fit nicely in that recently vacated lettuce or spinach bed—two cool-season crops whose harvest time has come and passed. With this discovery also will come a complete understanding of the basic concept of succession planning—a space-saving technique used by gardeners the world over to increase the yield of their beds and extend the duration of their harvest.

Succession planting also means enjoying a delightfully different "menu" of vegetables as the seasons progress. You may choose to replace one variety with another of the same type or to try planting entirely new vegetables. Many home gardeners plant early varieties in their first cycle, then sow longer maturing, more tasty cultivars a few weeks later. These strategies provide different flavors, looks, and tastes to their kitchen tables at different times.

Succession planting seems easy enough in concept, and the truth is, it is even easier to execute. Almost every gardener can use this simple principle to grow a wider variety of vegetables. The Vegetable Encyclopedia [see page 307] provides complete information on how succession plantings can ensure an ongoing harvest of desired vegetables, as well as which companion plants should be considered—the next topic of discussion.

COMPANION PLANTING. Companion planting is an old idea and one that stems from the belief that certain plants can deter plant pests. Modern agricultural research and many gardeners' personal observations have shed substantial doubt on this view that planting pest-resistant flowers near pest-susceptible vegetables brings beneficial results.

Regardless of its probable inefficacy in discouraging pests, companion planting has other significant benefits. Joint planting of symbiotic vegetables and flowers can help save space, increase the yield of plants, and enhance the aesthetics of a healthy, attractive garden.

Plants' growth habits vary. Some are tall and narrow, others low and wide. Some spread out, while others command little more space than that allocated at their planting. Some are short-lived; others go on growing, flowering, and fruiting until they are killed by frost, lack of water, or pests. Most are annuals, but others are

perennials that last from year to year with the proper care. Harvest cycles also differ, all to the home gardener's benefit.

Because vegetable habits are so varied, the unique characteristics of each can be used to develop companion relationships that conserve space. As we described earlier, rows of lettuce can yield to tomato bushes. A short-lived crop that is shade tolerant, such as peas, can be planted beneath a tall, narrow, and long-lived species, such as corn—at least in most areas of the country. The corn soon will sprout and climb

toward the sky, providing the 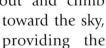 slow-starting peas with natural stakes for support.

A similar relationship mates cucumber vines, trained up a lattice, and spinach, which tends to bolt during the hot weather that accompanies the arrival of long-sunlight days. Spinach's tendency to bolt prematurely will be slowed if it is shaded beneath the broad leaves of the cucumber vines. The cucumbers benefit by being above mildew-nurturing damp soil, which also means the fruits will be straighter.

Other companion-planting opportunities exist for gardeners with the foresight to plant perennials, such as asparagus, in previous seasons. These hardy plants are purchased as root crowns, which then are buried deep in well-fertilized beds. In three years' time, the crowns sprout in spring to provide bountiful crops of tasty spears. Throughout the rest of the growing season, the spindly male shoots of the asparagus mature into feathery green fronds about 4 feet (1.2 m) tall. They provide an excellent protection from birds for low-growing strawberry plants, which can be set among the asparagus in the early spring. Take care, however: asparagus' hardy spears can penetrate right through young strawberry plants, making harvest of either crop difficult; strawberry and asparagus rows should be spaced at least 2 feet (60 cm) apart.

June

June 22nd
Set yellow onions out in old spinach bed

June 23rd
Pull radishes
plant melons + squash

58

ROTATION AND VARIATION. While companion planting can maximize yield and beautify any garden space and succession planting offers a means to control the timing and duration of harvests, the home gardener should consider one more technique when planning plantings: rotation of different vegetables through each individual planting area in the garden in succeeding seasons.

Certain plants have well-documented relationships with certain common diseases and pests. Garlic and onion, for instance, attract a flying pest called *Hylemya antiqua* that lays its eggs in the soil around the roots of the growing plants. Because it takes several generations for the insects to build up sufficient numbers to become a damaging nuisance, a vegetable gardener intent on a good crop of garlic may enjoy bountiful and beautiful heads the first year only to discover that a second or following year's crop is stunted and filled with boring maggots—the hatched young of the eggs from the flying adult pest.

Knowledgeable gardeners choose new locations to plant their onions and garlic each year since the pupae that hatch in the prior year's garlic patch die if no host plants are available to feed them. It is safe to replant them in the original bed after a few seasons have reduced the insect population—roughly a four-year cycle is best. During this time, immune crops such as squash, melons, beans, or peas, will grow perfectly well in these spots.

Other plants rapidly exhaust the soil of certain trace nutrients, causing plant vitality and yield to decline in subsequent years. This problem is of more concern to commercial growers than home vegetable gardeners since use of compost, fertilizer, and soil amendments in the home garden nearly eliminates the soil depletion cycle. Nonetheless, many gardeners tire of their garden's routine appearance and plantings each year, or conditions change in the garden due to young trees maturing and shading areas. For these and for many other reasons, gardeners usually try new planting locations for their standard crops or plant new varieties of vegetables in the old patch in a quest for the perfect garden.

Choosing a Beautiful Garden

There are beautiful vegetable gardens, and there are beautiful flower gardens, but it really comes down to the eye of the beholder. By nature, most gardeners prefer cultivating either vegetables or flowers, and those that enjoy growing both rarely do so to the same degree. It also is unusual for a member of either group to see the result of the other's labor as equal in beauty.

The beauty found in the home vegetable garden does not lie merely in its being a practical and bountiful source of fresh produce. Vegetable gardeners usually value the ordered neatness of their plantings as much as they do an abundant yield and the three telling characteristics of fine produce—large size, freedom from blemish, and outstanding taste. This competitive trait frequently culminates in informal contests or entry into local fairs, where perfect heads of cabbage, huge and succulent tomatoes, and luscious preserves are judged, complimented, and envied. No higher aesthetic award is attained by a vegetable gardener than receiving compliments on the taste, texture, and quality of one's garden produce from passersby or neighbors.

But if bounty and quality were the only considerations that mattered, home vegetable gardeners would miss out on the real joy the beauty of their gardens and pastime offers. The truth is, a vegetable garden is the best of two worlds. A growing ground also is a place of beauty, of solace, of contemplation, and of joy, not just a larder filled with fresh produce from Mother Nature. Gardeners bond with the earth in ways made unique by years of toil and observation—touching and seeing the soil, growing plants, and monitoring the effects of weather and climate. Through the acts of caring for and being rewarded by something outside one's own self, gardeners find a refuge from the workplace, from the outside world, and, sometimes, even from themselves.

Raised-bed Gardens. The ultimate in vegetable garden aesthetics is attained through raised-bed gardening, also termed "French intensive gardening." Neat wooden or stone borders and carefully tended pathways in such gardens serve to divide the many islands of produce and plenty. Each raised bed overflows with assortments of compatible plantings, providing a new view with every step.

Raised-bed gardens require somewhat more care than a simple plot, but not substantially more. The effort initially invested in the planning and installation of the beds themselves usually pays dividends to the gardener for many seasons. Once installed, raised-bed gardens weather into their surroundings and become eye-catching fixtures in the home's landscape, seldom requiring wholesale renovation.

Container Gardens. A vegetable gardener faced with limits on space, constraints on personal time—or who simply wants to bring the garden into closer proximity—may convert a patio, deck, rooftop, or vacant sideyard into an orderly, productive, and beautiful space. Container gardens take advantage of vertical space for employing innovative terraces, hanging planters, and climbing supports, trellises, and arches. These options convert precious space with filtered sunlight into a growing garden, almost out of thin air.

Row Gardens. Row crop gardens are reminders of a rich farm heritage. With neat and orderly row plants arrayed in arrow-straight lines and hill plantings ordered in squares, circles, and geometric patterns, row gardens once dotted backyards across the continent. In such gardens, beans and peas climb poles and string in tripod fashion, bushes are contained, care is apparent, and everything is in its place.

SPACE PLANNING

VEGETABLE	MAX. PLANTS PER SQ. YD.	MAX. PLANTS PER M²	VEGETABLE	MAX. PLANTS PER SQ. YD.	MAX. PLANTS PER M²
Artichoke	0.4	1.5	Pepper, Sweet	15	1.3
Asparagus	14	0.2	Potato	20	3.6
Bean, Broad	30	0.6	Potato, Sweet	20	1.8
Bean, Lima	55	0.5	Pumpkin	4	2.6
Bean, Snap	55	0.5	Radish	500	0.6
Beet	120	2.7	Rhubarb	2.5	0.4
Broccoli	8	1.3	Roquette	12	2.1
Brussels Sprouts	5	2.0	Rutabaga	50	3.1
Cabbage	8	3.4	Salsify	400	1.0
Cabbage, Chinese	18	3.5	Shallot	120	0.4
Cantaloupe	3	2.7	Spinach	50	0.9
Carrot	200	3.0	Spinach, New Zealand	15	0.9
Cauliflower	8	1.5	Squash, Summer	8	0.2
Celery	50	7.0	Squash, Winter	5	0.6
Collards	14	3.7	Sunflower, Seed	12	0.1
Corn, Popcorn	8	0.7	Swiss Chard	25	1.0
Corn, Sweet	8	1.1	Tomatillo	8	0.9
Cucumber	14	2.1	Tomato	5	1.3
Eggplant	14	2.9	Turnip	120	3.1
Endive	22	2.7	Watermelon	3	3.1
Garlic	60	2.2			
Greens, Various	12	2.7			
Kale	14	0.8			
Kohlrabi	8	2.7			
Leek	120	1.1			
Lettuce	14	3.1			
Melon	4	1.8			
Mustard	20	0.8			
Okra	15	1.9			
Onion, Drying	120	4.6			
Onion, Green	200	1.6			
Parsnip	120	1.1			
Pea, English	170	0.4			
Pea, Snap	150	0.4			
Pea, Southern	120	0.2			
Pepper, Hot	100	1.3			

Beyond Style to Space Planning

Whatever style you choose for your garden, whether for its aesthetic appeal or for more practical considerations, the outward appearance of bounty and lush growth will belie the fact that each plant must be provided with sufficient space, access to sunlight, and tender, constant care. This preparation before, during, and after planting is the final step in thoroughly planning your garden.

The Space Planning chart opposite provides the core information needed to space plants for an attractive and productive garden. Each plant, either at the time of seeding or at transplanting, must be given the opportunity to reach its full potential. This potential is realized by correctly spacing it from neighboring plants so that an adequate and continuing supply of water and nutrients (as well as pollen from nearby plants) can be obtained easily from the soil, air, and sunlight available.

The chart contains information for each type of garden—raised bed, container, row, and hill. Plant sizing information is given both in height and in horizontal spread so you can divide up available space among your crops and combine ones where appropriate. Information for transplant sizing is also provided so that you can determine easily when to move seedlings outdoors or know what size plantings to purchase.

DRAWING GARDEN PLANS. Nothing may be as helpful to a beginning gardener's space planning as the use of a kitchen table and a blank pad of graph paper. On the following page is a sample Garden Worksheet—before filling it in, you may want to make photocopies to plan out your succession plantings and for use in future seasons.

First, sketch your garden onto the grid, using a scale of one square to equal 1 square foot (or 1,000 cm^2). Next, add arrows to show the four compass directions. Sketch trees, fences, and other boundaries as well as any structures or yard features in their proper locations. Also indicate sources of water from downspouts, sprinklers, or irrigation risers.

WARNING: Always contact your local utility before digging in the vicinity of underground lines, pipes, and conduits.

Garden Worksheet

East-West Line

Gardener: Season:

Scale:

Finally, indicate any underground utilities, such as water pipes, outdoor lighting wires, conduits, or gas lines, if you know their locations.

After you've completed the scale drawing of the site, view, photograph, or videotape the garden area at various times of the day, including early morning, midmorning, noon, midafternoon, and late afternoon. Note where sunlight falls, keeping in mind that the day will be longer and the sun will be higher in the noonday sky in June than in February.

Back at your drawing board, sketch the boundaries of any areas that will remain in shade for more than two hours, then those that will remain in shade for more than four hours, then those shaded for more than six hours.

Once the backyard garden has been well defined, add to the worksheet the names of all the vegetable species that you want to grow. The Vegetable Encyclopedia [see pg. 307] contains pictures of growing plants and their fruits, with a description of each species and its notable features and habits. Be sure to try a few that are unusual, interesting, or just plain fun—such as popcorn, peanuts, or gourds. Next to each vegetable, note the information on spacing and plant sizing from the Spacing of Plants chart [see page 176]. Also add important information from the Planting Depths, Germination, and Harvest chart [see pg. 168]. Finally, take into account your available time and your expectations regarding consumption.

Next, take some scrap graph paper and draw a bed, row, or hill using the first vegetable on your list. Add plants until the harvest scale indicates that your planting has achieved the target consumption goal. Then do the same for your other vegetables. Next, considering their sunlight needs, try to fit them into the garden site. Make sure to add an access path wherever a bed, row, or hill extends more than 3 feet (90 cm) from any natural access point such as a border, pathway, or edge.

Garden Layout

Planning your garden's layout requires gathering your idea materials—photos, sketches, catalogs—and graph paper and colored pencils.

Measure your garden area carefully before beginning, noting the distance to all structures and utilities, such as water and power outlets. Draw a base plan of these items, then overlay it with your translucent graph paper. Trace the base plan and begin drawing your plan, Follow these easy steps:

1 Working in erasable pencil, sketch the basic layout of your planned beds to scale, adjusting them as necessary to fit the area and your plan concept. Refer to your source materials and this book when allocating space to each bed. When the placement is right, ink the lines.

2 Use colored pencils to shade areas depicting your choice of materials—paths in crushed bark or pea gravel, surrounding turf, planter edges, etc.—making a legend for later reference.

3 Indicate your vegetable plantings within the beds, labeling each for reference. Allocate space according to the expected yield for each crop or planting.

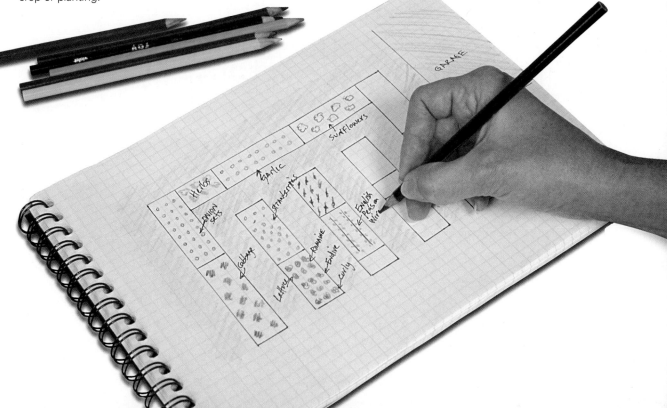

Try to think of the garden in three dimensions, placing low-growing varieties together and medium and tall plants in sites that do not block sunlight to other growing vegetables. Leave a space here and there for a wheelbarrow or a garden cart. Add, subtract, or move elements of the garden around until the desired effect is achieved.

In the best of all worlds you would experiment with a garden plan well before the season. The weather is still cold, and snow or rain makes the ground unworkable. Plenty of time remains to get the plan right. It is a time for research—reading seed catalogs, culling ideas from past seasons or other backyards, and leafing through gardening magazines for inspiration.

REALIZING THE PLAN. Eventually—usually later than the gardener really prefers—spring announces its presence with welcome thaws or dwindling rainstorms, sap rising in the trees, and shoots emerging from the newly warmed ground. As soon as weather conditions permit, go out to your garden site with a sack of flour, a tape measure, and your diagram to mark the outline of your plan on the ground. If you are considering raised beds, mark their edges by putting down boards and sprinkling flour along the edges.

When you finish marking the site, stand back and examine it very carefully. Imagine the growing vegetable plants, up to 7 feet (2.1 m) tall in the case of sunflowers and corn. Observe the site in the morning, at midday, and in late afternoon. Remind yourself that the sun will be rising farther north and climbing higher into the sky a few months further into summer, so any shadows will become shorter. Do you notice any problems with the bed placement? Now is the time to erase a bad start by scuffing the flour line into the surrounding soil and sprinkling in a revision.

When the garden plan is right, it will be readily apparent—it will "feel good." Old-time, experienced gardeners might chuckle at the above preparation. Most often, that chuckle would arise due to fond memories of their first efforts to bring forth bounty from the land in a backyard vegetable garden.

Vegetable gardening is a shared experience. It binds everyone to the common ground from which we all emerged. The cycle of planning, toil, care, and harvest of growing vegetables is a reminder of our own beginnings, youth, and maturity. Vegetable gardening is, after all, mostly an adult pastime; when undertaken by children at all, it usually is with an adult showing them how to dig, hoe, pick, and shuck. It may begin simply enough, with planning a vegetable garden; nevertheless, its impact often endures for generations. Gardening is the opportunity to share one's ideas and the fruit of one's labor with those who have enjoyed the journey already—or with those who someday will pick up the shovel.

Varietal Selection

When seed catalogs start arriving in the mailbox, and the garden centers and nurseries first put out seed displays for the coming season, the selection easily can seem overwhelming. Twenty varieties of corn, twelve different cucumbers, every squash under the sun—how can a gardener decide what to choose?

Though it may be hard for the beginning gardener to believe, the seed companies and local garden retailers have performed much of the hard work. Their years of experience already have determined which plants grow best in your climate, and which do not. Local retailers have refined their selection by only ordering varietals that have grown successfully in past seasons, or newly developed ones for which they have high hopes based on the literature or on seed companies' growing trials.

The goals you have set for your garden will let you know whether to choose a variety that yields an early harvest or full flavor in the fruit, one that will catch the eyes of passersby or be suitable for juicing, freezing, canning, or preserving.

Rather than be daunted by the wide selection, sit down with a catalog or step up to the seed rack. Have fun choosing the varieties that seem right for you and your tastes.

Carefully read the front and back of the package for each seed you are considering. Pay particular attention to the tiny map that sets forth the ideal planting seasons for each region of North America. Find your own location on it, then look for the recommended planting time that applies to your area. Remember that using hot frames or other early-start techniques that allow for earlier planting will extend the growing season. Next, notice the amount of time

Building a Potting Table

A potting table provides a convenient spot in the garden to transplant seedlings, clean containers, mix fertilizer, and perform other messy outdoor tasks. Many excellent models are offered for purchase at retail stores, but building your own custom table is a perfect winter weekend project.

The table shown here is made of durable pressure-treated lumber, pegboard, and readily available hardware. Cut and assemble it with common power and hand tools. Allow about 8–12 work hours total to complete the project.

Required Materials:

Pressure-Treated Lumber:

4	30-in. (76 cm)	2×6 (38×140 mm)	Legs
2	31-in. (79 cm)	2×6 (38×140 mm)	Top crossbraces
2	32½-in. (83 cm)	2×6 (38×140 mm)	Bottom crossbraces
4	12-in. (30.5 cm)	2×6 (38×140 mm)	Crossbrace blocks
4	5½-in. (14 cm)	2×6 (38×140 mm)	Castor mount blocks
6	72-in. (183 cm)	2×6 (38×140 mm)	Top surface planks
2	31-in. (79 cm)	2×6 (38×140 mm)	Top surface supports
4	66-in. (168 cm)	2×6 (38×140 mm)	Bottom shelf planks

Lumber:

1	52-in. (132 cm)	2×4 (38×89 mm)	Front apron support
1	66-in. (167.5 cm)	1×6 (19×140 mm)	Front apron
2	22-in. (55 cm)	1×6 (19×140 mm)	Side aprons

3	18-in. (46 cm)	2×8 (38×184 mm)	Vertical supports
1	72-in. (183 cm)	1×8 (19×184 mm)	Top shelf
1	34⅛-in. (86.5cm)	1×8 (19×184 mm)	Middle shelf

Pegboard Pressboard Sheet ⅜ in. (10 mm):

1	22×72-in. (56×183 cm)		Top shelf backing

Hardware and Materials:

100	No. 8×2½-in. (4×65 mm)	Galvanized deck screws
16	5/16×3½-in. (8×85 mm)	Hex bolts, nuts, washers
4	Caster assemblies with wheel locks and fasteners	
6	Pegboard hooks	
9	Vinyl-covered hanger hooks (screw-in)	
1	Bottle woodworker's exterior glue	

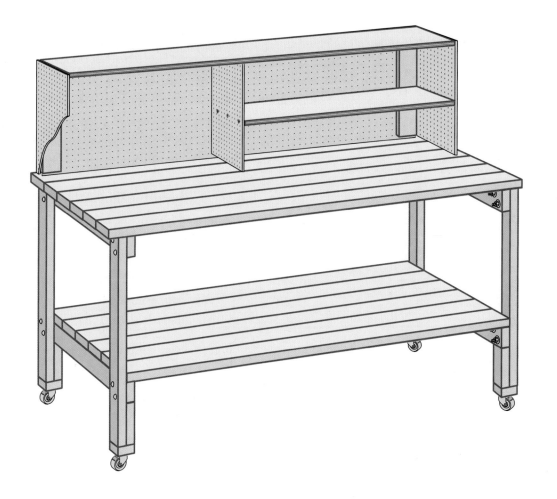

1 Construct leg assemblies: Cut legs, crossbraces, cross-brace blocks, and caster mount blocks. On a flat work surface, align 2 legs parallel, 33 in. (84 cm) apart. Flush top crossbrace to top corner of back leg and top of front leg, allowing 1 1/2-in. (38-mm) setback from front leg edge. Align crossbrace blocks parallel and flush to the bottom of each leg, then mark, drill, glue, and attach with 4 deck screws. Flush bottom crossbrace to outside edge of each leg, tight to the crossbrace block. Square and clamp the assembly, mark and drill two 1/4-in. (6-mm) bolt holes at each leg-crossbrace junction. Thread a washer onto each bolt, then drive the bolts through the legs and crossbraces with a hammer. Attach the final washer and nut on each bolt, then tighten until the wood just compresses. Release the clamps as each joint is secured. Align a caster block at the foot of each leg and attach with 4 deck screws. Repeat steps for second leg assembly.

2 Build the work surface: Cut top surface planks, top surface supports and front apron support. Loosely align the 6 planks, squaring them into a rectangle. Apply glue to each side edge of the 4 central planks, square, clamp tightly, and allow to dry overnight. When dry, release the clamps. Measure 4 1/2 in. (11.5 cm) from each of the 33-in. (84-cm) edges of the assembly and draw two lines. Place a work surface support on the inside of each line, flush with the assembly's back edge and 2 in. (50 mm) short of its front edge, and clamp. Drill 2 1/8×2-in. (3×50-mm) holes, 2 to each top plank, through the support, and into (but not through) the top planks. Attach both supports to the surface assembly with deck screws. Attach the front apron support between the work surface supports with deck screws.

3 Attach legs to work surface: Place the work surface assembly face down on a level surface. Stand each leg assembly on the work surface assembly, aligning each flush with the back edge and parallel and snug to a work surface support. Drill ⅛-in. (3 mm) pilot holes horizontally through the top crossbrace into a work surface support and fasten the leg assembly with deck screws. Repeat for other leg assembly.

Attach castors: Drill and install a caster assembly into the bottom of each leg, using the hardware supplied with the caster.

4 Attach bottom shelf: Cut 4 bottom shelf planks. Using a circular saw, rip ½ in. (10 mm) off of one plank, making it 5 in. (13 cm) wide. Stand the bench on its legs, checking it for square, and place the bottom shelf planks so that they span the bottom crossbraces. Flush each plank to the outer edge of the crossbraces, clamp, and drill 2⅛-in. (3 mm) pilot holes through each plank end into the crossbraces. Fasten with deck screws.

5 Construct the upper shelf unit: Cut vertical shelf supports, top, and middle shelf. Cut pegboard. On a flat surface, stand the shelf supports on edge, parallel and spaced 22½ in. (57 cm) apart. Fit the top shelf to their ends, drill ⅛-in. (3 mm) pilot holes, and fasten the shelf to the supports with 3 deck screws driven into each support. Measure 8¼ in. (21 cm) from the base of the middle and left shelf supports and mark a line with a square. Align the middle shelf between the 2 supports with its base on the line. Drill ⅛-in. (3 mm) pilot holes and fasten the middle shelf to its supports.

Next, square the pegboard to the shelf assembly, overhanging the bottom edge by 4 in. (10 cm). Fasten with deck screws to shelf and supports.

6 Attach the workshelf aprons: Cut the front and side aprons. Fit the side aprons flush against the top crossbraces, using them as a stop. Drill ⅛-in. (3 mm) pilot holes through the aprons and fasten them with deck screws. Fit the front apron onto its apron support, predrill and fasten it with deck screws.

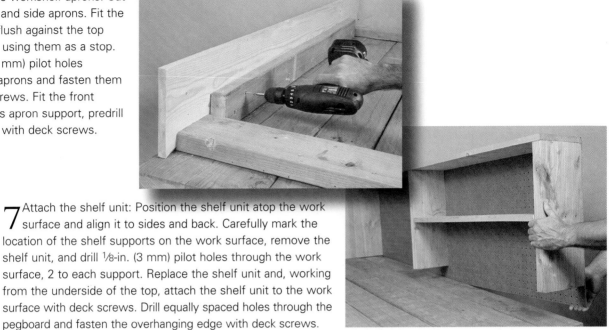

7 Attach the shelf unit: Position the shelf unit atop the work surface and align it to sides and back. Carefully mark the location of the shelf supports on the work surface, remove the shelf unit, and drill ⅛-in. (3 mm) pilot holes through the work surface, 2 to each support. Replace the shelf unit and, working from the underside of the top, attach the shelf unit to the work surface with deck screws. Drill equally spaced holes through the pegboard and fasten the overhanging edge with deck screws.

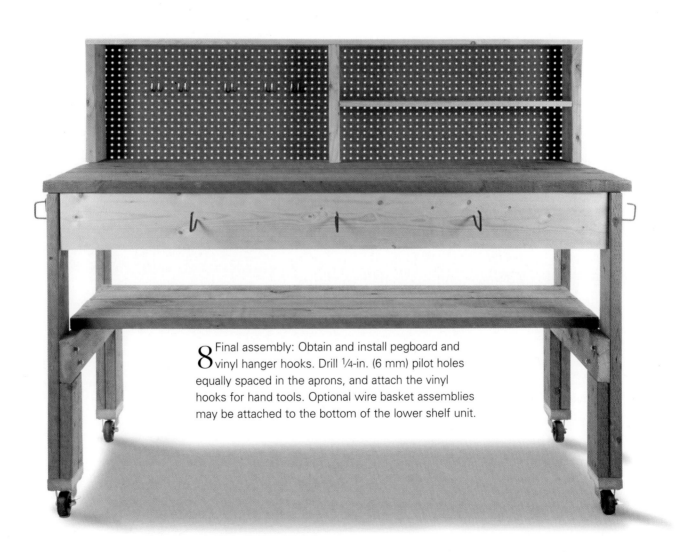

8 Final assembly: Obtain and install pegboard and vinyl hanger hooks. Drill ¼-in. (6 mm) pilot holes equally spaced in the aprons, and attach the vinyl hooks for hand tools. Optional wire basket assemblies may be attached to the bottom of the lower shelf unit.

from sowing to harvest. Look at the grower's plant spacing recommendation and compare it to the one found in the Space Planning chart [see pg. 124]. The seed package specifically describes the growth habit of the supplier's varietal contained within, while our chart provides general information applicable to all varietals in the species.

Especially note what the package says about disease resistance (this is usually shown on the label by letter codes; see the sample seed package label on page 132.) If you are uncertain or cannot choose between two options, describe your objectives to a knowledgeable clerk or nursery attendant and ask for a recommendation.

If the season has already advanced beyond the planting time suggested on the seed package, consider transplanting nursery-grown seedlings, especially if the growing season is short in your area [see Chapter Six: *Planting Your Garden*].

Transplants have been nurtured and cultivated to make them strong and healthy when they arrive in the store, and in-store care keeps them in that state; in fact, most retailers guarantee success with a plant replacement policy in the event of failure. Because the retailer has decided which varietals are best for the local climate zone and microclimates, purchasing nursery-grown starts also may be more reliable than cold framing or green-housing your own seedlings. You will trade off variety, however, since seedling selection is limited compared to seed. In other words, if your heart is set on a specific or unusual variety, it's very likely that only seeds will do.

The Vegetable Encyclopedia [see pg. 307] contains most information needed to understand each vegetable and its suitability to your area, its strengths and weaknesses, plus a listing of many varietals. Complete planting and care instructions are also provided. With this information, and that found on the Internet, from talking to fellow gardeners, and from consulting with professional associations or government offices, you should have everything you need to ask questions of nursery and garden store staff to make the vegetable selections that will accomplish the goals you have set for your garden.

Preparing Soil for Planting

In Chapter Three: *Gardening Basics*, we discussed the components of perfect garden soil [see Great Garden Soil, pg. 44]. In addition to good texture, ample supplies of nitrogen, phosphorus, and potassium are essential.

Now, with your garden planned and your seeds chosen, the weather warming and your tools at hand, let's look at what steps are required to prepare the beds to receive both seeds and transplants.

Over the winter, garden soil tends to compact. Part of this is due to settling, but a surprising amount results from the impact of rain and the weight of snow on the soil. Add to this the decay and reduction of the soil's organic components and your vegetable garden may be too dense to permit water to penetrate easily.

Before you can plant you must correct this deficiency. Loosening the soil is relatively easy—by double-digging or rototilling—but unless you deal with the texture and composition issues, it soon will be compacted again.

Good planting soil should be loose, filled with air, and comprise equal parts of mineral clay, silt, sand, and decomposed organic matter. In preparation for planting, add organic compost and well-rotted manure to increase both the nitrogen and organic components of the soil.

Now also may be the time to balance your soil's pH by applying lime to raise pH and increase alkalinity, or by adding sulfur to lower pH and make the soil more acidic. Allow about 4 pounds (1.8 kg) of lime and 1 pound (0.5 kg) of sulfur per hundred square feet (9 m^2) of garden in order to lower or raise pH one point. These water-soluble minerals will need to be replaced from time to time.

Finally, correct too-dense soils with gypsum and extra compost and quick-draining soils with fine-grained mineral silt and abundant compost.

It's unlikely that your garden will require all of these amendments—it probably will need a simple topdressing of compost and fertilizer and a quick tilling. Conduct soil and percolation tests to determine your beds' needs.

SOIL TESTING. The purpose of soil testing is to determine what your soil contains so that you will know what you need to add for growing vegetables.

There are two major tests every home gardener should know: acid-alkaline balance (pH) and nutrient analysis. Let's take a look at each of them:

CONDUCTING A pH TEST. Most garden retailers and nurseries sell electronic testers for measuring soil acidity. Such meters work by measuring the electric resistance between two electrodes when they are placed into a mixture of water and garden soil. Depending on the amount of dissolved salts in the liquid being tested, resistance to the meter's current decreases or increases. Alkaline soils tend to have low resistance to electricity while acidic soils have high resistance.

To use a pH meter at home, collect several samples of soil from around the garden. Take the samples from the soil at least 6 inches (15 cm) beneath the surface. Mix the samples in a clean container, then add distilled water (available at most grocery stores and drugstores) as the meter package instructions recommend.

Turn on the meter and insert its probe into the mixture of soil and water. In a few moments, it will register the pH of the soil in your garden.

A reading of 7.0 on the scale is considered neutral—neither acidic nor alkaline—and any measurement less than 4.0 or greater than 8.0 indicates a significant imbalance requiring correction if your vegetables are to survive. Low pH soils lack calcium, magnesium, and phosphorus. Plants in such soil often have purple-tinged foliage and poor vitality. Soils high in pH contain excessive salt, sodium, or calcium carbonate. These cause yellowing of leaves and stems followed by brown tips and edges. Plants do not perform well in soil conditions outside of their ideal range of 5.5–7.5.

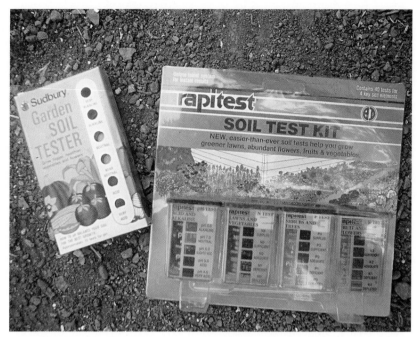

CONDUCTING A FERTILITY TEST. For many years the only way to test your soil was by digging up samples in the same manner as for a pH test, then packaging them up and mailing them away to a professional soil laboratory, which, in a few weeks, would send back an analysis.

Today, home test kits—available in most garden retail outlets and many seed catalogs—are reliable and accurate. They contain chemical reagents that react predictably to various soil components, either by changing color or otherwise signaling the test results.

Any good soil test should check for nitrogen salts, phosphorus, and potassium—the macronutrients. Conduct the soil test following the package instructions exactly in order to obtain accurate results. Even though most test kits do not check for micronutrients, a program of regular fertilization with organic fertilizers will assure that sufficient quantities are present in the garden.

Test your soil once a year, in the spring.

Testing Your Soil

Soil test kits are sold by most garden retailers. They determine the quality of soil and suitability for planting.

Inexpensive kits measure only nitrogen, phosphorus, and potassium. Better kits also test pH.

For accurate results, use the process shown here:

1 Use a shovel or spade to dig a hole at least 16-in. (40 cm) deep and 12-in. (30 cm) in diameter. Avoid testing surface soil in your garden—plant roots draw nutrients from subsurface soil and the reading may be inaccurate.

2 Using a clean trowel and collecting cup, remove soil sample from the side of the hole, at a point 12-in. (30 cm) deep. Follow test kit specific instructions to measure the nutrients and pH of the sample.

USING THE TEST RESULTS. Most soil test meters and kits include information suggesting corrective actions based on the results of your soil's test. Amend your soil as recommended. Till in the amendments, working them deep into the garden soil. Remember that your plants' roots will be 12–18-inches (30–45 cm) or more deep when fully grown. To be effective, amendments must extend to the furthest reaches of root growth.

DIGGING AND TILLING. Arguably the most labor-intensive part of vegetable gardening is preparing the soil for planting. In the past, this meant digging—often double digging [see Double Digging, pg. 50]—the garden with a spade or shovel. An excellent alternative is using a rototiller or garden tiller.

Tillers are easy to obtain and use. If your garden is small, purchasing one may not be practical; fortunately, rental yards offer these machines for hire by the hour at generally reasonable rates.

When using a garden tiller, remember that the goal of tilling is to loosen the soil to a depth of at least 16 inches (40 cm). Break all clods and remove any debris or rocks that the tiller unearths. Make two passes—one in one direction and the other perpendicular to it. This will ensure that the tiller thoroughly incorporates any amendments while loosening the soil. When finished, rake the area smooth and level before making rows and hills for planting.

Avoid tilling when the soil is sodden and sticky. Mechanical tillers tend to bog down in such soil and their digging arms can become clogged.

Constructing Raised Beds

When native soil is too clayey, rocky, or sandy, or when your garden site is not level, raised bed planters level the grade and allow gardening in rich, nutrient-filled soil. Such planters are easy to build, take only a few hours, and require a minimum of carpentry skills.

Never use pressure-treated lumber to construct vegetable beds. Such lumber contains poisonous compounds that may contaminate your plants. Avoid hazard by always using decay-resistant redwood or red cedar lumber.

1 Use flour, garden lime or sand to mark the edges of the raised bed area. Observe the result and adjust placement of the planter as necessary until fits your needs.

2 Excavate a perimeter trench 4–6-in. (10–15 cm) deep beneath the marked lines. Level the bottom of the trench, using a carpenter's level.

Required Materials:

Redwood or Red Cedar Lumber:

4	2×12-in. (38×286 mm)	Sideboards
	(dimension as required by site)	

Hardware:

12	No. 8×4-in. (4×100 mm)	Galvanized deck screws
24	No. 8×½-in. (4×12 mm)	Galvenized deck screws

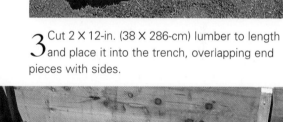

3 Cut 2 × 12-in. (38 × 286-cm) lumber to length and place it into the trench, overlapping end pieces with sides.

4 Drill pilot holes. Use a socket wrench or power driver to install three deck screws at each corner.

5 Drive wooden stakes 3-ft. (90 cm) apart and screw through them into, but not through, the sideboards. Fill the planter with rich soil and compost to ready it for planting.

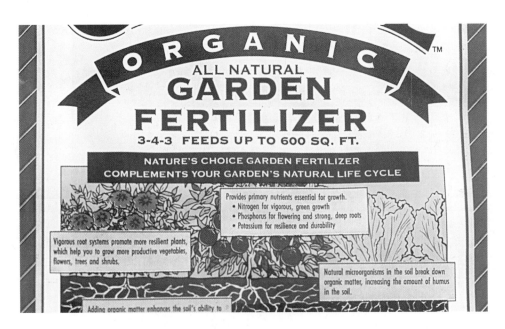

Now that you have a good grasp on garden planning fundamentals, have considered your interests and the amount of time you have, know the amount of space you have available for planting, and have weighed goals, sketched a garden plan, and chosen specific vegetable varieties, you're ready to learn how to plant your vegetable garden.

Planting Seeds or Planting Your Garden Seedlings

Is there a more enjoyable part of vegetable gardening than actually planting? While most people would guess the harvest, just ask any seasoned gardener: there is no moment quite as joyful and renewing to the spirit as kneeling in the soil on a warm, sunny day, coaxing seeds out of their packages, or seedlings out of their containers, then returning a few days later to find beds filled with tiny sprouts or plantings sporting new growth.

To understand this is to appreciate the weeks and sometimes months of preparation and planning that precede putting that first seed or transplant nurtured from seed in the soil. In fact, that single act of planting is no less than the culmination of work started—not only by the gardener but by the garden—at the end of last year's harvest.

Formed in the final days of the prior season from the fruit of fertilized flowers, seeds are the tiny messengers that bring the gardener continuity from year to year. Each seed contains a complete, embryonic plant awaiting the gardener's help to find it a nurturing place to grow in the coming season. Is it any wonder, then, that every vegetable gardener's heart fills with deep satisfaction at planting time?

Vegetable seeds hold within them the potential for new life, a new season of bounty, and a new fulfillment of promise. That is part of their magic. So too is every hour the gardener spends dreaming about the garden, designing its layout and new crops, poring through seed catalogs or nurturing seeds in flats indoors. All of this effort has led to this one crowning moment: planting.

Pause to think about just what this entails. Let's find out right now.

After selecting a site, laying out the garden, preparing the beds for planting, and choosing the vegetables you want to grow, the next step is to get your hands dirty. In this chapter, we explore the following major considerations when it comes to planting and transplanting vegetables:

- Deciding whether to plant seeds or nursery-grown seedlings

- Judging the weather and soil temperature for planting

- Choosing where to start seeds indoors

- Understanding how to plant seeds and how to buy seedlings

- Following the proper steps for hardening and transplanting

- Assessing proper seedling growth and problems

- Protecting young plantings from diseases and pests

Before we get to the potting soil and planting, however, we need to make an important choice: seeds or transplants.

Adding Beauty to Your Vegetable Plantings

In recent years, the selection of seeds offered by growers has increased dramatically. Among these new vegetables are many unusual, heritage—antique forms revived from the past—and colorful new plants that can add beauty to your vegetable plantings. Choose from such attractive and interesting options as decorative cabbages and Brussels sprouts, bright-colored scarlet runner beans, and yellow, gold, and zebra-striped tomatoes.

Seeds or Transplants

Growing vegetables from seeds and transplanting nursery-grown seedlings into the garden work equally well. Both will produce healthy, bountiful vegetable gardens. So how to choose?

The most common reasons to select seeds over transplants, or vice versa, have to do with your level of patience, your location, your desire to try unusual vegetable varieties, and a cost advantage (either slight or substantial depending on the size of your garden) over purchasing nursery transplants. An increasing number of gardeners prefer to get a head start on the season by using transplants—conveniently sold in so-called "six packs," or individually in 2- or 4-inch (5- or 10-cm) pots.

Transplants are available at most garden retailers and nurseries during the early months of the growing season. Both availability and selection wane with the progression of the gardening season.

Aside from convenience, your choice may be affected by the location of your garden, especially if it's in a high mountain region, the northern tier of states or Canada, or if it has a microclimate that reduces the growing season to a few short, frost-free months. For short-season gardens— or if you lack the time or facilities to start seedlings indoors, in a greenhouse, or in a cold frame—transplants may be your only real option. Refer to the plant hardiness zones maps [see pg. 81 or 408] for your area and ask lots of questions of garden store staff to find out when your region's frost danger will pass.

Whether planted in a special area of the garden or an interesting container—many earthenware pots sporting Italian, Spanish, and other motifs are available—decorative and unusual vegetables are a treat.

Many nurseries and garden retail stores have special sections for these decorative garden plants. Ask a clerk or other gardeners for ideas on dressing up your vegetable beds.

They'll be glad to give you advice.

Finally, don't forget flowers. It's very pleasing to view a vegetable garden adorned with them. Plant along paths, at row ends and in borders. They'll look great and attract bees, too!

Local gardening advice is especially important if the climate of your garden is different than that of the general surrounding region or area. Nearby mountains, angles of sunlight on hillside gardens, the presence of nearby bodies of water, wind exposure, and tree shade all can play a decisive role in how your garden will perform.

Even if your garden is blessed with a long growing season, you still may prefer transplants over sowing seed since there are numerous advantages to this quick-start approach.

Planting "Sets"

Some bulb vegetables—notably onion, garlic, and shallots—take two seasons to mature from seed. Many gardeners prefer to plant these slow-maturing species as sets.

Sets are the immature bulbs or cloves of many green-topped root vegetables, harvested by growers

Some gardeners are naturally born with a "time's a-wastin'" approach to life. For them, transplants provide immediate gratification. Bare soil quickly yields to neatly planted rows, taking little more than an afternoon. After a few weeks, plants are knee-high and the garden looks prosperous and well-established.

Other reasons for choosing transplants are to avoid the risks associated with failed germination, early disease, and uncertainty about the number of seeds needed to produce a desired crop. In addition, many transplants come in pest- and disease-resistant varieties.

Also, nursery-grown transplants are healthy and vigorous, with well-developed root systems ready for their move into the garden. Commercial transplants are grown in carefully prepared soils, meticulously watered and fertilized, and kept at ideal growing temperatures. They are rushed weekly from the grower to the retailer to assure that they are in peak condition when the home gardener comes to shop. Most nurseries and garden centers condition their transplant stock to the outdoors to preclude another common cause of failure.

There are lots of ways to pick one garden store, home center, or nursery over another, and as many ways or more to decide which particular plants are right for your vegetable garden. Later, we'll describe how to choose the "best of the best" transplants, if that's your choice. Despite these advantages, many gardeners prefer to pamper, cajole, and coddle their vegetables. For them, planting from seeds provides an engaging pastime as well as a means to enjoy unusual and interesting varieties not commonly found in other local gardens.

and sold each planting season in nurseries and garden stores.

Choose sets that are fresh—each bulb or clove should feel heavy and full and the dry "skin" should only be a layer or two thick.

In your garden's prepared bed, make a hole 2–3-inches (5–7.5 cm) deep for each set with your finger or the handle of a hoe. Space each hole about 4 inches (10 cm) apart for onions and shallots, 6 inches (15 cm) for garlic. Place each set in a hole with the root end down and pack the soil firmly around it.

Finish by topping your planting with a half-inch (12 mm) of topsoil or organic compost to cover.

In time at all, you'll see your first sprouts emerging.

Such gardeners make time and space for their hobby; many have greenhouses or have invested in cold frames to germinate their seeds. Others use sunny indoor windowsills to grow their tender seedlings. Special potting soil, hand-mixed foliar fertilizers and vitamin potions, and watchful eyes contribute to the success of the growing process.

Home gardeners who choose seeds often give as their reason that nurseries and garden centers cannot provide the same wide selection of varieties in transplants as can be found in seed packages purchased locally or through the mail. Though more than a hundred varieties of tomato exist in seed, space limitations in the nursery restrict transplants to a few options known to produce well in the local region. The uniqueness of the many varietal options of seeds—including many seldom seen as transplants—becomes a temptation to those tired of the usual choices.

The easiest way to take advantage of the wide selection of available seed vegetables is to purchase seeds from seed catalogs or at your nursery or garden retailer. Either method works well.

Early each year, seed companies mail catalogs of their entire vegetable line to gardeners on their mailing lists. Many major direct-to-consumer seed growers advertise in popular home and garden magazines. Others may be found in library reference books or through toll-free numbers in local telephone books. A partial listing of these direct-mail seed companies is included in the appendix [see Resources, pg. 413].

Purchasing seeds by mail is as simple as filling out an order card or calling the seed company's toll-free number. It's easy, reliable, and safe. Just allow four to six weeks from the order date to receive the seeds.

Even easier, especially if the garden season has already begun, is to visit a local nursery or garden retailer and pick seeds from their racks. They carry a wide selection of regionally successful vegetable seeds. By law, all seeds sold, regardless of method, must be fresh and meet governmental standards for germination.

Of course, there are some well-known downsides to choosing seed. While nursery-cultivated transplants usually are guaranteed to be disease free, seeds do not carry this promise since they rely so greatly on individual care and the choice of materials used for planting. If you decide to plant seeds, be sure to follow all the step-by-step instructions illustrated later in this chapter. They will assure successful plantings and help avoid any unwelcome surprises.

In the end, many gardeners choose the best of each method: planting certain vegetables from seed, others from transplants. When time runs out, leaving the season too far advanced to plant the seeds of long-harvest vegetables, transplants are the only option.

Whichever your preference—and the debate among gardeners is endless—the results obtained at harvest serve both sides of the patience scale. The truth is, vegetables respond to either start method by offering bountiful yields, so let's look at something that really matters: the weather.

Planting Weather

K iller frosts and late spring snows are the most obvious examples of weather obstacles to early gardening, but cold, drenching rains and chilling fogs can be equally harmful to young plants struggling to grow. In fact, any combination of cold and damp almost guarantees failure since such conditions promote fungus disease, which rots seeds and kills young seedlings. Better to move your gardening indoors until the danger of this weather has passed.

Soil temperature is key to successful germination and early growth of your vegetable plants. Don't try to grow vegetable seeds or seedlings in soil cooler than 40°F (5°C)—without exception, they'll rot instead of sprouting. The hardy vegetables that do tolerate soil temperatures of 40–50°F (5–10°C) are known as "cool season" plants—a reference to their tolerance of lower planting and growing temperatures, not their location or environment. Many other vegetables—the "warm season" varieties—require planting temperatures of 50°F (10°C) or higher. We'll give some tips later on how to know when it's time to plant them, or you can get timing tips from the garden experts at your nursery or garden retail center.

Most vegetables require soil temperatures above 50°F (10°C), and some prefer them to be as high as 95°F (35°C) on a sustained basis to reach maximum performance. They, not surprisingly, are called "warm season" vegetables. (Keep in mind that we are talking here about soil temperature, not air temperature. Garden soil takes longer to warm in the spring and cool in the autumn than does the atmosphere, but it holds heat long after the hottest part of the day has passed.) A complete table of minimum, maximum, and ideal soil temperatures for most vegetable crops is provided [see pg. 162]. Refer to this chart when deciding when to put in vegetable plantings.

To take soil temperature, use a stem thermometer such as the kind sold in photography, hobby, and many garden stores. Reading the temperature requires only a minute or two. However, experienced gardeners often rely on a more informal method. They pick up a handful of soil; when the soil a few inches beneath the surface feels cool but not cold to the touch, they know the bed is ready to plant.

Sunlight and the Planting Season

Sunlight makes plant growth possible. We all know that summers are warm because the sun's position in the sky during that season is higher than in winter. What you may not know is that some vegetables are very sensitive to the length of the day as well as its warmth.

Many vegetable plants time their growth by the length of the daylight hours. It tells them when to flower, when to mature fruit, and when to stop their growth.

Some leafy vegetables—spinach, lettuce, and their cousins—prematurely go to seed when daylight hours lengthen. This is called "bolt." In southern regions, it makes growing leaf crops in summer a bit difficult.

Other plants require long, full days of sunlight to set and mature fruit—tomatoes for one. Take advantage of sunlight by following closely the planting instructions in the temperature table [see pg. 162].

Another quick clue to soil temperature is a glance at the past five days' actual low air temperatures, found in the newspaper or on the weather report. Soil temperatures tend to lag behind the nighttime low until late spring, when the midday sun has risen quite high in the sky compared with its position on the first days of winter. If your area's daily low has been above 50°F (10°C) for several weeks, you can safely seed cool-season plants directly into the outdoor soil.

Old-time farmers used to say that planting conditions for warm-season vegetables weren't right until you could comfortably lie naked on the ground—surely an acid test for the high-80s (30–32°C) soil temperatures that warm-season crops prefer.

Cold rains or unseasonable frosts will cause soil temperatures to drop, usually more by the chilling effect of evaporation than by the moisture, hail, or ice crystals themselves. Seasoned gardeners in unpredictable climates usually protect their tender plantings by spreading weed-free straw or another loose insulating mulch over the planting bed. While providing insulation, mulch allows air to circulate and helps keep weeds to a minimum. As the material decomposes, it also provides a healthy source of nutrition to the growing plants [see Mulching, pg. 220].

MICROCLIMATES. Soil temperatures are influenced by shade from trees and structures, protection from or exposure to winds, and the slope of the site, among other factors. The soil near a wind-protected, sunlight-reflecting building may be as much as 20°F (11°C) warmer than garden soil just a few feet away; exposed sites may be colder. These microclimate differences can mislead even experienced gardeners' conclusions about a plot's readiness for planting. Use your measurements of soil temperatures to decide when to plant vegetables. It is especially important in early springtime, when the marginal differences in soil temperature can mean the difference between seed germinating or not. Later in the year, soil temperatures are not as vital.

A Head Start on the Season

If you prefer to grow some or all of your vegetables from seed, you can learn how to predict when the soil will be warm enough to support and nurture tender plantings. Depending on their type, seeds can take as few as 4 or as many as 25 days to germinate—that is, to swell and break through their hard, protective casings, develop roots, and emerge from the soil. Throughout this early stage, they must receive tender care and consistent moisture and be maintained in temperatures above their minimum recommended levels.

Dedicated gardeners use a greenhouse to assure that their seeds have a proper start. Those with less space or a lower budget can achieve equally good results using a "cold frame"—a thick-sided wooden box with a loosely fitting glass or plastic cover to trap sunlight and heat—or with a few other measures.

COLD FRAMES. A cold frame can get vegetable seedlings started many weeks before the garden is ready to receive them. Use of a cold frame extends the growing season in northern or high-altitude climates by as much as six to eight weeks, long enough for the long-harvest vegetables to be grown in climates that otherwise would not permit their fruit to ripen.

For use outdoors, a cold frame need not even have a bottom, although many gardeners prefer to have one so they can move their tender seedlings indoors at night if frost threatens. Such

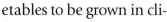

Building a Cold Frame

Warmth-loving vegetables can gain a head start on the season with this easily constructed cold frame. For maximum protection of tender plants on cool spring evenings, bury it deeply in the surrounding soil, allowing only the top to protrude. The translucent hinged top allows abundant air to circulate and, on warm days, may be opened to the sun.

The cold frame shown here is made of sturdy exterior-grade plywood with galvanized hinges and brass fittings. Paint the exterior for extra durability. Corrugated fiberglass panels are available at many building material retailers and often may be cut to size by store personnel. If you choose to cut them yourself, use a fine-toothed plywood blade in a handheld circular saw, and always wear a respirator—inhaled fiberglass dust is a health hazard.

Allow approximately 4–6 work hours total to complete the project, with extra time to gather materials and dry paint.

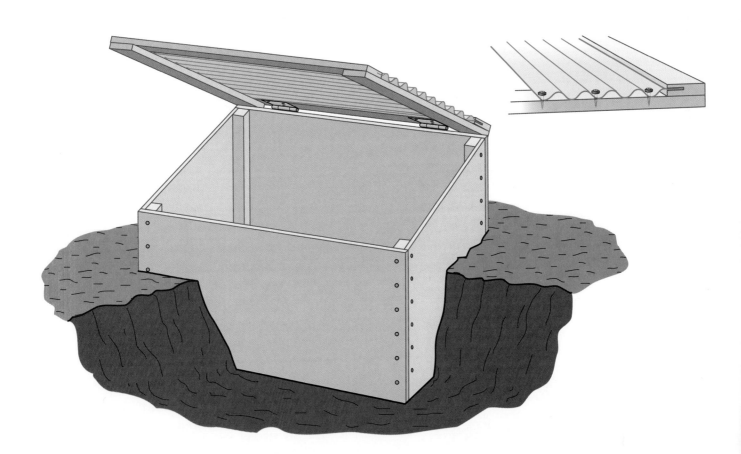

Required Materials:

Raw Materials:

1	48 × 96 × 3/4-in. (120 × 240 × 2 cm)	ABX plywood
1	26 × 36-in. (66 × 90 cm)	Corrugated fiberglass panel

Cut Plywood Panel to Following Components:

1	26 × 36-in. (66×90 cm)	Back panel
1	22 × 36-in. (56×90 cm)	Front panel
2	22 × 26 × 28 1/2-in. (56 × 66 × 72.4 cm)	Side panels
2	5 1/2 × 30 in. (14 × 76 cm)	Upright cover frames
2	4 × 36 in. (10 × 90 cm)	Horizontal cover frames

Hardware:

36	1/4 × 1 1/4-in. (6 × 30 mm)	Phillips brass wood screws
24	1/8 × 5/8-in. (3 × 16 mm)	Phillips brass wood screws
12	1/2 × 1/8-in. (12 × 3 mm)	Brass washers
2	2-in. (50 mm)	Galvanized butt hinges and wood screws

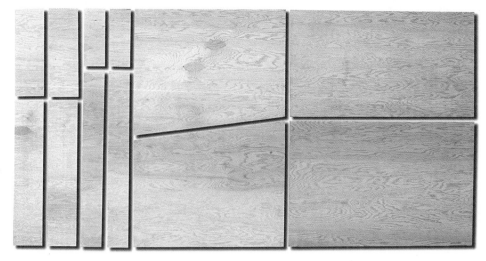

1 Cut plywood into front, back, and side panels, and into upright and horizontal cover frames following layout template shown. With a circular saw, cut a ½-in. (12-mm) kerf slot into one 30-in. (76-cm) edge of each upright cover frame.

2 Assemble cold frame box: Drill ⅛-in. (3-mm) pilot holes through front and back panels into edge of side panels and fasten with ¼-in. (6-mm) screws. Optional: Reinforce each corner with 2 X 2-in. (5 X 5-cm) corner braces.

3 Assemble cover: On a flat surface, fit fiberglass panel edges into kerf slots in upright cover frames. Loosely align horizontal cover frames flush at corners, overlapping the fiberglass and upright cover frames. Square and clamp assembly. Drill ⅛-in. (3-mm) pilot holes through corners and fasten with ¼-in. (6-mm) screws. Fasten panels to frames with ⅛-in. (3-mm) wood screws and washers.

4 Attach cover: Fit butt hinges 12 in. (30 cm) from each corner to back panel and edge of horizontal cover frame, and fasten with supplied hardware. Paint interior flat black with nontoxic exterior latex paint to aid solar heating.

5 Install the cold frame. In a sunny, protected garden site, dig a rectangular hole 36×42-in. (66×106-cm) square and 12–20-in. (30–50-cm) deep. Line it with plastic sheet, then mount the cold frame in the hole. Backfill around it with loose crushed bark or other material that has good insulating properties. Cap the fill area with building plastic and a coating of topsoil to create a water-proof weather barrier.

To use the cold frame, plant the seedlings in trays, then place the trays into the cold frame. Alternatively, plant the seedlings directly into the soil at the bottom of the cold frame.

Remember that the sun will cause temperatures to rise quickly in a cold frame. Open the top during warm sunlit hours; close the frame as temperatures drop in the evening. When your plants are nearly ready to set out into the garden, "harden" them by leaving the cold-frame top open unless a frost threatens. After a few more days, set them out in the garden, mulching around them with straw for protection from cold weather during the evenings.

SOIL TEMPERATURE FOR PLANTING (CS=COLD SEASON, WS=WARM SEASON, P=PERENNIAL)

VEGETABLE	TYPE	TEMP. °MIN	TEMP °IDEAL	USDA CLIMATE ZONES 3–4	5	6	7–8	9–10
Amaranth	WS	60°F/15°C	80°F/27°C	May-Jun	May	Apr	Apr	Mar
Artichoke	CS-P	40/5	70/21	Jun	May-Jun	Apr-Jun	Sep-Mar	Oct-Feb
Asparagus	CS-P	50/10	75/24	May-Jun	May	Apr	Apr	Mar
Bean, Asparagus	WS	60/15	80/27	Jun	May-Jun	May-Jun	Apr-Jun	Mar-Aug
Bean, Broad	WS	60/15	80/27	Jun	May-Jun	May-Jun	Apr-Jun	Mar-Aug
Bean, Lima	WS	60/15	80/27	Jun	May-Jun	May-Jun	Apr-Jun	Mar-Aug
Bean, Runner	WS	60/15	80/27	Jun	May-Jun	May-Jun	Apr-Jun	Mar-Aug
Bean, Snap	WS	60/15	85/29	Jun	May-Jun	May-Jun	Apr-Jun	Mar-Aug
Beet	CS	40/5	85/29	May-Jul	Apr-May	Mar-Apr	Feb-Apr	Jul-Oct
Broccoli	CS	40/5	85/29	May	Apr-May	Mar-Apr	Feb-Apr	Jul-Oct
Brussels Sprouts	CS	40/5	85/29	May	Apr-May	Mar-Apr	Feb-Apr	Jul-Oct
Cabbage	CS	40/5	85/29	May	Apr-May	Mar-Apr	Feb-Apr	Sep-Feb
Cabbage, Chinese	CS	40/5	85/29	May	Apr-May	Mar-Apr	Feb-Apr	Sep-Feb
Cantaloupe	WS	60/15	95/35	Jun	May-Jun	Apr-Jun	Apr-Jun	Apr-Jun
Cardoon	WS-P	60/15	80/27	Jun	May-Jun	Apr-Jun	Sep-Mar	Oct-Feb
Carrot	CS	40/5	80/27	May-Jun	Apr-Jun	Mar-Jun	Jan-Mar	Jan-Dec
Cauliflower	CS	40/5	80/27	May	Apr-May	Mar-Apr	Feb-Mar	Jul-Oct
Celery	CS	40/5	70/21	—	Apr-May	Mar-Apr	Feb-Aug	Feb-Aug
Collards	CS	45/7	85/29	May	Apr-May	Mar-Apr	Feb-Aug	Feb-Aug
Corn, Ornamental	WS	50/10	85/29	Jun	May-Jun	Apr-Jun	Mar-Jun	Mar-Jul
Corn, Popcorn	WS	50/10	85/29	Jun	May-Jun	Apr-Jun	Mar-Jun	Mar-Jul
Corn, Sweet	WS	50/10	85/29	Jun	May-Jun	Apr-Jun	Mar-Jun	Mar-Jul
Cress, Garden	CS	50/10	85/29	May-Jun	Apr-Jun	Mar-Jun	Aug-May	Sep-May
Cress, Water	CS	50/10	75/24	May-Jun	Apr-Jun	Mar-Jun	Aug-May	Sep-May
Cucumber	WS	6015	95/35	Jun	May-Jun	Apr-Jun	Apri-Jun	Apr-Jun
Eggplant	WS	70/21	85/29	Jun	May-Jun	Mar-May	Feb-Apr	Feb-Mar
Endive	CS	32/0	75/24	May	Apr-Jun	Mar-May	Aug-Sep	Jul-Sep
Garlic	Bulb	40/5	70/21	May	Mar-Jun	Apr-Jun	Mar-Jul	Sep-Mar
Gourd	WS	60/15	95/35	Jun	May-Jun	Apr-Jun	Apr-Jun	Mar-Jun
Greens, Various	CS	40/5	70/21	May-Jun	Apr-Jun	Mar-Jun	Aug-May	Sep-May
Herb, WS	WS	60/15	90/32	May-Jun	May-Jun	Apr-May	Feb-Mar	Jan-Mar
Herb, CS	CS	40/5	60/15	May-Jun	Apr-Jun	Mar-Jun	Aug-May	Sep-May
Kale	CS	40/5	75/24	May	Apr-May	Mar-Apr	Feb-Mar	Sep-Apr
Kohlrabi	CS	40/5	75/24	May-Jun	May-Jul	Mar-Aug	Feb-Sep	Jan-Dec
Leek	CS	40/5	75/24	May	Apr-May	Feb-May	Dec-Apr	Sep-May
Lettuce	CS	32/0	75/24	May-Jun	Apr-Jun	Mar-Jun	Aug-May	Sep-May

VEGETABLE	TYPE	TEMP. °MIN	TEMP °IDEAL	USDA CLIMATE ZONES				
				3–4	5	6	7–8	9–10
Melon	WS	60°F/15°C	95°F/35°C	Jun	May-Jun	Apr-Jun	Apr-Jun	Apr-Jun
Mustard	CS	40/5	75/24	Jun	May-Jun	Mar-Jun	Feb-May	Feb-Mar
Mustard-Spinach	CS	40/5	75/24	Jun	May-Jul	Mar-Sep	Feb-Oct	Jan-Dec
Mustard, India	CS	50/10	80/27	Jun	May-Jul	Mar-Sep	Feb-Oct	Jan-Dec
Okra	CS	60/15	95/35	Jun	May-Jun	Apr-Jun	Apr-Jun	Apr-Jun
Onion, Drying	Bulb	32/0	80/27	May-Jun	Apr-Jun	Feb-May	Dec-Apr	Dec-Mar
Onion, Green	CS	32/0	80/27	May-Jun	Apr-Jun	Feb-May	Dec-Apr	Jan-Dec
Parsnip	CS	32/0	70/21	May-Jun	May-Jun	Apr-Jun	Feb-Jun	Mar-Jun
Pea, English	CS	40/5	75/24	May	Apr-May	Feb-Apr	Jan-Sep	Jan-Sep
Pea, Snap	CS	40/5	75/24	May	Apr-May	Feb-Apr	Jan-Sep	Jan-Sep
Pea, Southern	WS	60/15	85/29	Jun	May-Jun	Mar-May	Feb-Apr	Feb-Mar
Pepper, Hot	WS	60/15	85/29	Jun	May-Jun	Mar-May	Feb-Apr	Feb-Mar
Pepper, Sweet	WS	60/15	85/29	Jun	May-Jun	Mar-May	Feb-Apr	Feb-Mar
Potato	CS	40/5	75/24	May	Apr-Jun	Mar-Jun	Feb-May	Oct-Feb
Potato, Sweet	WS	60/15	85/29	May-Jun	Apr-Jun	Mar-Jul	Mar-Aug	Feb-Sep
Pumpkin	WS	60/15	95/35	Jun	May-Jun	Apr-Jun	Apr-Jun	Apr-Jun
Radish	CS	40/5	85/29	May-Jun	Apr-Jul	Mar-Aug	Feb-Oct	Jan-Dec
Rhubarb	CS-P	50/10	75/24	Apr-Jun	Apr-Jun	Mar-Jun	Sep-Feb	Oct-Feb
Roquette	CS	50/10	60/15	May-Jul	Apr-Jul	Mar-Jul	Aug-May	Sep-May
Rutabaga	CS	40/5	85/29	Jun	Jun	Jul	Aug	Sep
Salsify	CS	40/5	80/27	May	Apr-May	Apr	Jun	Jun
Shallot	Bulb	60/15	75/24	May-Jun	Apr-Jun	Feb-May	Dec-Apr	Dec-Mar
Sorrel	WS-P	65/18	75/24	Jun	May-Jun	May-Jun	Apr-Jun	Mar-Aug
Soybean	WS	60/15	95/35	Jun	May-Jun	May-Jun	Apr-Jun	Mar-Aug
Spinach	CS	32/0	70/21	May-Jun	Apr-Jun	Mar-Jun	Aug-May	Sep-May
Spinach, N. Z.	WS	60/15	80/27	Jun	May-Jun	Apr-Jun	Apr-Jun	Apr-Jun
Squash, Summer	WS	60/15	95/35	Jun	May-Jun	Apr-Jun	Apr-Jun	Apr-Jun
Squash, Winter	WS	60/15	95/35	Jun	May-Jun	Apr-Jun	Apr-Jun	Apr-Jun
Sunflower	WS	60/15	95/35	May-Jun	May-Jun	Apr-Jun	Mar-Jun	Mar-Jul
Swiss Chard	CS	40/5	85/29	May-Jun	Apr-Jul	Mar-Aug	Feb-Sep	Jan-Dec
Tomatillo	WS	60/15	85/29	Jun	May-Jun	Apr-May	Feb-Mar	Jan-Mar
Tomato	WS	50/10	85/29	Jun	May-Jun	Apr-May	Feb-Mar	Jan-Mar
Tomato, Husk	WS	60/15	85/29	Jun	May-Jun	Apr-May	Feb-Mar	Jan-Mar
Turnip	CS	40/5	85/29	May-Jun	Apr-Jun	Mar-Jun	Aug-May	Sep-May
Watermelon	WS	60/15	95/35	Jun	May-Jun	Apr-Jun	Apr-Jun	Apr-Jun

types of cold frames also easily transport indoor "starts" to the garden when they must be hardened—that is, acclimatized to outdoor temperature fluctuations in preparation for planting [see Hardening and Transplanting, pg. 179].

A cold frame relies on two principles to nurture its contents: insulation and the trapping of light and heat.

Insulation is provided by the walls of the frame itself—usually thick wood, though some are made of plastic or Styrofoam. Old-time gardeners always have preferred hardwood cold frames because of their durability, but there is no reason why modern materials shouldn't work as well, season after season. For outdoor use, the cold frame should be buried in a mound of soft loam—loose, workable garden soil—along a south-facing wall in an area protected from chilling winds. Placing the cold frame in a protected location and burying it in the soil help protect plants from variations in air temperature.

The principle of insulation is only part of the story, however. There also must be a source of heat, provided to the cold frame by the early spring sun.

We all know the sun's infrared rays provide warmth as well as light. When they pass through the cold frame's glass cover, they heat the interior. This trip is one-way, though, because the glass does not allow the converted radiant heat to escape. Temperatures rise in the box, warming the soil and walls. As the temperature drops during the night, the cold frame's insulation holds the trapped warmth—often assisted by the gardener, who may choose to cover it with an old blanket, a plastic tarp, or some mulch. The result is that the variation in temperature is moderated and the soil becomes an ideal environment for the seeds to germinate.

OTHER PROTECTION. Similar to the cold frame are such temporary protective devices as a cloche—a bell-shaped glass cover just the right size for a single plant or two—or a large wide-mouth jug. Both of these glass containers provide a movable microgreenhouse environment to trap heat and increase soil temperatures.

Whichever means you use, remember that the sun is a powerful source of warmth. Direct sunlight can raise the temperature inside a cold frame to 140°F (60°C) or more very quickly, which will kill the seeds or tender plants within. If you anticipate direct sun exposure, use a garden thermometer to check the temperature inside the cold frame. Prop open the removable glass cover part way—or, when temperatures exceed 100°F (38°C), remove it entirely—to permit solar heat to escape during the day and maintain ideal growing conditions. Remember to replace the cover in the evening to protect the tender seedlings from any sudden drops in temperature.

By referring to the Soil Temperature for Planting chart [see pg. 162], you can determine when and if you can start seeds outdoors in a protected area, in a cold frame, or in a greenhouse. Another alternative used by many gardeners is to start tender seeds indoors, using a windowsill or other warm, sunny spot. The indoor temperature of most homes provides ideal growing conditions for many seeds through the germination stage.

Planting Seeds

Whether seeds are planted indoors or out, in cold frames or in the garden soil, their needs are the same.

The soil used for germinating seeds should be light, should retain moisture well, and should be deep enough to permit the roots of the developing plants to spread easily. Commercial potting soil is one ideal choice, as is organic compost made in a compost bin [see Building a Compost Bin, pg. 210]. If you choose compost, you will need to sterilize it by heating it in an oven or an outdoor gas barbecue to 140°F (60°C) for at least 20 minutes to destroy any fungus and disease organisms as well as any weed seeds that it may contain. Many commercial composts are certified sterile, but some are not; make sure to check the label for this important feature.

Next, check the recommended planting depth for each seed type. In general, the larger the seed, the greater the depth required. Refer to the Planting Depth, Germination, and Harvest chart [see pg. 168] for vegetable-by-vegetable recommendation or follow the planting instructions on the seed package. This typically varies from 1/16 inch (1.5 mm), for tiny, quick-germinating vegetables such as lettuce and spinach, to 1 inch (25 mm) for large, starchy seeds such as beans and peas.

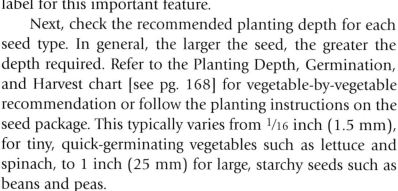

Planting Implements

Most planting in previously prepared beds can be done with a standard hoe and rake, but some other garden tools will prove useful.

To plant potatoes and other tubers and roots, shovels or spades are essential. The shovel has a sharp, "dished" face while the spade appears more flat and blunt. In loamy soils, a garden fork also is useful. Each comes with a variety of handles and hilts.

Small garden handtools, including cultivators, tined forks, and narrow and wide-bladed trowels, are ideal for potted plantings. Their small size makes them especially suited for work in containers and small plots.

Those made with cast handles are more durable than those with separately attached handles.

Other planting implements you'll surely find useful include: a watering can—select one with a strainer-ended spout; barrows or carts; dibs—peg-shaped tools for making planting holes for sets and seedlings; and a stem thermometer.

CAUTION: Chlorine bleach (sodium hypochlorite) is a powerful skin and eye irritant and is poisonous if ingested. Make sure you let any container dry thoroughly before using it to plant your vegetable seeds.

If you choose to plant seeds in a container, keep in mind the required planting depth and select a pot size that will permit the plants to form good, strong root systems. Many gardeners use peat pots because they are commonly available, hold moisture well, and decompose naturally. Other choices include plastic trays and pots, clay pots, discarded milk cartons, or other conveniently available containers.

Any planting container should be sterilized first. Soak it for a few minutes in a weak solution of household bleach and tap water. About a half-cup (120 ml) of chlorine bleach per gallon (3.8 l) of water is appropriate for most garden containers. Then rinse.

Avoid substituting "optical" bleaches that do not contain chlorine as they will be less effective for sterilization.

To plant seeds directly in containers, follow the step-by-step instructions [see Planting Seeds in Containers, pg. 172].

When directly planting seeds in the garden, first prepare the soil by turning it with a spade to a depth of at least 18 inches (45 cm), regardless of the particular seed's depth requirements. Add any amendments or compost you have chosen to improve workability and rake the surface level and smooth (see Chapter Three: *Gardening Basics*). After planting the seeds to the proper depth and recommended spacing according to the Spacing of Plants table [see pg. 176], or the back of the seed package, press down on the soil to firm it, using your hands for single hills and small containers or the back of a rake for larger plantings. This brings the seeds into contact with the soil and ensures moisture reaches them and begins to swell their casings.

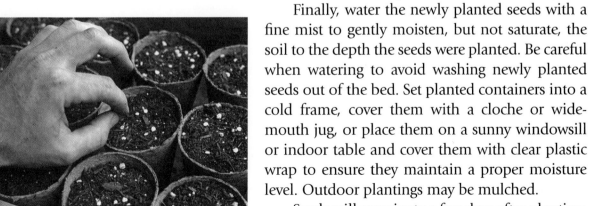

Finally, water the newly planted seeds with a fine mist to gently moisten, but not saturate, the soil to the depth the seeds were planted. Be careful when watering to avoid washing newly planted seeds out of the bed. Set planted containers into a cold frame, cover them with a cloche or wide-mouth jug, or place them on a sunny windowsill or indoor table and cover them with clear plastic wrap to ensure they maintain a proper moisture level. Outdoor plantings may be mulched.

Seeds will germinate a few days after planting.

PLANTING DEPTH, GERMINATION, AND HARVEST

VEGETABLE	DEPTH IN INCHES	DEPTH IN MILLIMETERS	GERMINATION DAYS	HARVEST DAYS
Amaranth	¼	6	10 to 12	40 to 56
Artichoke, Crowns	½	13	Plant crowns	Perennial
Asparagus, Crowns	6	150	Plant crowns	Perennial
Asparagus, Seed	½	13	14 to 21	Perennial
Bean, Asparagus	1 to 1½	25 to 40	7 to 10	75
Bean, Broad	1 to 1½	25 to 40	7 to 10	65
Bean, Lima	1½	40	7 to 10	65
Bean, Runner	1½ to 2	40 to 50	8 to 12	45 to 70
Bean, Snap	1 to 1½	25 to 40	7 to 10	55
Beet	1½	40	10 to 12	58
Broccoli	½	13	10 to 15	85
Brussels Sprouts	¼	6	10 to 15	100
Cabbage	½	13	10 to 15	75
Cabbage, Chinese	½	13	10 to 15	75
Cantaloupe	½	13	5 to 10	85
Cardoon	½	13	10 to 15	Perennial
Carrot	¼ to ½	6 to 13	14 to 25	68
Cauliflower	½	13	8 to 10	70
Celery	⅛	3	6 to 10	105 to 130
Collards	¼	6	10 to 15	75
Corn, Ornamental	1	25	5 to 7	105
Corn, Popcorn	1	25	7 to 10	85
Corn, Sweet	1 to 1½	25 to 40	7 to 10	77
Cress, Garden	¼	6	10 to 14	45 to 60
Cress, Water	⅛	3	7 to 10	50
Cucumber	½	13	8 to 10	57
Eggplant	¼	6	10 to 15	80
Endive	¼	6	7 to 14	95
Garlic	1½	40	Plant clove sets	90 to 100
Gourd	1	25	10 to 12	90
Greens, Various	¼	6	10 to 14	40
Herbs, CS	¼ to ½	6 to 13	14 to 21	45 to 60
Herbs, WS	¼ to ½	6 to 13	8 to 14	40 to 60
Kale	¼	6	10 to 14	55
Kohlrabi	½	13	12 to 15	45 to 60
Leek	½	13	10 to 14	150

VEGETABLE	DEPTH IN INCHES	DEPTH IN MILLIMETERS	GERMINATION DAYS	HARVEST DAYS
Lettuce	¼	6	7 to 10	45
Melon	½	13	5 to 10	110
Mustard	¼	6	8 to 9	45
Mustard-Spinach	¼	6	9 to 12	30
Mustard, India	¼	6	9 to 12	30
Okra	¾	20	10 to 14	56
Onion, Drying	½	13	Plant bulb sets	110
Onion, Green	½	13	12 to 14	60 to 110
Parsnip	½	13	21 to 28	95
Pea, English	1½	40	8 to 12	60
Pea, Snap	1½	40	6 to 10	70
Pea, Southern	½ to 1	13 to 25	7 to 10	78
Pepper, Hot	¼	6	10 to 12	80
Pepper, Sweet	¼	6	10 to 12	70
Potato	2 to 3	50 to 75	Plant seed potatoes	110 to 120
Potato, Sweet	2 to 3	50 to 75	Plant seed potatoes	110 to 120
Pumpkin	1½	40	8 to 10	120
Radish	½	13	4 to 6	26
Rhubarb, Crowns	4	100	Plant crowns	Perennial
Rhubarb, Seed	1	25	14 to 21	Perennial
Roquette	½	13	5 to 8	35
Rutabaga	½	13	7 to 10	90
Salsify	½ to 1	13 to 25	14 to 20	120
Shallot	½	13	Plant bulb sets	60 to 120
Sorrel	¼	6	7 to 10	Perennial
Soybean	1 to 1½	25 to 40	7 to 10	85
Spinach	½	13	8 to 10	45
Spinach, New Zealand	1	25	14 to 20	70
Squash, Summer	1	25	8 to 10	50
Squash, Winter	1½	40	8 to 10	120
Sunflower	1	25	10 to 14	65 to 80
Swiss Chard	¾	20	7 to 10	60
Tomatillo	¼	6	8 to 10	95
Tomato	¼	6	8 to 10	80
Turnip	½	13	8 to 12	45
Watermelon	½	13	5 to 7	73

Seeding in the Garden

Prepare soil in the plot by spading and raking. For rows and area plantings, prepare a flat, smooth surface, then mark the row with a string stretched between two stakes. For hills, raise each area 8-in. (20-cm) high by 18-in. (45-cm) wide, leaving a "moat" around the hill.

1 Following the string guide and using the handle of a hoe or rake, press down firmly to create a trench for the seeds. Follow package instructions for the depth of the trench.

2 Space the seeds along the row by gently tapping them out of the package.

3 Close the trench by raking soil with your hand or a rake onto the seeds. Press the soil down firmly around the planting, using your palms or the flat surface of a hoe. Mist the planted area with water.

Planting in Hills and Mounds

Hill crops, such as squash and pumpkin, require space to spread their vines. Raise a mound from the prepared soil and dig a trench surrounding it for easy irrigation of your plants.

1 Form hills 6–10-in. (15–25-cm) high and 12–14- in. (30–35-cm) wide by hoeing soil to the center of a mound from the surrounding area. This also creates an irrigation moat around the hill.

2 Evenly space 4–6 seeds atop each hill. Poke each seed into the hill to the depth recommended on the seed package. Sprinkle each seed with loose soil to cover it.

PUMPKIN
Spooktacular
NET WT. 2 grams
PERFECT SIZE FOR KIDS

3 Press the soil firmly to assure good contact with the seeds. Water by misting the planted area, then filling the trench surrounding the hill.

Planting Seeds in Containers

It's sometimes more convenient to plant seeds in small containers rather than flats. When only a small number of plants is required, space is conserved and individual care is easier. Choose new pots or thoroughly clean and sterilize those used in prior seasons since porous materials can promote fungal disease.

Disposable peat pots also are sold in many garden stores, either as flat "pellets" that expand when soaked in water or ready-to-plant. They are environmentally friendly but may cause rootbound plants or watering problems unless completely removed when plants are set in the garden.

When choosing a container, make sure it is large enough to allow unbounded root growth until such time as the plant is ready to be transplanted in the garden. Judge a container's suitability by imagining that the rootball will be equal in size to the plant's foliage, which should have 2–3 true leaves at time of transplant.

When planting seeds in containers, fill each pot with soil—either sterile potting soil or organic compost—then pack the soil tightly to avoid settling problems after watering. Seeds need good soil contact in order to germinate successfully.

Completely remove pots when transplanting.

1 Fill a container with sterile potting soil (available from garden-stores) or with organic compost.

2 Press the soil tightly with your fingers to remove excess air space between the soil particles.

3 Following package instructions, set 2–3 seeds on the soil and cover them to the specified depth.

4 Prepare a label for your planting, using either commercially prepared stakes or popsicle sticks. Use pencil since pens and markers can fade or run when the plant is watered.

5 Insert your label stick in the pot. Place the pot in a sunny location and mist with water. Seeds soon will germinate.

Selecting Transplants

If you choose to buy transplants rather than sow your own seeds, you soon will find yourself in a nursery or garden retail center scanning aisles and aisles of tables filled with a wide selection of young vegetable plants. There's an art as well as a science to choosing the best transplants at a retailer's. Let's look at some of the important considerations when it comes to selecting the best place to purchase your future vegetables:

Mulching

Where weather is still variable, gardeners often mulch the surface of recently planted beds with a layer 3–5 inches (7.6–12.7 cm) thick of weed-free straw, peat moss, or other loose, insulating organic mulch recommended by nursery or garden store staff. Mulch helps keep the surface of the soil a uniform temperature on cooler evenings and maintains proper moisture levels in the soil beneath.

Mulching is quick and easy. After you've planted your garden bed and given it its initial watering, just sprinkle the mulch over the bed. If the matter has large air spaces, like straw, make the layer a little thicker than you would if using a finer mulch medium, such as peat.

Because of the mulch, plants will reveal themselves a bit later than those in unmulched gardens. A quick examination of the seeded areas around the expected germination time will help identify the emerging vegetable plants.

- Are the seedlings placed in a protected spot to ensure they remain healthy until after they are purchased? Could they be buffeted by wind or subject to driving rain or damage from passersby? Look for display areas with wide aisles, good lighting, and ample protection from the elements.

- What is the general condition of the plants? Are they withered and neglected, mauled or riddled with insects? The best nurseries and garden stores have full-time attendants with regular maintenance duties. It's a good sign to see a nursery staff watering, arranging, and caring for the green goods.

- Is there a wide selection? Are there several sizes and many different varietals from which to choose, or only a few? Again, the best nurseries or garden center retailers try to satisfy their customers by providing a selection of individual-container plants, six-packs, and bedding trays, as well as several different cultivars of each vegetable.

• Is the stock moving? Do the plants look shopworn or leggy? Are they outgrowing their containers? Great gardeners tend to find excellent nurseries or garden stores with informative clerks. When the aisles are packed and a steady stream of plants is passing through the checkout, you can be assured that the transplants are fresh.

• What is the store's return or replacement policy? Will the management replace plants that fail after they have been put in your garden? Ask about the store's policies and what proof of purchase or other evidence staff may require.

These are just a few of the key questions to ask yourself as you shop for a garden store. Don't hesitate to stop other customers to ask them for advice or a recommendation. A good sign of an experienced gardener is a full shopping cart or tote. Feel free to inquire whether they have had good luck in the past with purchases from the store you are evaluating.

Transplanting into Containers

Choose your container carefully and sterilize it. The best containers are large enough to allow roots to develop fully. Remember to water and feed container plants frequently for best results. They need even more consistent and reliable care than plants grown in an open garden.

1 Fill the container you've selected with sterile potting soil or loose, organic compost. Container plants require good drainage, so avoid dense soils.

2 Gently remove the transplant seeding from its container. Inspect its development and roots.

After selecting your retail garden store, follow these steps to find great, healthy vegetable transplants:

- Choose fresh, green plants. Avoid those with yellow or brown foliage, which indicates poor past care. Also skip plants with purplish or whitish leaves; such symptoms may be due to poor fertilization or rapid changes in light conditions during growth. Plants with lush, complete foliage, strong stems, and good root systems will establish themselves quickly in your garden and grow well.

- Pick plants at the best stage of growth. Ready-to-transplant seedlings have between two and three true leaves above their "seed leaves." For every size except the largest containers, plants should not have flower buds, immature fruit, or other apparent signs of maturity.

- Select nursery stock appropriate to your space requirements and timing. If you are planting a large bed or row, pick flats containing 24 to 36 individual starts. For smaller areas, choose six- or jumbo twelve-packs. For container gardens or for late-in-the-season gardening, pick more mature plants grown in 2-, 4- or 6-inch (5-, 10-, or 15-cm) containers.

JUDGING PLANT QUALITY

CONDITION	DESCRIPTION OF CAUSES
Weak spindly foliage	Not enough light
Wilted leaves	Over-/underwatering
Purple foliage	Lack of phosphorus
Stunted growth	Container too small

3 Loosen the rootball by gently scoring it a few times with fork tines. This will help the plant become established in the new container.

4 After positioning the plant, press the soil down with your fingers until it is well packed. Thoroughly water the transplant.

SPACING OF PLANTS

VEGETABLE	BETWEEN ROWS (INCHES)	BETWEEN ROWS (CENTIMETERS)	BETWEEN PLANTS (INCHES)	BETWEEN PLANTS (CENTIMETERS)	BETWEEN HILLS (INCHES)	BETWEEN HILLS (CENTIMETERS)
Amaranth	24	60	24	60	—	—
Artichoke, Crowns	72 to 94	180 to 240	48 to 72	120 to 180	—	—
Asparagus, Crowns	24	60	18	45	—	—
Asparagus, Seed	24	60	18	45	—	—
Bean, Asparagus	36	90	6	15	—	—
Bean, Broad	36	90	6	15	—	—
Bean, Lima	36	90	3	8	—	—
Bean, Runner	36 to 48	90 to 120	3	8	—	—
Bean, Snap	18	45	3	8	—	—
Beet	18	45	1½	3.8	—	—
Broccoli	36	90	18	45	—	—
Brussels Sprouts	36	90	24	60	—	—
Cabbage	30	75	18	45	—	—
Cabbage, Chinese	30	75	18	45	—	—
Cantaloupe	48	120	—	—	48	120
Cardoon	36	90	20	50	—	—
Carrot	12	30	2	5	—	—
Cauliflower	36	90	18	45	—	—
Celery	24	60	6 to 10	15 to 25	—	—
Collards	36	90	18	45	—	—
Corn, Ornamental	36	90	12	30	—	—
Corn, Popcorn	36	90	20	50	—	—
Corn, Sweet	36	90	20	50	—	—
Cress, Garden	12 to 16	30 to 40	1 to 2	2.5 to 5	—	—
Cress, Water	—	—	2 to 4	5 to 10	—	—
Cucumber	72	180	—	—	48	120
Eggplant	36	90	15	38	—	—
Endive	24	60	12	30	—	—
Garlic	15	38	4 to 8	10 to 20	—	—
Gourd	—	—	18	45	48	120
Greens, Various	18	45	6	15	—	—
Kale	18	45	12	30	—	—
Kohlrabi	18	45	6	15	—	—
Leek	18	45	6	15	—	—

Spacing of Plants (continued)

Vegetable	Between Rows (Inches)	Between Rows (Centimeters)	Between Plants (Inches)	Between Plants (Centimeters)	Between Hills (Inches)	Between Hills (Centimeters)
Lettuce	12	30	10	25	—	—
Melon	48	120	—	—	48	120
Mustard	15	38	12	30	—	—
Mustard-Spinach	12	30	10	25	—	—
Mustard, India	12	30	10	25	—	—
Okra	36	90	18	45	—	—
Onion, Drying	18	45	6	15	—	—
Onion, Green	12	30	2	5	—	—
Parsnip	12	30	3	7.5	—	—
Pea, English	30	75	2	5	—	—
Pea, Snap	30	75	2	5	—	—
Pea, Southern	36	90	3	7.5	—	—
Pepper, Hot	24	60	18	45	—	—
Pepper, Sweet	24	60	18	45	—	—
Potato	36 to 48	90 to 120	10 to 18	25 to 45	36	90
Potato, Sweet	36 to 48	90 to 120	10 to 18	25 to 45	36	90
Pumpkin	96	240	—	—	96	240
Radish	10	25	1	2.5	—	—
Rhubarb	36	90	—	—	48	120
Roquette	16	40	6 to 8	15 to 20	—	—
Rutabaga	18	45	8	20	—	—
Salsify	18	45	4	10	—	—
Shallot	24 to 48	60 to 120	4 to 8	10 to 20	—	—
Sorrel	18	45	1	2.5	—	—
Soybean	18	45	3	7.5	—	—
Spinach	18	45	6	15	—	—
Spinach, New Zealand	24	60	12	30	—	—
Squash, Summer	48 to 60	120 to 150	48	120	48	120
Squash, Winter	48 to 60	120 to 150	96	240	72	180
Sunflower	—	—	18 to 24	45 to 60	10 to 14	25 to 36
Swiss Chard	18	45	6	15	—	—
Tomatillo	24	60	24	60	—	—
Tomato	24	60	24	60	—	—
Turnip	15	38	4	10	—	—
Watermelon	72	180	—	—	48	120

Spacing of Plants (continued)

- Choose plants that haven't outgrown their containers. Rootbound plants may be stunted or poor performers [see Hardening and Transplanting, opposite].

- Favor healthy plants. Get in close and look at each plant carefully. Notice insect damage and viral problems that may be identified by conspicuous spots on the foliage, withering, or other signs of disease.

- Examine growth habit. Strong, healthy plants will appear stocky and dense with foliage and will resist gentle pressure from your hand. Pass by those that appear leggy, spindly, or weak.

After-purchase care of live plants is as important as making wise choices. After selecting and purchasing vegetable transplants, be sure to transport them carefully to your garden. Hot automobile interiors and trunks are hazardous to young seedlings. In fact, in just a few minutes they can experience temperatures of 140°F (60°C) or higher!

If you do not plan to transplant purchased seedlings right away, place them in a protected spot in the garden. Water them with a fine mist and keep them damp if daytime temperatures are warm. Protect them at night from the cold according to the instructions given for hardening [see Hardening, pg. 180].

Hardening and Transplanting

Whether you've seeded yourself or purchased from a nursery, young vegetable plants quickly grow to transplantable size. When the foliage develops at least three true leaves, signaling that root development is established, the plants are ready for the garden.

Do not delay transplanting because once a transplant becomes rootbound, chemical messengers within send a signal that the vegetable should stop growing and it will be permanently stunted.

ROOT DEVELOPMENT. Root development is particularly easy to see in peat pots, as developing plant roots frequently will penetrate through the bottom and even the sides of these porous pots. If your transplants are in a plastic or clay container, checking root development also is easy. Carefully invert the plant so its stem is upside down between your fingers, then gently tap the bottom of the container to release the plant. Examine the plant's rootball; if you see white root hairs around its edges, the plant is ready for the garden.

FOLIAGE DEVELOPMENT. It's always amazing to watch nature perform its miracles. One of the most fascinating of these is the sprouting of seeds after germination has begun. In just a few days—seldom more than two weeks—bright green leaves begin to appear.

The first foliage to appear from freshly sprouted seed is the characteristic pair of so-called "seed leaves." These usually tiny, round leaves do not resemble the mature plant's leaves but were present in immature form while still part of the plant's embryo.

Their emergence from the soil is the first visible evidence that your planting was successful. Seed leaves are soon followed by true foliage development—leaves that are characteristic of the adult vegetable plant. Some are broad leaved, for example beans and squash; others are feathery, such as carrots; still others are narrow, swordlike, or toothed around the edges.

If you are like most gardeners, the welcome signs that foliage and roots are signaling transplant time are irresistible. Now is the time to make final preparation of your beds, including any amendments, take out hoe and rake, and get ready to transplant—almost. There's just one small task that must be attended to first.

Root and foliage development are the easiest measures of young plants' readiness for their move to the garden. Before transplanting, however, make sure you allow them time to adjust to the outdoors.

HARDENING. In preparation for transplanting, young plants must be acclimatized to the rigors of the weather, especially if they have been grown indoors or in a cold frame. The ups and downs of garden temperatures shock such tender plants and may kill them or stunt their growth. To harden plants grown indoors, put them outside, out of direct sunlight, for a few days, returning them indoors in the evening. To harden cold frame seedlings, remove their protective coverings during the day, then mulch heavily to protect them during their first nights outdoors. Gradually move them to full sunlight locations over a period of three to five days; in a day or two they will be ready for transplanting.

1 Space the plants as directed in the Spacing of Plants chart [see pg. 176].

Transplanting into the Garden

Whether grown yourself or purchased at a nursery, seedlings soon reach the stage of development making them ready for transplant to the garden. Follow the easy, step-by-step instructions shown for setting transplants into the garden.

2 Gently remove the plant by turning it upside down and tapping its container until the plant falls into your hand. Break up the roots if compacted. Position it in the hole, then backfill from the edges.

3 Firm the soil around the plant until it is well compacted. Water the plant whenever the soil is becoming dry. Do not overwater or soak the seedlings, especially if the ground temperature is still cool—such practices can promote disease and rot. Always water around the base of the plant, not onto the foliage, until the plant becomes well established.

Care of Established Plantings

The care of transplants, whether nurtured by the gardener from seed or purchased, is minimal, comprising simple fertilization and cultivation.

FERTILIZATION. There is no need to fertilize newly sprouted seeds because every seed contains a miniature nutrient factory within its shell. However, nursery-grown transplants and their seed-grown counterparts benefit from early fertilization to develop their roots and foliage. Organic compost, if used as a soil amendment or as a transplant medium, provides ample fertilizer for young plants. Adding extra fertilizer to a well-amended garden soil is simply unnecessary.

All fertilizers, whether organic or inorganic, natural or synthetic, are chemical compounds made up of nitrogen (for foliage development), phosphorus (for foliage growth), and potassium (for root growth). Tender young plants cannot distinguish between different types of fertilizer, but the risk of "chemical burning" is somewhat higher with concentrated synthetic fertilizers than with natural organic fertilizers made of fish emulsion or composted manure. Natural organics also provide numerous trace nutrients and minerals that synthetic fertilizer formulations frequently lack.

WARNING: Overapplication of chemical fertilizers may chemically burn or kill plants. Whichever brand you choose, always follow package instructions to the letter.

Fertilizer should be used sparingly around seedlings and never in direct contact with them. Ideally, it should be applied at the edges of the "root ring," an imaginary line that encircles the plant's root system. To determine the root ring, stand over the plant and look down on it. From this vantage point, circumscribe an imaginary line from the foliage to the ground. This circumference is about the same as that of the root system. Apply fertilizer around the outer edge of this rough circle for the greatest benefit to the plant.

After applying fertilizer to any vegetable plant, water thoroughly. Watering dilutes the fertilizer and carries its soluble nutrients down through the soil to the roots of the growing plant.

CULTIVATION. Cultivating, or hoeing around plants, provides another useful function beyond its purpose of eliminating weed sprouts. It also mixes surface soil nutrients and applied fertilizer with deeper, depleted soil down around the growing roots. Cultivate every four to six weeks or more frequently if necessary for weed control.

Problems with New Plantings

ost seedlings demonstrate their vigor and vitality shortly after transplanting with a remarkable growth spurt. This results from the foliage trying to keep up with the burgeoning root system, a balance dictated by the exchange of water, raw nutrients, and photosynthesis byproducts within the plant. Why do some plantings fail to develop properly, then? Poor, stunted plant growth may be traced to care factors, disease, or pests.

WATERING. The most common care problem is failing to irrigate properly. When a plant does not receive enough water to maintain what is called a hydrostatic balance, or internal cellular water pressure, the plant first wilts and then collapses. Conversely, when a plant's root system stands in waterlogged soil, it drowns and begins to rot. Like underwatered plants, overwatered ones appear listless and wilted. Because the soil around the roots lacks air, it cannot provide sufficient carbon dioxide and oxygen to the plant to permit photosynthesis. If you suspect overwatering, immediately cultivate deeply around the plant, working in more organic compost or other soil lighteners to help pull water away from the drowned root system. If the condition has not advanced too far, your quick action may save the plantings.

Correct watering is easy. Plants should be watered whenever their soil begins to feel dry or crumbly to the touch. A quick hoeing will reveal whether the soil has dried below the surface; if so, the plants need water. Always water deeply. If an open container placed nearby on the ground is filled to a depth of 1 inch (25 mm) or so, you can feel confident that the right amount is reaching the plants' roots. Do not water again until the soil begins to look or feel dry to the touch.

NUTRIENTS AND FERTILIZER. Another common care problem is underfertilization. Purple-tinged, underdeveloped young leaves and yellowed older foliage usually are symptoms of soil lacking sufficient nitrogen and phosphorus. Hoeing in organic fertilizer or compost should improve growth within a few days. If your plants remain listless after another week, or if they exhibit interveinal yellowing, suspect that the soil may need some additional iron. Soluble iron helps plantings combat salty, alkaline soils as well as promoting normal development.

Poor foliage also can result from lack of potassium in the soil and means the roots cannot provide adequate nutrients to the growing plant. Again, the prescription is to cultivate in organic compost or other amendments rich in potassium. Your plantings should improve noticeably in a few days.

DISEASE DAMAGE. The most common disease conditions in vegetable plants usually result from poor care. Weakened plants, whether due to under- or overwatering, poor nutrition, or compacted soil, are more susceptible to diseases.

Fungus infections are the most common of these, particularly if recent nights have been cool and if you have been overwatering a dense, claylike soil. After cultivating deeply to improve the soil's air circulation, cut back on watering and mulch the soil to help your plants recover. However, avoid fertilizing any fungus- or rot-damaged plants. These plant infections feed on fertilizer nutrients and will overwhelm healthy nearby plants rapidly.

First Care after Transplant

Young transplants need to be as carefully nurtured in their first few weeks in the garden as they were in the germination stage.

If harsh weather threatens, cover them with plastic dropcloths or roll film, two readily available materials that may be purchased at your nursery, garden or hardware store.

Keep the seedlings covered overnight, using wooden stakes to prevent the material from coming into contact with the tender leaves. Any such contact can transmit cold to the leaves and may kill the plant, or it can allow condensation from the warm soil to collect on the plant, which will promote rot.

Careful "construction" of these temporary shelters will help warm the soil and get the plants off to a good start.

Check your plantings daily and water whenever the topsoil appears dry. Water around your plants, never on top. Avoid overwatering or soaking the seedlings, especially if the ground temperature is still cool—the combination of cool temperatures with moist soil can cause disease or rot.

One common fungal disease of young seedlings is "damping off." The symptoms of this disease usually follow a set course: The seeds germinate normally and shoots emerge from the ground. Then, about the time they get their first true leaves, the gardener discovers one morning that the whole row of seedlings has fallen over and there is a brown discoloration at the base of each stem near the point where it comes into contact with the ground. Damping off almost always is caused by planting in soil that is moist and too cold.

If the entire planting is not affected, some plants may be saved by applying a layer of clear plastic on each side of the row. The plastic will absorb solar heat and warm the soil, killing the fungus that has caused the infection.

Another common category of disease is viral in nature. As with any virus, these are very difficult to treat. Infected plants will not recover to bear normal flowers or fruit. The only real treatment is to remove the infected plants and replace them with virus-resistant varietals. Local nurseries and garden retailers can help diagnose viral plant problems and suggest varieties that do not develop these distressing, incurable diseases easily.

PESTS. Pest problems are the bane of gardeners everywhere. Early recognition provides the best potential for stemming an infestation in your new plantings. In young plants, these usually are in the form of insects or mollusks (snails and slugs). Small and large mammals and birds also may attack young vegetable sprouts.

Insect pests attack plants in three main ways: by chewing, scraping, or sucking. Chewing insects bite holes in the leaves or eat the stems of young plants. Scraping insects rasp the surface layer of foliage, ingesting plant material and juices. Sucking insects drill into the leaf or stem, sucking plant juices from within. Insect pests can weaken an already diseased or poorly attended plant, but rarely will they kill the plant entirely unless the infestation is severe.

Mollusks are more voracious in their appetites. A single slug can decimate a row of newly planted seedlings in a single evening, when it emerges from its hiding place and becomes active. In daylight, look for shiny mucus trails near the damaged plants. Often the culprit will be nearby, under a stick, board, or rock. Venture out with a flashlight at night to look for them on your plants.

Larvae and grubs, different developmental stages of pre-adult insects, do their damage below the soil surface. They have strong, rasping teeth and eat plants at their roots, causing the entire plant to die.

Caterpillars, the juvenile forms of butterflies and moths, also eat plant foliage and stems. Large types, such as the tomato hornworm, can be several inches (8 cm or more) in length and can inflict damage on entire plants and their fruit.

Mammals—from mice, gophers, moles, and squirrels to larger animals such as raccoons, rabbits, opossum, and deer—are formidable predators of young plants.

Birds damage newly planted vegetable gardens by eating seeds, sprouts, and young plants, or by scratching and dusting themselves in the freshly turned soil.

All pest infestations are serious. An integrated approach to pest control in an organic garden actually welcomes predators as well as their nuisance prey. If your infestation reaches epidemic proportions, stronger methods may be necessary. A complete discussion of pest control using organic, chemical, and alternative methods is provided in Chapter Seven: *Pest & Diseases*.

AFTER-PLANTING CARE. Most vegetable gardeners log many seasons before encountering these pest, disease, and care problems. In fact, many gardens go for years without any significant problems. It all comes down to good garden practices—selecting a proper garden site, thoroughly preparing the soil, and taking care when sowing and transplanting to get your garden off to a good start.

With the beds planted and cultivated, let's turn our attention to the many enjoyable elements of mature garden care.

Tending to your Caring for a Garden Vegetables

WHEN SPRING HAS SPRUNG and your plantings have become well established, it's tempting to gaze down the orderly rows of your vegetable garden and consider your job completed. All that your plants need do, after all, is keep growing, bloom, set fruit, and ripen.

Much to the contrary, they still need your help—regular garden care.

Good garden care makes the difference between outstanding results and those that are so-so. Vegetables stand ready to give their all for us. Keep your plants healthy, well nourished, and free of weeds, and we assure you they will thrive and yield a bounty of produce.

While caring for your garden is a responsibility, it's also a joy. It's an opportunity to invest some time in gainful effort or to simply while away hours with your plants. Whatever your reason, there's lots to do and be done, so let's get started.

Your vegetable plants need each of the following to various degrees and in different frequencies:

- Watering
- Fertilizing
- Cultivating
- Mulching
- Pruning, thinning, and shaping
- Staking and supporting

We'll go into all of these in detail in a few pages, but first, let's quickly look at what each entails:

WATERING. Plants need an ample and regular supply of water to grow strong and healthy. To assure garden success, you need answers to these irrigation questions:

How frequently should I water? How much water is enough? What are the options for watering? How can I automate my watering, and how well do those sprinklers, soaker hoses, and other irrigation systems really work? We'll cover each of these in turn.

FERTILIZING. Another simple need of vegetable plants is a constant source of vital nutrients. All green plants obtain these nutrients from the soil, but it's mostly a one-way journey. Unless the supply is constantly replenished, the soil becomes depleted and plants become listless and are more prone to disease. Consider these issues:

What are the real differences between chemical fertilizers and the organic types? What effects does each have? How can I have a natural—and bountiful—vegetable garden using only organic fertilizers? What downsides are there to consider when applying fertilizer? Where can a constant, abundant supply of low-cost fertilizer be found? How do I apply fertilizers to plants, and when? All these questions are answered in the section on fertilizing.

CULTIVATING. Vegetables do best when they don't have to compete for nutrients and sunlight. Weed grasses and broadleaf plants are not only unsightly but crowd plantings, stealing water and nutrients from the soil. Fortunately, they are easy to control.

The best weed control is prevention rather than eradication. Some questions we'll address:

How does cultivating prevent weeds? How often should I cultivate? How does cultivation stimulate plants and make them healthier? To find out the answers, read the section on cultivation.

MULCHING. The best way to augment your cultivating is to mulch. Mulching not only prevents weeds from germinating, it increases soil temperature—most needed in early spring and late autumn—and helps fertilize the garden. The questions are:

Should I choose plastic fabric or an organic mulch? How does mulching insulate the soil? Why should a weed control program begin with mulching? We'll answer all of these queries.

PRUNING, THINNING, AND SHAPING. Vegetables sometimes have a way of getting out of control—spreading beyond their beds, developing too many blossoms for good fruit formation, or bolting and going to seed. There are plenty of tricks and tips for avoiding these common garden problems, but the best solution is pruning and thinning. Your questions may include:

How do vegetable plants grow? How can I control growth and concentrate their energy on developing and ripening fruit? How can I avoid overcrowding? When should I prune, pinch, trim, and shape? How do I know when there are too many flowers, and how should I select the ones to retain? We'll provide the answers—and pose a few more considerations.

STAKING AND SUPPORTING. A well-nourished vegetable plant can produce a yield beyond the plant's ability to support it. Besides these "intensive care" situations, using vertical space in gardens is just good common sense since getting plants up off the ground prevents a host of potential soil-borne disease problems. The questions we'll answer:

When are tomatoes, melons, and cucumbers too heavy for their vines? How and when should vegetable plants be supported? What's involved in staking a plant and providing supports, and when should I do it? How do I install a trellis support for plants that usually grow on or near the ground? How can I grow "trophy" produce? We've got the answers.

First up is watering—the most common source of questions and myths regarding a vegetable garden.

Watering

In Chapter Three: *Gardening Basics*, we described the simple watering needs of vegetable plants. Here we discuss in depth the watering and irrigation needs of your garden, including:

- How plants use water

- How to water vegetables

- How to install an in-ground irrigation system

- How to install a drip irrigation system

This overview provides the background plus step-by-step instructions on how to water. Then we go beyond the basics to dispel the mysteries of common watering problems. We'll look at hose and watering can solutions, as well as in-ground irrigation systems.

HOW PLANTS USE WATER.

All plants take water in through roots and transport it to the stems and leaves through well-understood physical processes. The critical interface takes place between the soil and a plant's "hair" roots, extremely fine roots with specialized cells that absorb water and dissolve soil nutrients mostly through a process called "osmosis."

Osmosis draws water—which bears dilute amounts of dissolved nutrient salts—through the cellular membranes of a plant's roots to the vessels and channels within the root structures. These internal structures contain water more salty than that found outside the roots. The salt solution in this water "attracts" the less-concentrated soil water, drawing it through the semipermeable root cell membrane. The result is a net transport of water from the low-salt concentration side of the cell membrane to the side with the higher salt concentration—in other words, from outside the plant to inside.

Although this process sounds complicated, it is actually very simple: water outside the plant continuously seeks to dilute liquids containing concentrated nutrient and waste salts within the plant.

This action, in turn, is driven by "transpiration"—evaporation through the foliage—and photosynthesis.

Transpiration is the evaporation of water from cells in the leaves of a plant, which allows the plant to "drink" water from the soil. As water evaporates from a plant's leaves, a tiny bit of salt is left behind. As more and more water transpires into the air, these leaf salts become more concentrated. To dilute the salt, osmosis draws water up into the leaves from the plant's roots through the plant's stem. Once in the leaf, the new water replaces that lost through transpiration.

Think of it this way: It's sort of like a miniature bucket brigade. The low-salt water in the soil passes through a cell to dilute its concentrated salts. This makes that cell less salty than its neighbors. The water, seeking to balance the salt levels between the two cells, transfers through the cell walls to the next cell and into the plant's vessels, and so on.

There's also a reverse flow taking place: the dissolved salts—along with nutrient starches and sugars produced by photosynthesis in the leaves—pass back through the cell membranes. This transfer assures that the roots and stem of the plant receive nutrition from the "food factories" located in its leaves.

When you consider it, the internal processes that balance all of these flows are quite remarkable.

WATERING PROBLEMS. Osmosis can only occur when a sufficient amount of water is present to balance the plant's internal salt levels. It stops whenever plants are not provided with enough water. Two of the most common problems affecting vegetable plants result when either heat or humidity is too high. Excessive heat causes transpiration to proceed at such a pace that cell-borne water cannot reach the leaves quickly enough to replace the liquid lost through transpiration. Excessive humidity halts transpiration entirely since the atmosphere already contains as much water as it can hold.

Under either condition, osmosis cannot keep pace and dilute the salts and starches in the leaves and the plant begins to wither. The breakdown of transpiration quickly reduces the amount of water in all the plant cells. The cells become toxic with excess salt and natural waste products and begin to die. Unless the balance is restored quickly, the plant cannot supply water to its withering parts and they will be damaged beyond repair or out-and-out destroyed.

These problems usually can be corrected easily, before they become dire. Simply water the plant during hot spells, and humid conditions seldom last long enough to cause permanent damage.

Another common problem is overwatering. While it is possible to drown a plant, the real problem usually is soil-borne fungus spores that are ever-present in dark, cool, and damp locations. Overwatering allows these spores to grow, killing the hair root cells, making them "leaky," or clogging their adjacent vessels with fungus. Either of these situations makes it impossible for osmosis to transport water up a plant's stem.

It's a strange coincidence, but the end result of over-watering is the same as that of underwatering. Not enough water reaches the stem and leaves, and the plant withers and dies from lack of water.

The secret to controlling overwatering damage is to make sure the soil is porous enough to permit lots of air to circulate around the roots. Soil fungal diseases grow poorly when they have lots of air circulating near their cells; conversely, they thrive in the absence of oxygen.

Watering Vegetables

There are three common ways to water vegetables. Choose the method appropriate for your plants.

A Overhead watering: Use a fine-spray setting with a hose-end nozzle to water leafy-green, cool-season plants. Always water early in the day so that foliage has a chance to dry completely before evening, which reduces the risk of fungal disease.

B Row irrigation: Water most row crops at the base of the plant by filling an irrigation furrow alongside. The water will diffuse slowly into the soil and reach the plant roots.

C Watering hills: Fill the basin surrounding each hill with water, taking care not to erode the hill. As the plant matures, avoid wetting the foliage by parting it when filling the basin.

WATERING CANS AND HOSES. With a traditional garden, once the texture of your soil is ideal [see Soil Texture, pg. 44], water regularly, which means neither too frequently nor too rarely.

Most vegetable gardeners supply their plants with water using simple hoses or watering cans (though watering cans usually are practical only for small-space and container gardens). The advantages of a hose irrigation system are low cost, simplicity, and good results, especially if furrows, trenches, and other watercourses have been dug to direct the flow of water from one area of the garden to another. The disadvantage is the time required to water and move hoses and sprinklers throughout the garden.

Some gardeners simplify their irrigation needs by installing "soaker hoses"—thick foam hoses designed to provide a steady trickle of water onto the ground through tiny perforations in their coverings. The foremost advantage of soaker hoses is that they prevent problems associated with overhead watering [see How to Water, pg. 199], and they also supply water to dense soils at a slow absorption rate. Such hoses can be costly, however, and intense sun may deteriorate them over time. Finally, if your water supply is too hard, it can clog their porous coverings with dissolved minerals, blocking the water's flow.

IN-GROUND IRRIGATION SYSTEMS. Even more time-saving than semipermanent soaker hoses is an in-ground watering system [see Installing an In-ground Irrigation System, pg. 200].

Such irrigation systems connect PVC pipe, controllers, timers, and a series of valves to your home's water supply. A backflow prevention valve assures that water in the irrigation system can't siphon back into the household water supply so it's a good idea to install one according to local code requirements. A so-called "gate valve" is simply a shut-off valve that allows you to drain the system and perform necessary repairs. It usually is installed in the water supply line, immediately after the backflow preventer. The supply line terminates in one or more irrigation control valves that open and close according to an electrical control timer; they permit water to flow to specific areas of the garden. Most systems include a pressure-relief valve that allows the system to vent if excess pressure builds up. It also is used at the end of the growing season to eliminate standing water in the pipes and avoid damage to the system under freezing temperatures.

Depending on the system design, an in-ground irrigation system can include sprinkler heads for overhead watering, bubbler heads for watering at the base of plants, and drip irrigation emitter heads for pinpoint watering. Depending on your needs and objectives, heads can be combined on a single watering circuit or divided and installed on several individual circuits.

Multiple watering circuits are used to meet the varying frequency needs of individual plantings. Some tender plants, including leafy greens, require daily watering, while others, such as pumpkins and squash, may require deep waterings as seldom as once a week. Some plants need to be flooded with water—melons, pumpkins, and squash come to mind—while others, including peas, beans, and spinach, need small, steady amounts of water delivered over the course of an hour or more. For best results, install at least two circuits—one to deliver bulk water and overhead sprays, and another to service drip-irrigation needs and fill your soaker hoses.

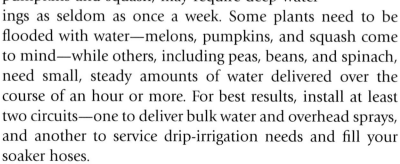

HOW TO WATER. Most vegetable plants—the exceptions are cool-season lettuce, cabbage, broccoli, cauliflower, and tall, upright plants such as corn and pole beans—should be watered at the base of the plant, above the fine hair roots [see Watering Vegetables, pg. 196]. It's also best to water most vegetables early in the day, after the chill of night air has left the garden but before the full force of the sun has begun to bear down. Watering at this time prevents water drops on foliage from catching sunlight, which some maintain can overheat spots on the plants' leaves, killing them. Avoid watering in the evening or before sunrise, when cool temperatures can promote the spread of fungal disease and rot.

Hydroponics

You may have heard of "hydroponic" gardening —growing plants without soil in water filled with dissolved nutrients. Hydroponics requires the gardener to take full responsibility for providing the plants with all their nutritional needs, which are met by mixing sometimes-exotic blends of nutrients into the water used to bathe the plant's roots.

Garden stores specializing in hydroponics sell all of the specialized equipment (and dispense the specialized advice) needed to establish tanks full of growing plants. This equipment includes special "grow lights," pumps, hoses, tubing, and plant support frames, along with water-soluble chemical nutrients, specialty fungicides, and pesticides to create the "water solutions" that bathe each plant's roots. Experimenting with hydroponics, especially in a green-house setting, can be lots of fun—and allows for fresh produce year-round.

Keep in mind, however, that maintaining a hydroponic garden is a responsibility equivalent to caring for a pet.

The amount of water required for optimum plant growth depends on daily temperature extremes and humidity, as well as on your plants' growth habits. Because these factors are different for every garden, observe conditions closely and use judgment to achieve a good balance between your plants' needs and your irrigation schedule.

To gauge your watering needs, dig up a soil sample from 2–4 inches (5–10 cm) beneath the surface and squeeze it in your palm. If the dirt quickly crumbles when pressure is released, it's time to water; if it stays balled and firm, test it again the following day. The rule of thumb is to add an inch (25 mm) of water to the soil with each irrigation [see Ideal Watering, pg. 61]. Water less if your soil is claylike or dense. Never water so much as to create runoff; it usually means you have overwatered, while good gardening practices mean conserving water.

Installing an In-ground Irrigation System

Permanent watering systems make caring for a vegetable garden easier and can ensure that plants receive adequate moisture according to a programmed schedule.

Installing such systems, while physically demanding, is easy to do and requires basic tools.

Plan your system carefully, using the readily available literature and worksheets available at your garden retail or hardware store. Allow for future expansion.

Follow these simple steps to automate irrigation in your garden:

1 From your water supply line and backflow prevention valve, trench and run 1-in. (25 mm), Schedule 40 pipe to the control valve location. Install a ¾-in. (18 mm) reducing bushing at the valve. Mount control valves below grade where freezing temperatures are likely.

2 Install a separate control valve for each water circuit. Use a ½-in. (12 mm) reducing bushing between each valve and the lines running to the sprinkler heads or drip emitters.

3 Cut pipe to length, using a PVC pipe-cutting tool, then join sections using two-step primer and adhesive. Allow glue to dry at least 24 hours.

4 Where each irrigation head is planned, install a 90° "street tee" or "ell" fitting, with slip joints to the pipe and a threaded coupler to the riser.

Irrigate slowly, allowing the water to completely penetrate the soil. When you believe you have watered enough, test it again. Dig some soil from the area next to your plants, to the depth of their roots. If the subsurface soil is dry, continue watering until it is uniformly wet to a depth of 4 inches (10 cm) [see A Simple Test for Proper Watering, pg. 62].

If you have an in-ground irrigation system, you can adjust the amount of time, and the flow, for your garden's watering needs. Always adjust your system to supply more water as temperatures climb. If you water with hoses or watering cans, times of drought and heat must be met with more frequent waterings. No matter which means of watering you use, check the soil every few days and adjust the watering patterns according to the differing impact of heat spells or rainy periods.

5 Install sprinkler spray housings or drip-system hose couplers atop each riser, using three wraps of teflon tape around each threaded fitting.

6 Turn on the gate valve and sprinkler manifold to clear line of debris, then turn off and install spray heads and drip lines. Finally, set controller.

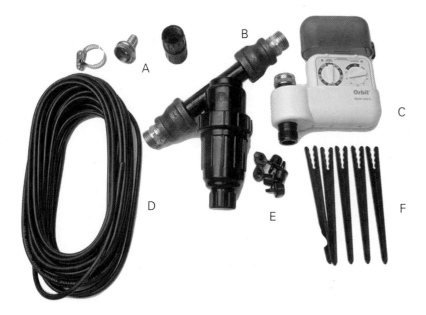

A Simple Drip System

Create drip systems quickly and inexpensively by attaching battery-controlled timers and filters to near-by faucets or hose bibs. Drip irrigation conserves by emitting a flow of water to each plant. A single system can water up to 30 plants, depending on the water pressure.

Components:

A   Couplers and fittings
B   Drip irrigation water filter
C   Battery-timed hose-bib irrigation valve
D   Drip irrigation line hose
E   Drip emitters
F   Line-placement stakes

1 Couple timer valve to hose bib, then install an in-line water filter to prevent clogged lines. Bushings may be needed where threads do not match exactly.

2 From the filter, attach the drip supply hose. This large-diameter hose carries pressurized water to the attachment for each drip line and may have several joints and junctions.

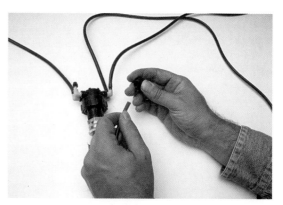

3 Wherever a drip line is needed, terminate the supply hose with a drip line coupler, available in 2-, 4-, and 8-connection models. Attach ¼-in. (6-mm) supply tubing and one or more emitters.

4 Attach a line-placement stake and position an emitter at the base of each plant to be watered. Vary water flow rates and the pattern of disbursement through your choice of emitter.

Fertilizing Vegetables

Like watering, proper fertilization is essential to producing great vegetable gardens. In Chapter Three: *Gardening Basics*, we introduced you to the various nutrients needed for good garden soil, including the three majors—nitrogen, phosphorus, and potassium—as well as certain micronutrients.

In the pages that follow, we provide in-depth coverage of fertilizer choices and their applications. You'll find out:

- Why vegetables need macronutrients

- How they absorb and use fertilizer

- How to determine the difference between chemical and natural fertilizers

- How much fertilizer you should apply, and how often

- What common fertilizing problems you may encounter

Let's start with how plants are nourished, and what and what quantity of nutrients they require to produce flowers, fruit, and foliage.

HOW PLANTS ARE NOURISHED. Plants get most of what they need for growth from adequately watered garden soil through a process called osmosis [see How Plants Use Water, pg. 193]. Two exceptions are oxygen and carbon dioxide, which plants obtain from the air surrounding their foliage. Another is sunlight energy, which the plants receive even on overcast days.

Plants are efficient at converting all of these elements into energy for their cellular tissues and structures. To obtain the basic building blocks they need for growth, flowering plants—including all vegetables—utilize special cells mostly located in their foliage. Within these cells, chlorophyll acts with sunlight energy and raw nutrients to build complex sugars, plant proteins, and amino acids in a process called photosynthesis. These, in turn, fuel the plant's growth. Over the growing season, a complete plant, with foliage, flowers, and fruit, results.

At a minimum, every green plant needs hydrogen (from water), carbon dioxide (from the air), nitrogen (in its dissolved soluble salt form, nitrate), plus phosphorus and potassium (from the soil) to grow. Three of these—nitrogen, phosphorus, and potassium—are considered the essential horticultural macronutrients. Together with a varied list of micronutrients, each element and compound has a role to play.

Oxygen and carbon dioxide are released from the leaves as by-products of the photosynthesis process—oxygen by day and carbon dioxide by night.

Nitrogen builds strong leaves and other foliage. Phosphorus promotes seed and root development and stimulates flower formation. Potassium buffers acids and carries carbohydrate sugars from the leaves to the stem and roots.

Plants depend on their hair roots to absorb water in the soil that contains these dissolved elements and mineral salts. Because these water-soluble nutrients are constantly being depleted from garden soil, it is up to the gardener to replenish the supply through regular applications of appropriate fertilizers.

FERTILIZER SELECTION. Choosing the type of fertilizer for your vegetable garden is mainly a matter of personal preference. Whether chemical or natural, solid or liquid, your primary consideration is the results you can expect in your garden. For best results, always read the label instructions carefully and follow them to the letter. It's an important step for getting good results

Most chemical and organic fertilizers contain varying ratios of the three key nutrients. These ratios are expressed on labels as a triad of numbers, such as 10-10-10. They refer to the relative amounts of soluble nitrogen ("N"), phosphorus ("P"), and potassium ("K") contained in the fertilizer—or its NPK ratio. Some fertilizers also list other trace mineral ingredients beneficial to plant growth, along with their inert ingredients—fillers with no nutritional benefit. While too numerous to discuss in detail, these micronutrients play important roles both in plant physiology and in the nutritional value of the plants' produce.

While it is a scientifically proven fact that plants are unable to distinguish between man-made and natural sources of nitrogen, phosphorus, and potassium, man-made chemical fertilizers seldom contain the multitude of trace minerals and micronutrients found in their organic and animal fertilizer counterparts. They are chemically "pure," meaning that, other than their inert component ingredients, they only contain the specified amounts of the three primary fertilizer components.

Chemical fertilizers cannot add balance to your soil in the same way and to the same extent that well-rotted manure, organic compost, and other natural fertilizers can. Organics also serve a garden's plants over an extended period of time, because their natural decomposition releases a continuous stream of nutrients.

Bone meal is one organic fertilizer that gardeners should avoid, at least until scientific evidence conclusively proves its safety. Recent scientific speculation has implicated bone meal components with infections from non-living, smaller-than-virus bodies called "prions." Prions are the suspected infectious agents of such neural diseases as "mad cow disease," or *spongiform encephalitis*, a deadly form of degenerative nerve disease thought to infect both bovine animals and man.

Bone meal is made from the ground, sterilized bones of cows, pigs, and other slaughtered animals, but prions cannot be destroyed by the sterilization techniques employed to kill bacteria and viruses. Until the evidence is in, prevent any potential hazard to you or your family by avoiding the use of bone meal.

Common beneficial organic fertilizers come in both solid and liquid forms. Two common solid fertilizers are fresh manure and rotted manure (the latter is made by allowing fresh, or so-called "green," animal manure to decompose, which reduces the amount of nitrogen it contains). During the growing season, pick composted or well-rotted manure to avoid overdosing your vegetable plants with nitrates, except in the autumn or early winter, when you are amending your garden's soil after the growing season is finished. Another solid fertilizer option is fish meal. Liquid fertilizer choices include fish emulsion—fertilizer made from fish protein and oil, which is high in nitrogen—and nutrient-rich "teas," which are made by soaking well-rotted manure in water, then draining off the liquid. Both solids and liquids are safe, effective, and easy to apply.

One of the most commonly used organic fertilizers is organic compost—decomposed plant matter purchased at a nursery or garden retail store or made right in your garden [see Building a Compost Bin, pg. 210]. Compost is made by piling waste plant materials from the garden in a suitable container and allowing natural bacteria to help them decompose into rich, fertile humus. An occasional turning of the pile with a garden fork—to move surface matter from the top of the pile to the bottom and incorporate air into the pile—is all that is necessary to obtain a ready source of fertilizer for your plantings. The entire process of conversion takes somewhere between four weeks and two months, depending on the temperature of the air, the level of moisture in the pile itself and in the surrounding air, and the number of times you turn the pile. A compost heap will yield about one-quarter as much volume as the amount you contribute in plant matter.

When adding to a compost heap, fruit and vegetable peelings are acceptable along with other garden waste, but avoid putting in meat or other greasy foods. They break down much more slowly than plant matter and may emit a foul odor. An active compost heap made exclusively from plant matter rarely emits bad smells. Whenever it does, the compost should be turned because aeration will kill most of its anaerobic bacteria—the source of the smell.

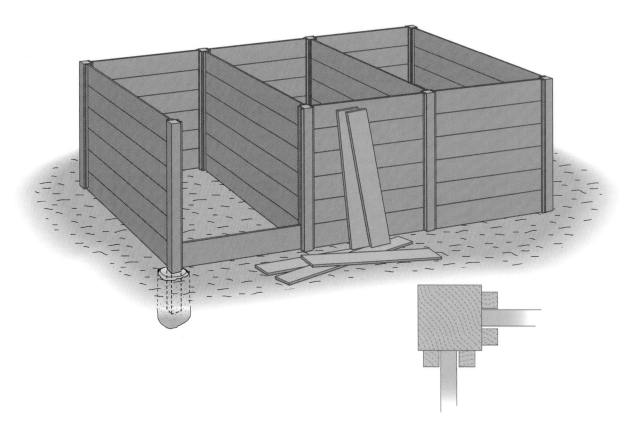

Building a Compost Bin

Adding compost to your garden soil improves it in three ways: decayed organic matter enhances workability, nutrients contained in the compost fertilize your vegetable plants, and neutral acidity compost buffers too-acidic or -alkaline conditions.

Making compost is easy and environmentally friendly. Many commercially manufactured compost bins are available for purchase at garden retailers, including some elaborate models that turn the compost mix with motors or weights. Most home gardens produce a steady stream of plant waste, so a large bin is the perfect solution to disposal.

The three-stage bin shown here has a 6×12-ft. (1.8×3.6 m) footprint, and processes 2–3 cu. yds. (1.5–2.3 m³) of vegetable matter per month. Raw waste is placed into the first section of the bin and allowed to decompose partially. After three to four weeks, it is turned into the second section. In another month, it is turned a last time into the final section, where it completes its decay and becomes available for use as mulch or a rich soil amendment.

The process is made easier by the way the bin is constructed—with slots containing fitted boards between each section. When the bin is turned, the boards slip out, making access easy and reducing the amount of lifting required.

Allow a couple of days for the project—six to eight hours to sink and set the postholes and another day to finish the bin. One day each on consecutive weekends works best.

Required Materials:

Redwood or Cedar Lumber:

8	6-ft. (180 cm)	4×4 (89×89 mm)	Posts
12	6-ft. (180 cm)	1×6 (19×140 mm)	Sideboards
12	6-ft. (120 cm)	1×6 (19×140 mm)	Section dividers
24	4-ft. (120 cm)	1×6 (19×140 mm)	Sideboards
40	33-in. (80 cm)	1×1 (19×19 mm)	Vertical slot guides

Hardware and Materials:

120	⅛ × 2-in. (3×50 mm)	Brass wood screws
8	Bags	Posthole concrete mix

1 Dig 8 footings, 20–24 in. (50–60 cm) deep, spaced 4 ft. (1.2 m) apart side-to-side and 6 ft. (1.8 m) apart front-to-back, face to face. Level, brace, and set posts in cement mix.

2 After posts have set, level their tops at 34 in. (86 cm) high. At each junction, install two 1×1-in (25×25 mm) vertical slot guides, spaced 1 in. (25 mm) apart. Attach them with wood screws installed into predrilled pilot holes. Into each slot, on the back and sides, insert 6 sideboards.

3 Install the section dividers and the front sideboards. These boards may be removed for easy access when turning the compost bin, or when removing finished compost for use in the garden. The bin is ready to receive its first load of garden waste.

The process of decomposition has an additional benefit: as plant matter breaks down into simpler components, it releases biotic heat, which sterilizes the compost. In the process, it also kills many weed seeds and speeds the plant matter's organic breakdown into compost. Organic compost is nearly weed free, though some hardy seeds may survive the process. Avoid composting fruits of tomato and pepper plants to prevent inadvertent seeding of these plants into other areas of your garden.

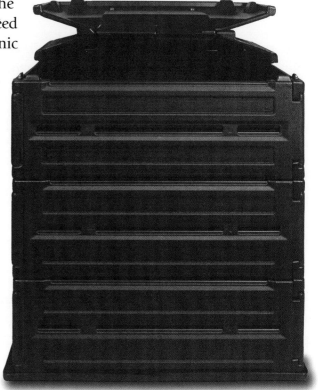

An even greater benefit of organic compost is its ability to buffer the acidity and alkalinity of natural garden soil. Compost made from decayed plant matter is nearly neutral in pH—naturally slightly acidic—whereas many garden soils tend to have either higher or lower pH values. The compost neutralizes the acids or bases in these soils, resulting in rich humus that is ideally suited for most vegetable crops.

Compost generally is considered a naturally "balanced" fertilizer—meaning that it often contains all three primary nutrients in equal amounts—because the plant matter from which it decomposes also contains a balanced ratio of macro- and micronutrients. Depending on your plants' specific needs, you may have to add more phosphorus or potassium. These so-called simple, or "specialty," fertilizers help vegetable plants develop stronger root systems and overall strength without triggering the development of excessive foliage. Apply them when blooms first appear, which will help the flowers set and develop fruit.

Applying Compost to Fertilize Plants.

Using nitrogen-rich organic compost to fertilize vegetables is an all-natural alternative to chemical fertilizers.

Because compost does not burn, it can be added more frequently than concentrated fertilizers. The best way to apply it is to cover the bed surface 4–6 inches (10–15 cm) away from rows and along the margins of hill crops. A layer 2–3-inches (5–7.5 cm) deep is about right. Gradually work the compost into the soil of the bed as you cultivate, being careful to avoid damaging any surface roots.

Using compost in this manner allows it to gradually supplement the natural nutrients in the garden's native soil, improve its texture and add trace minerals and micronutrients essential to plant health.

Another method of incorporating compost into the soil is to apply it more generously prior to planting. Garden soil that has lain fallow over winter often lacks sufficient organic matter since it decays over time.

There is one other class of inorganic fertilizer that is specifically compounded for application to foliage. So-called foliar fertilizers have become popular in recent years (mainly due to extensive promotional campaigns), and they are

effective. Foliar fertilizers are applied directly to plant leaves and foliage, and they bypass the usual transport from soil to root, root to stem, and stem to chlorophyll-bearing leaf cells. The fertilizer is absorbed by the plant's leaves, though more slowly than by root feeding. This allows the plant to gain vigor and strength quickly; it also means foliar fertilizers must be applied more frequently than soil fertilizers.

FERTILIZER TIMING AND AMOUNT. Fertilizing plants is an ongoing process. Before planting, apply fertilizer to the soil and work it in thoroughly as you cultivate.

About four weeks after sprouts appear, or soon after nursery starts are transplanted, apply a second feeding of fertilizer outside the "root zone" of each vegetable plant. A quick way to determine the root zone is to circumscribe an imaginary line around the outermost leaves of the plants to the ground. Applying fertilizer outside the plants' roots will encourage them to extend into the fertilized soil and will increase their vigor.

The best way to add compost prior to planting is to double dig the bed [see Double Digging, pg. 50] after applying a layer of compost 6–8-inches (15–20 cm) deep. As an alternative, till the compost into the bed with a mechanical tiller.

Container vegetable gardeners should especially consider use of compost in their planters. Because

compost holds moisture and air well, and resists compaction, it is a great amendment for container soils. Mix equal parts of compost, potting soil, and native soil prior to planting vegetables in containers.

As a fertilizer, compost is not "complete," however—depending on the plant matter used in your compost bin, it may lack sufficient

phosphorus or potassium to meet all of your plants' needs. Supplement these essential nutrients periodically throughout the growing season— about every two months is about right.

For each month thereafter, apply more fertilizer until fruit begins to set on the plants. Cut back on fertilization as soon as blossoms appear, or only use a specialty fertilizer with low or no nitrogen content—a 5–10–10 or 0–10–10 compound. Excessive nitrogen given to blooming plants diverts their energies away from forming fruit to producing more foliage.

Always apply fertilizer according to label instructions. Too much fertilizer may chemically "burn" your vegetable plants, though there's less risk if you use low-nitrogen and organic fertilizer products.

Always dilute liquid fertilizers as recommended on the label, and avoid spraying or sprinkling the solution on the plants' foliage unless such application is recommended.

Be sure to water your plants after each application of fertilizer—this vital step dilutes the concentrated nutrients contained within most fertilizers and further reduces the potential for burning foliage [see Applying Chemical Fertilizers opposite].

The best way to ensure that your plants receive a constant supply of needed nutrients is to mulch them with organic compost. A shallow layer of compost laid over the planting bed will slowly decompose, adding nutrients to the soil with each watering [see Applying Compost to Fertilize Plants, pg. 212]. Check fertilizing recommendations in the Vegetable Encyclopedia [see pg. 307] for those plants that require heavy fertilization; compost mulching alone may be insufficient for them.

COMMON FERTILIZER PROBLEMS. Most fertilizer problems are the result of a failure to follow mixing and application instructions completely. Always completely follow the manufacturer's recommended instructions for use.

Applying Chemical Fertilizers

Synthetic chemical fertilizers, along with many concentrated organics, contain either balanced amounts of nitrogen, phosphorus, and potassium, or they emphasize one nutrient more than the others.

Because their active ingredients are designed to dissolve and disperse quickly, they are effective and easy to apply.

Always follow all manufacturer recommendations closely regarding application and amounts. Wear waterproof gloves and avoid breathing fertilizer dust.

Measure carefully. Apply granular chemical fertilizers around your plants 6–8 in (15–20 cm) away from their stalks. Immediately work into the surface soil with a hand fork or rake, then irrigate. Avoid applying chemical fertilizers during very hot daylight hours.

Chemical fertilizers are highly concentrated and, if overapplied, can chemically burn or even kill vegetable plants. Even green manure, though natural and organic, can harm vegetables in a similar manner.

A more common failure is not fertilizing regularly or sufficiently, which results in plants losing vigor, dropping blossoms, or failing to set fruit. Regular feedings are essential to achieving the optimum plant growth and yield.

A less frequent fertilizer problem is due to lack of potency, either from misformulation at the time of manufacture or improper storage during transport, at the garden retail store, or at home. Always use fertilizer prior to the expiration date on the label.

Such underperforming fertilizer will not harm your plants, but it will have the same effect as underfertilization. If you suspect that your fertilizer is not performing well, return it to the retailer; most reputable retailers will exchange it gladly.

Cultivating Vegetables

It's no coincidence that cultivating is the image most vegetable gardeners hold in their mind's eye when they think about gardening. It's a simple act, and one that ties us to our gardening forebears. A gardener with a simple hoe or garden fork, working down a row of plantings, loosening the soil and eliminating young weeds, is in fact the essence of garden care.

In Chapter Three: *Gardening Basics* we covered some of the reasons cultivating is important to the success of your vegetables. Here we give you detailed instructions on how to cultivate your garden and share with you why and how cultivation helps plants grow.

CULTIVATING TO ENCOURAGE ROOT GROWTH. It's apparent that plants grow both up and down—above and beneath the soil's surface. For many plants, the foliage and branches above the ground are roughly equal in mass to the roots beneath the soil. This means that if foliage is damaged, the plant balances itself by sacrificing further root development until new growth has has a chance to fill in. In extreme cases, some roots actually may die if foliage is sufficiently damaged.

A plant performs this delicate balancing act of equalizing growth because the amount of nutrients produced by the process of photosynthesis in its chlorophyll-laden leaves must correspond to the needs of the entire plant, including its root system.

By the same token, a rootbound plant will fail to develop adequate foliage, flowers, or fruit because of the limited ability of its roots to provide water and nutrients to the above-ground parts of the plant.

The only thing that is necessary for strong root development is loose, fertile soil moistened by subsurface water. Loose soil, mixed with ample amounts of decayed organic matter, is best for ideal root development.

Whenever garden soil becomes compacted, root development slows or stops. Cultivation opens the soil to air and water, allowing it to harbor young, tender roots. If you regularly cultivate your vegetable garden, you will reap the reward of vigorous plants.

CULTIVATING TO PREVENT WEEDS. Most weeds—many non-natives that have been introduced to a region inadvertently—are plants with few natural enemies. In general they are far better adapted to growing in your garden than are most domesticated vegetable species. Every handful of garden soil contains a few weed seeds, waiting for optimum conditions to germinate, sprout, and grow. If allowed to do so, they will compete with your vegetable plants for water, nutrients, and space.

Weed *prevention* is better than any method of treating weed problems. Prevention also is quick, easy, and effective. In addition, stopping weeds when they first germinate eliminates the entire question of whether or not to apply chemical herbicides, meaning your garden ends up being a more healthful as well as attractive place.

Cultivating a Garden

Cultivating is an essential part of garden care that benefits plantings by loosening soil, controlling competitive weeds, aiding water penetration, and improving appearance.

For small areas, raised beds, or containers, use a hand fork or tined tool; in larger areas, use a hoe, cultivator, or specialty fork. The intent is to open the soil near the plants to the tops of their root systems, then dig deeply away from them, In other words, imagine each plant's rootball beneath the soil and then cultivate around it.

Observe carefully when you cultivate. If fine roots are disturbed, adjust the depth and location of your work. Follow these easy instructions:

1 Near the plants, unearth 4–6 in. (10–15 cm) of soil, removing weeds, rocks, and debris. Avoid disturbing plant roots. Break up clods. Incorporate any soil amendments you add.

2 About 12 in (30 cm) out from the plants, dig more deeply—10–12 in. (25–30 cm), or so. Bring deeply buried soil to the surface.

3 Work down the row and around any mounds. Avoid compacting finished areas by walking on the cultivated soil.

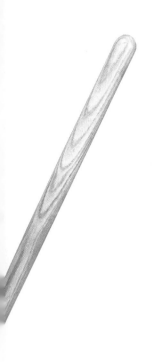

HOW TO CULTIVATE. Cultivating a garden is simply turning the surface soil with a hoe or garden cultivator [see Cultivating a Garden, opposite]. Any sprouted weeds are turned under in the process and quickly die. In addition, the soil is loosened, permitting water to reach vegetable roots more effectively.

When cultivating, limit your hoeing beneath the canopy of each plant to the top 3–4 inches (7.5–10 cm) of soil. As you cultivate outward from the plant, your hoe or cultivator will pass from the plant's canopy—the area in which water dripping from the foliage would hit the ground—to that area outside this imaginary boundary. Cultivating deeply beneath the canopy can damage the fine hair roots of the plant, but cultivating deeply just outside this boundary allows air to enter soil that may have become compacted or dense.

In these areas, your hoe or cultivator should overturn soil 8–10-inches (20–25-cm) deep or more. This cultivation outside the root line returns soil nutrients to the surface, where irrigation can dissolve them and carry them back down to the roots.

Cultivation also is an excellent time to add compost or fertilizer, which can be worked in with your hoe [see Cultivating a Garden, pg. 218]. The combination of fertilizing and cultivating will stimulate new root growth, which in turn will promote the overall growth of your vegetable plants.

Mulching

Mulching provides four major benefits to growing vegetable plants:

- Blocking sunlight to the soil

- Acting as a thermal blanket by holding solar heat within the bed

- Decomposing slowly, which provides a continuous source of fertilizer

- Protecting developing fruit from direct contact with the soil

Blocking sunlight to the soil prevents weed seeds from germinating. To germinate, weed seeds need a suitable environment, sunlight, and water, two of which every diligent gardener provides when preparing the soil and irrigating the vegetable plants. Mulching inhibits weed development by depriving the seeds of the sunlight needed to trigger germination and by disrupting the growth of any newly germinated sprouts.

Mulching is simply accomplished by covering the soil surrounding plants with either a barrier such as plastic sheeting or an organic layer of weed-free straw, organic compost, or other mulch material.

Many commercial growers use opaque black plastic sheeting to mulch their beds. The

Mulching with Plastic

Porous plastic weed barrier cloth allows air, solar heat, water, and most nutrients to penetrate to the soil beneath. Its black color blocks most light, preventing weed seeds from germinating. Use it in your vegetable garden to reduce the amount of cultivating required. Follow these simple steps to mulch your beds with plastic:

1 After soil is prepared and raked, roll out the weed barrier cloth, overlapping seams at least 8 in. (20 cm). Pin it to the ground with U-shaped aluminum stakes.

2 At the location planned for each planting, cut an X into the fabric with a sharp knife. Each opening should be slightly larger than each transplant's container.

3 Peel back the fabric and plant through the barrier cloth into the soil beneath.

4 Close the flaps to tightly surround the plant. Irrigate through the surface of the weed barrier fabric; it will penetrate to the roots beneath.

warmth of the sun is trapped by the plastic, much as it is in a greenhouse. Soil temperatures rise, plants increase their growth rates, and irrigation needs are reduced [see Mulching with Plastic on the previous page]. For hot-climate areas, where soil overheating is a concern, special plastic mulch material that is silvered on one side reflects solar energy and excess heat away from the planting bed back toward the sky.

Even better than plastic is organic mulch, whether with weed-free straw or any number of other materials. The insulating quality of organic mulch is superior to that of plastic sheeting, which is particularly important in the marginal periods of early spring and late autumn when plants are attempting to grow or produce is trying to ripen.

In addition, organic mulch applied in a layer 3–4 inches (75–100 mm) deep protects the soil surface from erosion or compaction. Because the mulch decomposes slowly, it also improves the soil texture during cultivation by adding beneficial organic matter [see Applying Organic Mulch on this page].

A final benefit of mulching is realized close to harvest, when produce such as melons, squash, and pumpkins lie close to the ground. Mulch prevents direct contact between the fruit and the soil, where bacteria and fungi can cause infection and rot.

Apply mulch immediately after each cultivation, beginning soon after planting. This will eliminate the need for frequent cultivation, weeding, and some fertilizing as your garden matures. Most important, is that you'll be rewarded with an attractive and productive garden.

Applying Organic Mulch

Applying organic mulch around your vegetables—weed-free straw, for instance—is an effective way to halt weeds by denying them sunlight, protect soil from erosion, and make your garden more attractive. Mulching also reduces the amount of care that your garden requires.

Cultivate and irrigate. Apply mulch. It's easy. Follow these steps:

1 Before mulching, always remove old mulch and cultivate the soil around your plants. This vital step eliminates weeds and loosens the soil to promote good root growth. It's also a good time to fertilize.

2 Use a rake or fork to scatter a layer of weed-free straw (available at most feed stores or where horses are boarded) at least 2-in. (25 mm) thick. Replace the mulch when it begins to decay.

3 Where ripening fruit and berries come in contact with the soil surface, build-up an extra thickness of straw. It will prevent the fruit from being infected by soil-borne diseases and limit damage to them by many pests.

Pruning

Plants sometimes grow without regard to our wishes. They may produce too much foliage, too many blossoms, or too much fruit, not to mention becoming unsightly in the process. A responsible gardener takes pains to restore balance to such plantings, though most often nothing more is required than pinching a blossom or bud here or there.

Let's look in turn at each of the three care processes that control a vegetable plant's growth: pinching, thinning, and pruning. Each of these addresses specific care needs.

PINCHING TO DIRECT GROWTH. The growth patterns of all plants are dictated by their genes—some grow upright, others twine and vine, still others grow close to the ground. One of the most common growth habits of vegetable plants is to grow, extend foliage, and develop a single bud on the end of each outermost branch.

There are two types of growth buds—dominant buds and secondary buds. By a growth process called "apical dominance," plants channel their energy to the outermost buds on the foliage, while developing secondary buds along the developing stems. This act of preference results in the plant quickly expanding its margins.

To control an errant or overly enthusiastic plant's growth, you can take advantage of this simple development process by pinching off the dominant buds. This will force the plant to retrench and select the nearest secondary bud for development. This process also will channel more of the plant's energy to the blooms and

Pinch Pruning

Many vegetable plants benefit from pinch pruning. To use this technique, nothing more than your fingers are required to remove all damaged and diseased foliage and fruit, as well as excess foliage and the tips of runners. Pruning forces a more compact growth habit and redirects nutrients to fruit and flowers. Follow these easy instructions.

1 Select a stem or leaf for removal. Terminal buds are ideal candidates for pruning.

2 Using your forefinger and thumbnail, pinch off the bud, leaf, or stem. Most annual vegetables have tender stalks and are easily pruned.

3 Removing terminal buds causes the plant to branch and develop more flowers.

developing fruit and conserves space in the garden. Choosing to pinch-prune dominant buds can exact an emotional toll on the gardener. After all, how much harm can there be in a leggy, overgrown tomato plant? The proof lies in the results: when excess foliage development is stifled, more of the plant's energy is channeled to its flowers and fruit. In a few weeks, branches that were barren are filled with clusters of ripening tomatoes. The same holds true for virtually every other vegetable, especially peppers, beans, and squash.

Pinch pruning is just what its name implies—squeezing off the dominant buds from the outermost branches of a plant, or excessive blossoms on already-flowering plants. Limiting the number of fruits increases their size and improves their succulent taste.

Pinch buds and blossoms whenever a plant begins to look leggy or has an abundance of flowers [see Pinch Pruning, pg. 225]. Pinching near the stem on young plants forces them to grow more upright, making harvest easier and the yield more satisfying.

THINNING. Leafy plants, such as lettuce and spinach, and small root vegetables, such as carrots and radishes, frequently are planted into the garden by a scattering of seeds over an area [see Planting seeds, pg. 166]. When the plants begin to grow, but before they fill in, thin the plantings to the desired spacing [see Spacing of Plants chart, pg. 176].

Thinning vegetable plantings to the recommended spacing is important because it prevents them from competing for sunlight, nutrients, and water. When weather is cool and moist, crowding also encourages fungal disease.

Thinning is easy [see Thinning Vegetables, opposite] and requires nothing more than removing the weaker sprouts that crowd the bed. For leafy vegetables, wait to thin until the plants are 3–4-inches (75–100-mm) tall. The thinnings provide tender salad greens even as you await the development of the plant.

On occasion, you may have to thin more mature plants if they are crowding their bedmates, but in general, keep the most mature and thriving plants and remove their stunted companions.

Thinning Vegetables

Seeding vegetables directly into the garden frequently results in too closely spaced seedlings. Always thin your plantings to the spacing recommended for that variety. It's easy to do:

1 These recently sprouted carrots are spaced much too close and require thinning. If allowed to grow, they will compete for water and nutrients, stunting the entire crop.

2 Follow the spacing recommended by the seed supplier or use the information contained in the Vegetable Encyclopedia [see page 307]. Protect closely neighboring plants by holding them gently between two fingers when pulling those to be thinned. Remove the weakest seedlings.

3 A few days after thinning, the remaining carrots already show vigorous new growth. They will grow large and straight.

Pruning and Shaping

Pruning plants with unruly growth yields larger fruit of better quality. Use sharp pruning shears. Always disinfect them in a mild solution of water and household bleach before pruning. Fungal diseases can be spread by contaminated tools.

1 Many bush plants and vines produce too much foliage and too few blossoms and fruit. Improve their performance by pruning non-productive leaves and stems.

2 After inspecting the plant, remove branches that grow back through the center of the plant line, along with any damaged or diseased foliage, with sharp offset pruning shears.

3 Three weeks after thinning, this tomato plant has set large fruit and is thriving.

PRUNING. Contrary to the popular belief that pruning is only for shrubs, trees, and flowering plants, it's also a useful technique in the vegetable garden. Branching plants, including tomato, tomatillo, and bush beans, as well as many vining berry varieties, can benefit from having their unproductive branches cut back. Use sharp pruning shears or hand clippers, cutting away the unwanted branches close to the stem [see Pruning and Shaping, above]. If you take care to not damage the stem, the wound will heal itself in a day or two. Never apply pruning compound, a sealant intended for use on ornamental shrubs and trees, to vegetable plants; if fungal infection is a concern, apply a fungicidal powder shortly after the cut is made. Within a week, the remaining foliage should become more robust as nutrients once destined for the removed branch are redirected to the rest of the plant.

Staking and Supporting

Gardeners use stakes and supports to shore up weak vining plants or to reduce the amount of space required by plants that tend to spread.

Supports usually are installed at the time of planting [see Supporting Heavy Vegetables, pg. 230]. After-planting supports are used to help vegetable plants hold their fruit, train plants to grow above the soil, and outfit the garden with a decorative touch.

Simple techniques accomplish all of these objectives.

TRAINING VEGETABLE PLANTS ONTO SUPPORTS. Training plants that normally spread to grow vertically not only takes up less space in the garden but exposes them to more sunlight. Among the plants that benefit by staking or trellising are pole beans and peas, vining plants, and berries. If the growth habit of your vegetable plants requires some supporting, install poles or cages at the time of planting. Most other vegetables can be trained onto supports during the early part of their growth cycles.

Choose either of two methods for supporting plants. The first is to install poles next to the plants and attach their stems to the uprights with sturdy twine or stretchy plastic plant tape and ties. The other is to install wooden or metal trellises beside the plants, or set cages or tripods around the plants.

Supporting Heavy Vegetables

Large squash, pumpkin, and melon can weigh 30 lbs. (13.5 kg) or more. Protect them from direct contact with the soil as they grow by training their vines onto a stout pyramid of poles. A strong support may be built in less than an hour, following these steps:

1 Cut 4 each 2-ft., 3-ft., and 4-ft. (60 cm, 90 cm, and 120 cm) poles of stock that is about 4 in. (10 cm) in diameter.

2 Lay 2 of the 4-ft. (120 cm) poles on the ground parallel to one another and equidistant from the center of the plant. Overlap them with the other pair. Create a strong joint by nailing through their junction.

3 Measure 6 in. (15 cm) in from the ends of the bottom square and lap a pair of 3-ft. (90 cm) poles. Again, nail the joints. Repeat for the second pair, then for each pair of the 2-ft. (60 cm) poles, as shown.

4 As the plant grows, blossoms, and sets fruit, train its vines onto the supports. Arrange the vines so that all of the fruit sets atop the poles and avoids contact with the soil.

Certain vegetables, including beans and peas, seek support and naturally entwine their strong tendrils around poles, string or lattice. For multiple plantings, install several uprights and tie string from one pole to the next Use stretchy plastic tape to loosely bind the vines.

Heavier vegetables such as melons, eggplants, and summer squash require more support than twine and poles can provide, even though some bear tendrils. It's easy to train these plants onto vertical supports—simply pick up the growing vine and drape it over the support, then loosely attach the vine to a sturdy cross brace with plant tape to secure it. Becoming accustomed to its new location and getting used to the support takes just a few days [see Supporting Heavy Vegetables, opposite].

In addition to the increased air and sunlight they receive—and the reduced potential they have for contracting soil-borne diseases—upright plants are easier to tend. It is much simpler to care for plants that are at eye level instead of on the ground and masked by excessive foliage. Fertilizing and watering also become easier, as does cultivating and harvesting, since most of the fruit is borne within close picking range.

SUPPORTING FRUIT. Large, heavy fruits, including tomatoes, eggplants, and summer squash, will frequently need support beyond that offered by their vines. This is especially true when the plant has been trained to grow vertically on supports, which leaves the fruit dangling in midair.

One common way to support heavy fruits is to nestle them in nylon or polypropylene mesh firmly attached to trellises or frames [see Supporting Heavy Vegetables, pg. 230].

Another technique is to prop both a plant's branches or vines and the fruit by tying the branches to a supporting frame installed near the plant's stem [see Training Vegetable Plants onto Supports, pg. 229]. This approach works particularly well for smaller fruits.

Always support fruits that are lying on the surface of the soil. Even tough-skinned vegetables such as pumpkins and melons can ripen unevenly or become misshapen if not supported and protected from direct soil contact.

DECORATIVE SUPPORTS. The increasing popularity of gardening over recent years has inspired many garden stores, nurseries, and catalogs to feature decorative supports for use in vegetable gardens. These whimsical options, more commonly associated with flower gardens, are not only attractive but functional.

Whether a simple frame of wrought iron or a sturdy wooden stand for container plantings, decorative supports often are more durable than temporary poles and trellises. Choose supports made from durable materials and weather-resistant finishes. Avoid any constructed of pressure-treated lumber, which is impregnated with toxic chemicals, making it unsuitable for use in an edible garden and a potential hazard to pets or children.

Whatever supports you select for your vegetables, they are sure to add both practical value and real visual interest to your garden.

Start with a clean slate—imagine how your garden will be transformed when you add vertical growth by allowing your vines and climbers to rise above nearby row crops.

Take the bare frame of a support—say the one pictured on this page—and picture it laden with green beans intertwined with scarlet runner beans. That's the idea.

It doesn't have to be so fancy. Simply use an existing fence to support pole crops, run some twine over a nearby tree's branch to train growth off of the ground.

Vertical gardening is an especially timely concept for those with small-space gardens. Where space is limited, a breakout to the upside opens more spacial volume to practical use. Consider it along patios and balconies—wherever enough room is an issue.

That's most of the story on how to care for your garden. The acts of caring for your garden by watering, fertilizing, cultivating, and mulching—or by pruning and staking —are among the most enjoyable and nurturing tasks you will perform for your vegetables. Whiling away the hours in the fresh air and sunshine, observing the minute changes

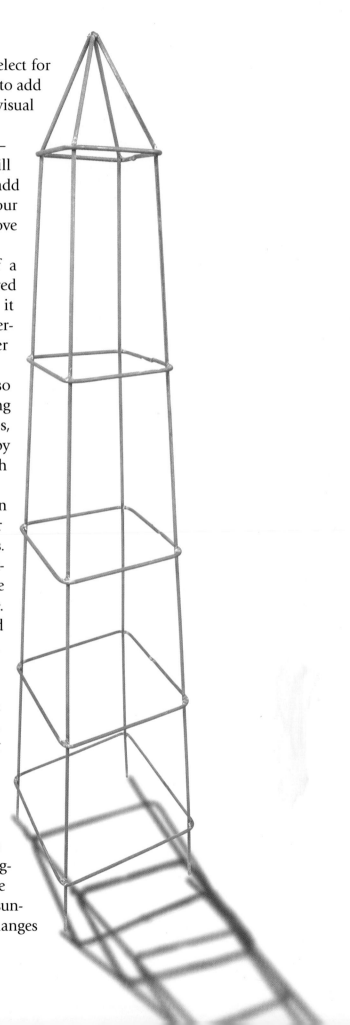

that take place in your plants from day to day, caring for their needs, and thinking about the eventual bounty fill a gardener with energy and satisfaction.

Unfortunately, there's also a dark side to garden care. There are pests standing ready to attack your healthy plants, not to mention diseases lurking in the air and soil. Next we'll discuss the actions necessary to prevent infestations and infections from becoming devastating concerns for your vegetable garden.

Keeping
Gardens

Pests & Diseases

Healthy

DESPITE THE BEST EFFORTS to choose vegetable varieties that are resistant to pests and diseases, every gardener sooner or later experiences problems related to them. While prevention is always the primary goal, quick identification of pest and disease problems—and a course of treatment to minimize the damage to vegetable plants and fruits—is a common reality.

Most gardeners prefer natural, organic methods of control, though they require both planning and vigilance. In the coming pages we'll discuss:

- How pests and diseases become established

- Methods for identifying pestilence problems

- Natural alternatives available for controlling infestations and infections

- Chemical alternatives for control

- Biointensive gardening for pest and disease control

Our goal is to provide the vital information you need to choose effective and responsible control methods. The simple truth is that some control methods actually can upset the natural balance of a well-established and totally organic vegetable garden.

A chewed leaf here and a scarred tomato there isn't cause for employing major chemical control. Most seasoned gardeners are willing to accept such minor damage as a trade-off for natural controls. The balance of nature dictates that, for nearly every pest, there are one or more foes to limit its spread and the damage it can inflict.

Moreover, spraying chemical insecticides in a vegetable garden has irreversible effects. Such controls indiscriminately kill all insects, including honeybees and other pollinating species. Worse yet, the severity of many infestations actually can increase after use of chemical control agents. With their natural predators eliminated, the pest population quickly rebounds to levels higher than they were initially. The same holds true for chemicals used to eliminate weeds and diseases.

Are there any circumstances when such extreme control measures are appropriate? Sure. Sometimes infestations and infections run rampant through a vegetable garden. Faced with total ruin, a gardener may choose a limited program of chemical control responsibly to try to restore balance. Professional horticulturists call this approach "Integrated Pest Management"—IPM for short [See Integrated Pest Management, pg. 264]. IPM emphasizes graded control in the garden—starting first with natural and organic methods, then with limited reliance on chemicals used selectively to achieve full control. In the following pages we'll discuss this and other methods for limiting pest and disease problems in your garden.

First let's explore how pests and diseases inflict damage in a garden, and how you can spot that damage before it becomes significant.

How Insect Pests Damage Vegetables

The largest group of potential pests are insects, followed by mollusks—slugs and snails—and then mammals and birds. There are important scientific distinctions between classes of insects, mites, spiders, and their near relatives, but for simplicity's sake we have categorized them according to the four distinct ways these pests can destroy your vegetable plants:

- Chewing
- Sucking
- Scoring and Rasping
- Boring

To make matters worse, many insect pests also can affect your garden by spreading plant diseases. We'll discuss that later, after describing each means of damage and suggesting effective control measures.

CHEWING PESTS. The most obvious signs of pest damage in a garden are chewed leaves, stems, flowers, and fruits. Most often, caterpillars, loopers, worms, and moth larvae are responsible, followed by cutworms and grasshoppers. Occasionally, chewing attacks come from such unexpected sources as leaf-cutting wasps, which use pieces of leaves to build their nests, or tomato hornworms, which appear almost magically at full size, stripping foliage and fruit from tomato plants.

The most notorious chewing pests are armyworms; tentworms; inchworms; cabbage loopers; cabbage and corn worms; asparagus, cucumber, bean, and other beetles; grape berry moth larvae; and rose chafers (which, despite their name, attack vegetable plants too).

The damage inflicted by chewing pests is the most easily identified: pieces of leaves and stems are gnawed or entirely missing. This damage causes sap to leak from the cuts and invites infection from fungal diseases that feed on sugary plant fluids. These pests can cause limited damage, or they can decimate an entire row of plants when infestation is severe.

Fortunately, most chewing insects are large and obvious, meaning you can spot them easily and pluck them from your plantings before they do significant damage. Plants generally recover quickly if limited areas of foliage are affected, but it still is best to prune those areas to reduce susceptibility to secondary fungal and viral infections.

A natural biological foe of many caterpillars and worms is a bacterium called *Bacillus thuringiensis* (BT), which infects the insects and quickly causes them to die. BT is sold in powdered and liquid formulations. Apply it with a hose-end sprayer or hand mister directly to both the tops and undersides of affected foliage. BT has been studied extensively and is harmless to humans, but it may have a negative effect on beneficial insects.

Applying *Bacillus thuringiensis*

Bacillus thuringiensis—commonly called "BT"—is a liquid solution or mixable powder of a living organism that infects insect larvae but is harmless to humans. Gardeners use BT as a natural organic control to limit damage from many of these chewing pests. Apply the BT solution directly to the pests and to any foliage on which they are feeding. The BT must contact the pests to be effective. Following these easy instructions:

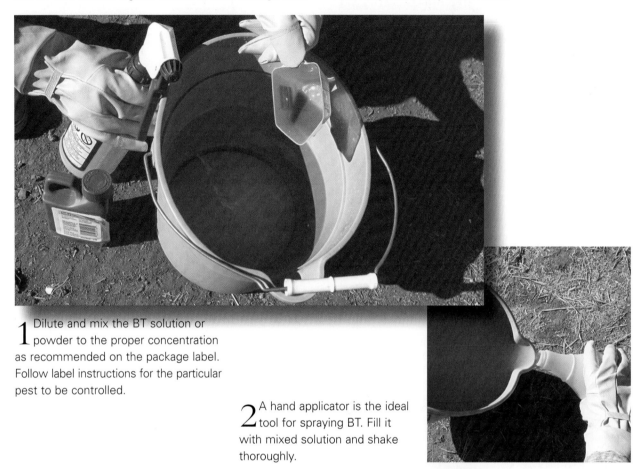

1 Dilute and mix the BT solution or powder to the proper concentration as recommended on the package label. Follow label instructions for the particular pest to be controlled.

2 A hand applicator is the ideal tool for spraying BT. Fill it with mixed solution and shake thoroughly.

3 Spray visible pests as well as the tops and undersides of all the foliage suspected of infestation. BT degrades quickly if no pest is present, so repeat applications may be required 7–10 days apart.

Detergents and mild insecticidal soap solutions add another level of control but because they are diluted quickly by dew and precipitation, must come in direct contact with the pest, and degrade quickly outdoors, they must be reapplied weekly. Such soaps smother pests, and the water in the solution washes larvae from the plants.

For serious infestations, you may need to apply an organic pesticide such as rotenone (extracted from the roots and stems of various tropical plants) to destroy pests and their eggs. Rotenone is most effective on many larval insects when applied directly to the pests. It decomposes quickly into harmless by-products when exposed to sunlight and a plant's acid neutralization process. Other naturally derived insecticides include pyrethrin, sabadilla, neem oil, and ryania. Before using them, always read the label carefully to make sure the one you are choosing is an effective control for the particular pest troubling your garden. Despite their natural origins, these are powerful chemical insecticides and should be handled strictly according to label instructions. Always wear protective gloves and clothing when applying any insecticides.

Last-resort chemical controls—used only when infestation damage is exceptionally severe—include malathion, sevin, and diazinon. Always apply these powerful insecticides in complete accordance with label directions, and never use sprays that combine one or more active chemical ingredients. Also recognize that these insecticides pose a potential hazard to humans and beneficial garden insects. Know that, even if you have adhered to the recommended waiting time before harvesting and have washed treated vegetables thoroughly, all pesticide residue still may not be removed.

Most chewing insect damage can be halted through prompt identification and a combination of hand and organic controls. Serious infestations usually occur when the natural balance between pests and their predators has been upset by indiscriminate pesticide use throughout a garden. Also remember that healthy plants are better able to defend themselves and repair damage than those weakened by poor nutrition, inadequate care, or improper watering.

Companion plantings won't have much effect on infestations of adult chewing pests. They may avert juvenile forms of the insects or deter adults from laying eggs, but the evidence is inconclusive.

Applying Insecticidal Soaps

Soap is an effective, nontoxic insect control suitable for use in vegetable gardens. Both soap and detergent contain "wetting agents" that break down the surface tension of water and fatty liquids. This, in turn, kills insect pests by making it impossible for them to breathe. The insecticidal soaps offered by garden retailers have been especially formulated for insect control.

   Insecticidal soaps are short-term answers for limiting the damage caused by juvenile and adult insect pests, bugs, mites, and spiders. They are effective, however, when applied directly to the insect. Repeat applications may be necessary.

1 Measure and fill a hose-end sprayer with soap concentrate, following the manufacturer's label instructions. Because some products contain insecticides as well as soap, wear protective gloves and exercise caution when handling.

2 Spray infested foliage and pests with soap solution. Avoid breathing the spray, wear a respirator, and never spray on windy days. Apply soap solution only to infested plantings.

SUCKING PESTS. Less obvious and therefore less quickly identifiable than chewing damage is that inflicted by sucking insects: whiteflies, thrips, aphids, harlequin bugs, beetles, their nymphs, and mites. These pests bore tiny holes into stems or into the undersides of leaves, then suck out vital plant juices. This deprives the plant of water and nutrients and interrupts the flow of fluids produced in the foliage to the stem and roots. These pests also introduce bacteria, fungi, and viruses to the plant.

Most sucking pests are minute, which means that you have to carefully inspect all foliage, top and bottom, for damage. The smallest of these pests may be seen only with a magnifying glass, so it's not possible to control them by hand. To identify the signs of sucking pests look for generally weakened, listless plants, damaged blooms, or fruit that appears to be stunted.

Soap and detergent solutions are effective low-toxicity controls for most sucking insects. As a preventative measure, apply one or the other to foliage and the soil surface weekly throughout the growing season. Soap control agents may be purchased in garden stores or nurseries and often include an insecticide; follow all label instructions. Detergent solutions can be made at home by diluting 2 tablespoons (25 ml) of soap flakes (do not use liquid concentrates) per gallon (3.8 l) of water. Be precise about these measurements because heavier concentrations can harm your plants. Whichever solution you choose, don't forget to apply it to the undersides of all leaves, where most sucking insects dwell.

Aphid infestations frequently result from the behavioral habits of ants, which, in themselves, rarely damage vegetable gardens directly and even provide some benefits. Ants actively support aphid colonies, however, by transporting aphid eggs to vegetable and other plants. Mature aphids, once their infestation is established, produce honeydew, which ants then harvest to feed their colonies. Eliminating ants from your vegetable garden is the first step toward controlling aphids.

The most effective ant control method is to follow the ant trail back to its source and dig up the colony. Start by carefully removing the soil over and around the colony, then soak the tunnels with an insecticidal soap solution. Thoroughly spade the area several times throughout the following week. Do not use this control method on the fire ant species common to the subtropical regions of North and South America and to a number of areas in the southern United States. These biting insects will vigorously defend their hills against human and animal attack by injecting an irritating poison beneath the skin. If you suspect that you have a fire-ant colony in your yard, consult with an expert at your local garden store, nursery, or the extension office of the United States Department of Agriculture for effective control measures.

Rarely is sucking insect damage extensive. Heavy infestations usually can be identified by large numbers of living and dead pests on leaves and stems, which may appear as a granular, dustlike coating on the undersides of foliage. This appearance, however, usually is caused by indiscriminate application of broad-spectrum chemical control agents. These agents only serve to deplete the garden of the natural enemies of sucking insects and other pests.

Effective chemical control agents, when used judiciously, include sevin, pyrethrin, malathion, and, for some species of sucking pest, rotenone. Before applying any control agent, be sure you have correctly identified the pest by comparing it to the profile on the pesticide label or by taking a sample of the infested foliage to your garden retailer or nursery.

Always choose an appropriate insecticide for your prey. To limit damage to beneficial insect populations, apply the control agent only to the infested area when the air is completely still and never when it's windy. Follow all label directions for use and disposal, and wear protective gloves and clothing whenever applying.

Though certain agents degrade more quickly than do others, never apply chemical controls within two weeks of harvest, and always wash harvested vegetables thoroughly with soap and water if they have *ever* been treated with insecticides.

Of course, the best preventative for any pest infestation is the vigor and health of your vegetable plants. Good care, including regular fertilization, watering, and cultivation, results in strong vegetable plants that are naturally able to resist all but the most severe infestations.

Though field trials indicate that companion plantings are limited in efficacy for deterring insect pests, many gardeners still swear by such measures— and they certainly can't hurt. Garlic and nasturtiums are believed to discourage aphids. Chrysanthemums are thought to repel colonies of whiteflies. Tomatoes are said to limit the proliferation of many types of beetles. Radishes may reduce mite problems.

Applying Organic Pesticides

Organic pesticides are naturally occurring extracts made from plants that bear insecticidal tendencies. They are no less toxic than synthetic pesticides, however, and should be used carefully in limited application only, in accordance with their package label instructions. To apply organic pesticides due to a severe infestation, follow these instructions:

1 Using a hose-end sprayer or a hand applicator spray bottle, mix the concentration of pesticide recommended for the specific infestation, as printed on the package label. Always wear protective gloves and wash them thoroughly with soap and water after mixing and applying organic pesticides.

2 When using an adjustable sprayer, set the application rate dial or other setting to the recommended rate on the package label. Read and follow all label warnings.

3 Spray conservatively all infested areas, including the undersides of leaves and the soil near plant stems. Avoid spraying unaffected plants. Never spray on windy days, and avoid breathing the spray solution by wearing a respirator when applying organic pesticides.

SCORING AND RASPING PESTS. This category of pest includes leafhoppers and leaf miners—larvae of a variety of moths, beetles, and flies—plus grasshoppers, which also chew.

Detecting damage from scoring and rasping pests is easy: the undersides of leaves will have brown or gray spots, veinlike tunnels, or a dry white encrustation (from dried plant fluids). Be especially watchful for tiny clustered deposits of round white or black eggs—they will hatch within days into tiny larvae that will feed on your vegetable plants' leaves. With severe infestations, entire leaves may turn yellow and curl.

Hand control is best for adult hoppers and beetles. Use soap solutions and pressurized sprays of water to dislodge and kill egg clusters on the undersides of leaves. Repeat treatment every three days until you have achieved control.

Established larvae that survive pressure spraying and soap solutions usually can be controlled with insecticidal soaps. Chemical controls, including pyrethrin, malathion, sevin, rotenone, or diazinon sprays are indicated only when damage becomes severe. As is true for all chemical insecticides, apply them only to infected areas, wear protective clothing and gloves, and follow package directions carefully and completely. In addition, always identify your pest problem to make sure you select the appropriate agent.

Applying Synthetic Chemical Pesticides

Synthetic chemical pesticides are used as a last resort measure when garden pest infestations cannot be controlled by less toxic measures. They always should be applied in a limited fashion, directly to the infested area, using the exact chemical recommended for the pest being controlled. Because some synthetic chemical pesticides may be long-lasting, they pose a hazard to the environment. Avoid eating produce that has been sprayed, and always wear protective clothing, gloves, and a respirator when mixing and spraying. Follow these steps for best results when applying chemical pesticides:

1 Wearing protective gloves, measure out the pesticide concentrate and dilute in water, according to package label instructions. Return any excess concentrate to the bottle and seal tightly since exposure to air may reduce its efficacy.

2 Carefully fill an applicator spray bottle with the mix solution, avoiding spillage. Mix only enough dilute pesticide for the application intended; do not store diluted mix. To apply, cap the spray bottle with its spray head and seal tightly.

3 Apply chemical pesticides directly to the infested plants, both tops and undersides. Avoid overapplying spray and never spray unaffected areas of the garden. Dispose of unused chemical mix and empty containers in accordance with the label instructions.

BORING PESTS. Perhaps the most frustrating vegetable garden pests are the borers. They make produce unattractive or inedible and are difficult to detect. The most common borers are larval worms and caterpillars of butterflies and moths, but earworms, fruitworms, weevils, wireworms, and maggots also can cause widespread damage to cabbage, corn, tomatoes, root crops, and members of the onion family.

The best way to detect a potential problem is to take notice of the moths and butterflies that are attracted to your vegetable garden. For instance, the cabbage moth, a white moth with a black spot on each wing, can cause widespread damage to leaf vegetables of the cole family by laying eggs that hatch into voracious larvae. In fact, a single hatch can destroy an entire cabbage head or stalk of Brussels sprouts.

If you suspect an infestation, peel back the outer leaves of cabbage, Swiss chard, lettuce, and other green-leaf vegetables and examine them for evidence. If you find any egg deposits, wash them away with a pressurized stream of water. If you observe any curled or rolled leaves, caterpillars are probably at work, spinning silk within the leaves of your vegetables; use hand control to eliminate them.

The living bacterial culture *Bacillus thuringiensis* (BT) infects and kills many larval worms, caterpillars, and immature moths but is harmless to humans and pets. Spray areas exhibiting these pests weekly throughout the plants' growth cycle.

Insecticidal soaps offer limited control potential since most of these agents easily wash off the surface of foliage.

They can provide additional control if applied to the undersides of leaves, but have little or no effect on borers that already have tunneled inside fruits and vegetables.

Even chemical controls, including pyrethrin, rotenone, sevin, diazinon, and malathion have limited effect on borers. Systemic insecticides, which travel through the plant, are effective for killing boring insects in nonfood crops but are unacceptable for both vegetables and fruits.

Regular garden care is all that is required to prevent damage from subsoil borers. The most significant pests in this category are cabbage root maggots, flea beetles, strawberry root weevils, and wireworms, which arrive in your garden when the adults lay their eggs on the soil surface. Thorough mulching prevents the adult flies from finding suitable places to lay their eggs; regular recycling of mulches will remove whatever eggs have been deposited.

If you have experienced an infestation from soil borers already, consider laying fine-mesh wire cloth or porous plastic mulch fabric in the bed before planting, then punching holes in it to place your plants.

Natural control methods for established subsurface borers are limited. BT sprayed on the soil and watered into the garden bed may eliminate some boring pests.

Dust or granular forms of diazinon and chloropyrifos have long duration cycles and may leave an unacceptable level of pesticide residue on produce. Use them as a last resort at the end of the garden season and follow all label instructions for mixing, application, and disposal. Even then, limit harvests of produce from the affected area for a season, and consider these measures in preparation for next year's crop.

Other Significant Pests

In addition to the previously mentioned pests, your vegetables may encounter problems from mollusks (slugs and snails), mammals, and birds. They can cause extensive damage but are relatively rare.

If your plants experience problems that don't seem to fall into any of these categories, consider the following:

NEMATODES. These minute worms make their homes in soil, causing damage to plants by feeding on the root systems. Nematodes are microscopic in size, leaving no visible clue as to why plants have lost vigor or begun to drop fruit. In fact, the only clue to a nematode infestation is knotlike swellings in plant roots, but many varieties of the pest do not even cause this effect. It should be noted that nearly all soil contains some nematodes, which come in both beneficial and harmful varieties.

Established nematode infestations are a real problem. Commercial growers use such agents as nemagon, methyl bromide, or vapam to sterilize problem soils, but these are too difficult to use and too hazardous for home gardens.

One natural control that has demonstrated effectiveness is rotating plantings of French marigolds through problem soil areas, which also repels the Colorado potato beetle. Another is the introduction of beneficial nematode populations, which can purchased from garden stores or nurseries, then introduced to the infested areas of the garden according to package instructions. To the degree that beneficial nematodes will compete with harmful varieties, they will reduce the population and therefore the severity of the problem.

If nematodes are suspected, plant resistant varieties genetically equipped to resist their damage.

Preplanting treatment of the soil in the vegetable bed by "solarization" also is an effective control: as soon as days turn sunny and hot, turn the earth in the garden and cover the infested soil surface with black plastic film, overlapping each section at least 12 inches (30 cm). Weight or stake the plastic so that wind will not lift or tear the film. Solar heat will raise the soil temperature beneath the plastic to temperatures high enough to kill the nematodes (and many other garden pests). After three to five days, lift the

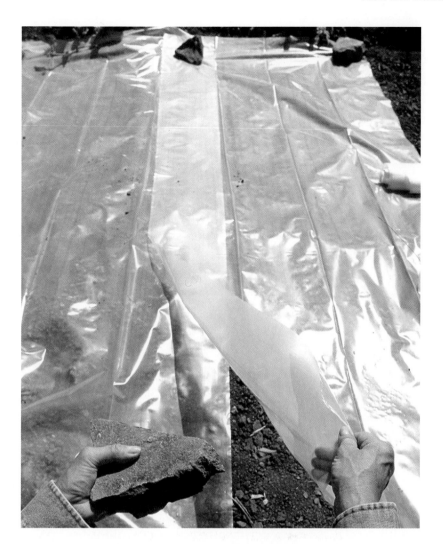

plastic, turn the soil again, and reapply the film—it may take several cycles of treatment to kill most nematodes throughout the entire depth of the soil.

If you have determined that your garden has a nematode infestation, give the affected plants extra water and fertilizer. This care won't negate the effects of the pests completely, but it may allow the plants to perform at acceptable levels. If you notice that particular plant varieties do not survive an infestation, avoid planting them for a season or two, or plant them in containers, using sterile potting mix rather than native soil. (Some gardeners plagued with nematodes have replaced infested soil wholesale, installed raised beds, and cycled the infested soil through their compost bins. This diligence, however, has not proven to solve the problem permanently.)

Without host plants, most nematode infestations dwindle after a season or two because natural enemies have a chance to proliferate and reduce the population.

SNAILS AND SLUGS. With or without a shell, these mollusks rank among the most common pests of vegetable gardens. Individually, they are capable of significant damage; collectively, they can devastate a garden in an evening. Evidence of slugs and snails is revealed by silvery slime trails on soil and foliage, chewed or cut plantings, and, during nighttime hours, the pests themselves.

If you suspect snails or slugs are culprits, visit your garden with a flashlight after dark, when these pests emerge to feed. Hand control is effective for most infestations of snails and slugs. Simply gather and kill all adults—immersing them in soapy water will do the trick. Turn over boards and rocks to expose them in their hiding places, or remove these items from the garden entirely. Neither like to live in gardens that offer limited shelter from sun and heat, and they rarely bury themselves beneath loose soil.

Also look for snail and slug eggs. These gelatinous, round, brown or gray eggs usually are laid in clusters about $1/12$ inch (2 mm) across. Destroy such clusters to prevent them from hatching and infesting your garden, or spade them into a bucket of soapy water.

Snails and slugs also are very sensitive to minute electrical charges, so barriers made of copper or copper foil—available in most garden stores and nurseries—installed around plantings or the base of containers housing plants will prevent these pests from crossing into your beds or climbing into your pots.

If hand control and preventative measures do not prove effective enough, chemical control is available. Liquid and pellet baits containing metaldehyde attract the pests, which die after feeding on them. More recently, harmless baits containing iron phosphate serve the dual purpose of killing snails and fertilizing your garden. Place baits along the margins of your garden and near likely hiding places, avoiding contact with the vegetable plants themselves. Many snail and slug baits are poisonous to animals, so take precautions to ensure household pets cannot ingest them. Finally, completely follow all label instructions and thoroughly wash all garden implements used to apply baits.

The common garden snail (*Helix aspersa*) was brought by commercial growers to the New World in the mid-1800s, and members of the species escaped into the wild. They are identical to the snails prized for eating in France and Belgium. If your tastes are so inclined, and your garden is strictly organic, garden snails may be cooked after harvesting them. Hold them for 72 hours or more in a sealed container partially filled with cornmeal, which allows them to eliminate any waste from feeding. Most epicures prefer snails sautéed or baked for about 10 minutes in a simple sauce of water, salt, butter, and minced garlic.

WHITEFLIES. These sucking pests cluster on the undersides of vegetable leaves, especially tomatoes, peppers, and other upright plants, and reveal themselves by flying about when the foliage is disturbed.

Though they are tiny—1/10–1/8-inch (2–3-mm) long—if an infestation becomes extensive, they will reduce your plants' vigor and may introduce diseases. Most of the damage is done by the immature nymphs that hatch from eggs laid on the plants. They appear on leaf undersides as tiny brown, black, or translucent scales.

Limit a whitefly population by hanging several traps containing sticky bait—available in most garden stores and nurseries— near infested areas. Adult whiteflies are attracted to these yellow traps, become entangled in the sticky attractant and die. Because whiteflies reproduce quickly, however, such measures have limited effectiveness.

Wash immature nymphs from leaves with mild soap or detergent solutions.

Chemical controls for whiteflies are mostly ineffective since they also kill the predator insects. Spraying pyrethrin or malathion according to label instructions will reduce the adult population for a few days, but most infestations will rebound or increase unless spraying is repeated at least weekly thereafter.

Unless a whitefly infestation is severe, some population can be tolerated.

SOWBUGS AND PILLBUGS. These $1/4$–$1/3$-inch (6–8 mm) arthropods are segmented, gray, and tend to roll up into a defensive posture when disturbed. They commonly are found in decomposing vegetable matter, though rich organic soils also provide suitable environments.

In themselves, sowbugs do limited damage to most vegetable gardens, primarily to soft fruits, such as strawberries, and to root vegetables, such as radishes, turnips, and rutabagas. Most of their damage occurs later, when they introduce fungal infections into the soil.

Protect aboveground plantings from sowbugs by mulching heavily prior to fruit formation. Add garden lime to the soil to limit damage to root vegetables.

BIRDS. Birds eat seeds and seedlings, as well as mature berries and ripening fruit. Often they will peck at nearly ripe fruit but not eat it. Despite this troublesome behavior, they provide a major check on other pests.

Protect plantings and ripening crops from bird attacks by covering the fruit with mulch or suspending porous netting attached to wooden supports over your plants. Reflective foil tape, scarecrows, and other eye-catching devices such as whirligigs and pinwheels also repel some birds, though these time-honored methods quickly lose effectiveness as the birds become accustomed to them; wait to use these devices until the crops begin to ripen.

Limit damage to low-growing greens by installing wire-mesh tenting over rows, taking care to bury the edges in the ground. This measure makes garden care more difficult, but prevents rabbits and deer from eating your produce.

GOPHERS AND MOLES. Invasion by gophers and moles is easily detected—you will see holes surrounded by displaced soil and mounds that betray underground tunnels. Damage by gophers is direct: they eat plant roots, tubers, and the bulbs of onions, radishes, garlic, shallots, and other bulb-bearing vegetable plants. Moles are omnivores that prefer to eat grubs, worms, and other insect life; they primarily damage the garden by uprooting and tunneling, not by consuming plants or produce.

If you live in an area prone to gophers or moles, prior to planting consider installing narrow wire mesh buried at least 16 inches (40 cm) down and around the perimeter of your garden beds to a height of at least 30 inches (75 cm). Such barriers prevent tunneling animals from entering your planting areas, and, by their nature, these animals are unlikely to enter your garden from aboveground.

Another barrier control worth trying is planting daffodils, crocus, or tulips along your garden's perimeter. Many bulb flowers contain substances—among them arsenic—that gophers and moles find offensive.

Once gophers or moles have gained access to your garden, your only choice is to eliminate them humanely. Traps are effective, but complete control may take some time. Flooding tunnels and dens may discourage or kill both gophers and moles, as will repellents and baits available at many garden outlets and nurseries. Such control agents are potentially hazardous to pets and humans so they always should be used in accordance with label instructions.

MICE AND OTHER RODENTS. Rodents are potently destructive garden pests that eat and contaminate fruit, vegetables, and produce. More important, they can transmit diseases. Droppings from mice and rats frequently contain viral and bacterial organisms—including hantavirus and bubonic plague—that are harmful, and even deadly, to humans. Rodents also harbor fleas, which may carry disease or infest pets.

If you suspect a rodent infestation, evidenced by droppings or by damage to plants, take immediate measures to keep these pests out of your garden. Install wire-mesh cages over and around all vegetable plantings, and remember that rodents are small and agile enough to squeeze through or climb most barriers. Effective rodent control requires the installation of ¼-inch (5 mm) mesh wire fabric at all potential access points to a plant—top, bottom, and all four sides.

If rodents have gained access to your garden already, mechanical traps are effective, baited with a small amount of peanut butter. Wear plastic gloves whenever disposing of dead rodents or handling live traps to avoid exposure to diseases carried by rodents and their parasites.

A variety of chemical baits and repellents also are available for controlling rodent infestations. In their action and effect they are devastating to mice and rats. Most rely on the chemical poison warfarin, which is a potent blood thinner that kills by causing anemia in mammals that eat the bait. However, this agent is also poisonous to children, household pets, and beneficial wildlife. Instruct children of the danger and install protective closures to prevent harm.

A less toxic control is a bait harmful only to rodents. It employs a chemical, related to one of the B vitamins, that rodents are unable to excrete; the cumulative effect of overdose causes death, often after a single feeding. Baits employing this active ingredient are harmless to most other mammals; nevertheless, follow all label instructions carefully.

RABBITS AND OPOSSUMS.

While jackrabbits, cottontail rabbits, and other species may seem desirable in the environment, they are significant problem pests when found in a vegetable garden. A single rabbit can decimate a garden in an evening, and opossums, which have similar nocturnal behavior, can do equal damage to a vegetable crop.

The most effective control for these pests is to fence the entire garden perimeter with ¹/₂-inch (10 mm) wire mesh fabric installed 6 inches (15 cm) below ground and raised 2–3 feet (60–90 cm) above ground.

If this is not wholly effective, some rabbits and opossums are deterred from eating produce that has been sprayed with cayenne pepper or other mixes and solutions containing capsaicin (a naturally occurring fiery compound found in hot peppers). If you wish to try pepper sprays, however, wear protective clothing, gloves, and eye protection—and avoid applying them on windy days.

A number of repellents targeting rabbits are available, but most rely on ingredients that contain dried blood, urine, or other organic compounds that are less than desirable in a vegetable garden. Avoid applying such repellents directly on or near any vegetable or fruit.

DEER. With their incursion into suburban and even urban areas, deer have become notorious garden pests. Just one deer can graze through most of a garden overnight, and what is not eaten likely will be trampled by sharp hooves.

A yard dog sometimes will deter deer; a more reliable deterrent is a fence at least 10 feet (3 m) tall. If you live in deer country, such a barrier is essential.

Hot-pepper sprays are of limited benefit. Many chemical and organic repellents targeted to repel deer may be effective if frequently applied, but like rabbit repellents, these compounds frequently contain such distasteful components as wolf and cat urine; they never should be applied directly on vegetable crops. Such compounds also frequently contain high levels of nitrogen-based salts, so you may need to adjust your fertilization to avoid chemical burn.

Though persistent, deer also are timid creatures. Scarecrows with billowing fabric, whirligigs, plastic foil tape, and other annoying, wind-activated garden fixtures may scare them.

A final defense is to install wire fabric barriers in the same manner described for discouraging bird pests [see Birds, pg. 258].

Applying Pepper Spray

Capsaicin, a substance found in hot peppers, is distasteful to many mammals. Gardeners take advantage of this by using nontoxic hot pepper sprays on crops to avoid nuisance animal damage.

While effective for many animals and some insect pests, pepper sprays and pepper waxes are less so for many others. Use a combination of defenses, from barriers and repellents to distasteful sprays, to limit damage from animal pests.

1 Pepper sprays irritate and can even blister skin and eyes so when applying them or even handling bottles and sprayers, always wear gloves, protective goggles, and a respirator. When application is completed, wash hands and clothing with soap and hot water to remove any residue of the spray, and clean equipment before using it to apply other sprays.

2 Pour pepper concentrate into a self-mixing hose-end sprayer. If the sprayer is adjustable, set the application level to the product rate recommendation described on the spray package. Seal the sprayer and attach it to a garden hose.

3 Spray foliage, especially tender young leaves. Always spray early in the day so that plants will have time to dry before cool nighttime temperatures begin. Avoid applying excess spray.

The Organic Garden

Organic vegetable gardeners subscribe to time-honored techniques for pest control. They believe that beneficial insects, extra care, and environmental balance in the garden are the best means for controlling pests. They also accept that superficial blemishes on produce and fruit are a small price to pay for a healthy, nutritious harvest.

The basis of organic gardening is that healthy plants, which have been nourished and given proper care, are best able to defend themselves against pests and diseases.

The most successful organic gardens are those with diverse plantings, those that even separate plantings of single species into several different garden locations. This helps prevent establishing critical mass—a habitat capable of supporting troublesome pests.

Next, we'll discuss this principle of controlling insect and other garden pests.

BENEFICIAL INSECTS AND ANIMALS. Gardeners seeking organic solutions to vegetable gardening problems should look first to nature's control measures: helpful insect and animal predators. The strongest argument for this approach is that chemical controls, whether natural or synthetic, kill a broad spectrum of beneficial and innocuous, as well as harmful, insects and pests. Their effects also extend far beyond their immediate application, harming waterways and wildlife.

Whether a gardener wants to limit chemicals in the garden because of distaste for additives entering the food chain, because of the persistence of such elements in the environment, or simply because of doubts about their efficacy, the garden benefits by having its natural balance restored.

A host of creatures inhabit the typical garden. By embracing a bio-intensive approach, the gardener not only benefits from these animals but

INTEGRATED PEST MANAGEMENT

Divide plantings into small areas.

Utilize natural controls, companion plantings.

Inspect frequently, use hand control and soap.

Apply low-toxicity agents directly to infestation.

Use local-area application of chemical controls.

preserves them. Ironically, to ensure their presence, a small population of their prey also must be maintained. The gardener can take heart by knowing that nearly seven out of eight species of insects are considered beneficial, or at least nonharmful. Among the insects that help control pests in your garden are praying mantis; lacewing flies and their larvae; ladybird, tiger and ground beetles; predatory wasps (tiny stingless insects); tachinid and syrphid flies; many species of carnivorous ants; and earwigs.

Toads, snakes, frogs, and lizards in the garden especially should be counted as blessings since they feed on harmful insects. A marsh or watercourse will encourage these voracious insect predators to set up housekeeping in your garden. For the same reason, install a birdhouse and a bat house to attract wrens, chickadees, orioles, flickers, and bats. Some birds devour more than 1,000 bugs a day; a single bat can consume as many as 10,000 flying insects in one night!

Many garden stores and nurseries sell packages of live ladybugs and mantis seed cases. After releasing these insects in your garden, keep them happy in their new home by providing ample feed and an environment that doesn't include broad-spectrum chemical sprays.

Regular use of organic fertilizers and compost will help create a biotic diversity in your garden soil, encouraging a healthy balance between beneficial and harmful organisms. Weeds are a draw to many pests so preventing their growth through regular mulching and eliminating them through cultivation will help ensure that your organic garden does not invite pests.

Finally, and perhaps surprisingly, some limited damage due to chewing insects may increase your harvest. Agronomists' tests reveal that 10 percent to 30 percent of leaf damage due to insects actually redirects a plant's nutrients to its blooms and fruit for greater yield.

Beneficial Plants

According to the theory of companion plantings [see Sucking Pests, pg. 244], many plants have insect-repelling defense mechanisms, so why not use those natural defenses to protect nearby plantings? Despite this common sense logic, companion planting never has been proven scientifically to control pests.

Still, many organic gardeners are ardent practitioners of it. Even if it doesn't help, at the very least, it diversifies your garden in beauty and yield. Here are some predators with their "natural enemies":

- Ants—mint, pennyroyal, pansy, sage
- Aphids—garlic, mint, nasturtium, chrysanthemum
- Moths—sage, thyme, rosemary, mint
- Potato bugs—eggplant, pepper
- Snails and slugs—oak leaf or evergreen-needle mulch
- Weevils—garlic, garlic chives.

Plant Diseases

The most common diseases that infect vegetable plants are either viral or fungal.

The most prevalent viral diseases—although each susceptible vegetable species has readily available resistant varieties—are:

- Cabbage yellows—a viral disease that infects, weakens, and kills cabbage, broccoli, cauliflower, and other cole crops
- Tobacco mosaic—a viral disease that stunts and kills tomatoes and tomato relatives

Treating established viral infections is beyond the capabilities of even professional horticulturists. Your best bet is to choose plants resistant to the common viral diseases found in your area. Viral infections, once established, will quickly spread to other vegetables. Uproot and burn (or otherwise dispose of) all infected plants as soon as you recognize the disease condition; do not compost them. Avoid planting similar species in beds infected in prior seasons.

Those who use tobacco products should be aware that tobacco mosaic virus inadvertently may be spread to susceptible garden vegetable plants by contact with cigarettes, cigars, or chewing tobacco. Always wash your hands thoroughly after smoking when handling tomato plants, or wear gloves.

Most fungal infections, even when established, are treatable, and in many cases resistant-plant varieties are available. Among the most prevalent fungal infections are:

- Fusarium wilt—a soil fungus that causes stems and foliage to wilt, yellow, and die
- Verticillium wilt—a soil fungus that clogs a plant's internal vessicles and capillaries, causing failure
- Cucumber anthracnose, mosaic, and scab—fungal diseases that deform and rot cucumber fruit

Gardeners will encounter a variety of fungus-caused diseases affecting their vegetables. The most common, with recommendations for treatment, are the following:

DAMPING OFF. Various fungal diseases can infect newly sprouted starchy seeds planted in too-cool soil. The stem of the seedling develops a telltale brown score where it comes into contact with the soil, then rots completely through, terminating growth. This so-called "damping off" may be prevented by delaying planting or transplanting when soil temperatures reach recommended levels.

Chemical preventatives to damping off include thirim or captan applied to seeds prior to planting.

DOWNY MILDEW. This fungal disease affects the leaves of squash, pumpkins, melons, and cucumbers. It is evidenced by brown spots on the tops and undersides of leaves and often by a cottonlike fibrous growth at the leaf margins. Downy mildew often causes plants to produce fewer flowers and fruits and reduces the length of time produce will store well. Wash the fungal spores from affected foliage with a solution of 2 tablespoons (50 ml) of household bleach (sodium hypochlorite) per gallon (4 l) of water.

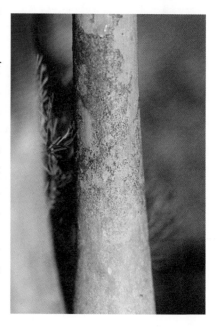

Downy mildew is aggravated by wetting foliage, especially with water splashed from the soil. Always water vine plants at the base of the stem.

Chemical controls include captan and maneb.

WARNING: Household bleach contains sodium hypochlorite, which is harmful if swallowed or in direct contact with the eyes. Use care and rubber gloves when handling.

Preventing Fungal Disease

Fungal infections of vegetable plants reduce their vigor, destroy blooms, mar fruit, or cause rot. These infections usually begin when spores in the soil are splashed onto the vegetables during irrigation. Always use proper watering techniques to prevent infection. A mild solution of household bleach will kill most mold and fungus. Apply it to your vegetables with a hose-end sprayer whenever mildew or mold is evident.

1 Prepare a weak solution of household bleach (sodium hypochlorite) by mixing 2 tbs (50 ml) of bleach with 1 gal. (4 l) of water. Pour the bleach mix into a hose-end sprayer or a hand-applicator bottle.

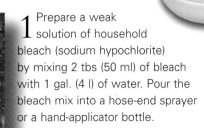

2 Liberally apply bleach solution to all infected plants, both tops and undersides of leaves, as well as the surrounding soil and mulch. Repeat the spraying every 7–10 days until control is achieved of all mold and fungus infections.

POWDERY MILDEW. This fungal disease is prevalent in cool, humid weather, especially when plants have been spaced too closely together, which prevents adequate air circulation. As with downy mildew, infection results in stunted and sparse produce.

Prevent powdery mildew by sprinkling garden sulfur dust on the soil surface prior to planting, then again two weeks later. Avoid overhead watering or splashing foliage with water that has been in previous contact with the soil.

If powdery mildew has become established, control it by applying the same weak bleach solution prescribed for downy mildew on the previous page. Choose a warm day with little to no humidity and apply it to the tops and undersides of all leaves as well as to the soil surface surrounding each of the plants.

Chemical controls include benlate and others, but most of them are slow to degrade and can contaminate the environment.

CLUB ROOT. This fungal disease deforms plant roots into twisted and swollen forms, stunting the plants and causing them to wilt. If you suspect that your plants have club root—it most commonly affects members of the cole family such as cabbage, broccoli, Brussels sprouts, and cauliflower—positively identify it by asking the opinion of a U.S. Department of Agriculture extension office agent or other plant expert.

If you confirm an infection, isolate, remove, and burn or otherwise destroy and dispose of all affected plants immediately. Do not compost them. Moreover, do not plant these crops in the same area of the garden for at least three years.

Chemical controls include terraclor and others, which, like benlate, are slow to decompose and may contaminate the environment.

Garden pests and diseases are the dark side of gardening—the truth is, a well-balanced and well-cared-for vegetable garden will produce well despite most of these problems. The greatest crop losses a gardener can expect, given due diligence and no pest or disease control effort at all, range between 5 and 10 percent. Chemical controls actually up the ante to between a 10 and 15 percent loss.

Next, we'll turn our attention to a topic that's certainly more pleasurable, the payoff—harvest. That's where all of your work and care yields handsome dividends. We'll give you tips and methods for getting your produce in from the field, plus instruction on how to prepare, store, and preserve it for enjoyment year-round.

Fresh from the
Harvest & Preserving
Garden

THE GREATEST JOYS OF HOME VEGETABLE GARDENING arguably come at harvest time. If harvest brings to mind barrows filled with produce in the crisp autumn air, the reality is even better. Harvest time is a continuous affair—a picking of corn here, a cutting of lettuce there, and the dinner table fills with fresh, succulent tastes throughout the gardening season. This is the dividend of our loving effort.

Because harvest extends for months as various vegetables ripen, understanding harvest and storage needs is as important as knowing everything that goes into the preparation for it.

Some vegetables reach a pinnacle of ripeness—and a peak of flavor—all at once, just as the plant matures; these include melon, eggplant, and squash. Other vegetables offer many opportunities throughout the season for gathering and tasting—spinach, all of the leaf lettuces, and sorrel among them. Then there are beets, carrots, potatoes, and other root crops, which can be stored right in the garden even after maturity. Protected by a covering of mulch to prevent them from freezing, they can be dug up a few at a time over a span of weeks.

Each vegetable has its own harvesting time and storage requirements. To help you prepare for the coming and continuous bounty, refer to the appendix for a concise listing of each vegetable and its storage needs [see Harvest and Storage, pg. 410]. In it you'll find convenient estimates of the maturity dates for most garden vegetables, recommendations for their ideal means of storage and their duration, as well as choices for methods and techniques of preserving them.

To provide information beyond that found in the chart, we'll offer additional advice on the following subjects:

- When vegetables should be harvested to achieve peak taste

- How fresh produce best should be stored

- What options exist for preserving vegetables

Our goal in this chapter is to help you reap—and maximize—the pleasure you receive from what you have sown, as well as to assure you a constant, healthy supply of fresh and preserved vegetables throughout the year.

Harvest

Look on the back of any seed package and you will find a description of the variety or cultivar, the length of time from sowing to germination, frequently a picture of the sprout's appearance, and an estimate of the time the vegetable needs to reach maturity from the time that the seeds are planted. Transplant stock usually bears descriptions and maturity information on the stakes inserted into the containers. We've summarized all of this information for each vegetable in the Vegetable Encyclopedia [see pg. 307] and also in the Harvest and Storage table [see pg. 410].

Information from growers and seed suppliers is useful for estimating the time it should take for plants to mature, but harvesting goes beyond calendar watching. When it comes to picking produce, an understanding of the three major categories of vegetables is essential. There are those that can be picked continuously throughout their growth cycle; those that should be picked upon their maturity; and those that, once mature, are quite durable and may be harvested at will until frost threatens.

CONTINUOUS-HARVEST VEGETABLES. Most leaf vegetables, plus a number of other plants, produce a series of harvestable crops as they mature. They include many varieties of the following crops:

Artichoke

Asparagus

Beans (green and snap)

Brussels sprouts

Chard

Chive

Corn

Cucumber

Eggplant

Endive

Horseradish (greens)

Lettuce (leaf varieties)

Mustard

Onion (green)

Pea

Pepper

Rhubarb

Sorrel

Spinach

Summer squash

Tomatillo

Tomato (indeterminate)

Continuous-harvest vegetable plants may be subdivided into two categories: those that grow at a steady rate, such as lettuce, spinach, peas, and beans, and then naturally die; and those that bear blossoms and then fruits, such as eggplant and tomato, until the plants are killed by frost. Given care and protection from the elements in mild-climate areas, the second of these two groups can produce crops long into the winter and in some areas even will flower and fruit year-round.

Leafy greens, including bok choy, cabbage, endive, horseradish greens, lettuce, mustard greens, sorrel, spinach, and Swiss chard, are at their tender best when the plants are young; thinning not only provides delicately flavored early salad makings but alleviates overcrowded beds. Because these plants grow from central buds, they yield a second harvest when their outermost leaves mature. Cut them, but do not cut the central growth bud; when it bolts, its flowering is beautiful and produces seeds for future plantings. Early harvests of leaf vegetables lack the stringy fiber and pronounced bitter taste of plants nearing bolt. Plant a succession of leafy greens for a continuous harvest, and plan your pickings for early in the day—soon after a watering provides optimum taste.

Rhubarb, Chinese cabbage, and Swiss chard also may be harvested by cutting from the largest, outermost leaf stalks as they reach full size.

Stalk vegetables—including Brussels sprouts and artichoke—produce a succession of ripening buds. Cut the lowest sprouts and developing chokes as they mature—for Brussels sprouts, when they exceed 1 inch (25 mm) in diameter; for artichokes, when the outermost leaves begin to loosen. When the sprouts or chokes are harvested, the plants will produce new buds.

Asparagus is ready for harvest in its third and subsequent years following planting. Cut the tender, succulent female spears at the soil line when they reach 5–8 inches (15–20 cm) in height but before their tips begin to loosen. When production slows, allow the last female spear or two from each plant to blossom, along with the much smaller, feathery male fronds. The foliage from these retained sprouts will provide nutrients to the subsurface root crowns and seed future seasons' harvests.

Fruiting vegetables that produce a succession of ripening crops, including eggplant, pepper, tomatillo, and indeterminate tomato varieties, should be picked when they develop peak color and their skins begin to thin. Test for this by gently pressing the skin with a fingernail; if the skin retains a dimple when pressure is released, the fruit is ripe. Picking vegetables at this stage ensures high sugar content and promotes additional bloom formation, sustaining the harvest. The same holds true for summer squash and cucumber. Pick them as soon as they reach peak color and their skins begin to thin—wait too long and they become pithy, starchy, seedy, or bitter. To assure mildest flavor in peppers, water your plantings heavily the evening before harvest, then pick in the early morning; withhold water and pick in the afternoon to yield a more piquant taste.

The ripeness of corn is more difficult to judge since its juicy ears are wrapped in husks. Experienced gardeners have developed a variety of ways to test corn for ripeness. The most reliable is to peel back very carefully the husk of the fullest ear an inch or two (2.5–5 cm) after the silk at the tip has begun to turn brown. If the kernels are swelling, the corn is at its peak of flavor—if not, rewrap the husk and wait a few days.

Remember, eating corn should be harvested within hours of cooking since kernel sugar is converted to tasteless starch very quickly after the ear is cut. Popcorn and decorative corn are harvested after the stalk and husk have completely dried.

Many vining plants, including peas, southern peas, and beans, offer two potential harvests: they may be picked green or after their pods dry; taste will dictate your choice. Many find drying varieties too tough for eating when steamed green. Picking snap beans and English peas as their young pods first fill yields tender, sweet peas and beans at the peak of flavor, causes new flowers to develop, and sustains the harvest. Pick sugar peas and other varieties suitable for stir-fry before their pods begin to swell. To pick beans when dry, follow the instructions for harvesting at maturity in the next section.

Green onion, bunching onion, and chive offer continuous harvests once they reach their desired size. Because onion sets frequently contain bulbs of various sizes, they mature at different times over a period of weeks. Pull green onions, wash them thoroughly to remove any clinging soil, and immediately refrigerate. Bunching onion and chive form perennial colonies of pungent shoots, which may be harvested throughout the gardening season. Pull or cut them at their base, according to the variety.

MATURE-HARVEST VEGETABLES. Most other garden vegetables, with the exception of some roots and tubers [see pg. 287], have fixed life spans and definite maturities. They grow, bloom, set fruit, or otherwise develop and ripen according to an internal clock that is affected only somewhat by growing conditions—sunlight, heat, and water. Mature harvest vegetables include:

Beans (drying)

Broccoli

Cabbage

Cauliflower

Celery

Garlic

Kohlrabi

Lettuce (head varieties)

Melon (all varieties)

Onion (drying)

Pea (drying)

Peanut

Potato

Pumpkin

Shallot

Sweet Potato

Tomato (determinate)

Winter squash

The Vegetable Encyclopedia [see pg. 307] indicates the length of time for such vegetables to reach maturity. A number of these will announce their harvest time when the green plant withers and dries.

Winter squash and pumpkin are the best examples of this kind of mature-harvest vegetable. At maturity, these vegetables sacrifice their foliage in order to develop the final sweetness in their tough-skinned fruits. As long as harvest weather conditions continue to be cool and dry, the fruit may remain in the field; if persistent rain or a hard freeze threatens, they should be harvested in entirety and placed in a cool, dry area.

To harvest mature vining plants, such as dried peas and beans, wait until the seedpods have dried and begun to open—all the foliage should be dead. Choose the first sunny, dry day and, immediately after picking, shuck the dried peas and beans from their pod and lay them out in a warm, dry place to cure for a week before storing or using.

Onion, shallot, and garlic plants usually require lodging to prevent their green tops from forming seed heads as they dry. Bend the stalks to the ground three to four weeks before harvest to limit further foliage development. This forces the plants to redirect their energy to developing roots and increases both the size and flavor of the heads. When the tops have nearly dried, dig up a head or two to make sure they are fully developed. Onions and garlic may be stored in the soil for a few weeks, but do not extend harvest much past that (shallots may be held in the ground for longer periods but are subject to damage in hard freezes). Choose a sunny, dry day for harvest, especially if the weather has been cool and damp. Hang the bulbs from their stalks in a warm, dry location for about 10 days, then move them to a cool, dry location or use them immediately.

Melons should be harvested from the growing vine when the stems begin to brown and the aroma of the fruit is engulfing. This is a sure sign that sugar content has peaked and the flesh is firm. Always cut a melon from the vine; breaking it off will damage the vine and prevent other fruits from ripening.

Head lettuce and most of the cole vegetables, including cabbage, cauliflower, and broccoli, are best harvested when they just reach maturity. Tight heads of lettuce or cabbage and immature flowers of cauliflower or broccoli signify harvest ripeness. Cabbage especially will continue to increase in size when daylight hours are long; flavor is intensified but the texture tends to become woody. Head lettuce left too long will split and develop seed heads. Water all of these varieties profusely the day before harvest to enhance crispness.

Tubers such as potato and peanut signify readiness for harvest when their foliage yellows and dies (an exception is new potatoes, which should be harvested when the plants are full size but before the foliage withers). They may hold for a time in the ground, as long as the weather remains cool and dry; otherwise they should be harvested as soon as they die back. Dig carefully around the margins of the plant with a garden fork and expose the potatoes or peanuts. Discard any potatoes that have significant areas of green skin; they are not tasty and may cause gastric distress. Leave newly harvested tubers to stand in the garden bed until completely dry, taking care that no moisture penetrates them. Gather them for holding in a warm, dry, and dark spot for about a week before storing them in a cool, dark, and dry location. Better yet, eat the newly dug potatoes immediately after harvest—the difference in taste and texture is startling when compared with commercially grown potatoes.

Celery should be harvested at the first sign of the plant forming a flower stalk in its center and by a general loosening of the bunch at its core. If you prefer white rather than green celery, you can blanch your plants about six weeks before harvest by wrapping them with dark paper or mounding soil around the plant.

Kohlrabi is a cole vegetable that grows a bulblike stalk with stems and leaves. It can be harvested when young for slicing into salads, or when mature by cutting the bulbs from the root and peeling the tough and fibrous outer skin back, then baking or steaming the bulbs.

Determinate tomatoes ripen nearly all at once, making them ideal for cooking, canning, and juicing. Such tomatoes often are fleshier and less sweet than the indeterminate eating varieties, but many tender and equally flavorful varieties of them exist. Pick them green for pickling or frying, when their skin first becomes tender; for storing or eating, pick them when fully ripe. They always should be eaten or prepared immediately after picking.

Unlike continuous-harvest vegetables, mature-harvest vegetables require some planning to spread out the bounty. Gardeners in areas with long growing seasons may extend the flavors of summer produce through autumn by using succession planting techniques [see Vegetable Succession Planning Chart, pg. 111].

DURABLE VEGETABLES. The last category of vegetables includes the durable plants—mostly root vegetables—which grow to maturity and lose little of their flavor or texture as they await our beckoning. The durable vegetables include:

Carrot

Celeriac

Fennel

Horseradish (root)

Jerusalem artichoke

Jicama

Leek

Parsnip

Radish

Rutabaga

Sweet potato

Turnip

True root vegetables—carrot, parsnip, many radish varieties, rutabaga, and turnip—are ideal plants for harvest timing. As long as weather conditions range from moderate to frosty (and a thick layer of mulch is applied to the soil), these vegetables are content to remain in the ground until the gardener chooses to harvest them. In very cold climates, the natural decomposition of a top coating of fresh manure applied heavily over plastic sheeting will generate the heat needed to warm the bed sufficiently. These vegetables can be dug up at any time after they have matured by peeling back the plastic carefully, then re-covering the bed to protect future harvests.

Other garden vegetables prized for their roots include Jerusalem artichoke (or sunchoke), kale, and horseradish. These vegetables are perennials, meaning they go dormant during the winter and allow harvesting at any time beginning midway through their second season. If you decide to harvest in summer or autumn, make sure to do so sparingly so that the plants can retain vigor and store energy for the coming winter.

Sweet or Florence fennel grows leafy overlapping stalks from a swollen junction near the root, permitting long in-garden holding periods before harvest. Leeks have similar characteristics, at least as far as tolerance to harvest is concerned. Pull and thoroughly wash them at any time after they reach 1 1/4 inches (3 cm) in diameter at their base, even through periods of heavy frost and snow with temperatures as low as 10°F (-12°C).

Many annual bulb and tuberous vegetables—such as celeriac, leek, jicama, kale, shallot, and sweet potato—tolerate long in-ground holding periods. Harvest them from maturity until the first hard frost.

Vegetable Storage

Perhaps the most compelling reason for home vegetable gardening is the opportunity it provides to eat produce fresh from the garden. Gardening also allows you to extend those flavors throughout the year through various means of preservation and storage.

A number of garden favorites, including berries, English peas, radishes, and corn, begin losing taste and texture from the moment they are picked. There is no substitute for eating them fresh.

For many others, including root and tuber vegetables, winter squash, pumpkin, and sweet potato, proper storage does not sacrifice flavor or texture and yields other benefits. Storage allows the gardener to take advantage of the bounty of an overproductive patch or extend the harvest season into autumn or even winter.

Storage needs vary depending on the vegetable, but generally can be divided along temperature- and humidity-lines to define the requirements for your storage areas.

WARM AND DRY. Among the vegetables that prefer to be stored in warm, dark, and dry locations are winter squash, pumpkin, winter melons, and sweet potatoes. These vegetables have thick rinds, which limit their loss of moisture; however, they also have high sugar content, which makes them susceptible to mold and fungus if temperatures drop below 40°F (5°C) or humidity climbs. They can be stored for two months or more at temperatures ranging between 55 and 65°F (13–18°C) and at a humidity level of 25 percent or less.

Such conditions also are perfect for ripening the last tomatoes of the season. It's true that tomatoes picked green lack the flavor of vine-ripened fruit, but they still will have better texture and better flavor than their counterparts from the supermarket.

When it comes to tomatoes, do not confuse redness with ripeness. Tomatoes develop their customary color because of the presence of ethylene gas—a green tomato placed in a plastic or wax paper bag with a bunch of bananas will turn red in a day or two, but it will not gain in sweetness nor become less hard. Ripeness is revealed by emission of a delicious scent and when a thumbnail pressed gently against the tomato's skin yields a dimple.

COOL AND DRY. Cool, dark, and dry storage areas are optimal for vegetables that are naturally dried, such as peas, beans, and southern peas; for those that are sun dried, such as tomatoes, peppers, herbs, and corn; and for those that are dried by a dehydrator, such as garlic, onion, chives, shallots, and leeks.

Dried and dehydrated vegetables are ideal for use in sauces, stews, soups, and braised meat dishes. When cooking with them, remember that their flavor is concentrated and also that you will have to add liquid volume to dishes to bring out yet dilute their flavor.

Dried and dehydrated vegetables may be stored for six to twelve months at temperatures ranging between 40 and 50°F (5–10°C) and at a humidity of 25 percent or less with no loss of flavor.

COOL AND MOIST. Adding humidity to a cool location reduces water loss and withering of fleshy vegetables. Good candidates for storage in such locations include green beans, cucumber, eggplant, peppers, summer squash, summer melons, okra, and new potatoes.

If your refrigerator has a vegetable keeper with a separate temperature and humidity control, set it no lower than 40°F (5°C) with humidity set at 90 percent. Most fleshy vegetables will store quite well for one week; some will retain their flavor and texture for up to three weeks.

Cold and Moist. The vegetables best stored in this kind of environment are asparagus, beets, leafy greens, celery, fresh peas, radishes, rhubarb, green onions, leeks, broccoli, head lettuce, and cabbage. The high moisture content of such vegetables makes them very susceptible to decay and fungal growth; cold temperature inhibits this while humidity helps them retain their moisture and crisp texture.

If carefully washed and dried, then stored in ideal cold and moist conditions of 34°F (1°C) and 90 percent humidity, most of these vegetables will keep their garden-fresh flavor and texture for two weeks to a month or more.

Storage Before Preserving. Keep in mind that these suggested storage recommendations apply only to produce being held for eating fresh or cooking. For best flavor and texture in preserved and frozen vegetables, always process them as soon as possible after harvest. Doing so assures the best-quality preserves.

Vegetable Preserving

For many centuries, a variety of methods have been used to preserve vegetables for later consumption. The primary methods used until the early 19th century—brining, drying, and pickling—sacrificed some of the flavor or texture of the produce. The invention of airtight cans and jar lids added heat processing, or canning, to the options, and a century later, modern refrigeration techniques made freezing vegetables widely practical for the first time.

For preserving original texture, taste, and nutrition, freezing remains the best option for long-term storage of vegetables. Every preservation method has its pluses and minuses, of course, and the total range of options allows the cook to achieve a vast array of flavors.

BRINING. Salt is a highly effective preservation agent. In many cultures, brined vegetables, with or without seasonings and herbs, are a staple. One of the most familiar of these is sauerkraut, simply brined and fermented cabbage. Most high-moisture leaf vegetables, or thin slices of fleshy vegetables, may be brined and fermented.

Traditionally, a ceramic crock with a loose-fitting cover is used to brine vegetables, but glass is an excellent alternative. Loosely pack cabbage leaves, Chinese cabbage, turnip greens, or spinach into a large jar and sprinkle coarse salt on every few leaves. For traditional sauerkraut, use shredded cabbage.

When the jar is filled, press down the leaves until they are firmly packed. Add just enough water to cover the top layer of leaves. Cover the container loosely with cheesecloth, drape a piece of kitchen plastic wrap over that, and store in a cool, dark place.

Once a week, remove the plastic, then the cheesecloth and rinse it clean. Skim off and discard any scum that forms on top of the brine. If necessary, add water to keep the leaves covered. In four weeks they will be ready. Remove them from the jar, rinse them thoroughly, and cook as you would sauerkraut or eat fresh in sandwiches and salads. Spinach prepared in this manner adds a unique, fresh taste to winter meals when warmed, dashed with lemon juice, and served with sweet potatoes, yams, turnips, or other sweet root vegetables.

WARNING: Brined vegetables generate carbon dioxide as they ferment, posing a significant risk of jars exploding if they are tightly capped. Never cap jars containing fermenting vegetables.

DRYING. Drying may be the most ancient food preservation method. Traditionally the heat of the sun was used to dry vegetables, but most gardeners today use a dehydrator—a rectangular or cylindrical container with racks and a heating element inside. Its great advantage is speed; a drying cycle often can be completed in one or two days.

Most legumes, peas, and beans dry naturally on their vines. When both the vine and the pods have turned brown, pick the pods carefully, then shuck the peas or beans. Lay them out in a warm, dry place for about a week. Fill freezer bags or sealed jars with the dried peas or beans and store at temperatures of 32–40°F (0–5°C). They will keep for more than a year.

Corn may be dried on the cob for grinding into meal. Shuck ears of eating corn and popcorn, then hang the cobs in a warm, dark, dry location until the kernels have lost all of their moisture, usually a few weeks. To remove the kernels, hold each cob vertically by the stem with the tip set firmly against a solid surface. Then, using a thick-bladed blunt knife, slice down the cob. Dried corn kernels may be stored in an airtight container in a cool, dark location at temperatures of 35–40°F (2–5°C) for up to one year. Corn ground into cornmeal will not keep as long, so it is best to grind the kernels as needed for immediate use, just as you would coffee beans.

Fleshy vegetables are good candidates for drying in a vegetable dehydrator. Eggplant, onion, garlic, leek, peppers, and cooking tomatoes can be arranged on the dehydrator's drying racks immediately after slicing; beets, carrots, kohlrabi, parsnips, rutabaga, and turnips first should be blanched for three minutes in boiling water, then patted dry. For best results, carefully follow the instructions provided by the dehydrator's manufacturer.

Vegetables, grapes, and berries with high moisture content may be sun dried in a protected area with low humidity, direct sun exposure, and temperatures that regularly exceed 100°F (38°C). Good air circulation is essential to preventing moisture becoming trapped inside the drying vegetables, so use a drying frame constructed of fine-mesh stainless-steel or copper-wire cloth, suspended at least one foot (30 cm) from the ground. Turn or winnow the drying produce daily. Many vegetables and berries with high moisture content will develop mildew unless they are bathed in an antifungal agent, such as sulfur, then dried thoroughly before being placed onto the drying rack. Allow seven to ten days for the drying process to be complete.

Detailed instructions for drying vegetables are available from agricultural extension offices of the U.S. Department of Agriculture.

PICKLING. Like brining, pickling relies on the natural antibacterial properties of salt for preservation. The use of vinegar also is essential since the acid it contains reduces the potential for bacterial growth in the brine.

Processing pickles, relishes, and giardiniera basically is a three-step procedure. First, carefully follow your recipe for preparing the brine solution; all contain vinegar, plus such optional spices as sugar, dill, pepper, and garlic. Boil according to directions.

In a separate, deep saucepan, invert clean, washed mason jars, their rings, and lids. Fill the saucepan with water, cover, and sterilize the jars at a rolling boil for at least 15 minutes. Clean the vegetables, prepare them for pickling, and blanch (according to the recipe instructions).

After the jars have been sterilized, carefully remove them one at a time from the water with tongs and pack them with the prepared vegetables. Add any spices or decorative garnishes, filling each jar to one-half inch (12 mm) below its

rim with hot brine solution. As each jar is filled, set the metal top in place and lightly tighten the ring. Do not tighten the ring completely, which will trap steam pressure and can cause the jar to break when boiled. As each jar is completely prepared, return it to the boiling water for an additional five minutes. Remove the jars from the water, fully tighten the rings, and check to make sure that the lids have sealed. (Most canning lids are designed to "pop" down into a concave shape when tightly sealed; listen for this distinctive noise as the jars cool, a sure sign that an airtight seal has been achieved.) Never rely on old-fashioned wire-closure jars with separate rubber seals; they are unreliable, may fail to form sterile seals, and thereby create a health hazard from bacterial contamination.

In six to eight weeks, the pickled vegetables will be well infused with the brine, vinegar, and spices. Unopened pickles and relishes may be stored at room temperature for up to three years.

Jams, Jellies, and Preserves

Sweet condiments that are canned at the temperature of boiling water, or water bath processed, rely upon the antibacterial power of sugar and the acidic nature of berries and fruits for safety. While there is little risk of food-bearing harmful bacteria if recipe instructions are followed exactly, it is nonetheless important to closely follow preparation guidelines if, for no other reason, than to make sure the results are flavorful.

Always process condiments using clean, undamaged Mason jars and new self-sealing lids. Avoid screw-top glass containers and those with loose rubber rings. Never reuse containers that originally held other foods.

The equipment for making jellies and jams is basic: a large saucepan, water bath canning pot, jar tongs, Mason or jelly jars, ladles, slotted spoons (for skimming foam from the boiling jelly), a sieve, a wide-mouth funnel, labels, and a candy thermometer.

Terms frequently seen in condiment recipes include:

Headspace: air space between the food and the top of the jar.

Jell point: temperature at which a recipe will thicken and set.

Pectin: jelling agent used to assist setting in berry preserves.

Sealing: airtight seal created during water bath processing.

Paraffin seal: household wax used to quick-seal jellies.

PRESERVING. Jams, jellies, chutneys, and condiments can all be preserved. The high sugar content of most jams and jellies serves to sterilize them naturally by creating a hostile environment to bacteria; still, always use the sterilization technique described opposite to add an extra element of safety. Most jams and jellies are distinguished from other canned preserves by their reliance on the jelling and thickening agent pectin, a natural extract of fruit (apples and citrus fruits are so high in pectin that they jell naturally when preserved). Jams and jellies usually are made from berries and fruit, though peppers, husk tomatoes and tomatillos, rhubarb and other vegetables also can be made into jelled preserves. Herbs, such as mint and others, serve as accents or flavoring agents for otherwise bland jellies such as apple, pear, and quince.

Vegetable chutneys are made from slowly cooked vegetables mixed with vinegar, spices, and sugar. Other preserve variants include vegetable butters (spiced and pureed vegetables reduced by cooking until they are thick and creamy), mustards (spreads made from that vegetable's seed), and conserves (multiple fruits or vegetables cooked with raisins, nuts, and sugar).

Always follow a recipe's instructions precisely when making preserves. They can be stored at room temperature for up to three years.

CANNING. Unlike storage processes that use high acid or sugar content to prevent spoilage, canning vegetables relies solely on high-heat processing to prevent bacterial growth. Because the canning jars and their contents must all be pre-sterilized, properly sealed, and boiled for a long period of time at temperatures exceeding 212°F (100°C), it's critical that a pressure cooker always be used. Improperly processed, low-acid vegetables bear a risk of botulism, a deadly bacteria. Carefully follow both the recipe's instructions and the manufacturer's recommendations for using your pressure cooker before proceeding. Canned vegetables are best if used within two years of processing.

Few home gardeners today can their own vegetables using a pressure cooker. The time and effort required simply are not worth the diminished flavors obtained from home canning. Most opt instead for freezing, which is the best way to preserve most home-grown vegetables for up to six months or more.

FREEZING. Home refrigerator-freezers are acceptable for short-term storage of vegetables—up to three months or so—but serious home gardeners will invest in a deep freezer to hold vegetables for periods of up to six or eight months. The difference between the appliances is simple: home refrigerator-freezers typically cool foods to 10–15°F (-9 to -12°C), while deep freezers can hold foods at 0°F (-18°C) or less.

Some vegetables are not suitable for freezing—they lose too much texture or flavor. Included are many of the leafy greens (except those suitable for steaming), celery, cucumber, melon, potatoes, and radishes. Other vegetables require processing—steaming or boiling, then mashing or pureeing—before they can be frozen. These include most varieties of squash, pumpkin, and root vegetables, such as beets, sweet potatoes, rutabagas, and turnips. Many others first must be cut into pieces and blanched to retain their optimum flavor and texture; do so with green beans, peas, broccoli, cauliflower, carrots, corn, rhubarb, and tomatoes.

The secret to achieving excellent frozen vegetables is to pick them at their peak of ripeness, then immediately immerse them in ice water before washing and drying in preparation for freezing. Many gardeners when they harvest carry a pail of ice water into the garden for this purpose. The ice water bath halts the ripening process, prevents sugars from converting to starch, preserves flavor, and prevents spoilage. Next, chill the vegetables to near freezing temperatures for an hour or so in the coldest area of your refrigerator, then freeze them quickly to 0°F (-18°C).

Always allow vegetables to dry thoroughly after washing or blanching, and arrange them in a single layer on cookie sheets for quick freezing. Only after the produce is fully frozen should it be placed into resealable heavy-gauge plastic bags for long-term storage. Airtight packages protect it from desiccation, or "freezer burn."

Whenever possible, store frozen vegetables in portion-size or premeasured quantities. Chopped onion, garlic, peppers, leeks, and shallots may be packed into ice cube trays or in cup-size (225 gm) portions and frozen. Do the same for pureed vegetables.

Prepare leafy greens—kale, mustard, spinach, and Swiss chard—by removing all stems, rinsing, drying, and steaming until just tender or cooking in a sealed container in the microwave. Place the greens in a colander or sieve to drain excess moisture and allow to cool to room temperature. Pack them into resealable plastic bags for quick freezing.

Blanch sliced vegetables, shelled peas, fresh beans, and corn on the cob before freezing to help them retain their flavor, color, and texture. Immerse them in boiling water for one to two minutes, then immediately place them in an ice water bath to stop the cooking process. Drain them and allow to dry thoroughly before packing into resealable bags or containers.

Freeze chopped fresh tomatoes, as well as tomato sauce, pureed tomatoes, and stewed tomatoes, after preparation. For extra-rich flavor, thicken sauces and purees before freezing by reducing them over heat more than their canned equivalents.

When thawing frozen vegetables, never allow them to stand at room temperature; add them to cooked dishes in their frozen state, thaw them quickly in a microwave, or allow them to thaw gradually in the refrigerator. The hazard of bacterial contamination exists whenever raw or partially cooked foods are thawed; avoid any hazard by following these instructions.

Proper harvesting, storing, and preserving of vegetables are the home gardener's sweetest reward because they allow the fruits of your efforts to extend to your next harvest. Every time a fresh vegetable flavor tantalizes your palate at mealtime, or a passing neighbor praises (and likely shares in) your garden's bounty, you will know the ultimate joy of home vegetable gardening.

Vegetable Encyclopedia

A

Amaranth

(Difficult)—A leafy vegetable similar in taste and appearance to spinach, amaranth is grown primarily in the tropics so is not generally well known in the United States and Canada.

Yield—Allow 4–6 plants per household member.

Planting Time—In spring, 3–4 weeks after last frost.

Planting Soil Temperature—60–80°F (15–27°C).

Growing Temperature—Prefers tropical climate with high humidity, optimally 72–86°F (22–30°C). If your climate doesn't meet these requirements, grow in a greenhouse or other protected location.

Soil Preparation—Have soil tested for adequate levels of nitrogen and, potassium, with, medium, phosphorus, content, and for proper acid-alkaline balance; maintain a 5.5–7.0 pH level.

Spacing—Sow seeds ¹/₄ inch (6 mm) deep, 8–12 inches (20–30 cm) apart, thinning successful plants to 4–6 inches (10–15 cm) apart, in rows 8–12 inches (20–30 cm) apart. Transplants should be 3–3¹/₂ inches (7.5–9 cm) tall and spaced 4–6 inches (10–15 cm) apart in rows 8–12 inches (20–30 cm) apart.

Care—Apply organic mulch to help keep plantings moist and free of weeds. Fertilize every 2–3 weeks with balanced fertilizer or organic liquid plant food. Pinch plants back when they are 7–8 inches (18–20 cm) tall to encourage greater production.

Companion Plants—Compact, leafy green vegetables, strawberries, and radishes, but not corn, pole beans, or melons.

Avoid—Planting in shaded areas; amaranth prefers full sun.

Maturity—6–10 weeks.

Harvest—When plant is about 6–8 inches (15–20 cm) tall by thinning outside leaves, then again whenever 4–5 new leaves have emerged to encourage continued production of tender, edible leaves.

Storage—In vegetable compartment of refrigerator for 1–2 weeks.

Varieties—Asian White, Burgundy, Fote Te, Golden, Mayo.

Tip—Leaves are primarily used raw in salads or steamed, similar to spinach.

Artichokes

(Moderate)—An edible thistle flower bud, the artichoke is a tasty garden addition. Plants require abundant space—at maturity they may reach 6 feet (1.8 m) in circumference and stand 3–4 feet (0.9–1.1 m) high. Consider their placement in the garden with mature size in mind. They are a perennial plant in all but the most severe winter climate areas.

Yield—Allow 1 plant per 1–2 household members, more if you are an artichoke enthusiast.

Planting Time—In late winter to early spring, about 2 weeks before last frost for root divisions.

Planting Soil Temperature—50–85°F (10–30°C).

Growing Temperature—40–75°F (5–24°C). Prefers mild winters and cool summers with consistent temperatures and precipitation.

Soil Preparation—Have soil tested for adequate levels of phosphorus and potassium, but there should not be excessive levels of nitrogen—abundant nitrogen encourages unnecessary foliage development. Amend soil to provide acid-alkaline balance at 6.0–6.8 pH level. Add compost and manure to loosen soil and improve drainage.

Spacing—Sow seeds ¹/₂ inch (12 mm) deep and 6 inches (15 cm) apart in every direction or, if planting in rows, thin successful plants to 6–8 feet (1.8–2.4 m) apart. Make rows 4–6 feet (1.1–1.8 m) to 6–8 feet (1.8–2.4 m) apart.

Care—Fertilize in spring and autumn with a low-nitrogen fertilizer such as 5–10–10. Water weekly, allowing soil to dry between waterings and avoiding saturated ground or standing water. Cut harvested stalks and leaves to the ground after all artichokes have been picked, forcing new growth. Plants should be replaced every few years.

Companion Plants—Perennial vegetables, such as asparagus, but not root vegetables or vines.

Avoid—Planting in areas with fewer than 100 days that are frost-free. In marginal climates, sow in a large container that can be moved indoors.

Maturity—No harvest in first year, annually thereafter.

Harvest—When buds are about the size of an apple and before they begin to open.

Storage—In vegetable compartment of refrigerator for up to 1 week, or in freezer after cooking. Also may be pickled or canned.

Varieties—Green Globe, Imperial Star, Violetto.

Tip—To eat, clean thoroughly under abundant running water, clip thorns off with kitchen scissors, and steam or boil until tender (about 20 minutes). Serve hot or cold, with butter or salad dressing; the soft part of the outer leaves and the entire heart are edible. Buds allowed to go to seed produce attractive purple thistle flowers for cutting or drying.

Asparagus   *(Difficult)*—A cool-season vegetable, this perennial member of the lily family is an early-spring delicacy. It requires 3 years for the plants to become established and begin fruiting, but they provide ample harvests every year thereafter for 20 years or longer. The harvested green spears are capped with a bud-forming top; if allowed to go to seed, the buds will sprout feathery, fernlike foliage.

Yield—Allow 30–50 roots to obtain enough for several meals for a household of 2–4 persons.

Planting Time—Indoors, about 12–14 weeks before the last frost. Transplant after all danger of frost has passed. Or, late winter or early spring for second-season root crowns.

Planting Soil Temperature—50–85°F (10–30°C).

Growing Temperature—30–95°F (0–35°C) when established, optimally 60–85°F (16–30°C). Tends to bolt above 95°F (35°C).

Soil Preparation—Have soil tested for adequate levels of nitrogen, phosphorus, and potassium and for proper acid-alkaline balance; maintain a 6.0–6.8 pH level by supplementing with lime.

Spacing—Sow seeds indoors in flats 1½ inches (4 cm) deep until 1 year old. Dig a trench 12 inches (30 cm) or more deep and add organic matter and pH-balanced fertilizer until the trench is about 8 inches (20 cm) deep. Plant the year-old crown in 2 inches (5 cm) of soil, filling the trench gradually with remaining soil after the plant emerges in spring.

Care—Add a high-nitrogen fertilizer before spears come up in spring and again after the last harvest, or dig in well-rotted manure alongside the rows. Keep free of weeds and cut back any foliage that feathers out once it has turned brown. Cut back to 1 inch (25 mm) in autumn. In severe winter climates, mulch with organic matter. Cover white varieties with black plastic supported by stakes to prevent the formation of green chlorophyll from sunlight.

Companion Plants—Tomatoes, parsley, and basil, but not root vegetables such as carrots or potatoes. Some gardeners claim tomatoes keep away asparagus beetle while asparagus defends tomatoes against nematodes.

Avoid—Cutting any spears from the first year's growth, and limit cuttings for crown plantings. Add an additional year for plants grown from seed.

Maturity—Spring of the third growth year.

Harvest—When spears are $1/4$–$3/4$ inch (6–20 mm) in diameter. Third-year spears may be harvested for up to 2 weeks; fourth-year, 4 or more weeks.

Storage—In vegetable compartment of refrigerator for 2–3 weeks; in freezer, after blanching. Also may be canned.

Varieties—Jersey Knight, Larac, Mary Washington, UC 157, Viking, Waltham.

Tip—Avoid overcooking and using metal utensils, which will discolor the asparagus.

B

BEANS—Many gardeners' favorite due to their ease of storage and use, beans are delicious eaten straight from the garden, as a main or side dish. Their seedpods come in a variety of shapes and sizes but are usually long and narrow. Primarily green in color, they also come in varying shades of yellow and purple. A number of varieties, such as snap beans, may be enjoyed in their entirety, or for their seeds, eaten in their fresh, green stage or dried. Some varieties grow as bushes while others, such as pole beans, vine and climb. For planting purposes, the bean family can be divided by growth habit into the following categories: *Dried Beans, Fava Beans, Garbanzo (Chickpea) Beans, Lima Beans, Snap Beans,* and *Soybeans.*

Beans are a cool-season, annual vegetable. As a member of the nitrogen-fixing legume family, they naturally add this vital growth nutrient back into soil depleted by previous plantings of lettuce, cabbage, or other leafy greens. Rotating bean plantings with greens in the garden from one season to the next also may help control soil-borne diseases.

Small dried beans grown indoors in a sunny spot as bean sprouts are excellent choices for tasty stir-fry dishes and can be used throughout the year to add a distinctive flavor to many meals [see Sprouts, pg. 368].

Beans—Dried *(Easy)*—Leaving the bean pod on the plant past full maturity, until the pod withers and dries completely, is the usual means of drying beans; however, in humid-climate areas, or in areas where precipitation is unpredictable, the fully matured bean pods can be gathered and dried off the plant in a dry, warm spot or in a vegetable dehydrator. An excellent source of protein in a convenient, storable form, the most common are pinto, white, navy, and kidney beans, used abundantly in many menus throughout the world.

Yield—Allow 4–8 plants per household member.

Planting Time—After all danger of frost has passed.

Planting Soil Temperature—60–85°F (15–30°C).

Growing Temperature—50–80°F (10–27°C), optimally 60–70°F (15–21°C).

Soil Preparation—Have soil tested for adequate levels of phosphorus and potassium and for proper acid-alkaline balance; maintain a

6.0–6.8 pH level. In first-time vegetable gardens, it may be necessary to add to the soil an inoculant with beneficial nitrogen-fixing bacteria; however, avoid using green manure or fertilizers that are high in nitrogen. Make sure soil is loose and drains well.

Spacing—Sow seeds 1½–2 inches (3.8–5.1 cm) deep, 2 inches (5 cm) apart, in rows 18–30 inches (45–75 cm) apart. Seeds planted more closely should be thinned when plants are well established.

Care—When weeding, do not hoe too deeply or you may cut through the beans' root system, which is shallow and widespread. Keep soil moist during flowering and pod formation.

Companion Plants—Potatoes, carrots, cucumbers, cauliflower, cabbage, and summer savory, but not onions, garlic, or gladioli.

Avoid—Using green manure or fertilizers high in nitrogen.

Maturity—65–70 days.

Harvest—When pods are completely dry or, in moist climates, pick pods when they first wither, then spread onto a flat surface in a warm, protected spot, and dry thoroughly. Fully dry pods will split open naturally to reveal the dried beans.

Storage—In fabric bags with good air circulation, not in plastic or glass containers, in a cool, dry location for up to 1 year.

Varieties—French Flageolet, French Horticultural, Great Northern, Navy, Pinto, Red Kidney, White Kidney, and any number of specialty varieties.

Tip—These beans also may be enjoyed at the green, shelling stage. So-called "shuckies," especially French Flageolet, French Horticultural, and Great Northern White Beans, can be eaten steamed with butter, or in soups and casseroles.

Beans—Fava, Horse, or Windsor

(Moderate)—A cool-season plant that grows to a height of 3–4½ feet (0.9–1.4 m), this bean produces large pods with somewhat flat and oval beans that come in a variety of colors, including white, yellow, green, and pinkish-red, but all of them may be harvested green for immediate use, canning, or drying for prolonged storage. Because beans are high in protein and grow well in cool climates, many cultures, including those of Italy, Spain, Peru, and Chile, include them in their dishes. They are common in chilies, stews, and soups that can warm the soul on a cold day.

CAUTION: Beans of this family may affect sensitive individuals, causing a severe allergic reaction, anaphylactic shock, or even death in those who lack a specific genetic enzyme. (Those of Mediterranean ancestries should pay particular attention to this hazard.)

Yield—Allow 4–8 plants per household member.

Planting Time—In early spring, as soon as the soil is able to be worked (early varieties), through mid-season. In mild-winter or reverse-season climates, in autumn for late winter or early-spring harvests. In short-season climates, start indoors or in a cold frame. They are not recommended as a summer crop in excessively hot, dry climates such as the desert southwest.

Planting Soil Temperature—50–85°F (10–30°C).

Growing Temperature—40–75°F (5–24°C), optimally 60–65°F (16–18°C).

Soil Preparation—Have soil tested for adequate levels of phosphorus and potassium and for proper acid-alkaline balance; maintain a 6.0–6.8 pH level. Avoid using fertilizers high in nitrogen or green manure. Make sure the soil is loose and drains well.

Spacing—Sow seeds 1 inch (2.5 cm) deep, 4–5 inches (10–12.5 cm) apart, in rows 18–30 inches (45–75 cm) apart.

Care—When weeding, do not hoe too deeply or you may cut through the root system, which is shallow and widespread. Keep soil moist during flowering and pod formation. Rotate with leafy-green and cole-family vegetables to prevent nitrogen depletion of soil.

Companion Plants—Potatoes, cucumbers, and summer savory, but not onions or garlic.

Avoid—Planting in areas that receive direct sunlight or excessive heat.

Maturity—80–100 days.

Harvest—When about half their final size of 1 inch (2.5 cm) for use fresh or after pods have dried on the vine for dried beans.

Storage—In vegetable compartment of refrigerator for about 1 week or dried for long-term storage.

Varieties—Aguadulce, Broad Windsor, Con Amore, Loretta, Sweet Lorraine, Windsor Long Pod.

Tip—Best eaten fresh, after steaming and dressed with garlic-seasoned olive oil or butter, then garnished with chopped fresh tomato.

Beans—Garbanzo, Gram, or Chickpeas

(Easy)—A bush with fernlike foliage standing 2–2½ feet (60–75 cm) tall, this bean produces fat green pods containing 1–3 tan-colored, pealike seeds. Also known as chickpeas or gram beans, they are neither true beans nor true peas. They can be eaten in their green stage, but are most often dried for later soaking and cooking. They have a unique flavor that is very popular for salads, and combined with grains they make a vegetarian meat substitute. They are a favorite in Mediterranean, Asian, and Indian cuisine.

Yield—Allow 4–8 plants per household member.

Planting Time—In spring, after all danger of frost has passed. In mild-winter and reverse-season climates, in late autumn.

Planting Soil Temperature—65–80°F (18–27°C).

Growing Temperature—50–80°F (10–27°C), optimally 60–70°F (16–21°C).

Soil Preparation—Have soil tested for adequate levels of phosphorus and potassium and for proper acid-alkaline balance; maintain a 6.0–6.8 pH level. Avoid using green manure or fertilizers high in nitrogen. Make sure soil is loose and drains well.

Spacing—Sow seeds 1½–2 inches (4–5 cm) deep, 3–6 inches (7.5–15 cm) apart, in rows 24–30 inches (60–75 cm) apart. Seeds planted more closely should be thinned when plants are well established.

Care—When weeding, do not hoe too deeply or you may cut through the root system, which is shallow and widespread. Keep soil moist during flowering and pod formation. Rotate legume crops throughout the garden to naturally boost soil nitrogen levels.

Companion Plants—Potatoes, cucumbers, corn, strawberries, celery, and summer savory, but not onions or garlic.

Avoid—Planting in areas that receive direct sunlight or excessive heat.

Maturity—100 days.

Harvest—When pods are completely dried out or, in moist climates, when they first wither; then spread on a flat surface in a warm, protected spot and dry thoroughly.

Storage—In airtight container after completely dried for up to 1 year. Also may be canned using a pressure cooker for storage up to 3 years, or blanched and frozen for up to 6 months.

Varieties—Chickpea, Garbanzo, Gram, Kabuli Black.

Tip—Fresh, boiled garbanzo beans, mashed with spices and olive oil, provide a healthy dip for crudites, crackers, chips, and crisps.

Beans—Lima or Butter

(Easy)—Also known as butter beans, limas come in bush and pole varieties bearing clusters of pods containing 3–4 large, flat, oval beans. A little fussy about temperature, they take longer to mature than other beans. Also available is a miniature variety of baby limas, only grown on a bush, that matures quickly but yields smaller beans.

Yield—Allow 4–8 plants per household member.

Planting Time—In regular climates, in spring, after all danger of frost has passed. In mild-winter climates, in autumn and late winter. In reverse-season climates, in late autumn and winter.

Planting Soil Temperature—65–85°F (18–29°C).

Growing Temperature—50–80°F (10–27°C), optimally 60–70°F (16–21°C). Temperatures of 80°F (27°C) or higher, or cold, wet conditions during flowering, will cause flowers to drop, preventing bean formation.

Soil Preparation—Have soil tested for adequate levels of phosphorus and potassium, and for proper acid-alkaline balance; maintain a 6.0–6.8 pH level. Avoid using green manure or fertilizers high in nitrogen. Make sure soil is loose and drains well.

Spacing—*Bush*: Sow seeds 1½–2 inches (4–5 cm) deep, 3–6 inches (7.5–15 cm) apart in rows 24–30 inches (60–75 cm) apart. *Pole*: Sow seeds 1½–2 inches (4–5 cm) deep, 6–10 inches (15–25 cm) apart in rows 30–36 inches (75–90 cm) apart. Seeds planted more closely should be thinned when plants are well established.

Care—When weeding, do not hoe too deeply or you may cut through the root system, which is shallow and widespread. Keep soil moist during flowering and pod formation.

Companion Plants—*Bush*: potatoes, cucumbers, corn, strawberries, celery, and summer savory, but not onions. *Pole*: corn, summer savory, scarlet runner beans, and sunflowers, but not onions, beets, or kohlrabi.

"God Almighty first planted a garden. And, indeed, it is the purest of human pleasures."

Francis Bacon

Avoid—Overhead watering, which may cause disease, fungal infections of the pods, or poor setting of fruit.

Maturity—*Bush*: 60–80 days. *Pole*: 85–90 days.

Harvest—When plump and fresh-looking. Prompt harvesting will encourage extended production of flowers and new pods.

Storage—In vegetable compartment of refrigerator for 1–2 weeks, or in freezer after blanching for 3–4 months. Also may be pickled or canned using a pressure cooker for storage 2–3 years, or dried and stored in fabric sacks.

Varieties—*Bush*: Baby Lima, Baby Thorogreen, Butter Bean, East Land, Excel, Fordhook, Henderson, Jackson Wonder, Packers, Thorogreen Early Bush.

Varieties—*Pole*: Aubrey Deane, Christmas, Florida Butter, Illinois Giant, King of the Garden, Prizetaker, Willow-leaf White.

Tip—Soak dried lima beans in hot water for at least 4 hours prior to use. Dried beans added directly to soups and stews will remain tough.

Beans—Snap, Wax, or Romano

(Easy)—As the most popular bean of home gardeners, new varietals and cultivars are added each season to old favorites to keep up with the demand for "different." It is available in flat or round pods; in green, purple, yellow, and speckled versions; and in bush and pole varieties. Bush beans typically produce earlier than pole varieties, but most do not yield as plentifully. Pole beans must be well supported since they can grow to 8 feet (2.4 m) in height or taller.

Yield—Allow 4–8 plants total of each variety or several varieties per household member.

Planting Time—In regular climates, after all danger of frost has passed. In mild-winter and reverse-season climates, in autumn through late winter. If growing season permits, plant succession crops of beans 2 weeks apart for longer harvests.

Planting Soil Temperature—60–85°F (18–29°C).

Growing Temperature—50–80°F (10–27°C), optimally 60-70°F (16–21°C).

Soil Preparation—Have soil tested for adequate levels of phosphorus and potassium and for proper acid-alkaline balance; maintain a 6.0–6.8 level. Avoid using green manure or fertilizers high in nitrogen. Make sure soil is loose and drains well.

Spacing—*Bush*: Sow seeds 1 1/2–2 inches (4–5 cm) deep, 2 inches (5 cm) apart, in rows 18–30 inches (45–75 cm) apart. *Pole*: Sow seeds 1 1/2–2 inches (4–5 cm) deep, 4–6 inches (10–15 cm) apart, in rows 36–48 inches (0.9–1.2 m) apart.

Care—When weeding, do not hoe too deeply or you may cut through the root system, which is shallow and widespread. Keep soil moist during flowering and pod formation. Rotate annually to plots where lettuce, squash, broccoli, Brussels sprouts, cabbage, cauliflower, or collards have grown in past seasons.

Companion Plants—*Bush*: celery, corn, cucumbers, potatoes, rosemary, strawberries, and summer savory, but not onions. *Pole*: corn, rosemary, summer savory, scarlet runner beans, and sunflowers, but not onions, beets, or kohlrabi.

Avoid—Crowding since beds planted too closely will reduce yield and increase the plants' susceptibility to disease.

Maturity—*Bush*: 45–60 days. *Pole*: 60–85 days.

Harvest—When pods are about 3 inches (7.5 cm) in length but before they begin to bulge. Prompt harvesting will encourage extended production of new flowers and of new pods.

Storage—In vegetable compartment of refrigerator for 1–1 1/2 weeks, or blanched and frozen for up to 3 months.

Varieties—*Bush* (Green): Blue Lake, Contender, Derby, Green Sleeves, Slenderette, Tender Pick, Tender Pod, Topper, Vernandon. (Yellow/Wax): Brittle Wax, Cherokee, Eastern Butterwax, Gold Crop, Gold Kissed, Gold Mine, Gold Rush, Golden Rocky, Improved Golden Wax, Kinghorn, Pencil Pod, Sunrae, Valdor, Wax Romano. (Purple): Purple Queen Bush.

Varieties—*Pole* (Green): Blue Lake Pole, Cascade Giant, Dade, Kentucky Wonder, Northeaster, Scarlet Emperor Runner, Violet-podded Stringless. (Yellow): Kentucky Wonder Wax, Rocdor, Yellow Annelinno. (Purple): Purple Peacock, Royal Burgundy, Royalty, Sequoia, Violet-podded Stringless.

Varieties—*Italian Green Beans*: Goldmarie, Musica, Romano.

Tip—Pickled snap beans usually require special care in canning due to botulism hazard; instead, for a crisp, fresh taste, preserve by packing blanched beans into sterile jars and covering with boiling, seasoned brine, then refrigerating for 2–3 weeks before use.

Beans—Soy *(Moderate)*—These fuzzy plump pods contain 2–4 beans apiece and grow on a bushy plant. Although they are known worldwide as an excellent source of protein, soybeans are relatively new to American gardens. They come in a number of varietals propagated to closely match regional conditions; check with a local nursery, garden center, seed company, or agricultural extension office to select appropriate varietals. Soybeans are determinate plants, meaning all the pods ripen at the same time.

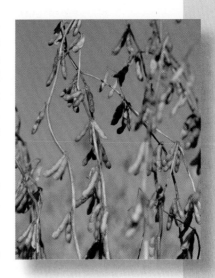

Yield—Allow 4–8 plants per household member.

Planting Time—In regular climates, after all danger of frost has passed. In mild-winter climates, in midwinter. In reverse-season climates, in late autumn.

Planting Soil Temperature—60–85°F (18–29°C)

Growing Temperature—50–80°F (10–27°C), optimally 60–70°F (16–21°C).

Soil Preparation—Have soil tested for adequate levels of phosphorus and potassium and for proper acid-alkaline balance; maintain a 6.0–6.8 pH level. Avoid using green manure or fertilizers high in nitrogen. Make sure soil drains well.

Spacing—Sow seeds 1 1/2–2 inches (4–5 cm) deep, 2 inches (5 cm) apart, in rows 24–36 inches (60–90 cm) apart.

Care—When weeding do not hoe too deeply or you may cut through the root system, which is shallow and widespread. Keep soil moist during flowering and pod formation.

Companion Plants—Most every garden plant except onion, garlic, and their relatives.

Avoid—Overhead watering after pods have set.

Maturity—45–100 days or more, depending upon climate.

Harvest—When pods are full, green, and dry, to prevent mildew.

Storage—Fresh in vegetable compartment of refrigerator for 1–2 weeks, or dried for storage up to 1 year.

Varieties—Black Jet, Envy, Hakucho, Kegon, Prize Vegetable, Verde.

Tip—If picked green, shell them by blanching in boiling water for a couple of minutes, then plunging into an ice water bath. Excellent for salads and stir-fries.

Beets *(Easy)*—This cool-season vegetable primarily is grown for its bulb-shaped root, which most often is red, but it also yields greens that can be eaten. Beets come in gold, yellow, white, and concentric- or candy cane-striped versions, which tend to be sweeter and milder. Beets are popular as a salad vegetable when cooked, chilled, and sliced, or pickled, and as a hot side dish.

Yield—Allow 5–10 mature plants per household member.

Planting Time—In regular climates, in spring, 2–4 weeks before the last frost has passed, then stagger succession plantings every 3 weeks until daily temperatures reach 80°F (27°C). Resume 6–8 weeks before the first frost for late-fall or winter harvest. In mild-winter areas, year-round. In reverse-season climates, in autumn, after daily temperatures have fallen below 80°F (27°C).

Planting Soil Temperature—50–80°F (10–27°C).

Growing Temperature—45–75°F (7–24°C). Beets will tolerate varying temperatures, provided that adequate water is supplied throughout the growing cycle.

Soil Preparation—Have soil tested for adequate levels of nitrogen, phosphorus, and potassium and for proper acid-alkaline balance; maintain a 6.0–6.8 pH level. Make sure soil drains well and is loose and loamy, with all hard clods and rocks removed.

Spacing—Sow seeds ½ inch (12 mm) deep, 1 inch (2.5cm) apart, in rows 18–24 inches (45–60 cm) apart. Cover seeds with ¼ inch (6 mm) of fine sand or compost. Thin when 3 inches (7.5 cm) tall to 3 inches (7.5 cm) apart.

Care—Weed and cultivate when soil begins to dry; maintain a regular and adequate supply of water since beets tend to stunt and become woody if their soil is allowed to dry out. Inspect often for boring pests, especially when plants reach maturity.

Companion Plants—Onions and kohlrabi, but not pole beans or other shading crops.

Avoid—Crowding.

Maturity—45–65 days.

Harvest—When bulb is 1–3 inches (2.5–7.5 cm) in width. Carefully pull up entire plant; rinse thoroughly to remove soil, then dry.

Storage—In vegetable compartment of refrigerator for 1–2 months or in damp sawdust in a cool storage location for use throughout winter. Also preserve by canning or pickling for storage up to 1 year.

Varieties—Action, Albina Verduna, Avenger, Baby Gladiator, Big Red, Burpee Golden, Chicago Red, Chioggia, Crimson King, Cylindra, Cyndor, Detroit Supreme, Early Wonder, Formanova, Forono, Green Top Bunching, Kestrel Crosby's Green Top, Little Ball, Long Season, Lutz Greenleaf, Mangels, Monopoly, Pablo, Pacemaker, Pronto, Red Ace, Red Ball, Ruby Queen, Sangria, Scarlet Supreme, Solo, Sweetheart, Warrior.

Tip—Beet leaves also are edible and taste best when young and tender.

Belgian Endive —See Chicory, Belgian Endive, Radicchio

BERRIES—Often used as decorative borders or screens to separate use areas in the yard, these perennials also are ideal for desserts or as a fresh-picked treat while gardening. Principally, berries are divided into two groups: bush berries and cane berries. Both types include many varieties and differences, but the feature all share is their tangy sweetness. Although individual berry types are very picky about their growng soil and climate, they often will try to take over the garden unless actively discouraged by deep, root-restraining borders. Strawberries are the one type that can be grown almost anywhere in the United States and Canada. Popular berry categories include *Blackberry, Blueberry, Currant* and *Gooseberry, Elderberry, Raspberry,* and *Strawberry.*

Berries—Blackberry *(Moderate)*—These small, cup-shaped perennials, which come in all shades of red to black, grow in clusters on canelike, thorny vines as long as 8 feet (7.5 m). They grow wild in many areas of the United States, but they also have been hybridized in a score of domestic versions. Some popular blackberry varietals include the common loganberry, ollalieberry, and boysenberry. Berries will begin to form 2 years after bareroot divisions are planted. The plants spread through aggressive root runners as well as from seeds that germinate from dropped fruit.

Yield—Allow 4–6 plants per household member for eating, twice as many for making jams or jellies.

Planting Time—In cold-weather climates, in early spring. In mild-winter climates, in early spring or autumn. Not recommended in excessively hot, dry climates.

Planting Soil Temperature—35–55°F (2–13°C) for bareroot divisions.

Growing Temperature—55–80°F (13–27°C).

Soil Preparation—Have soil tested for adequate levels of nitrogen, phosphorus, and potassium, and for proper acid-alkaline balance; maintain a 5.5–6.8 pH level through application of evergreen-needle compost or garden sulfur. Add well-rotted manure or compost to soil to keep it loose and ensure good drainage.

Spacing—*Erect*: Set out bareroot divisions 6 inches (15 cm) deep, 30 inches (75 cm) apart, in rows 10 feet (3 m) apart. Cover with 1 inch (2.5 cm) of soil. *Trailing*: Set out bareroot divisions 1 foot (25 cm) deep, 5–8 feet (1.5–2.4 m) apart, in rows 10 feet (3 m) apart. Cover with 1 inch (2.5 cm) of soil. Install edge boards or root-guard plastic barriers set at least 18 inches (45 cm) deep to prevent spreading of the plants from their roots as they grow and divide. Install trellises or support wires 6–8 feet (1.8–2.4 m) in height.

Care—Mulch with well-rotted manure or organic compost in spring. Train trailing varieties to grow on trellises or wire supports by tying the canes to the supports. Reduce watering after berries are harvested to retard cane growth. Prune away old canes after fruiting is completed [see Pruning, pg. 224], leaving new-season canes.

Companion Plants—Most garden vegetables, but not plants that prefer acidic soils such as potatoes, eggplants, peppers, and tomatoes.

Avoid—Planting in areas exposed to direct sunlight. Ideal sites should receive no more than 5 hours of direct sun per day.

Maturity—2 years from planting of bareroot divisions.

Harvest—When full-colored, sweet, plump, and easily pulled off the vine. Pick frequently as berries ripen to encourage additional flowers and fruit. Do not wash after picking.

Storage—In vegetable compartment of refrigerator for 1–2 weeks, or frozen up to 1 year for use in jams, jellies, preserves, or pies.

Varieties—Arapaho, Black Satin, Boysenberry, Darrow, Dew, Hull, Loganberry, Marionberry, Navaho, Sunberry, Sylvanberry, Tayberry, Thornless, Youngberry.

Tip—Thornless varieties produce fewer berries so make a choice between abundant picking and less pricking.

Berries—Blueberry

(Moderate)—A round, smooth-skinned, blue-colored berry, the blueberry grows on 1-year-old branches of established bushes, which should be trimmed back in autumn to remove all branches that have previously borne fruit. The blueberry plant blooms in late spring or early summer, displaying small, white blossoms with a slightly pink cast. In autumn, the foliage puts on a color show of bright red, orange, and copper leaves. The two main varieties are the high-bush blueberry, grown in cool, northern climates, and the rabbit-eye blueberry, grown mostly in the southeastern United States, where winters are mild.

Yield—Allow 3–5 bushes per household member.

Planting Time—High-bush varieties in early spring, rabbit-eye in late autumn or winter.

Planting Soil Temperature—35–55°F (2–13°C).

Growing Temperature—*High-bush*: 55–80°F (13–27°C). *Rabbit-eye*: 60–90° (16–32°C).

Soil Preparation—Have soil tested for adequate levels of nitrogen, phosphorus, and potassium, and for proper acid-alkaline balance; maintain a 4.0–5.5 pH level by supplementing soil with garden sulfur, peat, or evergreen-needle compost, or use acid planting mix. Add well-rotted manure or compost to ensure that roots retain moisture.

Spacing—Set plants 12–18 inches (30–45 cm) deep, 5 feet (1.5 m) apart, in rows 5 feet (1.5 m) apart. To discourage spreading, set plants in barrels or large pots planted into the soil.

Care—In winter, trim all lower, overlapping, weak branches; in spring, lightly trim the tops to reduce spreading. Weed and mulch soil with acidic organic matter. Cover with netting after flowers have set fruit to prevent birds from harvesting before you do.

Companion Plants—All acid-loving species and cole vegetables, but not mint.

Avoid—Overfertilizing, which will cause excessive foliage production and reduce yield.

Maturity—60–80 days after first bloom.

Harvest—When full-colored, sweet, plump, and easily pulled from the cluster. Determine timing of harvest by taste. The crop should yield abundant fruit for several weeks. Do not wash after picking.

Storage—In vegetable compartment of refrigerator for 2–3 weeks, or frozen for up to 6 months for use in pies, jams, jellies, or preserves.

Varieties—Blue Jay, Bluecrop, Blueray, Coville, Dwarf Top Hat, Elliot, Jersey, Northblue, Patriot, Saskatoon.

Tip—Bush berries, such as high-bush blueberries, make excellent garden borders.

Berries—Currant and Gooseberry

(Moderate)—Though they are close relatives, currants and gooseberries are cold weather–tolerant, neat, and tidy perennial bushes that grow 4–5 feet (1.2–1.5 m) tall. Both are frequently grown for their decorative nature as well as their fruit. Currants are smooth skinned, sweet in flavor, and high in vitamin C. Gooseberries, which come in green and red varietals, have a strong fragrance and are exceptional in size.

Yield—Allow 1–2 plants per household member, more if making jams or jellies.

Planting Time—In mild-winter climates, in winter. In cold-winter climates, in early autumn.

Planting Soil Temperature—45–60°F (7–16°C).

Growing Temperature—60–85°F (16–29°C).

Soil Preparation—Have soil tested for adequate levels of nitrogen, phosphorus, and potassium, and for proper acid-alkaline balance; maintain a 5.5–6.8 pH level by supplementing with peat, evergreen-needle compost, or garden sulfur. Add well-rotted manure or compost to ensure the roots retain moisture.

Spacing—*Currants*: Set bareroot divisions 5–6 inches (12–15 cm) deep, 4 feet (1.2 m) apart, in rows 10 feet (3 m) apart. *Gooseberries*: Set bushes 3–4 inches (7.5–10 cm) deep, 5 feet (1.5 m) apart, in rows 12 feet (3.5 m) apart. Install trellises or support wires when beds are established to at least 6 feet (1.7 m) in height.

Care—Prune annually [see Pruning, pg. 224] after fruiting is completed. Reduce watering after berries are harvested to retard foliage growth and increase yield in following year. Remove suckers from base to ensure best growth.

Companion Plants—Any plants that prefer acidic soils, but not potatoes, eggplants, peppers, or tomatoes.

Avoid—Mildew by careful pruning to allow air circulation, and by watering at roots.

Maturity—2 years.

Harvest—*Currants*: when full-colored, plump, and easily pulled from the cluster. *Gooseberries*: in late spring and early summer for cooking; in midsummer for sweet desserts.

Storage—In vegetable compartment of refrigerator for 2–3 weeks, or frozen for up to 6 months for use in pies, jams, jellies, or preserves.

Varieties—*Currants*: Red Lake, Wilder.

Varieties—*Gooseberries*: Josta, Pixwell, Welcome.

Tip—The tart flavor of currants and gooseberries makes them a natural companion for sweeter fruits such as strawberries, peaches, or nectarines.

Berries—Elderberry

(Easy)—A smooth, juicy, full-bodied, sweet bush berry with a deep purple color, elderberries grow in clusters on vinelike bushes that reach 10 feet (3 m) or more in height.

Yield—Allow 2 plants per household member (at least 2 are required for cross-pollination), more if making jams or jellies.

Planting Time—In cold-weather climates, in early spring. In mild-winter climates, in early spring or autumn. Not recommended in hot, dry climates such as the desert southwest.

Planting Soil Temperature—35–55°F (2–13°C).

Growing Temperature—50–90°F (10–32°C).

Soil Preparation—Have soil tested for adequate levels of nitrogen, phosphorus, and potassium and for proper acid-alkaline balance; maintain a 5.5–6.8 pH level by supplementing with evergreen-needle compost, peat, or garden sulfur. Add well-rotted manure or compost to ensure that roots retain moisture.

Spacing—Set out bareroot divisions in trenches 8 inches (20 cm) deep, 5 feet (1.5 m) apart, in rows 10 feet (3 m) apart. Cover with 1 inch (25 mm) of soil. Install trellises or support wires when beds are established to at least 6 feet (1.7 m) in height.

Care—Prune annually [see Pruning, pg. 224] after fruiting is completed. Reduce watering after berries are harvested to increase yield the following year. Cover with netting after flowers have set fruit to prevent birds from harvesting your berries before you do.

Companion Plants—Any plants that prefer acidic soils, but not potatoes, eggplants, peppers, or tomatoes.

Avoid—Planting in a site that does not receive at least 6 hours of full sunlight per day.

Maturity—2 years.

Harvest—When full-colored, sweet, plump, and easily pulled from the cluster. Do not wash after picking.

Storage—In vegetable compartment of refrigerator for 2–3 weeks, or frozen for up to 6 months for use in jellies or preserves.

Varieties—Adams, Johns.

Tip—The boiled juice of the elderberry makes a high-quality dry wine when fermented.

Berries—Raspberry

(Moderate)—This relative of the blackberry is as prolific and sweet. Raspberries grow both foliage and clustered fruit on canes, which may grow to 8 feet (2.4 m) or more in length, bearing fruit in their second year of growth. They come in 2 primary types: summer-bearing ("red") and autumn-bearing ("black"); each requires specific pruning care for best results [see Pruning, pg. 224].

Yield—Allow 2–4 plants per household member, more if making jams or jellies.

Planting Time—In cold-winter climates, in early spring. In mild climates, in early spring or late autumn.

Planting Soil Temperature—35–55°F (2–13°C).

Growing Temperature—55–80°F (13–27°C).

Soil Preparation—Have soil tested for adequate levels of nitrogen, phosphorus, and potassium and for proper acid-alkaline balance; maintain a 6–6.8 pH level by supplementing with peat, evergreen-needle compost, or garden sulfur. Add well-rotted manure or compost to ensure that soil drains well.

Spacing—Set out bareroot divisions 3 inches (7.5 cm) deep, 2 feet (60 cm) apart, in rows 4–6 feet (1.2–1.8 m) apart. Install root guard borders at least 18 inches (45 cm) on all sides of the bed to prevent spreading, and trellises or wire supports to at least 6 feet (1.7 m) in height.

Care—Protect from birds and pests with netting. Prune 2-year-old canes annually, after fruiting is completed, marking first-year canes with white spray paint to distinguish them from new canes. Reduce watering after berries are harvested.

Companion Plants—Any plants that prefer acidic soils, but not potatoes, eggplants, peppers, or tomatoes.

Avoid—Planting in any site that does not receive at least 6 hours of full sunlight per day.

Maturity—2 years.

Harvest—When full-colored, sweet, plump, and easily pulled off the cane.

Storage—In vegetable compartment of refrigerator for 2–3 weeks, or frozen for up to 6 months for use in pies, jams, jellies, or preserves.

Varieties—Bababerry, Blackhawk, Candy, Cumberland, Fall Gold, Fall Red, Goldie, Heritage, John Robertson, Mammoth Red, Nova, Red Latham, September Red.

Tip—Raspberries and strawberries are natural companions for superb berry pies.

Berries—Strawberry

(Easy)—These low-growing berries, notable for their brilliant red color, green leaves, and white flowers, reproduce by sending out foliage runners that start new plants the following year, or by root division. Strawberries are the only berry that bears seeds on the outside of the fruit, which gives them a unique appearance, texture, and taste. Plants grown in mild climates should be replaced every 3 years to maintain production, though the offspring of their runners can be transplanted to a fresh bed.

Yield—Allow 25 plants per household member, more if making pies, shortcakes, jams, or jellies.

Planting Time—In cold-winter climates, in early spring. In mild climates, in late autumn or early spring.

Planting Soil Temperature—45–60°F (7–16°C).

Growing Temperature—70–90°F (21–32°C).

Soil Preparation—Have soil tested for adequate levels of nitrogen, phosphorus, and potassium, and for proper acid-alkaline balance; maintain a 5.8–6.5 pH level by supplementing with peat, evergreen-needle compost, or garden sulfur.

Spacing—Set plants 12–14 inches (30–35 cm) apart in mounds 6 inches (15 cm) high, 6 inches (15 cm) wide, and 2 feet (60 cm) apart. In containers, plant 12–14 inches (30–35 cm) apart.

Care—Water in the morning to discourage disease and fungus, and check daily for signs of snails or slugs. Spread straw around plants as fruit starts to form to protect berries from direct contact with the soil. Remove straw immediately after harvest cycle ends, and cut plants back to the soil. In mild-winter climates, supply plants with potassium sulfate in winter. In severe-winter climates, transplant roots into containers filled with moist sawdust and place in a cool, dark place until spring.

Companion Plants—Low-growing plants that will not block sunlight, but not potatoes, eggplants, peppers, or tomatoes.

Avoid—Planting in a site that does not receive at least 6 hours of full sunlight per day.

Maturity—90–120 days from planting.

Harvest—When full-colored, sweet, plump, and full-flavored.

Storage—In vegetable compartment of refrigerator for 1–1 1/2 weeks, or frozen for up to 6 months for use in jams, jellies, or preserves.

Varieties—Alexandria, Alpine, Big Boy, Big Red, Cavendish, Dunlap, Early Glow, Ever Red, Fort Laramie, Guardian, Gurney's Giant, Ogallala, Ozark Beauty, Quinault, Ruegen Improved, Salva, September Sweet, Sequoia, Shortcake, Sparkle, Sure Crop, Sweetheart, Temptation, Tri Star, Tribute, White Alpine.

Tip—Strawberries are excellent candidates for small-space gardens; try terracotta pots, tiered planters, and other decorative plantings.

Bok Choy   —See Chinese Cabbage, Pak Choy, Celery Cabbage

Broccoli   *(Easy)*—Featuring broad leaves and a thick stalk, broccoli grows in tight clusters of tiny blue-green flower buds referred to as "heads." At maturity, plants are 2–3 feet (60–90 cm) tall and 2 feet (60 cm) in circumference. The size of the head varies by type (single, large head, or small head, which has multiple shoots). This cool-season member of the cole family is the easiest of the family to grow. It is subject to bolting in warm temperatures or when sunlight hours lengthen.

Yield—Allow 2–4 plants per household member.

Planting Time—Start indoors 5–6 weeks before the last frost. Transplant 2–3 weeks later after hardening for 4–5 days. In mild-winter and reverse-season climates, in autumn.

Planting Soil Temperature—50–85°F (10–29°C).

Growing Temperature—45–75°F (7–24°C).

Soil Preparation—Have soil tested for adequate levels of nitrogen (should be medium), phosphorus, and potassium (both should be high) and for proper acid-alkaline balance; maintain a 6.0–6.8 pH level by supplementing with compost. Change planting location annually to avoid soil nitrogen depletion.

Spacing—Sow seeds 1/4–1/2 inch (6-12 mm) deep, 2 inches (5 cm) apart in all directions or, if planting in rows, make rows 24–30 inches (60–75 cm) apart. Thin plants to 14–18 inches (35-45 cm) apart.

Care—Keep soil moist and free of weeds by mulching around plants. Water to maintain constant soil moisture, neither too dry nor too damp.

Companion Plants—Beets, celery, herbs, onions, and potatoes, but not pole beans, strawberries, or tomatoes.

Avoid—Overhead watering and planting in areas exposed to more than 2 hours per day of direct sunlight.

Maturity—55–85 days for transplants; 70–100 days for seed.

Harvest—When buds are still tight and green, cutting the main stem below the head to leave secondary shoots for smaller heads to develop.

Storage—In vegetable compartment of refrigerator for up to 2 weeks, or frozen (after blanching) for up to 3 months.

Varieties—Arcadia, Bonanza, Citation, DeCicco, Early Dividend, Emperor, Eureka, Green Comet, Green Goliath, Green Jewel, Green Valiant, Italian Sprouting, Land Mark, Legend, Love Me Tender, Marathon, Minaret, Packman, Paragon, Pinnacle Premium Crop, Purple Sprouting, Raab Spring, Rapine, Saga, Salad, ShoGun, Small Miracle, Sprinter, Super Blend, Super Dome, Thompson, Violet Queen, Waltham.

Tip—After harvesting, soak broccoli heads for a few minutes in warm water, vinegar, and salt to remove pests. Dry thoroughly before refrigeration.

Brussels Sprouts

(Moderate)—This cool-season member of the Cole family grows small, cabbage-shaped sprouts up a thick stalk featuring broad leaves. The sprouts mature from the bottom up, but if you pinch the stalk back at about 20 inches (50 cm) in height, they will all mature at about the same time (though yielding a smaller harvest). If a plant is allowed to grow to full height, it will reach about 3 feet (0.9 m). Cool temperatures experienced once the sprouts have formed will intensify and sweeten their flavor. Fresh Brussels sprouts provide an excellent appetizer when sliced and accompanied with a vegetable dip.

Yield—Allow 1–2 plants per household member.

Planting Time—Start indoors 16–20 weeks before the last frost. Transplant 4–6 weeks later after hardening for 5–7 days [see Hardening, pg. 179]. In mild-winter or reverse-season climates, in autumn, after late summer heat has ended.

Planting Soil Temperature—50–85°F (10–29°C).

Growing Temperature—45–75°F (7–24°C).

Soil Preparation—Have soil tested for adequate levels of nitrogen, phosphorus, and potassium and for proper acid-alkaline balance; maintain a 6.5–7.5 pH level by supplementing with compost. Change the planting location annually to prevent soil depletion.

Spacing—Sow seeds 1/4–1/2 inch (6–12 mm) deep, 2 inches (5 cm) apart in each direction, or in rows spaced 24–30 inches (60–75 cm) apart. Space transplants or thin seedlings to 12–18 inches (30–45 cm) apart

Care—Water at base of plants and keep soil moist and free of weeds by mulching.

Companion Plants—Beets, celery, herbs, onions, and potatoes, but not pole beans, strawberries, or tomatoes.

Avoid—Overmature sprouts; flavor is best when buds are small and tight.

Maturity—80–90 days for transplants; 100–110 days for seed.

Harvest—When sprouts are 1–1 1/2 inches (25–38 mm) in diameter, cutting at base of stem. In late autumn, cut the stalks and hang in a cool, dry spot to prolong enjoyment of fresh-picked Brussels sprouts. Note that tender young leaves found growing between the sprouts may be eaten as greens.

Storage—In vegetable compartment of refrigerator for 3–4 weeks, or frozen (after blanching) for up to 4 months.

Varieties—Bubbles, Catskill, Early Half Tall, Jade Cross, Long Island Improved, Oliver, Prince Marvel, Royal Marvel, Rubine, Seven Hills, Tasty Nuggets, Valiant.

Tip—Cutting off the top 6 inches (15 cm) of each plant 1 month before harvest time will mature all sprouts at once; however, the best flavor comes after a light frost, so don't take out the plants too soon. Water the evening before harvest for mildest flavor.

C **Cabbage** *(Easy)*—This cool-season mainstay of the cole family comes in a variety of colors, head shapes, and sizes. In addition to the standard green are the red and savoy, which are milder in flavor; the miniature, if space is a concern; and the ornamental, for its sheer beauty. Using methods of succession planting [See Succession Planting, pg. 114] will allow for a continuous variety throughout the entire growing season.

Yield—Allow 4–8 plants per household member.

Planting Time—In cold-winter climates, start indoors 4–6 weeks before the last frost has passed; transplant to the garden after hardening for 5–7 days. In mild-winter climates, start outdoors as soon as the soil can be worked. In such climates, seed may be sown in late summer for a winter or spring harvest. In reverse-season climates, plant in autumn once the summer heat has passed.

Planting Soil Temperature—45–90°F (7–32°C).

Growing Temperature—45–75°F (7–24°C), but may withstand light frost. Tends to bolt above 80°F (27°C).

Soil Preparation—Have soil tested for adequate levels of nitrogen, phosphorus, and potassium and for proper acid-alkaline balance; maintain a 6.5–7.5 pH level by supplementing with organic compost.

Spacing—Sow seeds ¹/₂ inch (12 mm) deep and 1 inch (2.5 cm) apart in all directions, or in rows that are 2–4 feet (60–120 cm) apart. Thin plants to 15–24 inches (38–60 cm) apart.

"Training is everything. The peach was once a bitter almond; cauliflower is nothing but cabbage with a college education."

Mark Twain

Care—Water at base of plants and keep soil moist and free of weeds by mulching. Failure to water evenly may cause stunted or cracked heads. Fertilize when plants are established with a fertilizer high in nitrogen, such as 10–3–3. Rotate to new locations annually to avoid soil depletion and prevent damage from disease and pests.

Companion Plants—Beets, celery, fragrant herbs, onions, and potatoes, but not pole beans, strawberries, or tomatoes.

Avoid—Planting in areas exposed to more than 3 hours per day of direct sunlight.

Maturity—50–100 days for transplants; 70–120 weeks for seed.

Harvest—When heads are filled out, firm, and 4–10 inches (10–25 cm) in diameter at base of stem.

Storage—In vegetable compartment of refrigerator for 3–4 months or cured with brine as sauerkraut and canned for up to 1 year.

Varieties—*Early*: Bergkabis, Charmant, Danish Ballhead, Derby Day, Discovery, Dynamo, Early Jersey Wakefield, Golden Acre, Jingan, Julius, Mini Cole, Parel, Primo, Stonehead.

Varieties—*Red*: Barteolo, Bentley, Cardinal, Copenhagen Market Red, Lasso, Lennox, Mammoth Red Rock, Red Acre, Red Debut, Red Drumhead, Red Rodan, Red Rookie, Rona, Rougette, Ruby Perfection, Solid Red.

Varieties—*Midseason*: Blue Vantage, Copenhagen Market, Fortuna, Savoy.

Varieties—*Winter*: Brunswick, Danish Ballhead, Gloria, January King, Late Flat Dutch, Savonarch, Solid Blue, Wivoy.

Tip—Pickled or blanched leaves, rolled around a spicy ground meat filling, produce savory cabbage rolls.

Carrots *(Easy)*—This popular cool-season vegetable is grown for its orange root, which reaches 3–10 inches (7.5–25 cm) in length depending on the variety. Though the standard variety is tapered, other varieties come in cylindrical and ball shapes. Carrots adapt to a variety of growing conditions and, if properly planted, can provide a continuous harvest over several months. They are an excellent source of beta-carotene, a nutrient recognized for health benefits.

Yield—Allow 30 plants per household member.

Planting Time—In early spring, early summer, midsummer, and even late summer, except in the northernmost tier of states and Canada. In reverse-season climates, in autumn, winter, and early spring.

Planting Soil Temperature—40–85°F (4–29°C).

Growing Temperature—45–75°F (7–24°C).

Soil Preparation—Have soil tested for adequate levels of nitrogen, phosphorus, and potassium and for acid-alkaline balance; maintain a 5.5–6.8 pH level by supplementing with peat, evergreen-needle compost, or garden sulfur. A light topcoat of wood ash will ensure the potassium needed for optimum growth. Make sure soil is loose, clod free and rock free, and drains well.

Spacing—Sow seeds ¼–½ inch (6–12 mm) deep, ½ inch (12 mm) apart in all directions, or in rows 12–24 inches (30–60 cm) apart. Thin plants to 4 inches (10 cm) apart in beds and 2 inches (5 cm) apart in rows.

Care—Keep soil moist and free of weeds by mulching around plants after they are 2–3 inches (5–7.5 cm) tall. Mulching also prevents chlorophyll discoloration at the top of the carrot root.

Companion Plants—Chives, onions, leeks, tomatoes, peas, and rosemary, but not dill.

Avoid—Using fresh manure in the soil mix.

Maturity—50–80 days; 30–40 days for baby carrots.

Harvest—When fingerlong for tapered varieties; ¾ inch (19 mm) in diameter for round varieties.

Storage—In mild climates, leave in soil until ready for use. In cold-winter climates, dig in late autumn and, with soil clinging to the hair roots, pack in damp hardwood chips in a cool, dark place. In vegetable compartment of refrigerator for 1–3 months; frozen after slicing and blanching for up to 6 months; or pickled in vinegar brine (after boiling) for up to 1 year.

Varieties—*Tapered (Long)*: Apache, Blaze, Caro-Choice, Cheyenne, Condor, Discovery, Eagle, Fanci Pak, Goliath, Healthmaster, Imperator, King Midas, Long Red Surrey, Navajo, Orangette, Spartan Premium, Sunrise, Tamino, Touchon.

Varieties—*Tapered (Medium)*: Armstrong, Artist, Bolero Hybrid, Caroline, Coreless Amsterdam, Danvers, Kuroda, Mokum, Nanco, Nantes, Nantes Tip Top, Napoli, Nelson, Nevis, Orange Rocket, Park's Eurosweet, Presto, Primo, Royal Chantenay, Scarlet Keeper, Spartan Bonus, Sweetness II, Tendersweet, Tim Tom, Toudo.

Varieties—*Tapered (Short)*: Amador, Chantenay Red Chord, Early Scarlet Intermediate, Imperial Chantenay, Kinko, Kuroda, Little Finger, Minicor, Short 'n Sweet.

Varieties—*Ball Shaped*: Marche de Paris, Parisian Rondo, Parmex, Partima, Thumbelina.

Tip—Short, round varieties generally are easier to grow and tend to be sweeter than the tapered varieties.

Cauliflower and Broccoflower

(Moderate)—These cool-season vegetables consist of many small, tightly formed, curd-shaped clusters that comprise the edible head. Known primarily for its mostly white or cream color, cauliflower also comes in purple and green varieties. A hybrid cross between broccoli and cauliflower with characteristics of both, broccoflower bears distinctive green heads. Both are finicky about growing temperature.

Yield—Allow 1–2 plants per household member.

Planting Time—In cold-winter climates, in early spring to midsummer. In mild-winter climates, in autumn, after summer heat has ended, to winter. In reverse-season climates, in late autumn to early winter.

Planting Soil Temperature—65–85°F (18–29°C).

Growing Temperature—45–75°F (7–24°C), optimally 60–65°F (15–18°C).

Soil Preparation—Have soil tested for proper levels of nitrogen, phosphorus, and potassium and for proper acid-alkaline balance; maintain a 6–6.8 pH level by supplementing with organic compost. Make sure soil is loose and drains well.

Spacing—Sow seeds ½ inch (12 mm) deep, 1 inch (2.5 cm) apart, in rows 2–3 feet (60–90 cm) apart. Thin plants to 15–24 inches (38–60 cm) apart.

Care—Keep soil moist by mulching around plants and cultivate to keep beds free of weeds. Tie leaves of non-self-blanching varieties over developing heads when heads are about 2 inches (5 cm) wide to protect them from the sun and ensure a white color. Check at least weekly for insects, pests, or disease.

Companion Plants—Beets, celery, herbs, onions, and potatoes, but not pole beans, strawberries, or tomatoes.

Avoid—Direct sunlight; cauliflower and broccoflower prefer semishaded conditions.

Maturity—55–80 days for transplants; 70–120 days for seed.

Harvest—When heads are firm and reach 4–8 inches (10–20 cm) in diameter.

Storage—In vegetable compartment of refrigerator for 2–3 weeks; frozen (after blanching) for up to 4 months; pickled in vinegar and brine and canned for up to 1 year.

Varieties—*White*: Amazing, Arbon, Arctic, Avalanche, Candid Charm, Cashmere, Cumberland, Dominant, Fremont, Inca Winter, Incline, Majestic, Mantono, Minuteman, Ravella, Rushmore, Serrano, Sierra Nevada, Sira, Snow Ball, Snow Crown, Snow Grace, Snow King, Snow Peak, Solide, Starbright, White Rock, White Sails, Yukon.

Varieties—*Purple*: Burgundy Queen, Early Purple Sicilian, Purple Cape, Rosalind, Violet Queen.

Varieties—*Green and Broccoflower*: Alverda, Brocoverde, Chartreuse, Green Goddess.

Tip—If your cool-weather season is short, try growing fast-maturing varieties, such as Rosalind, Snow Crown, and Violet Queen, which require just 55–60 days when grown from transplants.

Celery Cabbage

—See Chinese Cabbage, Pak or Bok Choy, Celery Cabbage

Celery, Celeriac

(Difficult)—These tall, leafy, cool-season vegetables are grown for the stalk of the former and the root of the latter. Today's celery descends from harsh-tasting ancestors found growing wild in marshes. Selection and hybridization have cultivated it into the mild and widely consumed vegetable enjoyed today, eaten raw as a snack and in salads, and cooked as an addition to stews and soups. Celery generally reaches a height of 15-20 inches (38–50 cm). Celeriac is a close relative with similar growth habits, cultivated primarily for its tasty, egg-shaped root. Both can be difficult to grow because of their simultaneous demanding requirements for cool weather and limited sunlight, and their specific care needs during growth. Celery requires 4 months of continuous cool growing season without excessively long sunlight hours to mature successfully.

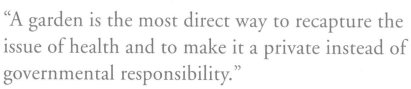

Yield—Allow 5 plants per household member.

Planting Time—In cold-winter climates, in early spring. In mild-winter climates, in winter, spring, or autumn. Not recommended for reverse-season climates due to its low tolerance for heat and dry conditions; experiment by trying late fall plantings, sowing seeds indoors about 3 months before outdoor planting and transplanting when 5–6 leaves have emerged.

> "A garden is the most direct way to recapture the issue of health and to make it a private instead of governmental responsibility."
>
> ***Wendell Berry***

Planting Soil Temperature—50–65°F (10–18°C).

Growing Temperature—60–70°F (16–21°C).

Soil Preparation—Have soil tested for adequate levels of nitrogen, phosphorus, and potassium and for proper acid-alkaline balance; maintain a 5.8–6.8 pH level by supplementing with organic compost.

Spacing—Sow 1/4–1/2 inch (5–10 mm) deep, 6–10 inches (15–25 cm) apart, in rows 2 feet (60 cm) apart. Seeds planted more closely should be thinned when they are well established.

Care—Water whenever soil becomes dry to the touch. Apply liquid fertilizer or mulch with organic compost a month after transplanting and water in. If celery is not a self-blanching variety, blanch when plants reach about 12 inches (30 cm) tall by mulching with soil or straw or by wrapping with paper. Celeriac does not require blanching since its foliage is not harvested.

Companion Plants—Lettuce, spinach, and English peas, but not pumpkins, cucumbers, or squash.

Avoid—Planting in areas that receive direct sun and excessive heat.

Maturity—90–120 days.

Harvest—When celery plant reaches 12–18 inches (30–45 cm) in height, cut outer stalks as needed; the plant will continue to produce stalks from the inside out. Harvest the entire plant by cutting at the root before frost or sustained heat. Harvest celeriac when roots reach 2–3 inches (5–7.5 cm) in diameter. Celery roots also may be harvested for use in salads and cooked dishes.

Storage—In vegetable compartment of refrigerator for 4–6 weeks.

Varieties—*Celery*: French Dinant, Giant Red, Golden Plume, Golden Self-blanching, Large Smooth Prague, Pascal, Red Stalk, Scarlet, Solid White, Utah, Ventura.

Varieties—*Celeriac*: Brilliant.

Tip—To increase the intensity of flavor, withhold water from celery plants for 2 days prior to harvest; mild flavor may be enhanced by watering 4–8 hours prior to harvest.

Chayote *(Easy)*—A member of the gourd family, chayote looks like an odd-shaped green pear and tastes like a squash with a mildly nutty flavor. A perennial vine, it grows best in areas with mild-winter climates and moderate summer temperatures such as the coastal regions of western North America and the Gulf Coast. These sprawling plants can reach 50 feet (15 m) or more in length and require good support because their fruit will suffer damage from direct soil contact.

Yield—Allow 1 vine per household of up to 4 persons.

Planting Time—In spring, after all danger of frost has passed.

Planting Soil Temperature—65–85°F (18–29°C).

Growing Temperature—65–80°F (18–27°C).

Soil Preparation—Have soil tested for adequate levels of nitrogen, phosphorus, and potassium and for proper acid-alkaline balance; maintain a 6.0–6.8 pH level by supplementing with organic compost. Make sure soil is loose and drains well.

Spacing—Set plants 6–8 inches (20–25 cm) deep, at least 10 feet (3 m) apart. Install sturdy trellises or wire supports able to support vines up to 50 feet (15 m) long.

Care—Keep soil moist, cultivate (taking care not to cut the plant's shallow, spreading roots), and fertilize with balanced fertilizer or organic compost monthly throughout growth. In colder climates, apply mulch 8–12 inches (20–30 cm) thick before cold weather sets in.

Companion Plants—Pumpkin, peppers, squash, and corn, but not celery, mint, or snap beans.

Avoid—Damaging vines; train them onto supports as they grow.

Maturity—Fruits in autumn of first season, annually thereafter in early autumn.

Harvest—When 4–6 inches (10–15 cm) in diameter.

Storage—In vegetable compartment of refrigerator for 4–6 weeks. Also may be canned for up to 1 year.

> "Nature is crafty, but for a good end."
>
> ### *Goethe*

Varieties—Cultivars adapted to specific regions are available; obtain recommendations from local nursery or garden store staff.

Tip—A wholly edible plant, its soft seeds may be sliced and eaten in salads or chopped and used as a nut substitute; the tender young vine tips may be eaten raw in salads or used in stir-fry dishes; the leaves may be steamed and eaten, and the tubers may be boiled or baked. Also remember to eat the chayote fruits, steamed or sautéed.

Chickpeas —See Beans, Garbanzo, Gram, or Chickpeas

Chicory, Belgian Endive, and Radicchio *(Moderate)*—These

leafy cool-season perennials are grown primarily for their leaves or root. The green leaves of chicory are a tasty addition to the salad bowl, while the dried and ground root may be used to substitute for or add its distinctive flavor to coffee. Radicchio is simply a broad-leafed red version of chicory with a biting, tangy flavor. Belgian endive bears dense, white leaves bearing a crisp texture and mildly bitter taste.

Yield—For chicory, allow 1–2 chicory plants per household member; for radicchio, 5–6 plants; for Belgian endive, 6–8 plants.

Planting Time—For chicory and Belgian endive, in cold-winter climates, in spring and early summer; for mild-winter climates, in autumn and winter; in reverse-season climates, in winter. Cooler temperatures produce a sweeter crop while warmer temperatures produce a slightly bitter flavor. For radicchio, in cold-winter climates, in spring or late spring; in mild-winter climates, in late summer or autumn; in reverse-season climates, in autumn. Plants tend to bolt if days are too long when heads begin to form. Cool weather causes radicchio to develop its distinctive purplish-red coloration and become milder in taste.

Planting Soil Temperature—50–85°F (10–29°C).

Growing Temperature—45–75°F (7–24°C).

Soil Preparation—Have soil tested for adequate levels of nitrogen, phosphorus, and potassium and for proper acid-alkaline balance; maintain a 5.0–6.8 pH level by supplementing with organic compost and garden sulfur.

Spacing—Sow seeds ¼ inch (6 mm) deep, 1–2 inches (2.5–5 cm) apart in rows 2–3 feet (60–90 cm) apart. Thin plants to 6–12 inches (15–30 cm) apart.

Care—Keep soil moist and cultivate to control weeds. Blanch around radicchio plants (mulch with porous matter to force upright growth and head formation and mound soil around each head). During periods of consistent heat, protect plant by installing shade cover fabric. Belgian endive harvests leaves for salads identically to chicory during its first year until frost is experienced. First, trim leaves to 1 inch (2.5 cm) from the stems. Dig carefully from the garden, transplant immediately into damp sand at a 45° angle so the tips are just covered, then store in a cool, dark location until they form the distinctive tight, pale-green, succulent heads typical of Belgian endive.

Companion Plants—Leafy green vegetables, including lettuce and spinach, but not peas or beans.

Avoid—Blanching while leaves are wet since this may cause the plant to rot.

Maturity—85–100 days.

Harvest—*Radicchio*: When heads are tightly formed and 3–5 inches (7.5–12 cm) in diameter, cutting at the base of the leaves. *Chicory*: When leaves are 5–6 inches (12–15 cm) in height, cutting 1 inch (25 mm) above the neck so the plant will resprout and provide continuous harvest. *Belgian endive*: When heads are tightly formed and 3–5 inches (7.5–12 cm) in diameter. If only leaves are cut, the plant will resprout and provide a continuous harvest.

Storage—*Chicory*: in vegetable compartment of refrigerator for 1 week; roots 4–5 months. *Radicchio* and *Belgian endive*: in vegetable compartment of refrigerator for 1 week.

Varieties—*Chicory*: Biondissima Trieste, Ceriolo, Dentarella, Puntarella, San Pasquale, Spadona, Sugar Loaf.

Varieties—*Radicchio*: Carmen, Castle Franco, Chioggia, Early Treviso, Giulio, Milan, Prima Rossa, Red Treviso, Red Verona, Rossa de Verona, Rossana Radicchio, Rouge de Trevise, Rouge de Veron.

Varieties—*Belgian endive*: Flash, Galla, Red C, Witloof Robin, Witloof Zoom.

Tip—Exclusive Belgian endive is really just the heart of chicory. If planting for the endive, simply tie the outer leaves of each chicory plant over the developing heads 2–3 weeks before harvesting.

Chinese Cabbage, Pak or Bok Choy, Celery Cabbage

(Easy)—These members of the mustard family produce tall, loose, crinkle-leafed heads and are notable for their milder- and sweeter-than-cabbage flavor. They are prime ingredients in many Asian dishes but also can substitute for regular cabbage in other cuisines. Cool-season vegetables, they are subject to bolting when garden temperatures rise and daylight hours lengthen, but even their flower buds are edible.

Yield—Allow 6–8 heads per household member, assuming up to 3 resprouts from each head after harvesting by cutting just above the base of the leaves; otherwise, sow 16–20 heads per household member.

Planting Time—In cold-winter climates, early summer; in mild-winter climates, mid-summer to early autumn; in reverse-season climates, autumn.

Planting Soil Temperature—40–85°F (4–29°C).

Growing Temperature—45–75°F (7–24°C).

Soil Preparation—Have soil tested for adequate levels of nitrogen, phosphorus, and potassium and for proper acid-alkaline balance; maintain 6.5–7.5 pH level by supplementing with garden lime.

Spacing—Sow seeds ½ inch (12 mm) deep, 4 inches (10 cm) apart, in rows 24–30 inches (60–75 cm) apart. Thin plants to 12–18 inches (30–45 cm) apart.

Care—Water whenever soil is dry to the touch.

Companion Plants—Cabbage, cauliflower, Brussels sprouts, and Chinese cabbage, but not tomatoes, peppers, okra or potatoes.

Avoid—Planting in exposed, hot locations that receive more than 6 hours per day of direct sunlight.

Maturity—50–85 days.

Harvest—When at least 5 inches (12 cm) tall, picking outside leaves sparingly. Pick again when sprouts mature.

Storage—In vegetable compartment of refrigerator for about 1 month, or blanched and frozen for 3–4 months.

Varieties—Blues, Bouquet, China Express, China Flash, China Pride, Jade Pagoda, Japanese White Celery Mustard, Joi Choi, Kasumi, Lei Choi, Lettuce Type, Mei Quing Choi, Michihli, Monument, Orient Express, Season Chinese, Summer Top, Tah Tsai, Tropical Delight.

Tip—The younger the leaves, the more subtle the flavor.

Chives, Garlic Chives

(Easy)—Cool-season perennials, these onion relatives are prized for their tangy, hollow green leaves rather than their roots. Chives grow to 18 inches (45 cm) tall and form colonies as expansive in area as permitted. Chives bloom in late spring or early summer—regular chives with a blue flower; garlic chives with white. They may be grown from seed, or planted by root division from an established chive colony, and are hardy to temperatures of –40°F (–40 °C).

Yield—Allow 1 bunching colony per household.

Planting Time—In spring after ground has warmed and is workable. In reverse-season climates, in autumn. Chives may also be grown indoors.

Planting Soil Temperature—35–65°F (2–18°C).

Growing Temperature—40–85°F (–40–29°C).

Soil preparation—Have soil tested for adequate levels of nitrogen, phosphorus, and potassium and for proper acid-alkaline balance; maintain a pH level of 6.0–6.8 by applying organic compost to native soil.

Spacing—Broadcast seeds over a 100-square-inch (650 cm²) area, cover with ¼–½ inch (6–12 mm) of loose potting soil, then compact the soil with the palms of your hands. To plant root divisions, purchase transplant stock or divide an existing chive cluster with a sharp garden spade or shovel. Trim the green tops, expose them 1 inch (25 mm) aboveground, and cover the entire planting with ½ inch (12 cm) of soil.

Care—Keep soil moist and shade plant from direct sun in hot climates with porous shade fabric installed on wooden supports. In cold winter climates, trim to the ground every autumn and fertilize with organic compost every spring; chives will grow through the winter in milder climates. If grown in a container, move indoors in extremely hot weather. Divide bunches every 3–4 years to maintain vitality of the colony.

Companion Plants—Cress and mint.

Avoid—Overharvesting before the young colonies become established.

Maturity—75–90 days.

Harvest—When 3–4 inches (7.5–10 cm) in height, clip one-third of the crop, allowing the rest to continue growing. Clip another third when 5–8 inches (13–20 cm) in height. Leave the final third to develop flowers and expand the colony through root division.

Storage—Most flavorful if used fresh. Chives also may be chopped and frozen in sealed plastic bags, or chopped and dried.

Varieties—Nonvarietal.

Tip—Chopped chives are used primarily as a flavor note on baked potatoes, in fresh green salads, and as a garnish for cream soups.

Collards

(Easy)—A member of the mustard family, collards are a leafy green that produces plants up to 3 feet (90 cm) tall and wide, with bluish-green leaves. Grown primarily in the South because it can tolerate the regional heat and grow well into late autumn, the plants also are quite frost hardy and actually improve in flavor after temperatures drop.

Yield—Allow 2–3 plants per household member.

Planting Time—In cold-winter climates, in spring, late summer or early autumn. In mild-winter climates, in spring. In reverse-season climates, in winter.

Planting Soil Temperature—50–85°F (10–29°C).

Growing Temperature—45–75°F (7–24°C).

Soil Preparation—Have soil tested for adequate levels of nitrogen, phosphorus, and potassium and for proper acid-alkaline balance; maintain a 5.5–6.8 pH level by supplementing with organic compost.

Spacing—Sow seeds 1/4 inch (6 mm) deep, 2 inches (5 cm) apart, in rows 3 feet (90 cm) apart. Thin plants to 15–18 inches (38–45 cm) apart.

Care—Fertilize soil with a balanced fertilizer or well-rotted manure before planting, then again 1 month later. Mulch surrounding soil with straw or clear plastic film in autumn.

Companion Plants—Tomatoes, southern peas, and peppers, but not celery, potatoes, or yams.

Avoid—Crowding; collards require ample space to produce abundantly.

Maturity—60–90 days.

Harvest—When about 12 inches (30 cm) tall.

Storage—In vegetable compartment of refrigerator for about 1 week.

Varieties—Blue Max, Champion, Georgia, Top Bunch, Vates.

Tip—When thinning, save trimmings as tender and tasty greens for salads or steaming.

Corn, Popcorn, Decorative Corn

(Moderate)—This member of the grass family, corn was first noticed by Europeans upon their discovery of the New World, and it now is a main staple food around the world. Stalks of sweet corn can reach heights of up to 9 feet (2.8 m) tall, with ears forming on the side of the stalk about three-quarters of the way up. The top of the stalk terminates in a flowering tassel that produces pollen, which is carried by the wind and pollinates silky threads on the ears. Each of the silks is connected to an unfertilized kernel; the ear develops as many kernels as the number of silks that were pollinated. Giving the cornstalk a little shake can aid this natural process and will produce fuller ears of corn. Other corn varieties include popcorn and decorative corn.

Yield—Allow 12–20 plants per household member.

Planting Time—In all climates, sow early, midseason, and late varieties in spring after the last danger of frost has passed for a continuous harvest throughout the growing season.

Planting Soil Temperature—50–90°F (10–32°C).

Growing Temperature—50–95°F (10–35°C).

Soil Preparation—Have soil tested for adequate levels of nitrogen, phosphorus, and potassium and for proper acid-alkaline balance; maintain a 5.8–6.8 pH level by supplementing with organic compost, well-rotted manure, and high-nitrogen fertilizer.

Spacing—Sow seeds 1–2 inches (2.5–5 cm) deep, 4–6 inches (10–15cm) apart, in at least 4 rows 2–3 feet (60–90 cm) apart to form a square. Thin to 12–18 inches (30–45 cm) apart.

Care—Keep soil moist and add high-nitrogen fertilizer or organic compost when stalks reach 12 inches (30 cm) in height; repeat when stalks are 30 inches (75 cm) in height.

Companion Plants—Potatoes, peas, beans, cucumbers, pumpkins, and squash, but not cane berries and pole beans.

Avoid—Planting in areas that do not receive at least 6 hours per day of direct sunlight; planting more than one variety closer than 20 feet (6 m) apart (preferably in 2-week intervals); or planting in rows perpendicular to prevailing winds.

Maturity—60–100 days.

Harvest—When silks turn brown and kernels yield a white milky fluid when pinched.

Storage—In vegetable compartment of refrigerato, for 2–4 days after plunging freshly picked ears into ice water to preserve sweetness by slowing the conversion of sugar in the kernels into starch, or in the freezer for 3–6 months after blanching on the cob, plunging into an ice bath, and cutting the kernels from the cob.

Varieties—*Sweet and Supersweet (Yellow)*: Bodacious, Buttergold, Earlivee, Early Sunglow, Golden Bantam, Illini Xtra-Sweet, Kandy King, Kandy Kwik, Northern Xtra-Sweet, Polarvee, Suger Buns, Tuxedo. *(White)*: Alpine, Argent, Divinity, How Sweet It Is, Platinum Lady, Pristine, Silver Queen, Sparkle, Stowell's Evergreen, Sugar Snow, Summer Sweet. *(Bicolored)*: Athos, Clockwork, Cotton Candy, Dancer, Delectable, Double Gem, Eagle, Fantasy, Honey & Cream, Jumpstart, Pilot, Quickie, Skyline, Sugar & Gold.

Varieties—*Popcorn*: Black, Chocolate Pop, Early Pink, Japanese Hulless, Pennsylvania Butter-flavored, Robust, Tom Thumb, Top Pop, White Cloud.

Varieties—*Decorative/Indian*: Calico Indian, Fiesta, Indian Fingers, Laser, Little Jewels, Mini-Blue, Mini-Pink, Painted Mountain, Strawberry, Wampum.

Tip—Late-season varieties have larger kernels, sweeter flavor, and stronger growth habits than early varieties.

Coss —See Lettuce, Romaine

Cucumbers

(Easy)—Most often cucumbers are cylindrical, with a smooth dark-green skin bearing prickly protrusions and a whitish crisp, juicy interior. They usually grow on vines, but some hybrid bush varieties also have been developed. Cucumbers come in many varieties, including green, yellow, white, seedless, spineless, and burpless, plus such novelties as the round, yellow lemon, and odd-shaped, ribbed Armenian. Some extremely succulent hothouse varieties are seedless and self-fertilizing, and are grown from embryonic genetic clones or cuttings—buy them as nursery transplants. Pickling cucumbers are picked when as short as 2 inches (5 cm), compared to slicing varieties, which are picked at lengths as great as 15 inches (38 cm). So-called *Gynoecious* cucumbers require a male pollinator plant, usually included in seed packages; a single male plant will fertilize 6 or so female plants.

Yield—For eating, allow 6 plants of a single variety or mixed varieties per household member. For pickling varieties, 3–4 plants per quart.

Planting Time—In spring, after all danger of frost has passed.

Planting Soil Temperature—60–90°F (16–32°C).

Growing Temperature—60–90°F (16–32°C).

Soil Preparation—Have soil tested for adequate levels of nitrogen, phosphorus, and potassium and for proper acid-alkaline balance; maintain a 5.5–6.8 pH level by supplementing with organic compost.

Spacing—Sow 4–6 seeds 1 inch (30–35 cm) deep in mounds 16 inches (40 cm) in diameter, raised 10 inches (25 cm) above the soil surface, spaced 4–6 feet (1.2–1.8 m) apart. With your palms, compress each mound's soil firmly around the seeds. Thin to 2–3 seedlings per mound. Set trellises or support wires 18–24 inches (45–60 cm) in height if gardening in a small space.

Care—Weed every 7–10 days. When watering, fill the moat surrounding each mound until water stands in the basin. Do not worry if vines temporarily wilt on hot days—they will recover overnight.

Companion Plants—Beans, corn, peas, pumpkins, and squash, but not potatoes and herbs.

Avoid—Disease by planting resistant varieties. Cucumbers are sold graded with letter codes indicating their resistance to common diseases, including leaf spot (LS), anthracnose (A), wilt (BW), mosaic (M), scab (S), and mildew (DM). Prevent cross-pollination between varieties by separating plantings 6–8 feet (2–2.5 m) apart. Also avoid allowing soil to completely dry.

Maturity—55–65 days.

Harvest—*Slicing*: when 6–10 inches (15–25 cm) in length. *Pickling (sweet or baby dills)*: when 1–6 inches (2.5–15 cm) in length; *(regular dills)*: when 3–4 inches (7.5–10 cm) in length. English or Armenian varieties grown in a hothouse or under glass should be harvested when 12–15 inches (30–38 cm) in length.

Storage—*Pickling* and *slicing cucumbers*: in refrigerator for 1–2 weeks. *Hothouse cucumbers*: in refrigerator for 1–2 days. Pickled cucumbers may be stored for up to 1 year.

Varieties—*Pickling*: Bush Baby, Calypso, Cross Country, Edmonson, Green Spear, Lafayette, Little Leaf, Napoleon, Pik-Rite, Regal, Salty, Spear-It, Sumter.

Varieties—*Slicing*: Ashley, Comet II, Dasher II, General Lee, Jazzer, Marketmore, Medalist, Panther, Poinsett, Raider, Revenue, Slice King, Spacemaster, Speedway, Supersett, Sweet Slice, Tasty Green, Thunder, Ultraslice, White Wonder.

Varieties—*Novelty*: Armenian, Crystal Apple White Spine, English Telegraph, Lemon, Painted Serpent, Suyo Long, White Wonder.

Varieties—*Bush*: Fanfare, Salad Bush

Tip—Harvest 3–4 times each week as cukes mature to allow the setting of new flowers and fruit. Hot caps used in cold-winter climates will encourage early sprouting and flowering.

Curly Endive   —See Endive, Curly

Cress   —See Watercress (Cress, Garden Cress, and Early Winter Cress)

Eggplant

(Moderate)—Large, egg-shaped, warm-season vegetables with smooth, glossy skin, eggplant are commonly deep purple, though varietals have been developed in yellow, green, and white. A tomato and pepper cousin, this annual resembles the pepper both in appearance and growth habit, ranging in length from 5–12 inches (13–30 cm) in length. The heavy fruit of full-size varieties—a single eggplant can reach 2 pounds (0.75 kg) or more—burdens the bushy, foliage-bearing stem, requiring support once the plant becomes heavy with developing fruit. This attractive addition to any garden lends itself well to Greek and Italian dishes featuring cheese, tomatoes, onions, and garlic. It is a common substitute for pasta in lasagna and other Mediterranean casserole dishes.

Yield—Allow 1–2 plants per household member.

Planting Time—Sow seeds indoors 6–8 weeks before temperatures reach 65–70°F (18–21°C). In cold-winter climates, harden and transplant when seedlings bear at least three true leaves and soil temperature reaches 65°F (18°C); soil may be warmed by adding a black plastic cover.

Planting Soil Temperature—60–85°F (18–29°C).

Growing Temperature—65–90°F (18–32°C).

Soil Preparation—Have soil tested for adequate levels of nitrogen, phosphorus, and potassium and for proper acid-alkaline balance; maintain a 5.5–6.8 pH level by applying organic compost. Make sure soil is loose and drains well.

Spacing—Sow seeds 1/4–1/2 inch (6–12 mm) deep, 3–5 inches (7.5–13 cm) apart, in rows 36 inches (90 cm) apart, thinning successful plants to 24 inches (60 cm) apart. Transplants 6–8 weeks old should be spaced 24–30 inches (60–75 cm) apart.

Care—Fertilize in first and second months with liquid fertilizer or organic compost mulch to keep soil moist and free of weeds. Thin fruit of large varieties to one per branch. In the desert southwest, protect with shade covers or plant in early spring to avoid temperatures above 100°F (38°C). In marginal climates, plant in containers that allow the soil to retain heat and can be moved to protected locations.

Companion Plants—Bush beans and southern peas, which naturally fix nitrogen in their roots, but not tomatoes or corn.

Avoid—Planting where peppers, tomatoes, potatoes, or eggplants were grown during the past 2 years, and cool locations because blossoms will drop if temperatures fall below 50°F (10°C).

Maturity—100–140 days from seeds; 60–95 days from transplants.

Harvest—When glossy, firm, and full-colored—avoid overripening.

Storage—In vegetable compartment of refrigerator for about 1 week.

Varieties—*Purple*: Agora, Baby Bell, Bambino, Black Beauty, Black Bell, Blacknite, Classy Chassis, Dusky, Early Black Egg, Highbush Select, Imperial Black Beauty, Long Purple, Mini Finger, Short Tom, Slim Jim, Vernal, Violetta Lunga, Violette Di Firenze, Vittori. *Green*: Apple Green, Asian Bride, Thai Long Green. *White*: Alba, Casper, Easter Egg, Ghost Buster, Osterei, Snowy White, White Beauty, White Sword. *Red*: Machiaw, Neon, Rosita, Turkish Gem, Turkish Italian Orange. *Bicolor*: Italian Pink, Listada De Gandia, Louisiana Long Green, Rosa Bianca. *Oriental*: Ichiban, Millionaire, Osaka.

Tip—For short-season climates, plant fast-maturing varieties.

Endive—Belgian   —See Chicory

Endive—Curly and Escarole

(Easy)—Endive is a ruffled-leaf vegetable grown for its strong flavor; by contrast, escarole is smooth-leaved but similar in taste. Both are cool-season annuals that bear light-green leaves in the center, gradating to dark-green outer leaves. These tasty additions to the salad bowl may be blanched, which gives them a paler appearance and slightly milder flavor. Though commonly associated with chicory or Belgian and French endives [see Chicory, Belgian Endive, Radicchio, pg. 328], there is no relation between the two species. Endive and escarole are members of the sunflower family and commonly are carefree plants with few disease problems.

Yield—Allow 2–3 plants per household member.

Planting Time—In cool-season climates, in early spring as soon as danger of frost has passed, to produce a sweeter-tasting crop. In warm-season climates, in early autumn, to produce the highly prized, bitter-tasting crop preferred by many salad lovers. In mild-winter and reverse-season climates, in late autumn, which will yield leafy greens throughout the winter.

Planting Soil Temperature—50–85°F (10–29°C).

Growing Temperature—50–80°F (10–27°C).

Soil Preparation—Have soil tested for adequate levels of nitrogen, phosphorus, and potassium and for proper acid-alkaline balance; maintain a 5.0–6.8 pH level by supplementing with organic compost. Make sure soil is loose and drains well.

Spacing—Sow seeds ¼ inch (6 mm) deep, 1–2 inches (2.5–5 cm) apart, in rows 2–3 feet (60–90 cm) apart, thinning successful plants to 6–12 inches (15–30 cm) apart.

Care—Keep soil moist but not sodden and free of weeds. To blanch, tie outer leaves loosely around the heart of the plant when 4–5 inches (10–13 cm) tall.

Companion Plants—Radish, turnip, and parsnip, but not pumpkin or squash.

Avoid—Blanching while foliage is wet, which will cause fungal disease.

Maturity—85–100 days.

Harvest—When 5–6 inches (12–15 cm) in length, 1 inch (25 mm) above the soil, to allow plants to resprout and provide a continuous harvest. Alternatively, cut only outer leaves as needed.

Storage—In vegetable compartment of refrigerator for 2 weeks.

Varieties—*Endive*: Frisan, Galia, Green Curled Ruffec, President, Salad King, Tosca, Tres Fine Endive.

Varieties—*Escarole*: Broad-leaf Vatavian, Coral, Florida Deep Heart, Full Heart Batavian, Sinco, Sinco Escarole.

Tip—Blanching is worth the effort for the mild, distinctive taste it lends to both escarole and endive.

Fava Beans —See Beans, Fava, Horse, or Windsor

Garlic *(Moderate)*—A bulb plant related to the onion, garlic is made up of heads, protectively wrapped in white papery skin, that contain clusters of individual cloves. If used raw, a little garlic goes a long way, but when cooked, it makes a tasty addition to many dishes. Roasted garlic can be used as a mild-flavored spread for appetizers. In addition to its strong flavor, garlic is thought by herbalists to possess a number of curative and protective powers; in fact, references to garlic appear as far back as pre-biblical times in many cultures. Modern medicine has documented garlic's beneficial effects on the immune system, as well as its efficacy in reducing cholesterol levels and blood pressure. Garlic is susceptible to a soil-borne pest, however, and may be difficult to raise in areas with endemic infestation—check with your local USDA extension office to learn whether your area is affected.

Yield—Allow 12–16 plants per household member.

Planting Time—In cold-winter climates, in early spring and again in early autumn. In mild-winter climates, in spring and autumn. In reverse-season climates, in winter.

Planting Soil Temperature—35–90°F (2–32°C).

Growing Temperature—45–85°F (7–29°C). Garlic will tolerate a wide temperature range; however, it requires two months of 32–50°F (0–10°C) temperatures once its stalk has developed to promote bulb growth.

Soil Preparation—Have soil tested for adequate levels of nitrogen, phosphorus, and potassium and for proper acid-alkaline balance; maintain a 5.5–6.8 pH level by supplementing with organic compost that does not contain garlic or onion waste. Make sure soil is loose and drains well.

Spacing—Set large single cloves 1 inch (25 mm) deep, 4–8 inches (10–15 cm) apart, in rows 15 inches (38 cm) apart. Reserve the small center cloves from each head for cooking—do not plant them. Avoid planting grocery store garlic; it likely has been treated to prevent sprouting.

Care—Keep soil moist and free of weeds. Pinch off all blossoms as they form to promote maturity. After flowers form and stems yellow, bend the stems sharply to the ground, taking care not to break them. This process, known as "lodging," promotes bulb formation and the drying and withering of plant tops. Discontinue regular watering about one month later, except in very hot, dry climates, where soil moisture should be maintained.

Companion Plants—Beets, lettuce, strawberries, summer savory, and tomatoes, but not beans and peas.

Avoid—Planting in the same location in subsequent seasons [see Planning Plantings, pg. 99].

Maturity—90 or more days, depending on climate.

Harvest—2–3 weeks after lodging, when heads are fully formed and pull easily from the stem. Brush off any clinging soil and allow heads to dry for 3–4 weeks in a protected outdoor space until outer skins turn papery.

Storage—In a well-ventilated container or nylon net bag in a dry, cool, and dark place. As cloves are used, store in porous terracotta containers. Peeled garlic cloves also may be canned or frozen.

Varieties—Brown Tempest, California White, Chesnok Red, Chet's Italian Purple, Elephant, Georgian Crystal, German Extra Hearty, Hillside Rocambole Og, Inchelium Red, Italian Purple Skin, Leningrad, Lorz Italian, Machashi, Mild French Silverskin, New York White, Polish White, Red German, Red Touch, Romanian Red, Spanish Rojo, Yugoslavian.

Tip—Partially dried garlic may be braided into decorative strands for short-term storage.

Gourds *(Easy)*—Though closely related to squash and pumpkin, most gourds are inedible. Because they naturally grow in unusual shapes, sizes, and colors, the primary use of these warm-season annuals is decorative. Some may be dried for making bowls, rustic canteens, and ladles; others may be carved into musical instruments; and one variety, "luffa," is grown commercially for making exfoliating sponges. Plant each variety of gourd in an isolated area of the garden since cross-pollination will produce hybrids with shapes, sizes, colors, and flesh much different from the expected.

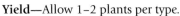

Yield—Allow 1–2 plants per type.

Planting Time—In cold-winter climates, in spring, after all danger of frost has passed. In extremely hot, dry climates such as the desert southwest, in late winter. In short-season climates, start indoors about 4 weeks before transplanting.

Planting Soil Temperature—68–86°F (20–30°C).

Growing Temperature—50–90°F (10–32°C). For best results, nighttime temperatures should remain warm throughout flowering and fruiting.

Soil Preparation—Have soil tested for adequate levels of nitrogen, phosphorus, and potassium and for proper acid-alkaline balance; maintain a 5.5–6.8 pH level. Add sand and abundant decomposed organic matter to aid rooting.

Spacing—Sow 2–3 seeds, 2 inches (5 cm) deep, 12 inches (30 cm) apart, in rows or hills 4 feet (1.2 m) apart, thinning successful plants to 2–4 feet (60–120 cm) apart.

Care—If space is a consideration, set trellises or support wires 3–5 feet (90–120 cm) in height at the time of planting. Water into basins or moats when soil is dry to the touch, taking care not to wet foliage, flowers, or developing fruit.

Companion Plants—Corn, beans and peas, but not pumpkins, squash, or melons.

Avoid—Direct soil contact of fruits.

Maturity—85–100 days from seeds; 55–70 days from transplants.

Harvest—When stems turn tan, after vines have dried, but before the first frost. Complete drying in a warm, protected space until seeds rattle when the gourd is shaken.

Storage—When dried, gourds can be stored indefinitely.

Varieties—Birdhouse, Chinese Okra, Dipper, Hercules Club, Luffa, Pear Bicolor, Round Orange, Spoon, Turk Turban, Warted.

Tip—To extend preservation and enhance beauty, coat dried gourds with shellac or other clear finish. To process luffa sponges, cook mature fruit in slowly boiling water 4–5 hours, or soak in cold water for several days. When sodden and pliable, remove skin and flesh from the tough, fibrous core of the gourd. Bleach, rinse thoroughly, trim, and dry in a protected, sunny spot.

CAUTION: Household bleach contains sodium hypochlorite, which is harmful if swallowed or in direct contact with the eyes; use care when handling.

Gram Beans —See Beans, Garbanzo, Gram, or Chickpeas

Ground Cherry —See Husk Tomatoes, Ground Cherries, or Tomatillos

Horse Beans —See Beans, Fava, Horse, or Windsor

H

Horseradish *(Easy)*—This perennial plant, which grows wild in many parts of the world and features a brownish, rough skin and white interior, is prized for its pungent flavor when added to relishes, or as a dry, powdered seasoning. Horseradish is best grown in containers, due to its spreading habit. Plant it as an annual; second-year and older roots develop tough fibers and are not as flavorful as those newly grown.

Yield—Allow 1 plant per household.

Planting Time—In spring, when all danger of frost has passed.

Planting Soil Temperature—45–85°F (7–29°C).

Growing Temperature—40-75°F (4–24°C). Prefers cool, moist conditions.

Soil Preparation—Have soil tested for adequate levels of nitrogen, phosphorus, and potassium and for proper acid-alkaline balance; maintain a 5.5–6.8 pH level by adding garden sulfur, if needed. Add abundant sand or compost to soil to permit easy digging of roots at harvest.

Spacing—Set out an 8–14-inch (20–35 cm) root cutting at an angle of 30°, 3–4 inches (7.5–10 cm) deep, and cover with 2–3 inches (5–7.5 cm) of soil. If planting more than 1 root, space 30–36 inches (75–90 cm) apart. Set wooden, metal, or masonry borders at least 24 inches deep around the bed to restrict unintentional spreading.

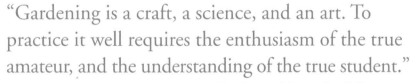

"Gardening is a craft, a science, and an art. To practice it well requires the enthusiasm of the true amateur, and the understanding of the true student."

Louise and James Bush-Brown

Care—Keep soil moist at all times and fertilize monthly with organic compost or balanced chemical fertilizer.

Companion Plants—Potatoes and yams, but not beets.

Avoid—Leaving pieces of harvested roots in the soil unless you want more plants.

Maturity—140–160 days.

Harvest—When leaves are about 12 inches (30 cm) long and roots are 3–4 inches (7.5–10 cm) in diameter. Carefully expose root and cut 12-inch (30 cm) sections, covering the remainder with soil for additional growth and later harvest.

Storage—In vegetable compartment of refrigerator for 10–12 months or packed in damp sawdust and placed in a dark, cool place for replanting in the spring. Also may be pickled or made into relishes.

Varieties—Nonvarietal root vegetable.

Tip—To make tangy horseradish relish, grind and combine 3 parts of the root with 1 part boiling white wine vinegar seasoned with a dash of salt. Keeps 3–6 months refrigerated.

Husk Tomatoes, Ground Cherries, or Tomatillos

(Moderate)—This warm-season plant bearing fruit about the size of a cherry tomato is covered with a green papery husk and resembles the beautiful orange Chinese lantern plant, a close cousin. Depending upon the variety, peeling back the husk reveals a green or purplish, seedy solid fruit that tastes either sweet or tangy. The bush reaches heights of 18–48 inches (45–120 cm), and the fruit should not be harvested until the husks become tan-colored and the fruit drops from the plant. Depending upon the variety, the pulp is suitable for jams, pies, or salsas. All varieties cultivate well in similar conditions to those required for tomatoes but without the need for consistent heat.

Yield—Allow 1–2 plants per household member.

Planting Time—Start plants indoors 4–6 weeks before transplanting. In warm climates, in spring, 4–6 weeks after the last danger of frost has passed.

Planting Soil Temperature—65–85°F (18–29°C).

Growing Temperature—50-75°F (10–24°C). Prefers cooler temperatures.

Soil Preparation—Have soil tested for adequate levels of nitrogen, phosphorus, and potassium and for proper acid-alkaline balance; maintain a 6.0–6.8 pH level by supplementing with organic compost.

Spacing—Sow seeds 1/8 inch (3 mm) deep, 2 inches (50 mm) apart, in rows 2 feet (60 cm) apart, thinning successful plants to 10 inches (25 cm) apart.

Care—Keep soil moist and free of weeds. Deep-water mature plants every 5–10 days, depending on temperature, or when soil becomes dry to the touch.

Companion Plants—Tomatoes and beans, but not melons, squash, or pumpkins.

Avoid—Frost. To protect the plants or extend harvest, cover plants with clear plastic whenever temperatures dip.

Maturity—120 days.

Harvest—When husks turn a tan color, open, and fruit begins to drop from the plant.

Storage—In husks, in vegetable compartment of refrigerator for 2–3 weeks, or canned as salsa, jam, or preserves for up to 1 year.

Varieties—Aunt Molly's, Cossack Pineapple, Golden Tomatillo, Goldie, Indian Strain, Purple De Milpa, Toma Verde, Tomate Verde, Verde Puebla Tomatillo, Yellow Husk.

Tip—Fruit tends to be sweeter after a light frost.

Indian Corn   —See Corn, Popcorn, Decorative Corn

Jerusalem Artichokes or Sunchokes

(Easy)—An edible variety of perennial sunflower that grows 6–10 feet (1.8–3 m) tall and is topped with a yellow flower, the plant is not related to the artichoke commonly found in grocery stores nor is it valued for its seeds, as are true sunflowers. Instead, it produces a tuber similar in appearance to a potato but with a flavor resembling water chestnuts. Some believe that the "Jerusalem" designation for the plant was an English corruption of the French name for sunflower, "girasol," or that the plants were brought from Jerusalem to Europe by Crusaders during the Middle Ages. Sunchokes will take over the garden if given the opportunity so plant where spreading will be limited. They will survive severe winter conditions or even a hard freeze when protected by an overlayer of soil or mulch.

Yield—Allow 5–10 plants per household member.

Planting Time—In cold-winter climates, in spring, 4–6 weeks after the last frost. In mild-winter climates, in late winter. In reverse-season climates, in winter.

Planting Soil Temperature—50–85°F (10–29°C).

Growing Temperature—65–90°F (18–32°C).

Soil Preparation—Have soil tested for adequate levels of nitrogen, phosphorus, and potassium and for proper acid-alkaline balance; maintain a 5.8–6.2 pH level by supplementing with organic compost. Add sand or abundant organic compost to keep soil loose and ensure easy harvesting.

Spacing—Set tubers 4–6 inches (10–15 cm) deep, 24 inches (60 cm) apart, in rows 36–40 inches (0.9–1 m) apart.

Care—Limit growth of foliage and spread of roots by installing wood, plastic, metal, or masonry barriers at least 24 inches (60 cm) deep in the soil. Keep soil moist and free of weeds. When cultivating, do not hoe too deep or you may cut the developing tubers on the roots, 8–16 inches (20–40 cm) beneath the outer edge of the foliage. When leaves turn yellow, either lodge [see Mature Harvest Vegetables, pg. 284] or cut stalks to 3 inches (7.5 cm) in height.

Companion Plants—Corn, rhubarb, and peanuts, but not tomatoes.

Avoid—Excess foliage growth due to application of fertilizer. Do not leave roots or stray tubers in the soil unless you want sprouts the following season.

Maturity—110–150 days.

Harvest—When tubers are 3–4 inches (7.5–10 cm) in diameter. Tubers are frost-hardy and may be dug even after hard frosts have killed other garden plants.

Storage—In vegetable compartment of refrigerator for 2–3 weeks, or in damp sawdust in a cool location for up to 6 months.

Variety—Stampede.

Tip—Sunchokes tend to have a sweeter flavor if harvested after a light frost. Because they lack starch that turns to sugar when digested, they are a perfect and tasty alternative to potatoes for diabetics. As plantings, they also provide an effective and attractive windbreak.

Jicama, Yam Beans, or Mexican Potatoes

(Easy)—A subtropical, warm-season annual vine that reaches 30 feet (9 m) in length, jicama is grown for its root, though it also yields beautiful white to lavender flowers resembling sweet peas. The bulbous root, which can weigh 1–6 pounds (0.3–2.2 kg) and attain a diameter of 8 inches (20 cm), has a brownish-gray skin with a crisp, white interior. Because of its refreshing, crisp texture, it can be enjoyed raw, cut into slices for salads, finger-size sticks for crudites and in salads, or cooked in sauces, soups, and stir-fry dishes. It is extremely popular in Mexico, where the plant is a New World native. Because it requires a growing season of 9–10 months featuring several months of moist heat, it is only practical for those climates that can support it.

WARNING: Ripe pods, seeds, and leaves of jicama contain a narcotic substance that is toxic to humans and pets. Avoid leaving seeds where young children may ingest them, and surround growing plants with sturdy fencing or other protection.

Yield—Allow 1–2 plants per household member.

Planting Time—In cold-winter climates, in spring, about 4 weeks after the last danger of frost has passed. In mild-winter climates, in early spring. In reverse-season climates, in winter.

Planting Soil Temperature—65–85°F (18–29°C).

Growing Temperature—75–95°F (24–35°C). Moist heat and tropical conditions lasting a minimum of 4 months are ideal with mild weather before and after the summer heat.

Soil Preparation—Double-dig abundant amounts of organic compost and sand equal to the amount of native soil and supplement with garden sulfur, gypsum, or lime and a high-nitrogen 10-0-0 fertilizer. Maintain a 5.8–6.5 pH level.

Spacing—Soak seeds overnight, then sow 2 inches (5 cm) deep, 4 inches (10 cm) apart, in rows 12 inches (60 cm) apart. Or transplant seedlings grown indoors for 8–10 weeks. Set trellises or support wires about 12 inches (30 cm) in height, about 24 inches (60 cm) apart.

Care—Add a high-nitrogen fertilizer monthly throughout plant growth. Keep soil free of weeds, but do not hoe deeply or you risk cutting the growing roots, which may extend up to 5 feet (1.5 m) from the stalk. Train developing vines onto their supports.

Companion Plants—Cactus.

Avoid—Allowing seedpods to develop, which will stunt the tubers.

Maturity—9 months.

Harvest—Anytime after flowering declines but before the first frost.

Storage—In vegetable compartment of refrigerator for 2–4 months.

Varieties—Nonvarietal.

Tip—Excellent low-calorie appetizer.

Kale *(Easy)*—A hardy member of the cabbage family, this leafy vegetable does best in mild to cool growing conditions and is often planted for its beauty as well as its sweet taste, which actually improves after frost has reduced most other garden vegetables to memories. The most common leaf color is green, but kale also comes in shades of blue-green and in variegated shadings that range from red to white and yellow to white. When mature, the plant reaches 24 inches (60 cm) in height and width.

Yield—Allow 4–5 plants per household member.

Planting Time—In spring or autumn, when there is no danger of temperature dropping below 10°F (–12°C).

Planting Soil Temperature—55–75°F (13–24°C), but kale can perform well over a wide range of cooler temperatures, provided the soil drains well and does not harbor mold and fungus spores.

Growing Temperature—45–75°F (7–24°C). All but the coldest temperatures affect kale's taste more than its ability to grow; for optimal flavor, grow in cool, temperate weather.

Soil Preparation—Have soil tested for adequate levels of nitrogen, phosphorus, and potassium and for proper acid-alkaline balance; maintain a 5.5–6.8 pH level. Do not overfertilize at time of planting. If soil is dense and claylike, add sufficient organic matter to improve drainage.

Spacing—Sow seeds 1/4 inch (6 mm) deep, 1 inch (25 mm) apart, in rows 24 inches (60 cm) apart, thinning successful plants to 12 inches (30 cm) apart.

Care—Keep soil moist. Fertilize by topdressing the soil around each plant with organic compost every 6 weeks, working it in during cultivation. After plants have reached 6 inches (15 cm) in height, pile straw around the stems to prevent direct contact with the soil. If white cabbage butterflies appear around the plants, inspect undersides of leaves for egg clusters; wash infested plants with dilute soap solution to remove and kill the eggs.

Companion Plants—Beets, celery, herbs, onions, and potatoes, but not pole beans, strawberries, or tomatoes.

Avoid—Growing during the heat of summer, which will turn kale's sweetness bitter.

Maturity—55–75 days.

Harvest—When plants reach 8–10 inches (20–25 cm) in height by thinning outside leaves. When the plants are mature, but before they bolt, cut at the stalks, about 2 inches (5 cm) above the soil, and leave the roots in place. In mild climates, the roots will sprout new heads in 1–2 weeks.

Storage—Harvest as needed. In vegetable compartment of refrigerator for 1–2 weeks, or blanched and frozen for up to 6 months.

Varieties—Blue Armor, Blue Curled Scotch, Blue Knight, Dwarf Blue Curled, Dwarf Siberian, Greenlance Hybrid, Hanover Salad, Konserva, Lacinato, Premier, Red Russian, Redbor, Squire, Vates, Verdura, Winterbor.

Tip—Remove the middle rib of the leaves before eating. Kale may be used raw in salads, much the same as spinach, or chopped to add body to soups and stews.

> "Nothing takes place all at once…nature never makes leaps."
>
> ### *Gottfried Leibnitz*

Kohlrabi   *(Easy)*—A cool-season vegetable, this annual member of the cabbage family also is related to mustard. Kohlrabi's swollen stem resembles an aboveground turnip; long-stemmed leaves sprout in a fan from a light-green or purplish globe. Though the plant may continue to grow larger and taller, it is ready for harvest when the bulbous stem reaches 2–3 inches (5–7.5 cm) in diameter.

Yield—Allow 4–5 plants per household member.

Planting Time—In spring, or in late summer for autumn harvest. In reverse-season climates and the desert southwest, in autumn for harvest in early winter, in early spring at higher elevations.

Planting Soil Temperature—50–85°F (10–29°C).

Growing Temperature—40–75°F (4–24°C). Once established, these hardy plants can withstand most temperatures but prefer late summer planting for autumn harvest.

Soil Preparation—Have soil tested for adequate levels of nitrogen, phosphorus, and potassium and for proper acid-alkaline balance; maintain a 5.5–6.8 pH level by amending with organic compost and garden sulfur as needed. If soil is not porous and light, amend with gypsum and abundant organic matter to improve texture.

Spacing—Sow seeds 1/4–1/2 inch (6–12 mm) deep, 1 inch (25 mm) apart, in rows 30 inches (75 cm) apart, thinning successful plants to 5–8 inches (13–20 cm) apart.

Care—Keep soil moist, cultivate for weed control, and topdress the soil with fertilizer or organic compost after plants reach 4–5 inches (10–13 cm) in height. If white cabbage butterflies appear around the plants, inspect the undersides of leaves for egg clusters; wash infested plants with dilute soap solution to remove and kill the eggs.

Companion Plants—Beets, celery, herbs, onions, and potatoes, but not pole beans, strawberries, or tomatoes.

Avoid—Allowing the stem to grow larger than a baseball, which will cause it to become woody and lose flavor.

Maturity—45–60 days.

Harvest—Bulb and leaves when the stem reaches 2–3 inches (5–7.5 cm) in diameter.

Storage—In vegetable compartment of refrigerator for 1–2 weeks.

Varieties—Early Purple Vienna, Early White Vienna, Express Forcer, Gigante, Gigante Winter, Grand Duke, Komet, Purple Danube, Rapid, Superschmelz, Triumph, Waldemar, White Danube, Winner.

Tip—Kohlrabi bulbs can be eaten raw, similar to an apple, or shaved with a vegetable grater and added to salads. The tangy, cabbage-flavored leaves are also prized as salad greens.

Leeks   *(Easy)*—A cool-season vegetable, this annual is a member of the onion family. Its white stem, topped with deep-green fanlike foliage, is prized for its mild flavor. Though leeks are easily grown, they mature slowly. They are worth the wait, however, since they are among the more expensive items in the produce market.

Yield—Allow 12–15 plants per household member.

Planting Time—In early spring; in mild-winter climates, in late winter; in reverse-season climates, in late autumn.

Planting Soil Temperature—35–90°F (2–32°C).

Growing Temperature—45–85°F (7–29°C).

Soil Preparation—Have soil tested for adequate levels of nitrogen, phosphorus, and potassium and for proper acid-alkaline balance; maintain a 6–6.8 pH level by achieving a balance of equal parts of native soil, well-rotted manure, sand, and compost. Prepare trenches 5 inches (13 cm) deep to receive transplants.

Spacing—Sow seeds indoors 1/8 inch (3 mm) deep, 1 inch (25 mm) apart, in flats filled with loose potting soil at least 3 inches (7.5 cm) deep. Transplant into the garden when plants are 3 inches (7.5 cm) tall, spacing them 2–4 inches (5–10 cm) apart in trenches 5 inches (13 cm) deep spaced 6–10 inches (15–25 cm) apart.

Care—Water only when soil is dry to the touch. If weather turns cold, cover soil with mulch to insulate the plants. To blanch, apply sand mulch to each stem just below the leaf junction. Add more as the plants grow until the trench is filled and forms a mounded row.

Companion Plants—Carrots, celery, garlic, and onions.

Avoid—Applying sand mulch around plants higher than their leaf junctions to prevent sand lodging in the leek's leaves and stem.

Maturity—120–170 days.

Harvest—When stems reach 1–2 inches (2.5–5 cm) in diameter and the leaves reach 6–8 inches (15–20 cm) in height.

Storage—Harvest as needed; leeks do not store well out of the garden.

Varieties—Albinstar Baby Leek, American Flag, Arkansas, Bleu de Solaise, Carina, Durabel, Gabilian, Giant Carentan, Giant Musselburgh, King Richard, Laura, Lyeon, Otina, Primor, St. Victor, Splendid, Tadorna, Titan, Unique.

Tip—For longer harvests, leek plantings must be sequenced; allow 3 weeks between plantings. In colder climates, cover the bed with straw mulch to hold soil temperatures through early winter. The mild flavor of leeks makes them a perfect accompaniment to potatoes, yams, and other mild-flavored tubers; leeks and potatoes are the primary ingredients in vichyssoise, a creamy, cold summer soup.

LETTUCE *(Easy)*—These cool-season leafy green salad vegetables come in many sizes, shapes, textures, flavors, and colors, and more than a hundred different varieties. Lettuce is the perfect choice for beginning gardeners: it tolerates poor soil preparation and requires very little care once established. In fact, lettuces have only one fault: they bolt to form tall flowering heads when the weather becomes too warm. If harvested properly, lettuce rejuvenates new leaves, providing an abundant supply of fresh salad greens over a lengthy period [see harvest instructions for each variety].

There are five major categories of lettuce, each comprising many varieties with differing textures and tastes. They are: *Butterhead* or *Bibb, Celtuce, Crisphead* or *Iceberg, Leaf* or *Looseleaf,* and *Romaine* or *Cos.* Salads are often made up of more than one type of lettuce to add a variety of tastes as well as visual interest. Similarly, gardeners frequently use lettuce as a decorative border to frame other garden plots.

See separate listings for Amaranth; Endive, Curly, and Escarole; and Chicory, Belgian Endive, Radicchio.

Lettuce—Butterhead or Bibb

(Easy)—This leafy green bears heads with cream-yellow leaves at their centers. Preferred by many lettuce connoisseurs for its smooth texture and delicate flavor, it ranges in size from miniatures of about 4 inches (10 cm) in diameter to large heads about 7 inches (18 cm) in diameter.

Yield—Allow 6–10 heads per household member, replanting in succession as other crops are harvested.

Planting Time—From seed, start indoors 4–6 weeks before the last expected frost, then outdoors continuously to early autumn. In mild-winter climates, year-round. In reverse-season climates or areas with very high summer temperatures, in winter. For transplants, after danger of frost has passed. For succession harvesting, plant beds every 3–4 weeks throughout the recommended growing season.

Planting Soil Temperature—40–75°F (4–24°C).

Growing Temperature—45–75°F (7–24°C). Warmer temperatures and long days will cause plants to bolt.

Soil Preparation—Have soil tested for adequate levels of nitrogen, phosphorus, and potassium and for proper acid-alkaline balance; maintain a 6.0–6.8 pH level. Apply generous amounts of organic compost. Lightly fertilize soil before planting, taking care not to overfertilize, which causes lettuce leaves to become bitter.

Spacing—Sow seeds ¼ inch (6 mm) deep, 1–2 inches (25–50 mm) apart, in rows 16–24 inches (40–60 cm) apart, or broadcast over an area. Thin successful plants to 6–8 inches (15–20 cm) apart.

Care—Keep soil moist and weed free. As plants mature, avoid overhead watering in direct sun to prevent leaf blemish. Protect from frost by covering with protective plastic or straw mulch whenever cool nighttime temperatures are anticipated. Avoid bolt during hot, sunny days by erecting shade covers made of porous shade cloth above each bed.

Companion Plants—Carrots, cucumbers, radishes, and strawberries.

Avoid—Overcrowding plants, which will prevent heads from forming properly, and excessive shade, which will produce leggy plants.

Maturity—65–80 days.

Harvest—As soon as the loose heads form, but before the inner leaves turn yellow. To harvest the whole head, cut at the top of the stem, beneath the head. Roots left in the ground will sprout new foliage, though resulting plants will not be as tender as those first harvested.

Storage—In vegetable compartment of refrigerator for 2–3 weeks.

> "You may drive out nature with a pitchfork, yet she still will hurry back."
>
> ***Horace***

Varieties—Ace of Hearts, Audran, Bronze Arrow, Brune d'Hiver, Buttercrunch, Capitane, Catalogna, Cobham Green, Continuity, Dark Green Boston, Delta, Dolly, Ermosa, Escort, Esmeralda, Italian Red Perella, Jacqueline, Juliet, Kinemontpas, Kwick, May King, Merveille Des Quatre Saisons, Mescher, Nancy, North Pole, Optima, Parris Island Cos, Prado, Red Sails, Red Vogue, Rigoletto, Rougette du Midi, Salad Bowl, Schweitzer's Mescher Bibb, Sierra, Sucrine, Susan's Red, Tania, Valdor, Webb's Wonderful, Yugoslavian Red.

Tip—An area 4 feet (1.25m) square will yield salads for a family of 3 for about 1 month; plant 2 such beds in succession 3 weeks apart for continuous harvests.

Lettuce, Celtuce

(Easy)—This novelty lettuce has the appearance and taste of leaf lettuce before reaching maturity, then sprouts stalks that resemble celery.

Yield—Allow 4–6 heads per household member.

Planting Time—In late summer or early autumn; in reverse-season and mild-winter climates, in winter.

Planting Soil Temperature—40–75°F (4–24°C).

Growing Temperature—45–75°F (7–24°C); with sun protection, up to 85°F (29°C). If early hot weather is a threat, start indoors to allow the celtuce to become established before transplanting.

Soil Preparation—Have soil tested for adequate levels of nitrogen, phosphorus, and potassium and for proper acid-alkaline balance; maintain a 6–6.8 pH level. Apply generous amounts of organic compost. Fertilize soil lightly before planting taking care not to overfertilize, which will cause the lettuce leaves to become bitter.

Spacing—Sow seeds 1/4 inch (6 mm) deep, 2 inches (5 cm) apart, in rows 18 inches (45 cm) apart, or broadcast over an area. Thin successful plants to 12 inches (30 cm) apart.

Care—Keep soil moist and weed free. Protect from frost by covering with protective plastic or straw mulch whenever cool nighttime temperatures are anticipated. Avoid bolt during hot, sunny days by erecting shade covers made of porous shade cloth above each bed.

Companion Plants—Carrots, cucumbers, radishes, and strawberries.

Avoid—Stripping leaves excessively if you intend to harvest stalks.

Maturity—65–90 days.

Harvest—Trimmings when plant reaches 1½–2 inches (4–5 cm) in height, and stalks when stem reaches 4–6 inches (10–15 cm) tall but before it starts to produce flower buds.

Storage—In vegetable compartment of refrigerator for 2 weeks.

Varieties—Nonvarietal.

Tip—Use greens as you would any other lettuce; use stalks as you would celery.

Lettuce—Crisphead or Iceberg *(Moderate)*—

This leafy green forms a firm, compact head of pale-green crisp leaves and is more tolerant of heat than are the leaf lettuces. It is the most common commercially grown lettuce but tends to be the most difficult lettuce to grow in a garden patch, if the objective is tight, perfect heads such as are found in groceries. Fortunately, imperfect crispheads are identical in flavor and texture to their idealized sisters.

Yield—Allow 6–10 heads per household member.

Planting Time—In early spring or late summer; in mild-winter and reverse-season climates, in autumn.

Planting Soil Temperature—40–75°F (4–24°C).

Growing Temperature—45–75°F (7–24°C); with sun protection, up to 100°F (37°C).

Soil Preparation—Have soil tested for adequate levels of nitrogen, phosphorus, and potassium and for proper acid-alkaline balance; maintain a 6–6.8 pH level. Apply generous amounts of organic compost. Fertilize soil lightly before planting, taking care to not overfertilize, which will cause the lettuce leaves to become bitter.

Spacing—Sow seeds ¼ inch (6 mm) deep, 1–2 inches (25–50 mm) apart, in rows 16–24 inches (40–60 cm) apart, or broadcast over an area. Thin successful plants to 12 inches (30 cm) apart.

Care—Keep soil moist and weed-free. Protect during hot, sunny days to prevent bolting.

"We must cultivate our garden."

Voltaire

Companion Plants—Carrots, cucumbers, radishes, and strawberries.

Avoid—Watering midday, which may create downy mildew and imperfect leaves; instead, water early in the morning to allow the lettuce time to dry before full sun hits the bed. Also, avoid watering in the evening if overnight temperatures below 50°F (10°C) are predicted to avoid fungal infection.

Maturity—80–90 days.

Harvest—When heads are tight and turn yellowish-green. Cut heads from the stem about 1 inch (25 mm) above the soil to encourage resprouting; remove any loose outer leaves.

Storage—In vegetable compartment of refrigerator for 2–3 weeks.

Varieties—Calmar, Cerise, Crispino, Diamond Head, Gemini, Great Lakes, Ithaca, Mini Green, Montello, Nevada, Prizehead, Queen Crown, Red Grenoble, Salinas, Summertime, Tennis Ball, Vanity.

Tip—Discard the outer leaves before rinsing to prevent premature spoilage of the head.

Lettuce—Leaf or Looseleaf

(Easy)—These yellow, green, red, or purplish lettuces with loose, circular patterns of leaves surrounding the central growth bud are the most visually interesting of the varieties. They sport leaf margins that are smooth, ruffled, variegated, or resemble oak leaves, are the easiest lettuces to grow; and are less subject to bolt than the headed varieties.

Yield—Allow 6–10 plants per household member.

Planting Time—In early spring or late summer; in mild winter or reverse-season climates, in autumn. For succession plantings, every 3–4 weeks.

Planting Soil Temperature—40–75°F (4–24°C).

Growing Temperature—45–75°F (7–24°C); with sun protection, up to 85°F (29°C).

Soil Preparation—Have soil tested for adequate levels of nitrogen, phosphorus, and potassium and for proper acid-alkaline balance; maintain a 6–6.8 pH level. Apply generous amounts of organic compost. Fertilize soil lightly before planting, taking care not to overfertilize, which will cause the lettuce leaves to become bitter.

Spacing—Sow seeds 1/4 inch (6 mm) deep, 1–2 inches (25–50 mm) apart, in rows 12–24 inches (30–40 cm) apart, or broadcast over an area. Thin successful plants to 4–8 inches (10–20 cm) apart.

Care—Keep soil moist and weed-free. Reduce overhead watering once the plants have reached 4–6 inches (10–15 cm) in diameter to prevent leaf blemish. Water in early morning so that plants are completely dry by the time full sun hits the bed.

Companion Plants—Carrots, cucumbers, radishes, and strawberries.

Avoid—Cutting the central growth bud when harvesting outer leaves.

Maturity—40–50 days.

Harvest—By thinning or by cutting outer leaves 1–2 inches (25–50 mm) above the soil before leaves turn yellow or the plant bolts.

Storage—In vegetable compartment of refrigerator for 2–3 weeks.

Varieties—Australian Yellow, Biondo Lisce, Black Seeded Simpson, Brunia, Cocarde, Deer Tongue, Fire Mountain, Grand Rapids, Green Ice, Impulse, Lollo Biondo, Lollo Rossa, Mascara, Merlot, Monet, Oak Leaf, Piroga, Pom Pom, Purple Oak Leaf, Red Deer Tongue, Red Fire, Red Sails, Red Salad Bowl, Redina Red Leaf, Rossa d'Amerique, Rossa di Trento, Royal Green, Royalty, Ruby, Salad Bowl, Samantha, Simpson Elite, Slo-Bolt, Sunshine, Tango, Thai Oakleaf, Tomahawk, Two Star, Vulcan, Waldman's Dark Green, Winter Marvel.

Tip—If summer temperatures tend to be extreme, plant the Slo-Bolt variety, which is more heat tolerant than others.

Lettuce—Romaine or Cos

(Easy)—This leafy green grows to 8–9 inches (20–23 cm) in height, with an open, upright, cylindrical or oval head. Its compact greenish outer leaves and greenish-yellow center leaves are crisp and somewhat sweeter than other varieties.

Yield—Allow 6–10 plants per household member.

Planting Time—4–6 weeks before the last expected frost, then again in late summer or early autumn. In reverse-season climates, in winter. For succession plantings, every 3–5 weeks. In short-season areas, start indoors and transplant when 3–4 inches (7.5–10 cm) tall.

Planting Soil Temperature—40–75°F (4–24°C).

Growing Temperature—45–75°F (7–24°C) or, with sun protection, up to 85°F (29°C).

Soil Preparation—Have soil tested for adequate levels of nitrogen, phosphorus, and potassium and for proper acid-alkaline balance; maintain a 6.0–6.8 pH level. Apply generous amounts of abundant organic compost. Fertilize soil lightly before planting, taking care not to overfertilize, which will cause the lettuce leaves to become bitter.

Spacing—Sow seeds ¼ inch (6 mm) deep, 1–2 inches (25–50 mm) apart, in rows 16–24 inches (40–60 cm) apart, or broadcast over an area. Thin successful plants to 6–8 inches (15–20 cm) apart.

Care—Keep soil moist and weed free. Prevent bolt during hot, sunny days by erecting covers made of porous shade cloth above each bed from mid-May through August in hot climates.

Companion Plants—Carrots, cucumbers, radishes, and strawberries.

Avoid—Overcrowding plants, which will prevent heads from forming well-developed, broad leaves.

> "What a man needs in gardening is a cast iron back, with a hinge in it."
>
> ***Charles D. Warner***

Maturity—80–85 days.

Harvest—Once heads form, thin until plant begins to bolt. Cut the head of early spring plantings 1 inch (25 mm) above the soil and a new head will sprout and mature by autumn.

Storage—In vegetable compartment of refrigerator for 2–3 weeks.

Varieties—Cimarron, Cosair, Cosmo, Green Towers, Ideal Cos, Jericho, Little Gem, Lobjoit's, Kalura, Majestic Red, Olga, Parris Island, Red Winter, Redcurl, Romance, Romulus, Rosalita, Rouge D'Hiver, Ruben's Red, Valmaine, Verte Mar, Winter Density.

Tip—The main ingredient in Caesar salads, romaine leaves are best eaten torn, not cut. Dry leaves thoroughly after rinsing; wet greens will dilute the flavor of the lettuce and its dressing.

M   **MELONS** *(Difficult)*—A warm-season cousin of the gourd family, this vining annual bears two main types of fruit: *Summer Melons*, which include Cantaloupe, or Muskmelon, and Watermelon; and *Winter Melons*, which include Casaba, Crenshaw, Honeydew, and Persian. These are heat-loving plants, requiring 2½–4 months of hot weather. Melons range in size from ½–30 pounds; in shape from round to oblong; in exterior color from shades of greens and yellows to orange; in interior colors from greens and oranges to reds, yellows, and whites; and in exterior textures from smooth to rough webbed. Their succulent flesh is prized as a flavorful addition to salads and desserts.

Melons—Summary

(Difficult)—Summer melons—cantaloupe, or musk-melon, and watermelon—are round or oval in shape with a firm rind surrounding light-green, yellow, orange, or red flesh. The cantaloupe or muskmelon has a rough, web-patterned rind and seldom exceeds 4 pounds (1.5 kg) in weight. Watermelons come in solid and striped green varieties, seedless or bearing seeds, in oblong, round, and egg-shaped husks. It is not uncommon for watermelons to grow to 30 pounds (11 kg) or more.

Yield—Allow 2 plants per household member, pinching back flowers to permit only 4 fruits to form per vine.

Planting Time—2 weeks after all danger of frost has passed and when soil has warmed.

Planting Soil Temperature—60–90°F (16–32°C).

Growing Temperature—70–90°F (21–32°C), with many days exceeding 80°F (27°C) for the plant to set flowers and develop fruit. If temperatures exceed 90°F (32°C) for numerous days during bloom, however, flowers will drop without setting fruit.

Soil Preparation—Have soil tested for adequate levels of nitrogen, phosphorus, and potassium and for proper acid-alkaline balance; maintain a 6–6.8 pH level by double-digging in abundant amounts of organic compost. Apply a 10-0-0 or other high-nitrogen fertilizer to the soil at the time of planting. Prepare mounds 2–3 feet (60–90 cm) in height, 2 feet (60 cm) in diameter, spaced 4–6 feet (1.2–1.8 m) apart. To support fruit, install tripod-shaped trellis or rail supports.

Spacing—Sow 4–6 seeds 1 inch (25 mm) deep, 12 inches (30 cm) apart, in mounds. Thin successful plants to 2 vines per hill.

"Nurture overcomes nature."

James Howell

Care—Keep soil continuously moist around the moat surrounding each hill. Apply 10-0-0 or other high-nitrogen fertilizer monthly throughout growth. Support heavy fruits in damp soil with a nylon net hammock strung beneath a stout wooden tripod, or place melons on a raised board to prevent direct soil contact.

Companion Plants—Corn, radish, and nasturtium.

Avoid—Overhead watering, which will promote mildew.

Maturity—70–100 days.

Harvest—When full size, stems have turned brown, fruit is easily detached from the vine, and the stem-hold has a strong, sweet aroma. Limit water for about a week before harvesting to concentrate sweetness.

Storage—In refrigerator for about a week.

Varieties—*Cantaloupe (Muskmelon)*: Alaska, Ambrosia, Athena, Banana, Blenheim Orange, Burrell's Jumbo, Canada Gem, Charentais, Delicious, Earli Dew, Earligold, Early Dawn, Early Hanover, Early Nutmeg, Early SugarShaw, Eclipse, Eden Gem, Edisto, Fast Break, Four-Fifty, French Orange, Gallicum, Gold Star, Golden Crispy, Golden Jenny, Grande Gold, Hale's Best, Hearts of Gold, Imperial, Iroquois, Kansas, Luscious Plus, Magnum, Minnesota Midget, Morning in Dew, New Charm, Northern Arizona, Old Time Tennessee, Orange Blossom, Oregon Delicious, Passport, Peach

Vine, Pike, Planters Jumbo, Primo, Pronto, Pulsar, Rising Star, Roadside, Saticoy, Scoop II, Sleeping Beauty, Solid Gold, Sparkle, Star Headliner, Starship, Super Market, Superstar, Swan Lake, Sweet Granite, Sweet 'n Early, Tam Mayan Sweet, Top Mark, Touchdown, Treasure.

Varieties—*Watermelon*: Allsweet, Arikara, Arriba, Black Diamond, Black Diamond Yellow Belly, Blacktail Mountain, Calsweet, Carolina Cross, Crimson Sweet, Desert Storm, Fiesta, Garden Baby, Golden Crown, Ice Cream, Imperial Seedless, Jade Star, Jubilation, King & Queen Mini Jubilee, Moon & Stars, Navajo Sweet, Northern Sweet, Orchid Sweet, Park's Whopper, Regency, Royal Majesty, Sangria, Strawberry, Sugar Baby, Sun Sweet, Super Sweet, Sweet Favorite, Sweet Heart, Tiger Baby, Yellow Doll, Yellow Shipper.

Tip—Melon rinds may be made into preserves, chutneys, and sweet pickles.

Melons—Winter

(Difficult)—The winter melons—casaba, charental, crenshaw, honeydew, and Persian get their name from their long development cycle and the fact that they generally are not ready to harvest until late autumn or early winter in most areas. They come in a variety of sizes, shapes, flavors, and colors and are an interesting addition to any garden.

Yield—Allow 2 plants per household member, pinching back flowers to permit only 4 fruits to form per vine.

Planting Time—2 weeks after all danger of frost has passed; in subtropical areas of Hawaii, Florida, the coastal southern tip of Texas, and the low-desert regions of California, Arizona, and New Mexico, in midwinter for harvest in early summer.

Planting Soil Temperature—50°F (10°C).

Growing Temperature—45–95°F (7–35°C), with numerous days exceeding 80°F (27°C) for the plant to set flowers and develop fruit. If temperatures exceed 90°F (32°C) during bloom, however, flowers will drop without setting fruit.

Soil Preparation—Have soil tested for adequate levels of nitrogen, phosphorus, and potassium and for proper acid-alkaline balance; maintain a 6.0–6.8 pH level by double-digging equal amounts of native soil and organic compost into the bed. Apply a 10-0-0 or other high-nitrogen fertilizer to the soil at the time of planting. Prepare mounds 2–3 feet (60–90 cm) in height, 2 feet (60 cm) in diameter, spaced 4–6 feet (1.2–1.8 m) apart. To support fruit, install tripod-shaped trellis or rail supports.

Spacing—Sow 4–6 seeds 1 inch (25 mm) deep, 12 inches (30 cm) apart, in mounds. Thin successful plants to 2 per hill.

Care—Keep soil moist. Apply 10-0-0 or other high-nitrogen fertilizer monthly, working it into the soil surrounding each mound. Support heavy fruits in damp soil with a nylon net hammock strung beneath a stout wooden tripod, or place melons on a raised board to prevent direct soil contact.

Companion Plants—Corn, radish, beans, and nasturtium.

Avoid—Overhead watering, which will promote mildew. Also avoid allowing the fruits to stand in the field beyond maturity, which makes them mushy and seedy.

Maturity—110 days.

Harvest—Full-size, stems have turned brown, fruit is easily detached from the vine, and the stem-hold has a strong, sweet aroma.

Storage—In refrigerator for about 1 week, but some sweetness and flavor will be lost after a few days.

Varieties—*Casaba*: Casaba Golden Beauty, Marigold, Sungold Casaba, Tam Mayan.

Varieties—*Charental*: Alienor, Charmel, Pancha, Savor.

Varieties—*Crenshaw*: Early Hybrid Crenshaw.

Varieties—*Honeydew*: Honey Ice, Honey Orange, Honeybrew, Honeymoon, Magic-to-Dew, Morning Dew, Orange Blossom, Sharlyn, Silverworld.

Varieties—*Persian*: Galia Perfume, Haogen Israeli, Small Persian.

Varieties—*Miscellaneous* (*Butterscotch*): Sweetie. (*Oriental*): Snow Charm. (*Spanish*): Santa Claus, St. Nick Christmas, Sonora Canary. (*Tropical*): Passport.

Tip—Place fruit on an aluminum reflector to enhance heat in colder climates; this also protects the melons from soil-borne fungal diseases.

Mexican Potatoes —See Jicama, Yam Bean, or Mexican Potato

Mustard *(Easy)*—A cool-season leafy green, this annual has curly leaves with a peppery flavor

Yield—Allow 6–10 plants per household member.

Planting Time—4–6 weeks before the last expected frost; in mild-winter and reverse-season climates, in autumn or early winter. For succession plantings, every 4–6 weeks. In short-season, cold-winter, and dry, hot climates, start seeds indoors on wads of damp newspaper or paper towels in a sunny area, then transplant.

Planting Soil Temperature—40–65°F (4–18°C).

Growing Temperature—45–75°F (7–24°C).

Soil Preparation—Have soil tested for adequate levels of nitrogen, phosphorus, and potassium and for proper acid-alkaline balance; maintain a 5.5–6.8 pH level by applying organic compost. If necessary, amend dense soil with organic matter, sand, and gypsum to ensure it drains well.

Spacing—Sow seeds 1/4 inch (6 mm) deep, 1 inch (25 mm) apart, in rows 15–30 inches (38–75 cm) apart, or broadcast over an area. Thin successful plants to 4–6 inches (10–15 cm) apart.

Care—Keep soil moist and weed free.

Companion Plants—English peas, snap beans.

Avoid—Planting in full-sun locations.

Maturity—30–40 days.

"All gardening is landscape painting."

Alexander Pope

Harvest—When bottom leaves are 6–8 inches (15–20 cm) in long, harvest the inner leaves that are 3–4 inches (7.5–10 cm) in long. Harvest entire plant before sustained warm weather is established.

Storage—In vegetable compartment of refrigerator for 2–3 weeks.

Varieties—Black Mustard, Florida Broadleaf, Green Wave, Osaka Purple, Red Giant, Savanna, Southern Giant Curled, Tendergreen.

Tip—Mustard sprouts are a tasty addition to stir-fry dishes and for use as a sandwich garnish.

O **Okra** *(Moderate)*—This tropical-appearing annual grown for its edible seedpods requires the midsummer heat of the deep South for best growth. Okra plants reach 4–7 feet (1.2–2.1 m) in height. The seedpod is deep green (occasionally red) and best if harvested when 3–5 inches (7.5–13 cm) long. The most commonly cultivated varieties have sharp spines, though some hybrids are spineless. Sustained summer heat is necessary for proper development; try northern varietals if climate conditions are questionable.

Yield—Allow 6 plants per household member.

Planting Time—In spring after all danger of frost has passed, and in summer. In short-season areas, start indoors 4–6 weeks before transplanting outdoors.

Planting Soil Temperature—65–95°F (18–35°C).

Growing Temperature—65–95°F (18–35°C). Numerous days above 85°F (29°C) are required for proper growth, flowering, and pod development.

Soil Preparation—Have soil tested for adequate levels of nitrogen, phosphorus, and potassium and for proper acid-alkaline balance; maintain a 6.0–6.8 pH level by applying abundant organic compost. If soil is claylike, add organic matter and, if necessary, gypsum to improve drainage.

Spacing—Sow seeds ½ inch (12 mm) deep, 6 inches (15 cm) apart, in rows 30–48 inches (75–120 cm) apart. Thin successful plants to 12–20 inches (30–50 cm) apart.

Care—Keep soil moist and weed free.

Companion Plants—Melons, peppers, southern peas.

Avoid—Breaking or bruising pods; they contain a sticky sap that may be difficult to remove from clothing and utensils.

Maturity—55–65 days.

Harvest—Every other day, when pods are 2–4 inches (5–10 cm) long, which will induce new pods to form.

Storage—Use promptly. Okra does not store well.

Varieties—Annie Oakley, Artis, Blondy, Burgundy, Cajun Delight, Cajun Jewel, Clemson Spineless, Dwarf Green Long Pod, Evertender, Gold Coast, Green Best, Jade, North and South, Perkins Dwarf, Red Okra, Red River, Star of David.

Tip—Wear gloves when harvesting to prevent potential skin irritation. Okra is the primary vegetable ingredient and thickener in gumbo as well as in a number of other soups and stews.

Onion *(Easy)*—A cool-season perennial member of the lily family, onions have been an important part of cooking since ancient times. While some varieties are harvested when young for their raw green and white stems (known as scallions), most are grown for their mature bulb of white, brown, or red. The bulb has a papery sheath covering layer upon layer of crisp, juicy, distinctively pungent flesh that is abundant in vitamin C. The strong-smelling, eye-irritating scent is a distinctive feature of the onion group and its close relatives—garlic, shallots, chives, and leeks. Onions can be grown in most gardens throughout the United States and Canada as well as in other temperate regions of the world. Onions may be started from seed, planted as transplants, or planted as sets (the immature bulbs commercial growers raise for sale to home gardeners).

Yield—Allow as many plants per household member as space permits if you use green and mature onions nearly every day for cooking.

Planting Time—Sow seeds indoors 4–6 weeks before the last expected frost, then transplant as soon as the garden soil can be worked. For onions grown from sets, plant 3–4 weeks before the desired harvest of green onions, 3–4 months before the desired harvest of mature bulbs. In mild-winter and reverse-season climates, in late autumn.

Planting Soil Temperature—35–90°F (2–32°C).

Growing Temperature—45–85°F (7–29°C).

Soil Preparation—Have soil tested for adequate levels of nitrogen, phosphorus, and potassium and for proper acid-alkaline balance; maintain a 6–6.8 pH level by achieving a balance of well-rotted manure, native soil, and organic matter.

Spacing—Sow seeds 1/2 inch (12 mm) deep, 1/2 inch (12 mm) apart, in rows 18–25 inches (45–63 cm) apart, or broadcast over an area. Thin successful plants to 4 inches (10 cm) apart. Space sets 3 inches (7.5 cm) apart.

Care—Keep soil moist and weed free. Apply liquid fertilizer when leaves start to appear. If planning to harvest mature bulbs, crease, or lodge—bend them to the ground to halt foliage development and hasten bulb formation—but do not break stalks before immature flower buds begin to open atop the plants. For bunching onions, trim off the flowers after they have died and remove any brown stalks. In severe-winter climates, mulch heavily with straw and a covering layer of soil to propagate for the following season.

Companion Plants—Beets, lettuce, strawberries, summer savory, and tomatoes, but not beans or peas.

Avoid—Planting onions in beds used for garlic during previous seasons. Avoid leaving onions in soil throughout flowering, which will rob the onion of taste, turn it mushy, and cause the bulb to divide.

Maturity—80–150 days.

Harvest—For green onions, when bulbs are no more than 1/2 inch (13 mm) in diameter. For bunching varieties, when bulb divisions reach 1–2 inches (2.5–5 cm), by splitting them off from the outside of the bunch. For mature bulbs, when tops become withered and brown and bulbs are 3–5 inches (7.5–13 cm) in diameter.

Storage—For green and bunching varieties, in vegetable compartment of refrigerator for 2–3 weeks. For bulbs, either cut them 1 1/2 inches (4 cm) above the bulb, or leave tops on and braid into strands. Dry for 10–20 days in a moderately warm, dry area, then hang or store in a cool, dry place. Chopped onions also may be dried in a vegetable dehydrator and stored indefinitely in plastic containers, or placed fresh into bags and frozen for use in cooking.

Varieties—*Red*: Benny's Red, California Wonder Red, Giant Red Hamburger, Jon, Lucifer, Mars, Mercury, Red Baron, Red Burgermaster, Red Dutch, Red Globe, Red Mac, Redman, Rio Kyda Von, Southport Red Globe, Stockton, Wethersfield. *Yellow or White*: Ailsa Craig, Bingo, Blanco Duro, Buffalo, Burgos, Capable, Celebrity, Condor, Copper King, Copra, Duration, Early Yellow Globe, Eskimo, Fiesta, First Addition, Frontier, Gazette, Giant Zittau, Granex, Gringo, Headliner, Joint Venture, Kelsae Sweet Giant, Legacy, Lisbon White, New York Early, Norstar, Prince, Reliance, Riverside Sweet Spanish, Simcoe, Southport, White Globe, Sweet Sandwich, Sweet Spanish Hybrid, Tarmagon, Texas Yello Grano, Valiant. *Sweet/Eating*: Walla Walla, Yellow Sweet Spanish, Vidalia. *Green Onions/Scallions*: Any of the above before bulbs are fully developed.

Tip—Save large onion sets for growing green onions since they do not perform well, even when lodged, for producing mature onions.

P

Pak Choy —See Chinese Cabbage, Pak or Bok Choy, Celery Cabbage

Parsnips *(Easy)*—These close relatives of the carrot are cool-season, biennial root vegetables usually grown as an annual. Parsnips tend to be cream or light rust colored, growing to 4–9 inches (10–23 cm) in length and 2 inches (5 cm) in diameter at their tops, tapering down to a pointed tip. Cool weather conditions prior to harvest will increase their sugar content, and they can be left in the ground all winter long for harvest as needed, provided they are heavily mulched in severe-winter climates.

Yield—Allow 10 plants per household member.

Planting Time—In late spring; in mild-winter climates, in early summer; in reverse-season climates, in late autumn.

Planting Soil Temperature—40–75°F (4–24°C).

Growing Temperature—45–75°F (7–24°C).

Soil Preparation—Have soil tested for adequate levels of nitrogen, phosphorus, and potassium and for proper acid-alkaline balance; maintain a 6.0–6.8 pH level by double-digging in organic matter to a depth of 18 inches (45 cm).

Spacing—Sow seeds 1/2 inch (12 mm) deep, 1 inch (25 mm) apart, in rows 24 inches (60 cm) apart, or broadcast over an area. Thin successful plants to 3–4 inches (7.5–10 cm) apart.

> "What is a weed? A plant whose virtues have not yet been discovered."
>
> *Ralph Waldo Emerson*

Care—Apply a balanced fertilizer or carefully work well-rotted manure around the plants 4–6 weeks after seeds are sown. Water frequently and consistently during the growth period to prevent the roots from splitting. Keep weed free, especially when plants are young; once well established, parsnips require minimal care. In severe-winter climates, before the first hard freeze, mulch the bed with 6–10 inches (15–25 cm) of straw or loose wood chips, then cover it with 4–6 inches (10–15 cm) of soil; in milder climates, simply mulch the patch to protect the ground from freezing.

Companion Plants—Beets, carrots, rutabagas, and other root vegetables, but not tomatoes, tomatillos, or such cole vegetables as broccoli, Brussels sprouts, cabbage, or kale.

Avoid—Allowing volunteer growth in second and subsequent seasons, or allowing parsnips to remain in the ground once winter is past; they will be too fibrous to eat the second season.

Maturity—100–130 days.

Harvest—As needed after the first frost. Peel back the mulch and top cover of the area being harvested, harvest, then replace to protect the remaining bed. Dig carefully with a garden fork, taking care not to damage the parsnips. In mild-winter and reverse-season climates, complete harvest before the onset of hot weather.

Storage—In vegetable compartment of refrigerator for 2–4 months, but some flavor and texture will be lost. For storage in ground, see above.

Varieties—All American, Andover, Avon Resister, Cobham Improved Marrow, De Guernesey, Gladiator, Hollow Crown, Lancer, Offenhan, Student, Tender & True.

Tip—As a vegetable side dish, parsnips can be steamed, mashed, or grilled much the same as carrots; they also contribute their distinctive flavor to stews and soups.

Peanuts *(Difficult)*—Unlike tree nuts, this warm-season annual begins life as pealike flowers, which then extend their stems to grow underground seedpods. Various varieties produce from 2–6 nuts per pod.

Yield—Allow 10–12 plants per household member. Peanuts produce 2–3 pounds (0.75–1.1 kg) of nuts per 10-foot (3 m) row.

Planting Time—In spring, after all danger of frost has passed; in areas with long, hot, and humid growing seasons, when soil has warmed. In shorter-season areas, start indoors under glass 4–6 weeks before transplanting.

Planting Soil Temperature—65–85°F (18–29°C).

Growing Temperature—65–90°F (18–32°C) with numerous days exceeding 85°F (29°C) throughout the long growth cycle.

Soil Preparation—Have soil tested for adequate levels of nitrogen, phosphorus, and potassium and for proper acid-alkaline balance; maintain a 5.8–6.2 pH level by applying evergreen needle compost or garden sulfur. If soil is dense, double-dig in organic matter and garden gypsum to a depth of at least 8 inches (20 cm).

Spacing—Start indoors or sow the raw, shelled peanuts keeping their papery skin coverings 1 1/2 inches (40 mm) deep, 6–8 inches (15–20 cm) apart, in rows 36 inches (90 cm) apart.

Care—Water regularly, allowing the soil to dry between waterings. Cultivate around each plant to keep weed free and maintain loose soil consistency. Work a fine coating of garden gypsum into the soil when plants begin to flower.

"Nature provides exceptions to every rule."

Margaret Fuller

Companion Plants—Beets and potatoes, but not tall vegetables such as corn and pole beans.

Avoid—Watering during flower development to assist pollination.

Maturity—110–150 days.

Harvest—When leaves turn yellow and wither, digging with a garden fork. Shake off loose soil and hang the plants in a warm, dry place for 2–3 weeks. When completely dry, remove the peanuts

Storage—If raw, in the shell, in a dry, dark area with ventilation, for up to 3 months; if roasted, in a container or the freezer for up to 1 year.

Varieties—*Virginia—2 nuts per pod*: Jumbo. *Spanish—3–6 nuts per pod*: Pronto, Tennessee Red, Valencia.

Tip—Peanuts are infinitely easier to buy, but they are a particularly fun crop to grow because of their surprising habit of starting life aboveground, then developing their tasty nut pods below the soil's surface. Children especially love peanut butter, which can be made by parents in minutes using a household blender or food processor.

PEAS *(Easy)*—As a cool-season bush or vining annual, some varieties of peas are grown for their green seedpods and the peas contained within. As a warm-season annual, other varieties are grown for their beanlike peas, which must be shelled. The major varieties are: *Garden, Snap,* and *English peas, Southern Peas* (black-eyed peas, cowpeas, and crowder peas), and *Sugar,* or *Snow Peas.* As a cool-weather crop they usually will survive a light frost once they are established, but their starchy seeds are subject to rot or damping-off if planted into soil that is too cold. In cold-winter climates with mild summer temperatures, a spring crop may be followed by another in early autumn. Bush varieties can provide a windbreak for your garden. Pole varieties, which may reach 8 feet (2.4 m) in height when supported on poles, wires, strings, or trellises, generally produce more heavily but require more care.

Peas—Garden, English, or Snap

(Easy)—These cool-season annuals are grown for the succulent green peas found within their pods, and though super-sweet varieties are abundant, many prefer the traditional sweet English pea. It generally grows 6–10 peas in each 4–6 inch (10–15 cm) pod, on either a knee-high bush or a climbing vine that reaches up to 6 feet (1.8 m) in length. As a rule, plants will not tolerate temperatures that exceed 80°F (27°C).

Yield—Allow 30 plants per household member.

Planting Time—From early spring through midsummer, every 2–3 weeks for continuous harvests. In mild-winter and reverse-season climates where summer temperatures regularly exceed 80°F (27°C), in mid- to late autumn.

Planting Soil Temperature—40–70°F (4–21°C).

Growing Temperature—50–75°F (10–24°C).

Soil Preparation—Have soil tested for adequate levels of nitrogen, phosphorus, and potassium and for proper acid-alkaline balance; maintain a 5.5–6.8 pH level by applying well-rotted manure or organic compost. Raise rows 6–8 inches (15–20 cm); install wire or string supports between wooden stakes for bush varieties, sturdy poles for pole varieties.

Spacing—For rows: sow 2 seeds 2 inches (5 cm) deep, 2–3 inches (5-7.5 cm) apart in a diagonal pattern, in rows 3–4 feet (90–120 cm) apart. Thin successful plants to 4 inches (10 cm) apart, preserving the alternating diagonal pattern. For poles: sow 1 seed at a time 2 inches (5 cm) deep, 2 inches (5 cm) apart, in a circle 8–10 inches (20–25 cm) from the pole. Thin to 8 successful plants around each pole.

Care—Keep soil moist along each side of the rows or in each basin around poles. Use porous shade cloth erected on wooden supports to protect peas from early heat in hot climates.

Companion Plants—Beans, carrots, corn, cucumbers, radishes, and turnips, but not garlic, gladioli, onions, or potatoes.

Avoid—Overusing high-nitrogen fertilizer, which will prevent blooms from setting pods.

Maturity—55–70 days.

Harvest—When pods are bulging but before they are full size to encourage regrowth. Shell early for sweetest texture and flavor. Any withered or yellowed pods may be harvested for dried peas.

Storage—In vegetable compartment of refrigerator for 1–3 weeks in the pod, 1 week shelled. Snap peas also can be blanched, chilled in an ice water bath, dried, and stored in the freezer for 4–6 months. To dry peas, shell and lay them out on a water-proof cloth in a sunny, warm, and protected area. When completely dry, bag or jar them for use within 1 year.

Varieties—Alaska, Alderman, Bolero, Bounty, Cascadia, Daybreak, Early Sweet, Freezonian, Frosty, Green Arrow, Hatif De Annonay, Lincoln, Little Marvel, Maestro, Novella, Olympia, Oregon Pioneer, Oregon Trail, Patriot, Pea Succession, Petit Provencal, Progress, Spring Knight, Sprite, Sugar Ann, Sugar Bon, Sugar Daddy, Sugar Mel, Sugar Snap, Tall Telephone, Thomas Laxton, Utrillo, Wando.

Tip—For pods to be used for stir-fry and salad dishes, select stringless varieties and pick when 1–2 inches (25–50 mm) long, shortly after the flower drops, or plant sugar or snow varieties (see below).

Peas—Southern

(Easy)—Native to the Middle East, southern peas are a group of warm-season vegetables, including *Black-eyed Peas, Cowpeas,* and *Crowder Peas,* that do not tolerate even the mildest frost. Their green, cream, or pink seedpods enclose "peas" that are usually beige colored with a black notch and are not peas at all—most resemble bushy snap beans. They can be picked at the green-shell stage, when the pods first become full, or left to fully mature and dried for storage.

Yield—Allow 30 plants per household member. Sequential plantings every 6–8 weeks will allow continuous harvests throughout the growing season.

Planting Time—In hot-summer climates, in spring 2 weeks after all danger of frost has passed and when soil has warmed. For succession plantings, every 4 weeks.

Planting Soil Temperature—60–70°F (16–21°C).

Growing Temperature—70–95°F (10–24°C), with numerous days exceeding 85°F (29°C) during the growth cycle.

Soil Preparation—Have soil tested for adequate levels of nitrogen, phosphorus, and potassium and for proper acid-alkaline balance; maintain a 6.0–6.5 pH level by applying abundant organic compost. Peas prefer a sandy, loamy soil. Raise rows 6–8 inches (15–20 cm) since southern peas do best in raised beds. Install wire or string supports between wooden stakes.

Spacing—Sow seeds 1 inch (25 mm) deep, 2 inches (5 cm) apart, in rows 3 feet (90 cm) apart. Thin successful plants to 4 inches (10 cm) apart.

Care—Water regularly without wetting foliage or blossoms.

Companion Plants—Beans, carrots, corn, cucumbers, radishes, and turnips, but not garlic, gladioli, onions, or potatoes.

Avoid—Overusing high-nitrogen fertilizer or fresh manure, which will prevent blooms from setting pods.

Maturity—60–70 days.

Harvest—For green peas, when the pod is bulging but has not yet begun to dry or become fibrous. Shuck the peas, rinse, and dry. For dry peas, when the pods are completely dry but have not split open. Shell and spread on a waterproof cloth in a protected, sunny spot to dry.

Storage—In vegetable compartment of refrigerator for 1–3 weeks. Southern peas in the green-shell stage can be blanched, cooled in an ice water bath, dried, and stored in the freezer for up to 6 months. All peas may be dried and stored for up to 1 year.

Varieties—Big Red Ripper, Calico Crowder, California Black Eye, Knuckle Purple Hull, Mississippi Purple, Mississippi Silver, Pinkeye Purple Hull, Queen Anne, Running Conch, Zipper Cream.

Tip—You can substitute green southern peas for snap beans in most recipes.

Peas—Sugar or Snow *(Easy)*—These cool-season annuals are genetically selected for the tenderness and sweetness of their flat, green pods. Unlike their pea-bearing cousins, they are meant to be eaten when immature, before the seeds begin to swell in their pods. They do not tolerate well any temperatures that exceed 80°F (27°C).

Yield—Allow 30 plants per household member.

Planting Time—From early spring through midsummer, every 2–3 weeks while moderate temperatures persist for continuous harvests.

Planting Soil Temperature—40–70°F (4–21°C).

Growing Temperature—50–75°F (10–24°C).

Soil Preparation—Have soil tested for adequate levels of nitrogen, phosphorus, and potassium and for proper acid-alkaline balance; maintain a 5.5–6.8 pH level by applying well-rotted manure or organic compost. Raise rows 6–8 inches (15–20 cm); install wire or string supports between wooden stakes.

Spacing—Sow 2 seeds 2 inches (5 cm) deep, 2–3 inches (5–7.5 cm) apart in a diagonal pattern, in rows 3–4 feet (90–120 cm) apart. Thin successful plants to 4 inches (10 cm) apart, preserving the alternating diagonal pattern.

Care—Water regularly, avoiding excessive wetting of foliage. Limit watering when flowers appear; resume after pods begin to form.

Companion Plants—Beans, carrots, corn, cucumbers, radishes, and turnips, but not garlic, gladioli, onions, or potatoes.

Avoid—Overusing high-nitrogen fertilizer, which will prevent setting of pods.

Maturity—55–70 days.

Harvest—When pods are 1½–2½ inches (40–60 mm) long and peas are just barely visible within the pods, which also encourages new blooms and second crops.

Storage—In vegetable compartment of refrigerator for 1–2 weeks. Snow pea varieties also may be blanched in boiling water, chilled in an ice water bath, dried, and stored in the freezer for up to 3 months, though some desirable texture will be lost.

Varieties—Carouby De Maussane, Chinese Snow, Corgi, Dwarf Gray Sugar, Little Sweetie, Mammoth Melting Sugar, Mega, Norli, Oregon Giant, Oregon Sugar Pods, Snow Flake, Snowbird, Sugar Anne, Sugar Bon, Sugar Mel, Sugar Snap, Sweet Snap.

Tip—Sugar pea pods are excellent in stir-fry dishes, eaten raw as a snack, or in salads.

PEPPERS *(Moderate)*—These warm-season annuals are grown on medium-sized bushes for their spicy or mild podlike fruits. Peppers vary widely in color—they come in dark purple, green, yellow, red, and variegated shades; in size and shape—short and long, fat and round, skinny and long; and in flavor—from sweet to tangy to picante to unbearably hot, according to the level of fiery capsaicin they contain. The seeds and outer skin membrane of the pepper especially contain concentrated amounts of this agent, so beware! Peppers are divided into two major categories: *Hot* or *Chili*, which include *Jalapeño, New Mexico, Serrano,* and *Habañero,* and *Sweet,* which include *Hungarian Wax, Bell,* and *Banana.* The larger, drying varieties often are braided into southwestern *ristras,* providing a functional decoration in the kitchen. Though peppers prefer tropical and subtropical climates, with a little added care they can be grown in most parts of North America.

Peppers—Hot or Chili

(Moderate)—Hot peppers range in size from 1–7 inches (2.5–18 cm) in length, come in green, red, gold, and yellow colors, and range from mild to extremely hot. Hot peppers vary in spicy temperature, even from the same plant and from hour to hour, depending on their care.

Yield—Peppers vary from only a few fruits per plant to the proverbial "too many for Peter Piper to pick." The number of plants per household member depends on the type selected. Read seed package information carefully when estimating yield in your region. Peppers store well so plan to vary the types grown each season.

Planting Time—In mild to hot climates, in late spring when soil has warmed, about 90 days before the hottest summer temperatures. For succession plantings, every 3–4 weeks until the peak of summer heat. In short-season climates, sow seeds indoors, under glass, broadcasting seed 5–8 inches (12–20 cm) apart in a planting tray 4–6 inches (10–15 cm) deep filled with loose potting soil, 6–8 weeks before outdoor soil begins to warm. Transplant when 4–6 inches (10–15 cm) tall.

Planting Soil Temperature—65–90°F (18–32°C).

Growing Temperature—70–95°F (21–35°C). In climates with daily highs exceeding 105°F (41°C), protect shade plants by using porous shade fabric erected on wooden supports.

Soil Preparation—Have soil tested for adequate levels of nitrogen, phosphorus, and potassium and for proper acid-alkaline balance; maintain a 5.5–6.8 pH level by applying organic compost.

> "When I go into my garden with a spade and dig a bed, I feel such an exhilaration and health, that I discover that I have been defrauding myself all this time in letting others do for me what I should have done with my own hands. But not only health but education is in the work."
>
> **Ralph Waldo Emerson**

Spacing—Sow 2 seeds ½ inch (12 mm) deep, 18–24 inches (45–60 cm) apart, in rows 28–36 inches (70–90 cm) apart. Thin to the more successful of each planting pair. For seedlings, transplant according to the spacing instructions above.

Care—Water more frequently when fruits begin to form, allowing soil to nearly dry between waterings. In especially hot midsummer climates shade as described above or blossoms may drop without setting peppers. Water profusely 4–8 hours before harvest for milder peppers; withhold watering to enhance spiciness.

Companion Plants—Beets, garlic, onions, and parsnips.

Avoid—Planting in plots previously used to grow peppers, eggplants, or tomatoes.

Maturity—60–95 days.

Harvest—When peppers are full size and have obtained mature color.

Storage—In the vegetable compartment of the refrigerator for up to 1 week, or in a cool, dry spot for up to 2 weeks. If roasted, peeled, and stored in the freezer, for up to 6 months. If dried, whether in a vegetable dehydrator, hung in garlands, or laid out in loose flats in the sun, for up to 1 year. If pickled whole, cooked, and canned, for up to 2 years.

Varieties—Ammazzo, Anaheim, Ancho, Bellingrath Gardens Purple, Bulgarian Carrot, Cascabella, Cayenne, Cayenne Long Red, Charleston Hot, Cherry Bomb, Chili Grande, Copacabana, Crimson Hot, Czechoslovakian Black, Delicias, Diablo Grande, Early Scotch Bonnet, Española Ristra, Firecracker Piquín, Firenza Jalapeño, Flash, Garden Salsa, Golden Prolific, Green Leaf Tabasco, Habañero, Hero, Hot Portugal, Hot Stuff, Hungarian Wax, Inferno, Jalapa, Jalapeño, Large Cherry, Louisiana Hot, Marble, Mirasol, Mitla, Mulato Isleno, Numex Big Jim, Orange Habañero, Orozco, Ortega, Paper Dragon, Paprika, Pasilla Bajio, Pimiento Elite, Pretty Hot Purple, Red Savina Habañero, Riot, Romanian Hot, Rooster Spur, Royal Black, Santa Fe Grande, Señorita, Serrano, Serrano Huasteco, Sizzler, Super Chili, Surefire, Szentesi Semi Hot, Tam Jalapeño, Thai Dragon, Thai Hot.

Tip—Read seed packages carefully regarding the degree of sweetness or "heat" of each variety. Some hot peppers are a favorite for pickling; when dried, they can be ground into powder in a food mill; both versions lend a fiery flavor to many salsas and chutneys. Cayenne pepper is the main ingredient in tabasco sauce.

WARNING: Capsaisin is an oily skin and eye irritant that clings to the outer skin, juice, and seeds of fresh and dried hot peppers. Use disposable rubber gloves when handling peppers to prevent burns to the skin, and never rub your face with your hands after handling peppers or their plants. If you experience skin or eye irritation after handling peppers, flush the affected area with abundant running water; see a licensed medical practitioner or other qualified health care professional if burn symptoms persist more than 30 minutes or if red welts appear.

Peppers—Sweet

(Moderate)—Sweet peppers come in many different shapes, but the most common is the bell. Other sweet pepper favorites include the long and slender banana pepper; the short, round cherry pepper; the small, bright-red, heart-shaped pimiento; the slender, yellow-green Hungarian yellow pepper; and the pointed, multicolored Italian frying pepper. Colors of sweet peppers range from shades of red, orange, and yellow to purple and green, which are actually unripe red or yellow bell peppers picked early to encourage a second fruiting. All sweet peppers grow on compact, broad-leafed bushes to a height of 1 1/2–2 feet (46–60 cm). Some sweet pepper varieties are nearly as spicy as their hot pepper cousins. If you prefer milder flavors, water the plants profusely the evening before picking the mature fruits.

Yield—Allow 2–3 plants of each type per household member. If space is limited, plant 1–2 plants and pick peppers when green to increase production.

Planting Time—In late spring, after all danger of frost has passed and soil has warmed. For succession plantings, plant every 3 weeks through the summer.

Planting Soil Temperature—65–90°F (18–32°C).

Growing Temperature—65–80°F (18–27°C); in much higher temperatures, established fruit will ripen, but plants will drop blossoms. In short-season climates, sow seeds indoors in trays or pots, covering with 1/2 inch (12 mm) of loose potting soil, compacted down, 6–8 weeks before soil begins to warm. Add tomato fertilizer to encourage early growth and root formation.

Soil Preparation—Have soil tested for adequate levels of nitrogen, phosphorus, and potassium and for proper acid-alkaline balance; maintain a 5.5–6.8 pH level by applying organic compost.

Spacing—Sow 3 seeds ¼–½ inch (5–12 mm) deep, 18–24 inches (45–60 cm) apart, in rows 28–36 inches (70–90 cm) apart. Thin to the 2 most successful plants in each trio. For nursery stock and indoor starts, transplant according to the spacing instructions above.

Care—Water more frequently when fruits begin to form to prevent flower drop. Cultivate soil 8–12 inches (20–30 cm) from the plants, adding 1–2 inches (25–50 mm) of organic compost monthly.

Companion Plants—Beets, garlic, onions, parsnips, and radishes.

Avoid—Planting in a plot previously used to grow peppers, eggplants, or tomatoes.

Maturity—60–95 days.

Harvest—When full size, 12–14 weeks after transplanting, depending on desired use, color, and flavor. For pickling, best if picked before seeds fully develop.

Storage—In vegetable compartment of refrigerator for 2–3 weeks. If blanched, in the freezer for 4–6 months. If dried in a vegetable dehydrator or laid out in loose flats in the sun, for up to 1 year. If pickled whole or canned, for up to 2 years.

Varieties—*Bell*: Ace, Admiral, Aladdin, Apple, Aruba, Bell Captain, Big Bertha, Big John, Blackbird, Blockbuster, Blue Jay, Bonanza, Bull Nose, California Wonder, Camelot, Canary, Cardinal, Chocolate Beauty, Corona, Dove, Elisa, Emerald Giant, Enterprise, Fajita Bell, Flamingo, Gigaro, Gold Finch, Hercules, Islander, Ivory, Jackpot, Jingle Bells, Jupiter, King Arthur, Klondike Bell, La Bamba, Little Dipper, Merling, Midway, North Star, Ori, Orobelle, Peppourri, Peto Wonder, Purple Beauty, Rampage, Redstart, Redwing, Robin, Secret, Summer Sweet, Sunrise Orange, Valencia, Verdel, Whopper Improved, Yankee Bell, Yellow Belle, Yolo Wonder.

Varieties—*Other*: Biscayne, Cadice, Canada Cheese, Corno di Toro, Cubanelle, España, Figaro, Golden Arrow, Guantanamo, Gypsy, Islander Lavender, Italian Sweet, Ivory Banana, Laparie, Marconi, Matador, Navarone, Pepperoncini, Perfection, Queen, Red Cherry, Red Heart Pimiento, Red Ruffled, Sofia, Sugar Banana, Super Shepherd, Super Sweet Banana, Sweet Banana, Sweet Cherry, Tequila Sunrise, Vidi, Yellow Cheese Pimiento.

Tip—All sweet peppers can be eaten raw, and many varieties are suitable for roasting and use in stir-fry dishes and casseroles. They also may be pickled or added to relishes. Sweet peppers are the main ingredient in the Mexican chiles rellenos—roasted, peeled and deseeded, stuffed with cheese, dipped into beaten egg whites and fried—but beware, some bell-shaped peppers are surprisingly hot.

Popcorn —See Corn, Popcorn, Decorative Corn

Potatoes

(Easy)—A cool-season annual, this South American native was introduced to the United States by Irish immigrants in the 1700s and has flourished to become a staple food crop. In fact, the United States consumes more potatoes annually by weight than any other vegetable, a staggering 100–125 pounds (37–46 kg) per person—baked, fried, mashed, as potato chips, and in a score of other food products, including bread and pastries. An unlikely seeming relative of the tomato and peanut, it shares similar- appearing vines with the latter, producing swollen tubers that grow underground from the plants' roots. Potatoes come in red, purple, brown, tan, and yellow; many are accompanied by unique flavors and textures. Shapes are primarily oval or round, though unusual varieties grow in finger- and clusterlike shapes. Individual sizes range from bite size to about a pound (0.3 kg) for the baking varieties. Varieties include early, midseason, and late-season potatoes.

Yield—Allow 1 plant for every 5–10 potatoes desired, planning on about 10 plants per 10-foot (3 m) row.

Planting Time—*Early*: In spring, 4–6 weeks before the last expected frost for summer harvest; in areas where soil temperatures do not climb above 85°F (29°C), in late spring for autumn harvest. *Midseason*: In spring, 4–6 weeks before the last expected frost for early autumn harvest. *Late*: In late spring for autumn harvest.

Planting Soil Temperature—50–85°F (10–29°C).

Growing Temperature—45–80°F (7–27°C); however, due to their variety, potatoes differ widely in their growing temperature requirements. Check planting instructions carefully or rely on advice from an experienced gardener familiar with your region and plant selection.

> "Nature is whole and yet never finished."
>
> *Goethe*

Soil Preparation—Have soil tested for adequate levels of nitrogen, phosphorus, and potassium and for proper acid-alkaline balance; maintain a 4.8–5.4 pH level by applying abundant organic compost and garden sulfur. Dig a trench 4 inches (10 cm) deep for each row, fertilize along each side of the trench with 5-10-10 fertilizer, then work it into the soil. After planting, place an additional 2 inches (5 cm) of soil atop the trench.

Spacing—Dust the cut surfaces of seed potatoes with garden lime, then plant them 10–14 inches (25–35 cm) apart in trenches 28–34 inches (70–85 cm) apart.

Care—When sprouts emerge, add 2 inches (5 cm) of soil to the trench. Form a large hill around the base of each plant to protect developing tubers from sunburn and to prevent greening. Keep soil mounded and moist, but do not overwater, which increases the risk of disease. Carefully cultivate around the plants until they form flowers.

Companion Plants—Beans, cabbage, corn, eggplant, horseradish, and marigolds, but not cucumbers, pumpkins, raspberries, squash, sunflowers, or tomatoes.

Avoid—Changing levels of temperature, nitrogen, and soil moisture, which may result in abnormally shaped potatoes. Also avoid overusing nitrogen, which will encourage foliage growth at the expense of tuber development.

Maturity—*Early*: 90–110 days. *Midseason*: 100–120 days. *Late*: 110–140 days.

Harvest—For new potatoes, when flowers begin to fade. For mature potatoes, when the foliage dies. Dig carefully with a garden fork, 8–10 inches (20–25 cm) away from the plant, then work closer to the vine until all the potatoes have been gathered. Brush but do not wash clinging soil from the tubers.

WARNING: Sunburned and green potatoes and potato foliage are hazardous when consumed. Remove all potato eyes before eating.

Storage—Use new potatoes promptly; they do not store well. For mature varieties, store in a dark, well-ventilated area with a constant temperature of 40°F (4°C) for up to 6 months.

Varieties—*Russets (Early to Midseason)*: Norgold, Russet Burbank. (*Midseason*): Frontier Russet, Newleaf, Russet Norkotah, Viking. (*Late*): Butte Gold Rush, Ranger Russet.

Varieties—*Long Whites (Midseason)*: Carola, Rose Fin Apple, Russian Banana. (*Mid- to Late Season*): Peanut, Yellow Fin. (*Late*): Austrian Crescent, German Yellow, Green Mountain, Ozette Fingerling, Swedish Peanut, Tobique.

Varieties—*Round Reds* (*Early*): Dark Red Norland, Red Sun, Sangre Red. (*Early to Midseason*): Redsen. (*Mid- to Late season*): Red Pontiac, Rose Gold. (*Late*): Alaska Sweetheart, Elba, German Butterball, Red Pontiac, Royal Pimpernel.

Varieties—*Round Whites* (*Early*): Epicure, Irish Cobbler, Onaway. (*Early to Midseason*): Red La Soda, Yukon Gold. (*Midseason*): Beltsville, Saginaw Gold, Superior. (*Late*): Bintje, Island Sunshine, Katahdin, Kennebec, Mainstay.

Varieties—*Novelty*: (*Early*): Caribe. (*Midseason*): All Blue, Brigue Purple Viking. (*Late*): Purple Marker.

Tip—To harden the potato skins, water for the last time 2 weeks before harvest; 10 days later, cut the foliage away; 4 days after that, harvest during a cool part of the day.

Potatoes, Sweet —See Sweet Potatoes or Yams

Pumpkins

(Easy)—A warm-season annual, this orange-colored, round or oval, squashlike vegetable has a firm, smooth rind scored with vertical grooves radiating down from its stem. Pumpkins are grown on the vine for their orange flesh and tasty, meaty seeds, as well as for Halloween and Thanksgiving decorations. Pumpkins range in size from a few ounces (mgs) to 400 pounds (00 kg) or more for the giant, squashlike varieties such as Big Max. Though most varieties are orange, a few are white. They need plenty of room to grow.

Yield—Allow 1–2 plants per household member.

Planting Time—In late spring after all danger of frost has passed and when soil has warmed. In extremely hot and dry climates, after the summer heat has broken; excessive heat literally will cook pumpkins on the vine. In reverse-season climates, in winter for harvest in mid to late spring.

Planting Soil Temperature—65–90°F (18–32°F).

Growing Temperature—50–90°F (10–32°F).

Soil Preparation—Have soil tested for adequate levels of nitrogen, phosphorus, and potassium and for proper acid-alkaline balance; maintain a 6.0–7.5 pH level by applying well-rotted manure and abundant organic compost. Work the ground until loose, then raise hills 8–12 inches (20–30 cm), 6–8 feet (1.8–2.4 m) apart; install a tripod with sturdy rails if space is a consideration.

Spacing—Sow 5–6 seeds 1 inch (25 mm) deep, 3–4 inches (7.5–10 cm) apart, in hills 6–8 feet apart. Thin successful plants to 2–3 per hill.

Care—Keep soil moist and weed free. For larger pumpkins, remove the female flowers, which bear immature pumpkins beneath their blossoms, after 2–3 pumpkins have reached the size of a small peach; do not remove the male, pollen-bearing blossoms, which appear intermingled with the female blossoms. If not supported on tripods, place pumpkins on wood planks to prevent contact with damp soil, which may cause them to rot.

Companion Plants—Corn, but not potatoes or squash because of competition for space.

Avoid—Wetting leaves during watering, which may promote leaf diseases or affect the developing pumpkin.

Maturity—90–120 days.

Harvest—When deep orange or golden white, depending on the variety; when a fingernail will not easily penetrate the rind; when the vines have turned dry and brown, and, for best flavor, shortly after the first frost. Cut from the vine with pruning shears, leaving about 4 inches (10 cm) of stem on each pumpkin.

Storage—Cure in the garden under direct sun at a temperature of 75–80°F for 2 weeks, then store in a cool, dry, ventilated area for up to 3 months. If pureed and frozen, for up to 6 months. If canned, for up to 1 year.

Varieties—Appalachian, Aspen, Atlantic Giant, Autumn Gold, Baby Bear, Baby Boo, Baby Pam, Big Autumn, Big Max, Big Moon, Buckskin, Bush Spirit, Casper, Cinderella, Connecticut Field, Dill's Atlantic Giant, Frosty, Funny Face, Ghost Rider, Gremlin, Half Moon, Harvest Moon, Howden, Jack O'Lantern, Jack Of All Trades, Jack-Be-Little, Jack-pot, Japanese Pumpkin, Jarrahdale, Lady Godiva, Little Lantern, Long Island Cheese, Long Pie, Lumina, Montana Jack, Munchkin Mini, New England Pie, Oz, Pankow's Field, Potimarron, Prizewinner, Pro Gold, Rocket, Rocky Mountain Pie, Rouge D'Etampes Cinderella, Rouge Vif D'Etampes, Small Sugar, Spirit, Spookie, Spooktacular, Sweetie Pie, Tallman, The Great Pumpkin, Tom Fox, Trick or Treat, Wizard.

Tip—Pumpkins can be "personalized" by scoring the soft green rind of the early fruit; as they mature, the scratches will harden into a white callus. When carving a pumpkin into a jack-o'-lantern, do not forget to remove the tasty seeds, which can be dried and roasted for eating.

Radicchio   —See Chicory, Belgian Endive, Radicchio

Radishes

(Easy)—A cool-season annual root crop, radishes range from zesty mild to extremely hot. Though most varieties are red and globe shaped, some vary in shape and color, including long, tapered forms in red, purple, and cream, and others in black, cream, and yellow. Radishes grow quickly and reliably in most climates.

Yield—Allow 15 plants per household member per month, replanting every 2 weeks to ensure continuous harvests.

Planting Time—In spring or autumn. In mild-winter and reverse-season climates, in late autumn and early winter.

Planting Soil Temperature—45–85°F (7–29°C).

Growing Temperature—50–75°F (10–24°C).

Soil Preparation—Have soil tested for adequate levels of nitrogen, phosphorus, and potassium and for proper acid-alkaline balance; maintain a 5.5–6.8 pH level by double-digging in abundant organic compost, which also will loosen the soil and permit the radishes to form.

Spacing—Sow single seeds $1/2$ inch (12 mm) deep, 1 inch (25 mm) apart, in mounded ridges 10–16 inches (25–40 cm) apart. Thin successful plants to 4 inches (10 cm) apart.

Care—Keep soil moist, but do not overwater or overfertilize with high-nitrogen fertilizers or green manure; either will encourage excessive foliage growth at the expense of root development.

Companion Plants—Cucumbers, lettuce, nasturtiums, peas, and peppers.

Avoid—Leaving in ground past maturity, which causes radishes to become hollow and pithy, with an excessively earthy flavor.

Maturity—22–70 days.

Harvest—When roots have swollen to 1 inch (25 mm) in diameter and have attained full color. Rinse thoroughly to remove clinging soil and immediately chill without cutting tops.

Storage—In vegetable compartment of refrigerator for 3–4 weeks.

Varieties—All Seasons, April Cross, Black Spanish Long, Black Spanish Round, Cavalier, Champion, Cherriette, Cherry Belle, Chinese Misato, Chinese Rose, Chinese White, Comet, Crunchy Red, D'Avignon, Early Scarlet Globe, Easter Egg, Fancy Free Altari, Flamboyant, Fluo, French Breakfast, Gala, Galahad, Hailstone, Icicle, Little Tokyo,

Marabelle, Mexican Bartender, Minowase, Miyashige, Munich Bier, Novired, Parat German Giant, Pink Beauty, Plum Purple, Rave, Red Beret, Red Boy, Red Flame, Red King, Red Meat, Red Prince, Redball, Ribella, Rose of China, Saxa, Scarlet Globe Special, Shunkyo, Snow Belle, Sora, Sparkler White Tip, Spring Light, Spring Song, Sukurajima Mammoth, Summer Cross, Tae-Baek, Tricolor, Valentine, Vintage, White Globe, White Icicle.

Tip—Radishes are enjoyed fresh and whole or sliced as a flavor note in green salads.

Rhubarb *(Easy)*

A broad-leafed cool-season perennial with edible reddish or green stalks 10–15 inches (25–38 cm) long when harvested, rhubarb is so attractive in the garden that it often is grown for decoration. Rhubarb may require 4 years to produce a full harvest, but this hardy plant is well worth the wait.

Yield—Allow 2–3 plants per household member, since rhubarb plants each offer only 2 pounds (0.7 kg) of edible stalks per year.

Planting Time—In early spring, as soon as the soil is workable. In mild-winter climates, in autumn after the summer heat has broken. Rhubarb is not easily grown in desert and hot-summer climates.

Planting Soil Temperature—40–85°F (5–29°C).

Growing Temperature—35–90°F (2–32°C). Shade with porous shade cloth erected on wooden supports whenever temperatures are expected to exceed 90°F (32°C).

Soil Preparation—Have soil tested for adequate levels of nitrogen, phosphorus, and potassium and for proper acid-alkaline balance; maintain a 5.0–6.8 pH level by applying abundant organic compost to native soil. If soil is dense, add sand or gypsum. Use a 5-10-10 fertilizer at the time of planting to help roots become established. Raise mounds 14 inches (35 cm), 5–6 feet (1.5–1.8 m) apart, in rows 4 feet (1.2 m) apart.

Spacing—Set out crowns no deeper than 1 inch (25 mm) below the surface of the soil in mounds raised 6–8 inches (15–20 cm).

WARNING: The leaves of rhubarb are hazardous to humans and animals if consumed. Fortunately, they are also bitter and unpalatable.

Care—Cut and remove flower stalks once they appear. Keep soil moist, except in winter, but do not allow the plants to stand in water. Remove dead leaves in spring. Fertilize each year with well-rotted manure or low-nitrogen fertilizer, and mulch the soil with organic compost in autumn.

In severe-winter climates, cut the stems to the crown in autumn, mulch with 1–2 feet (30–60 cm) of straw, and cover with 1–2 inches (25–50 mm) of soil to protect the crowns from freezing. Remove the straw in spring after air and soil temperatures have warmed. Rhubarb will yield 4 years of good harvest. Divide the plant's root crowns in the third year and replant in another area of the garden to sustain the planting.

Companion Plants—Artichokes, asparagus, and cole vegetables such as Brussels sprouts, cabbage, sprouts, and kale but not legume or root vegetables.

Avoid—Ingesting the leaves, which contain poisonous concentrations of oxalic acid.

Maturity—2–4 years to attain its first full harvest.

Harvest—When stems reach 2 feet (60 cm) in length and plants are 3 feet (90 cm) in diameter. Cut outer stalks at their base, but leave a few young central leaves to replenish the crowns.

Storage—In vegetable compartment of refrigerator for 2–4 weeks. If cut and blanched, in the freezer for 3–4 months. If canned, for up to 1 year.

Varieties—Cherry Red, Chipman's Canada Red, Crimson Red, Glaskin's Perpetual, Red, Valentine, Victoria.

Tip—Rhubarb can be made into a wonderful sauce suitable for hotcakes, waffles, crepes, and ice cream. Chop the tart, stringy stalks into 1–2 inch (25–50 mm) pieces, then boil in water to cover and add sugar to taste.

Rutabagas or Swedish Turnips

(Easy)—This cool-season annual produces a swollen root with a generally yellow interior and crisp texture. The most common rutabagas are globe shaped and sometimes are confused with turnips; however, rutabagas tend to be larger—often reaching 3–5 pounds (1.1–1.8 kg)—and sweeter than their turnip cousins. Young rutabaga leaves may be used in the same manner as turnip greens.

Yield—Allow 5–10 plants per household member.

Planting Time—In late summer for autumn harvest. In mild-winter climates, in spring for summer harvest; then again in early autumn for winter harvest. In reverse-season climates, in late autumn for winter harvest.

Planting Soil Temperature—50–70°F (10–21°C).

Growing Temperature—40–75°F (4–24°C).

Soil Preparation—Have soil tested for adequate levels of nitrogen, phosphorus, and potassium and for proper acid-alkaline balance; maintain a 5.5–6.8 pH level by applying abundant organic compost. If soil is dense, add organic matter or gypsum. Soil is best if green manure is dug into the bed before the end of the prior season.

Spacing—Sow seeds ¹/₂ inch (12 mm) deep, 1 inch (25 mm) apart, in rows 15–36 inches (38–90 cm) apart. Thin successful plants to 4–6 inches apart.

Care—Keep soil moist and weed free. When the root begins to swell, trim the outer foliage or "lodge" plants to enhance root development and sweetness.

Companion Plants—Beets, carrots, and turnips, but not where berries may send runners into the bed.

> "Don't judge each day by the harvest you reap, but by the seeds you plant."
>
> *Robert Louis Stevenson*

Avoid—Watering sporadically, which may crack the developing roots.

Maturity—60–90 days.

Harvest—When tops are 12 inches (30 cm) tall and tubers are 3–5 inches (7.5–12 cm) in diameter. If soil is too dense to allow harvesting by pulling without breaking, carefully dig up roots with a garden fork.

Storage—In the ground, unless temperatures drop below 24°F (–4°C) or exceed 80°F (27°C). In vegetable compartment of refrigerator, for 2–4 months. If diced and frozen, for 3–4 months, though some flavor and texture will be lost.

Varieties—American Purple Top, Gilfeather, Joan, Laurentian, Marian, Pike, Swede Purple Top.

Tip—Rutabaga greens are prized for their unique texture and delicious flavor. Steam them as you would mustard or turnip greens, or add them to leafy green salads.

S **Salsify** *(Easy)*—A cool-season biennial often referred to as "vegetable oyster" or "oyster plant,"salsify resembles a long thin carrot in shape. Its flavor depends on the age of the root and growing conditions. Young salsify is both tender and mild in flavor; older plants are fibrous and strong, reaching 2–3 feet (60–90 cm) in height. In its second year, it forms a ball-shaped purple flower that resembles blooms of onion or garlic. The roots store well in the ground, even after frost.

Yield—Allow 10 plants per household member.

Planting Time—2–4 weeks after the last expected frost or as soon as soil is workable. In mild-winter and reverse-season climates, in early autumn for autumn and winter harvests.

Planting Soil Temperature—40–80°F (4–27°C).

Growing Temperature—45–85°F (7–29°C).

Soil Preparation—Have soil tested for adequate levels of nitrogen, phosphorus, and potassium and for proper acid-alkaline balance; maintain a 6.0–6.8 pH level. Apply abundant organic compost to a depth of 18 inches (45 cm). Soil is best if green manure is dug into the bed before the end of the prior season.

Spacing—Sow seeds 1/2 inch (12 mm) deep, 1/2 inch (12 mm) apart, in rows 20–30 inches (50–75 cm) apart. Thin successful plants to 3–4 inches (7.5–10 cm) apart.

Care—Keep soil moist and weed free.

Companion Plants—Carrots, turnips, rutabaga, potatoes, and sweet potatoes.

Avoid—Applying fresh manure at the time of planting, which will cause the root to split.

Maturity—120–150 days.

Harvest—When 1–1 1/2 feet (30–45 cm) long, or as needed, unless soil temperature warms above 85°F (29°C). If harvest is planned after freezing temperatures, mulch the bed with 1–2 feet (30–60 cm) of straw and 1–2 inches (25–50 mm) of soil late in autumn. If soil is too dense to allow harvesting by pulling without breaking, carefully dig up roots with a garden fork.

Storage—In vegetable compartment of refrigerator for 3–4 weeks.

Varieties—Giant Russian, Sandwich Island Mammoth, Scorzonera.

Tip—Because of its oyster flavor, salsify can be substituted whenever that taste is desired. It can be served raw as a fresh vegetable for dips, boiled and mashed for canapes, or battered with egg and cracker crumbs and fried in butter.

Shallots *(Easy)*—This cool-season perennial relative of the onion contains garliclike cloves that taste like a cross between onion and garlic. The heads, which generally contain 3–4 cloves apiece, are 3/4–1 1/2 inches (19–38 mm) in diameter, and each clove is protected by a brown papery sheath. A hardy plant, shallots can remain in the ground from year to year, dividing into multiple plants, or shallot "bunches."

Yield—Allow 4–6 plants per household member.

Planting Time—2–4 weeks after the last expected frost and as soon as the soil is workable. In mild-winter climates, in autumn after soil temperatures have dropped to 50°F (10°C) or lower for harvest in spring, or in late winter for harvest in midspring.

Planting Soil Temperature—35–90°F (2–32°C).

Growing Temperature—40–85°F (4–29°C); however, shallots need a dormant period lasting at least 1 month soon after planting, with temperatures 32–50°F (0–10°C).

Soil Preparation—Have soil tested for adequate levels of nitrogen, phosphorus, and potassium and for proper acid-alkaline balance; maintain a 5.0–6.8 pH level by applying organic compost, peat, or garden sulfur.

Spacing—Plant stock cloves, broad end down, covering the tips with 1/2 inch (12 mm) of soil, 5–8 inches (12–20 cm) apart, in rows 2–4 feet (60–120 cm) apart.

Care—Keep soil moist and weed free. For a quicker harvest, "lodge" the stalks when they have reached 16–18 inches (40–45 cm) in height, which will force the bulbs to mature in 3–4 weeks.

Companion Plants—Beets, lettuce, strawberries, summer savory, and tomatoes, but not beans or peas.

Avoid—Planting in beds previously used to grow garlic.

Maturity—60–120 days.

Harvest—When tops are yellow and dry. Allow harvested bulbs to dry for a month in a warm, dry area before use or storage.

Storage—In a cool, dry, dark, well-ventilated area for up to 6 months. If minced, packed into ice cube trays, frozen, then sealed in plastic bags and stored in the freezer for up to 1 year; each cube contains approximately 2 tablespoons (25 ml).

Varieties—Ambition, Atlantic, Bonilla, Creation, Dutch Yellow Shallot, Ed's Red, French Red Shallot, French Shallot, Gray Shallot, Maine Organic, Pikant, Success.

Tip—Use shallots as you would onions in quiche, omelets, coq au vin, and other delicately flavored dishes. Sauteed with wine and butter, they also make excellent sauces for prime rib and other red meats. The greens of the immature shallot may be chopped and used like chives.

Spinach   *(Moderate to Difficult)*—There are three varieties of spinach: a cool-season, dark-green annual with a frustrating tendency to bolt quickly under warm temperatures, a warm-season annual leafy plant, and a warm-season perennial vine. The cool-season plant is the traditional spinach; the warm-season varieties are either New Zealand or Malabar spinach. Warm-season varieties require less, and significantly different, care than cool-season spinach. Both cool-season and New Zealand spinach yield 6–8 waxy, semisucculent leaves per plant, and Malabar spinach yields 20 or more leaves per vine.

Yield—*Spinach/New Zealand*: Allow 15 plants per household member. *Malabar*: Allow 3 plants per household member.

Planting Time—*Spinach*: In spring, 6–8 weeks after all danger of frost has passed, then every 2–3 weeks for a continuous harvest. In mild-winter and reverse-season climates, in late autumn for winter harvest. Refrigerate seeds 1 week before sowing to help germination. *New Zealand/Malabar*: In spring after the soil has warmed. In mild-winter climates, in early spring. In reverse-season climates, in autumn.

Planting Soil Temperature—*Spinach*: 50–65°F (10–18°C). *New Zealand/Malabar*: 60–85°F (16–29°C).

Growing Temperature—*Spinach*: 60–70°F (16–21°C); it will tolerate light frost but bolts quickly in excessive heat. *New Zealand/Malabar*: 55–90°F (13–32°C); it does best with nighttime temperatures exceeding 60°F (16°C).

Soil Preparation—Have soil tested for adequate levels of nitrogen, phosphorus, and potassium and for proper acid-alkaline balance; maintain a 6.0–6.8 pH level by applying abundant organic compost. Add high-nitrogen fertilizer or well-rotted manure once plants are established. For Malabar, install wire or trellis supports at time of planting.

Spacing—*Spinach/New Zealand*: Sow seeds 1/2 inch (12 mm) deep, 1 inch (25 mm) apart, in rows 12–24 inches (30–60 cm) apart. Thin successful plants to 3–4 inches (7.5–10 cm) apart. *Malabar*: Sow 2 seeds 3/4 inch (20 mm) deep, 12 inches apart, in rows at least 3 feet (90 cm) apart. (For New Zealand and Malabar varieties, presoak seeds for 8 hours before planting to aid germination.)

Care—Keep soil moist, without wetting leaves, unless the plant will dry quickly before nightfall, and cultivate to keep weed free. For Malabar, pinch ends of vines once they are 18–24 inches (45–60 cm) long; this will encourage spreading to 40–50 inches (1–1.2 m) as vines grow laterals on wire or trellis supports.

Companion Plants—Strawberries, but not tall plants such as corn or pole beans.

Avoid—*Spinach*: Bolt by growing in temperatures below 75°F (24°C). *New Zealand/Malabar*: Exposing to frost or sustained temperatures below 60°F (16°C).

Maturity—*Spinach*: 40–50 days. *New Zealand*: 50–75 days. *Malabar*: 70–75 days.

Harvest—*Spinach*: When leaves are 4–7 inches (10–18 cm) long on heads with 6–8 leaves. Thin leaves to allow central growth bud to continue producing leaves. If leaves are picked too late, they will have a gritty texture, caused by the mineral silica deposited in the cell walls of the leaves as they mature. When plant begins to bolt, cut 3 inches (7.5 cm) above the soil to force regrowth. *New Zealand*: When leaves are 3–5 inches (7.5–12 cm) long, every 5 days, until the first frost. *Malabar*: When leaves are 3–5 inches (7.5–12 cm) in length, every week, until the first frost.

Storage—In vegetable compartment of refrigerator for 10–14 days. If blanched and chilled, in the freezer for 4–6 months.

Varieties— Bolero, Correnta, Giant Noble, Hector, Imperial Summer, Indian Summer, Italian Summer, Long Standing Bloomsdale, Mazurka, Medania, Melody, Nobel, Nordic, Norfolk, Olympia, Patience, Skookum, Space, Steadfast, Strawberry, Teton, Tetragone Cornue, Tetragonia, Tomina, Tyee, Vienna, Winter Bloomsdale, Wolter.

Tip—Spinach yields a high content of vitamins and minerals, whether raw or cooked. It is the basic green in many salads, adds flavor to stews and casseroles, and is an ingredient in many pasta dishes.

SPROUTS *(Easy)*—Sprouts are nothing other than the young seedlings of grasses and vegetable plants, harvested for use before they become tough or develop true leaves. Vegetable sprouts such as *Alfalfa, Bean, Cress, Mustard, Southern Pea*, and *Radish* are an efficient way of attaining fresh garden tastes year-round, in all climates.

Planting Time—Year-round indoors.

How to—Grow sprouts by soaking small seeds in a water-filled container for 3–4 hours, overnight for larger seeds. Empty them into a sieve or strainer, then layer into a shallow clear, sealable plastic or glass container. Place the container in a warm spot out of direct sunlight. Once a day, open the cover and add enough water to keep the seeds moist, but drain any standing water. In 3–10 days, seeds will begin to sprout. Harvest the sprouts when they are 1–2 inches (25–50 mm) long and use immediately. The container will produce sprouts for 7–10 days. Replant frequently to assure a continuous supply.

Tip—Buy only organic seeds that are specifically intended to be grown for sprouts. Sprouts can be enjoyed in salads, sandwiches, and stir-fry dishes. They contain several nutrients that aid the body's processing of carbohydrates.

SQUASH *(Easy)*—A many-member group of the gourd family, squashes are warm-season annuals that grow on bushy vines that will survive most of the temperature variations found throughout North America. The plants require plenty of space—6–8 feet (1.8–2.4 m) in all directions—and generally are planted in hills or on vertical supports when space is limited. Squash comes in two main types: *Summer*, which includes Crookneck, Scallop, Spaghetti, Straightneck, and Zucchini; and *Winter*, which includes Acorn, Banana, Butternut, Hubbard, Spaghetti, Sweet Potato, and Turban. Summer Squash is harvested in that season and eaten while its rind is still soft. Winter Squash is so named because of its ability to store well throughout that season after harvest in autumn. All squash varieties are prolific, so plan your plantings carefully.

Squash, Summer

(Easy)—Crookneck, Scallop, Straightneck, and Zucchini—Squash varieties vary in shape from round, gourdlike and cylindrical to—as their names imply—scallop- and crookneck-shaped fruits. Plants bear very broad leaves, frequently the size of a dinner plate, which rise from each of the 4–6 vines growing from the central root.

Yield—Allow 1–2 plants per household member, or up to 8 total.

Planting Time—In spring, after soil has warmed and all danger of frost has passed. In reverse-season climates, in late summer.

Planting Soil Temperature—60–85°F (16–29°C).

Growing Temperature—60–75°F (16–24°C); established fruit will ripen in temperatures as high as 100°F (38°C), but flowers will drop without setting fruit.

Soil Preparation—Have soil tested for adequate levels of nitrogen, phosphorus, and potassium and for proper acid-alkaline balance; maintain a 5.5–6.8 pH level by applying abundant organic compost, a low-nitrogen 5–10–10 fertilizer or well-rotted manure. Raise mounds 12 inches (30 cm), 6–8 feet (1.8–2.4 m) apart if plants are allowed to spread, and 4 feet (1.2 m) apart if plants are supported on wooden tripods.

Spacing—*Hills*: Sow 4–5 seeds 2–3 inches (5–7.5 cm) deep, 3–4 inches apart, in hills spaced 6–8 feet (1.8–2.4 m) apart. Thin to 2 successful plants per hill. *Rows*: Sow 2 seeds 2–3 inches (5–7.5 cm) deep, 10 inches (25 cm) apart, in rows 3–5 feet (90–150 cm) apart. Thin successful plants to 3 feet (90 cm) apart.

Care—Keep soil basin around each hill or alongside each row saturated with water and weed free. Apply 5–10–10 or other low-nitrogen fertilizer monthly, irrigating the fertilizer into the soil. If not supported on vertical tripods, place developing squash on wood planks to prevent direct soil contact.

Companion Plants—Nasturtiums, bush peas, and beans, but not tall plants.

Avoid—Wetting foliage or planting in soil that has not warmed sufficiently.

Maturity—50–65 days.

Harvest—For all varieties, when the rind is tender and before seeds have developed. For zucchini, when 5–10 inches (13–25 cm) long for slicing into rounds, 3–5 inches (7.5–13 cm) long for use whole. For yellow varieties, when 4–7 inches (10–18 cm) in length. For scallop varieties, when 3–5 inches (7.5–13 cm) in diameter.

Storage—In vegetable compartment of refrigerator for 2–3 weeks. If cooked, in the freezer for 6–8 months.

Varieties—*Crookneck*: Aztec, Bandit, Crescent, Early Summer Yellow, Golden Dawn, Horn of Plenty, Medallion, Milano, Seneca, Sundance, Supersett. *Scallop*: Benning's Green Tint, Golden Bush, Patty Pan, Peter Pan, Scallop White Bush, Scallopini, Sunburst. *Straightneck*: Early Prolific, Enterprise, Gold Slice, Goldbar, Multipik, Precious, Seneca Prolific, Sunbar. *Zucchini*: Ambassador, Arlesa, Aristocrat, Black Beauty, Black Jack, Butterstick, Chefini, Clarimore, Cocozelle, Condor, Costata Romanesco, Dark Green, Elite, Embassy, Gold Rush, Golden Dawn, Goldfinger, Greyzini, Jackpot, Lebanese Light Green, Magda, Midnight, Milano, Onyx, Raven, Ronde de Nice, Round, Seasons, Seneca, Spacemiser, Spineless Beauty, Tatume, Tipo, Viceroy. *Novelty*: Cousa, Cucuzzi, Florentino, Ghada, Tromboncino, Vegetable Marrow Bush, Zahra, Zapallo del Tronco, Zucchetta Rampicante.

Tip—The first flowers will not set fruit because they are female blossoms requiring pollination by a male flower. Later blossoms will be either female or male, resulting in pollination and fruit setting. (Female flowers are distinguished by an immature bud found at the base of the petals, which the slightly smaller male flowers lack.) Summer squash can be eaten in its entirety. Sliced, it can be steamed, boiled, broiled, baked, or grilled. It is particularly tasty when coated with butter, wrapped in foil, and barbecued or baked. Do not forget the blossoms, which, when dipped in batter and fried until brown and crunchy, are a true delicacy—and a sure way of limiting vine production

Squash, Winter

(Easy)—These squash varieties come in a wide array of shapes and colors, and their succulent flesh varies in consistency, texture, and taste. Some grow fruits as long as 30 inches (75 cm), and all of them store well.

Yield—Allow 1 plant per household member. Each plant requires 5–8 feet (1.5–2.4 m) of space unless trained onto vertical supports.

Planting Time—In spring, when soil has warmed and all danger of frost is past. In reverse-season climates a second crop may be planted in early autumn for harvest in winter.

Planting Soil Temperature—65–85°F (18–29°C).

Growing Temperature—50–90°F (10–32°C); established fruit will ripen in temperatures exceeding 100°F (38°C), but flowers will drop without setting fruit.

Soil Preparation—Have soil tested for adequate levels of nitrogen, phosphorus, and potassium and for proper acid-alkaline balance; maintain a 5.5–6.8 pH level by applying organic compost or well-rotted manure to the native soil. Add low-nitrogen 5–10–10 fertilizer before planting. Raise hills 12 inches (30 cm), 20 inches (50 cm) in diameter, and 6–8 feet (1.8–2.4 m) apart if plants are allowed to spread, or 4–5 feet (1.2–1.5 m) apart if plants are supported on sturdy wooden tripods.

Spacing—*Hills*: Sow 4–5 seeds 2–3 inches (5–7.5 cm) deep, 3–4 inches apart, in hills 6–8 feet (1.8–2.4 m) apart. Thin to 2 successful plants per hill. *Rows*: Sow 3 seeds 2–3 inches (5–7.5 cm) deep, 12–18 inches (30–45 cm) apart, in rows 6 feet (1.8 m) apart. Thin to 2 successful plants, 4 feet (1.2 m) apart.

Care—Keep soil basin around each hill or alongside each row saturated with water and weed free. If not supported on tripods, place squash on wood planks to prevent direct soil contact. Support hanging fruit in nylon netting or with other sturdy supports.

Companion Plants—Nasturtiums, bush peas, and beans, but not cabbage or other cole vegetables.

Avoid—Overhead watering.

Maturity—60–110 days.

Harvest—When rinds are full color and firm (though some varieties of acorn squash will remain green, with semihard rinds), stems and vines are hard and dry, and before the first hard frost. Cut the stems 2–4 inches (5–10 cm) above the fruit for longer storage, using pruning shears or other shearing cutters. Wipe off any clinging soil but do not wash.

Storage—Cure in the garden at temperatures of 75–80°F (24–27°C) or in a warm, protected area, then in a cool, dry, ventilated area. If cooked, in the freezer for 4–6 months.

Varieties—*Acorn*: Autumn Queen, Bush Table Queen, Carnival, Cream of the Crop, Ebony Acorn, Gill's Golden Pippin, Heart of Gold, Jade, Table Ace, Table Gold, Table King, Table Queen, Tay Belle, Tuffy Acorn. *Banana*: Pink Banana Jumbo. *Butternut*: Early Butternut, Harris Butternut, Nicklow's Delight, Ultra Neck Pumpkin, Waltham Butternut, Zenith Butternut. *Hubbard*: Baby Blue Hubbard, Little Gem, New England Blue Hubbard, Sweet Meat, Warted Chicago Hubbard. *Spaghetti*: Pasta, Pasta Spaghetti, Stripetti, Tivoli Spaghetti, Vegetable Spaghetti. *Sweet Potato*: Delicata, Sugar Loaf, Sweet Dumpling, Thelma Sanders' Sweet Potato. *Turban*: Ambercup, Autumn Cup, Bitterroot, Burgess Buttercup, Buttercup, Churimen Abobora, Emerald Bush, Honey Delight, Sweet Mama, Turk's Turban. *Other*: Doe, Flat White Boer, Futtsu Early Black, Gold Nugget, Hopi Pale Grey, Lower Salmon River, Mayo Blusher, Red Kuri, Silver Bell, Sweet Meat, Tahitian. *Novelty*: Luffa, Pasta, Stripetti, Tivoli Spaghetti, Turk's Turban, Vegetable Spaghetti.

Tip—Exposure to cold weather actually lends a sweeter flavor and better texture. Squash adds flavor and body to creamy soups and casserole dishes. The novelty spaghetti squash may be roasted whole, then split and scraped for its spaghettilike, stringy flesh for use with creamy pasta sauces, butter, or olive oil.

> "Earth is here so kind, that just tickle her with a hoe and she laughs with a harvest."
>
> ***Douglas Jerrold***

Sunflowers *(Easy)*—This warm-season, annual, gentle giant usually grows to heights of 5–12 feet (1.5–3.7 m), though dwarf varieties also exist. It is prized by gardeners of all ages for its bright golden-yellow, composite flower, which can reach as much as 18 inches (46 cm) in diameter. The center of the flower is a pithy bed bearing several hundred tasty seeds. Sunflowers also attract pollinating bees to the garden. They may require staking, unless planted in a group, to support their heavy heads.

Yield—Allow 4 plants per household member of the large varieties, keeping in mind that one flower bears 1–2½ pounds (400–900 g) of dried seeds. Double the number of plants for dwarf and miniature varieties.

Planting Time—In spring, 4 weeks after all danger of frost has passed and when the soil has warmed.

Planting Soil Temperature—65–85°F (18–29°C).

Growing Temperature—60–105°F (16–41°C).

Soil Preparation—Have soil tested for adequate levels of nitrogen, phosphorus, and potassium and for proper acid-alkaline balance; maintain a 5.8–6.2 pH level by applying organic compost and garden sulfur.

Spacing—Sow seeds ½ inch (12 mm) deep, 8–12 inches (20–30 cm) apart, in rows 30–36 inches (75–90 cm) apart. Thin successful plants to 18 inches (45 cm) apart.

Care—Water regularly, allowing the soil to dry out between waterings.

Companion Plants—Cucumbers and pole beans, but not peanuts, potatoes, or tomatoes. Use sunflowers as organic stakes for vining plants such as beans, Malabar spinach, and peas.

Avoid—Planting in areas that will cause the mature sunflowers to block sunlight to other crops.

Maturity—70–80 days.

Harvest—When seeds are hard and become loose in the flower head. Cut the stalk about 12 inches (30 cm) below the flower and hang the head upside down in a warm, dry area until the seeds are completely dry.

Storage—Remove raw seeds and store in a cool, dry place for up to 6 months. If roasted, packed into plastic storage bags and frozen, for up to 1 year.

Varieties—Black, Giant Russian, Giganteus, Helianthus, Large Grey Striped, Lemon Queen, Mammoth, Mammoth Gray Stripe, Sun, Sunspot, Velvet Queen.

Tip—If planted in a staggered row, sunflowers will provide a windbreak for other plants in the garden. To roast seeds, spread on a cookie sheet and bake at 250°F (120°C) for about 60 minutes. Raw or roasted seeds will also feed birds throughout the winter.

Swedish Turnips —See Rutabagas or Swedish Turnips

Sweet Potatoes or Yams Sweet Potatoes or Yams

(Moderate)—These warm-season perennial tuber plants resemble elongated potatoes and require a long, hot growing season to flourish—indeed, no other vegetables are as heat tolerant. The skin of the tuberous root usually is light brown or red, and the sweet flesh is yellow or gold. Sweet potatoes are relatives of the morning glory, and their plants resemble tropical vines, yielding colorful pink to purple flowers. The tuberous roots of both plants grow underground from the vine's central shoot and continue to develop in size as long as the season permits.

Yield—Allow 5 plants per household member.

Planting Time—In spring, when soil has warmed but does not exceed 85°F (29°C). In cold-winter climates, start seed tubers indoors 6–8 weeks before soil has warmed. Dust the cut surfaces with garden lime, then cover each cutting with 4 inches (10 cm) of moist sand and maintain at a temperature of 80°F (27°C) for 3–4 weeks. Reduce the temperature to 70°F (21°C) when sprouts are 3–4 inches (7.5–10 cm) long.

Planting Soil Temperature—60–85°F (16–29°C).

Growing Temperature—65–95°F (18–35°C); however, they also will thrive at temperatures as high as 100°F (38°C) if soil is kept continuously moist.

Soil Preparation—Have soil tested for adequate levels of nitrogen, phosphorus, and potassium and for proper acid-alkaline balance; maintain a 5.0–6.5 pH level by applying organic compost and garden sulfur. Add low-nitrogen 5–10–10 fertilizer, working it into the soil to a depth of 6–8 inches (15–20 cm) 2 weeks before planting.

Spacing—Set out cuttings 2–3 inches (5–7.5 cm) deep, 12–18 inches (30–45 cm) apart, in rows raised 12 inches (30 cm), 3–4 feet (90–120 cm) apart.

Care—Begin watering once the soil has dried following planting, keeping it moist but allowing no standing water. Do not pinch or cut the vines back. If desired, train the vines onto vertical supports made of lattice or wire strung between sturdy poles.

Companion Plants—Other long-cycle root vegetables such as beets, parsnips, and salsify.

Avoid—Using high-nitrogen fertilizer, which will result in lush foliage but poorly developed sweet potatoes.

Maturity—110–150 days.

Harvest—When test diggings reveal fully developed potatoes, beginning at 4 months. If vines begin to wither or turn yellow, or if there is frost, harvest immediately. Dig carefully with a garden fork, 8–10 inches (20–25 cm) away from the plant, then pull potatoes gently from the vines, taking care to avoid brusing the tubers.

Storage—Cure in the garden in a sunny, protected area for 3–4 hours, then move to a humid area between 80–85°F (27–29°C) for 10–15 days; after that, store in a dry, cool place for 8–24 weeks.

Varieties—Centennial, Georgia Jet, Jewell, Puerto Rico.

Tip—Sweet potatoes and yams can be baked, boiled, steamed, or mashed and are an excellent source of vitamin A and C.

Swiss Chard *(Easy)*—A cool-season annual and close relative of the beet, Swiss chard is grown for its large, shiny green leaves and white or red stalks. The plant reaches 12–16 inches (30–40 cm) in height when mature and will tolerate considerable heat as well as light frost. It rejuvenates itself for several pickings after its leaves are harvested before finally bolting into a flowering stalk.

Yield—Allow 2–3 plants per household member.

Planting Time—2–4 weeks after all danger of frost has passed. In mild-winter climates, in early autumn or late winter. In reverse-season climates, in autumn after summer heat has passed.

Planting Soil Temperature—50–85°F (10–29°C).

Growing Temperature—40–80°F (4–27°C), but will tolerate light frost and short periods of heat; however, extended hot weather will cause the plant to bolt.

Soil Preparation—Have soil tested for adequate levels of nitrogen, phosphorus, and potassium and for proper acid-alkaline balance; maintain a 6.0–6.8 pH level by applying abundant organic compost.

Spacing—Sow seeds 1/2 inch (12 mm) deep, 1–2 inches (25–50 mm) apart, in rows 15–25 inches (40–65 cm) apart. Thin successful plants to 8–12 inches (20–30 cm) apart.

Care—Keep soil moist and weed free. If the plant begins to bolt, pinch back the central stalk to slow maturation. Inspect frequently for chewing and sap-sucking insect pests. Apply well-rotted manure or a high-nitrogen fertilizer every 4–6 weeks.

Companion Plants—Chicory, garlic, leeks, mustard, onions, but not legumes, potatoes, or tomatoes.

Avoid—Growing in areas of excessively hot sun, which will cause leaves to turn bitter.

Maturity—45–55 days.

Harvest—When plants are 6 inches (15 cm) in height. Beginning at one end of the row, thin or cut outer leaves at the base of the stalk, slightly above the soil, moving down the row in succession. The first plants will be ready to harvest again when the end of the row is reached. Rinse and dry cut leaves thoroughly before storing.

Storage—In vegetable compartment of refrigerator for 2–3 weeks. Swiss chard also may be stored in the freezer for up to 6 months after removing the stem and center rib, blanching, and chilling in an ice water bath.

Varieties—Bright Lights, Broadstem Green, Candy Stripe, Fordhook Giant, French Green, Large White Rib, Lucullus, Perpetual, Rhubarb Chard, Ruby Red, Silverado.

Tip—Swiss chard greens taste like a milder version of spinach and can be used similarly, either raw in salads, steamed or boiled. Chard also provides a colorful thickener to soups and stews.

Tomatillos —See Husk Tomatoes, Ground Cherries, or Tomatillos

TOMATOES *(Easy)*—It will come as no surprise to anyone who has eaten a store-bought tomato that the most commonly homegrown vegetable throughout nearly every region of North America is the tomato. Most varieties are red, but others come in yellow, striped, pink, orange, and even whitish-green shades. Most are round, including the large beefsteak and diminutive cherry, but others are pear-shaped, oblong, or tear drop shaped. All tomatoes are either determinate or indeterminate. Determinate plants flower at the end of the stalk and produce fruits that ripen all at once; indeterminate varieties produce a succession of fruits on branching spurs that form beneath the foliage.

There are more than 1,000 tomato varieties, but they divide into three major categories, based on use: *Cherry* or *Miniature*, *Cooking*, and *Slicing and Eating*.

Tomatoes are a warm-season annual, requiring full sunlight and hot days to ripen fruit—although temperatures above 85°F (29°C) will prevent blooms from setting fruit. In cool climates, where the growing season is short or where inclement weather makes vine ripening difficult, green tomatoes may be picked and ripened indoors in a warm spot.

Tomatoes are also subject to a variety of plant diseases, both viral and fungal. The most common have prompted plant geneticists to develop disease-resistant strains, identified by a letter code: "V" (verticillium wilt), "F" (fusarium wilt), "N" (nematodes, a microorganism that causes cankers on the roots), and "T" (tobacco mosaic virus—tomatoes are a relative of tobacco, and subject to viral diseases of that plant species). Consult with your nursery or garden center staff to choose the varieties that are most resistant in your area.

Many heirloom varieties of tomato are available, allowing gardeners to sample unusual flavors and textures known only to a few.

Tomatoes—Cherry or Miniature *(Easy)*—The smallest variety of tomatoes, cherries range from 3/4 –1 1/2 inches (20–40 mm) in diameter and are a perfect snack food for toiling gardeners. They come in hues of red, yellow, and even zebra-stripe green.

Yield—Allow 1–4 plants of each desired variety, mixing early and late cultivars.

Planting Time—Sow seeds indoors 10–14 weeks before the soil is expected to warm, hardening seedlings 7–10 days before transplanting outdoors, or transplant nursery-grown seedlings 4–6 weeks after all danger of frost has passed. In mild-winter climates, after soil has warmed to 55°F (13°C). In the hottest climates, in late spring, or in early autumn, when at least 3 months of warm weather remain.

Planting Soil Temperature—55–85°F (13–29°C).

Growing Temperature—65–90°F (18–32°C); however, fruit may not set in temperatures exceeding 85°F (29°C) and may require shade covers to prevent sunburn in direct-sunlight areas exceeding 90°F (32°C)

Soil Preparation—Have soil tested for adequate levels of nitrogen, phosphorus, and potassium and for proper acid-alkaline balance; maintain a 5.5–6.8 pH level by digging in to a depth of 3 feet (90 cm) a mixture of compost, peat moss, and garden gypsum, or decomposed ground bark equal to one-half the volume of the native soil. If planting in containers, select only the largest and deepest to allow for good drainage

Spacing—Sow 2–3 seeds ½ inch (12 mm) deep, 18–48 inches (45–120 cm) apart, thinning successful plants to 3 feet (90 cm) apart. Plant seedlings 18–48 inches (90–115 cm) apart, in rows 35–45 inches (1–1.2 m) apart. If the plants will require staking, set them 12–24 inches (30–60 cm) apart, in rows 35–45 inches (90–115 cm) apart. For container plants, install a cage at the time of planting to support the plants' foliage and fruits.

Care—Keep soil moist, taking care not to wet the fruit, vines, or foliage. Mulch to help root development and to maintain soil temperature during the night. Apply a low-nitrogen fertilizer only until fruit begins developing. If heat becomes extreme, shade the plant with porous shade fabric installed on wooden supports. Inspect for hornworm, a very large, voracious, green moth larva that all but disappears among the stems and foliage. Identify it by the damage it does to leaves and fruit, or from its round black droppings on leaves.

Companion Plants—Asparagus, carrots, chives, marigolds, nasturtiums, onions, and parsley.

Avoid—Using high-nitrogen fertilizers, which will produce abundant foliage but stunt the fruit.

Maturity—50–90 days.

Harvest—When full color and desired size but before the first frost. Support the vine in one hand and gently pull the fruit to prevent damage to the plant. Pick green for pickling.

Storage—At room temperature for 7–10 days. If pickled, for up to 2 years.

Varieties—Consult your garden retailer.

Tip—Cherry or miniature tomatoes can be grown in a container indoors year-round. As winter sets in, use ultraviolet "grow lights" to promote flowering and fruiting—tomatoes require a minimum of 6 equivalent full-sun hours per day. Cherries come in red and yellow hues and are a favorite in salads and vegetable trays; when green, they are an old-time favorite for pickling.

Tomatoes, Cooking

(Easy)—Cooking varieties generally are oblong or pear shaped, with a meatier, less juicy flesh than the eating varieties, but with a sweeter flavor. Because most ripen at a single time, they provide sufficient quantities for canning and sauces. They are a core ingredient for many cuisines of the Mediterranean—Spain, Italy, France, the Balkans, and Greece, among others—which would not be nearly as enticing without their contribution

Yield—Allow 3–6 plants of each desired variety, which will yield 8–10 quarts of each type of tomato. Allow sufficient time to cook, can, and freeze beginning 4–5 weeks after transplanting greenhouse seedlings of the early varieties to the garden, and every 3–4 weeks thereafter.

Planting Time—Sow seeds indoors 10–14 weeks before the soil is expected to warm, hardening seedlings 7–10 days before transplanting outdoors, or transplant nursery-grown seedlings 4–6 weeks after all danger of frost has passed. In cold-winter and short-season climates, sow seeds indoors 3–4 weeks before soil is expected to reach 60°F (16°C).

Planting Soil Temperature—55–85°F (13–29°C).

Growing Temperature—65–90°F (18–32°C); however, fruit may not set in temperatures exceeding 85°F (29°C) and may require shade covers in direct sunlight areas exceeding 90°F (32°C) to prevent sunburn.

Soil Preparation—Have soil tested for adequate levels of nitrogen, phosphorus, and potassium and for proper acid-alkaline balance; maintain a 5.5–6.8 pH level by digging in to a depth of 3 feet (90 cm) a mixture of compost, peat moss, and garden gypsum, or decomposed ground bark equal to one-half the volume of the native soil.

Spacing—Sow 2–3 seeds ½ inch (12 mm) deep, 18–48 inches (45–120 cm) apart, thinning successful plants to 42 inches (1.1 m) apart. Plant seedlings 18–48 inches (45–120 cm) apart, in rows 40–50 inches (1–1.2 m) apart. If the plants will require staking, set them 12–24 inches (30–60 cm) apart, in rows 36–48 inches (90–120 cm) apart.

Care—Keep soil moist, taking care not to wet the fruit, vines, or foliage. Mulch to aid root development and to maintain soil temperature during the night. Apply a low-nitrogen fertilizer only until fruit begins developing. If overnight temperatures below 40°F (4°C) are anticipated, protect plants with plastic or fabric coverings, taking care not to allow the coverings to come in contact with foliage or fruits. If heat becomes extreme, shade the plant with porous shade fabric installed on wooden supports. Inspect for hornworm, a very large, voracious, green moth larva that all but disappears among the stems and foliage. Identify it by the damage it does to leaves and fruit, or from its round black droppings on leaves. Cooking tomatoes are especially prone to a growth disorder, known as "blossom-end" rot, that appears as a brown, scablike area on the blossom end of the fruit. Water the plants regularly and dust the soil with crushed oyster shell, gypsum, or other high-calcium supplements, or plant resistant varietals. Mulch the soil with straw to retain moisture.

Companion Plants—Asparagus, carrots, chives, marigolds, nasturtiums, onions, and parsley.

Avoid—Using high-nitrogen fertilizers, which will produce abundant foliage but stunt the fruit.

Maturity—50–90 days.

Harvest—For determinate varieties, when the clusters of fruit reach full color and desired size but before the first frost. For indeterminate varieties, when the fruit is at the peak of color but not yet soft and emits a strong aroma. Support the vine with one hand and gently pull the fruit to prevent damage.

Storage—At room temperature for 7–10 days. If cut and packaged, in the freezer for 3–4 months. If canned, for up to 2 years. If dried, either sliced and laid flat on drying trays or in a vegetable dehydrator, for up to 1 year. Never refrigerate fresh whole tomatoes.

Varieties—Consult your garden retailer.

Tip—If tomatoes become overripe, freeze them or use immediately for fresh food preparations. Never can such tomatoes, because they have lost much of their natural acidic balance, which increases the risk of botulism even when they are processed in a pressure cooker.

Tomatoes—Slicing and Eating   *(Easy)*—Gen-

erally, these varieties are the largest, juiciest, most flavorful tomatoes. In long-growing-season locales, they may produce a bountiful series of harvests; in frost areas, the entire season may be required to produce a single, yet high-yield, picking. They come in both early-season and longer-developing varieties; those with longer growth periods have enhanced taste and texture.

Yield—Allow 1–4 plants of each desired variety per household member, mixing early and late cultivars. Double the number of plantings if the fruit is intended to be crushed for juice.

Planting Time—Sow seeds indoors 10–14 weeks before the garden soil is expected to warm, hardening seedlings 7–10 days before transplanting outdoors, or transplant nursery-grown seedlings 4–6 weeks after all danger of frost has passed. In mild-winter climates, after soil has warmed to 55°F (13°C). In the hottest climates, in late spring, or in early autumn when at least 3 months of warm weather remain.

Planting Soil Temperature—55–85°F (13–29°C).

Growing Temperature—65–90°F (18–32°C); however, fruit may not set in temperatures exceeding 85°F (29°C). Shade covers may be required to prevent sunburn in direct sunlight areas exceeding 90°F (32°C).

Soil Preparation—Have soil tested for adequate levels of nitrogen, phosphorus, and potassium and for proper acid-alkaline balance; maintain a 5.5–6.8 pH level by digging in to a depth of 3 feet (90 cm) a mixture of compost, peat moss, and garden gypsum, or decomposed ground bark equal to one-half the volume of the native soil. Install support stakes or wire cages.

Spacing—Sow 2–3 seeds ½ inch (12 mm) deep, 18–48 inches (45–120 cm) apart, thinning successful plants to 42 inches (1.1 m) apart. Plant seedlings 18–48 inches (45–120 cm) apart, in rows 40–50 inches (1–1.2 m) apart. If the plants will require staking, set them 12–24 inches (30–60 cm) apart, in rows 36–48 inches (90–120 cm) apart.

Care—Keep soil moist, taking care not to wet the fruit, vines, or foliage. Mulch to help root development and to maintain soil temperatures during cool nights. Apply a low-nitrogen fertilizer only until fruit begins developing. If heat becomes extreme, shade the plant by installing porous shade fabric on wooden supports. Inspect for hornworm, a very large, voracious, green moth larva that all but disappears among the stems and foliage. Identify it by the damage it does to leaves and fruit, or from its round black droppings on leaves.

Companion Plants—Asparagus, carrots, chives, marigolds, onions, and parsley.

Avoid—Using high-nitrogen fertilizers, which will produce abundant foliage but stunt the fruit.

Maturity—50–90 days.

Harvest—When full color and desired size but before the first frost. Support the vine in one hand and gently pull the fruit to prevent damage to the plant. Pick green for frying or pickling.

Storage—At room temperature for 7–10 days. If pressed for their juice, in the freezer for up to 6 months. If pickled, for up to 2 years.

Varieties—Consult your garden retailer.

Tip—These are the eating tomato of choice for sandwiches, salads, and pizza; they may also be pickled or breaded and fried when green.

Turnips *(Easy)*—This cool-season annual produces edible greens and a bulbous root with a white interior and crisp texture. The most common varieties are globe shaped, though oval forms are also common. Turnip greens sometimes are grown as the only crop, either by harvesting before the root forms or by planting varieties that do not develop swollen roots.

Yield—Allow 5–10 plants per household member.

Planting Time—In late summer for early autumn harvest. In mild-winter climates, in early spring for summer harvest, then again in early autumn for late autumn harvest. In reverse-season climates, in late autumn for winter harvest.

Planting Soil Temperature—40–75°F (4–24°C).

Growing Temperature—40–75°F (4–24°C); if temperatures exceed 75°F (24°C) for extended periods, roots will be slow to develop and may fail.

Soil Preparation—Have soil tested for adequate levels of nitrogen, phosphorus, and potassium and for proper acid-alkaline balance; maintain a 5.5–6.8 pH level by applying organic compost and well-rotted manure. If soil is dense, add sand or gypsum. Soil is best if green manure is dug into the bed before the end of the prior season.

Spacing—Sow seeds 1/2 inch (12 mm) deep, 1 inch (25 mm) apart, in rows 15–36 inches (40–90 cm) apart. Thin successful plants to 4–6 inches (10–15 cm) apart.

Care—Keep soil moist and weed free. Mulch with loose straw to protect the tops of the root from sunburn.

Companion Plants—Bush beans, peas, and southern peas.

Avoid—Leaving in the ground past maturity, which will cause turnips to become woody and lose flavor.

Maturity—30–60 days.

Harvest—When greens are 12 inches (30 cm) long and tubers are 2–3 inches (5–7.5 cm) in diameter. For greens, thin the outside leaves, leaving the central growth bud to resprout. For tubers, dig carefully with a garden fork.

Storage—In vegetable compartment of refrigerator, 7–10 days for greens and 2–3 months for tubers. The roots also store well in the ground at soil temperatures of 35–80°F (2–27°C). If cooked, in the freezer for up to 6 months.

Varieties—All Top, Amber Globe, American Purple Top Yellow, De Milan, Gilfeather, Hakurei, Just Right, Market Express, Purple Top White Globe, Red Milan, Royal Crown, Seven Top, Tokyo Cross, Tokyo Market, Tomson Laurentian, Topper, Vertus, White Egg, White Lady, Yori Spring, York.

Tip—Turnip greens are prized for their delicate flavor and because they are generally unavailable in most grocery stores. They are delicious raw as an addition to salads, or steamed. The turnip bulb, with its unique, sweet flavor, may be eaten raw, baked, or boiled and mashed.

Watercress *(Easy)*—These cool-season, zesty-flavored, small green plants are used for spicy greens and garnishes. The three major varieties include perennial *Watercress*, annual *Garden Cress*, and biennial *Early Winter Cress*. The first of these is the most common and the most commonly available; it grows, rooted in soil, in pure, gently running water, which makes it ideal for planting in backyard watercourses and decorative ponds. Garden cress, also known as peppergrass, and early winter cress are parsleylike plants that thrive in damp-soil locations.

Yield—*Watercress* and *Early Winter Cress*: Allow 1 plant per household. *Garden Cress*: Allow 1 plant per household, planted every 2 weeks to ensure a continuous supply.

Planting Time—*Watercress* and *Garden Cress*: In spring, when soil becomes workable and water temperature reaches 50°F (10°C). In reverse-season climates, in late autumn for winter harvest. *Early Winter Cress*: In late summer, sparingly for autumn and winter harvests, allowing for new growth the following year. Not recommended for reverse-season climates.

Planting Soil Temperature—50–85°F (10–29°C).

Growing Temperature—40–85°F (10–29°C).

Soil Preparation—Maintain a 6.0–6.8 pH level by amending with organic compost. *Watercress*: This water plant grows in containers with a rich soil, sand, and compost mixture submerged in running water or artificial watercourses constructed for ornamental use. Prepare pots, then submerge after planting. *Garden Cress* and *Early Winter Cress*: Continuously moist soil requiring rich organic, sandy loam. The submerged, wet environment necessary for watercress is not desirable for these plants.

Spacing—Broadcast seeds over the area and cover with 1/8 inch (3 mm) of loose soil. Thin successful plants to 6–8 inches (15–20 cm) apart. For seedlings, transplant and space accordingly.

Care—*Watercress*: Provide a moving, well-aerated supply of water in an area free from excessive sunlight. Pinch main runners to limit spreading. *Garden Cress*: Keep soil moist and weed free. Prune branching foliage to prevent overgrowth. *Early Winter Cress*: Keep soil moist and weed free. Remove seed stalks to promote new foliage development.

Companion Plants—Bunching onions, chives, and garden peppermint, spearmint, and wintergreen.

Avoid—Planting in areas that receive direct sunlight.

Maturity—*Watercress*: 55–70 days. *Garden Cress*: 10–14 days. *Early Winter Cress*: 40–50 days, then again 21–28 days after resprouting the following spring.

Harvest—*Watercress*: Pick individual leaves and tender sprouts at the tips of runners. *Garden Cress* and *Early Winter Cress*: 12–16 days after planting, when plants are 4–5 inches (10–12 cm) tall.

Storage—In vegetable compartment of refrigerator for 3–5 days.

Varieties—Nonvarietals.

Tip—Watercress and garden cress are mainly used to lend a peppery flavor to salads. The bitter flavor of early winter cress is best when cooked with milder-tasting vegetables.

Windsor Beans —See Beans, Fava, Horse, or Windsor

Yams —See Sweet Potatoes or Yams

Yam Beans —See Jicama, Yam Beans, or Mexican Potatoes

Zucchini —See Squash, Summer

"I have a garden
of my own.
Shining with every hue,
I loved it dearly
while alone.
But I shall love it more
with you."

Thomas Moore 1835

Garden Tools

Aerator, Compost   An aerator is inserted into the compost pile to stir and add oxygen to the mix. It's a 3-foot (30-cm) long tool with small paddlelike blades that easily penetrate the compost and loosen it up. Galvanized-steel tube poles are best.

Apron/Vest, Gardeners   To keep the smaller tools of the trade right by your side, an apron or vest keeps seed packages, trowels, gloves, and many other items secured in big pockets or loops. Aprons generally are made from heavy cotton duck-cloth or poly denier fabric, and vests from light cotton material. A vest offers the added advantage of backpocket storage.

> "One of the healthiest ways to gamble is with a spade and a package of garden seeds."
>
> ***Dan Bennett***

Ax   This heavy-duty implement fells trees, splits logs, and clears brush. The ax blade should be broad and constructed out of forged and tempered steel. A hickory handle is considered best, but any high-quality, close-grained hardwood will do. The average ax weighs between 4 and 5 pounds (1.8–2.3 kg). A smaller ax, the hatchet, is also useful for chopping kindling and other, lighter tasks.

Belts, Tool   When a single holster is not enough and an apron is too heavy, a tool belt is a good bet. Most garden tool belts are constructed out of cotton canvas duck, but if you prefer leather there are tons of choices at any home supply depot. A good tool belt should offer space for trowels, stakes, seed packages, gloves and small folding knives, to name just a few items.

Bench, Kneeling   A kneeler is a padded bench with rigid tubular handles that helps take the grunt out of getting up and down. Once down, your knees are protected by a foam cushion. Flip the device over and you've got yourself a seat. A sturdy steel frame and well-padded bench indicate a quality product.

Bill/Brush Hook   The billhook, and its longer-handled cousin, the brushhook, are among the most ancient of cutting tools. A few swipes of the broad, hook-ended blade will clear out your garden space in no time. A quality model has a double-edged blade forged out of solid steel and handles that are flat and made of hardwood.

Bin, Compost   Soil is nourished by compost, which is made up of organic material. With a compost bin you can produce your own by recycling your food scraps (though avoid composting any meats or other fatty foods). Compost bins are made of wood, metal, or plastic and come in various shapes and sizes, but they should be at least 3 X 3 X 3 feet (90 X 90 X 90 cm). There should be at least one removable door or lid to allow for turning and collecting purposes.

Bin, Potato   If you lack the space for a potato crop of any magnitude, potato bins offer the solution. Fifty pounds (23 kg) of tuber will grow in one of these polyethylene bins. Just layer the bottom with potting soil, insert the seed potato starters, then layer with soil and straw. Open the side of the container at harvest time and the potatoes spill right out. Most bins adjust from 1–3 feet (30–90 cm) in diameter.

Blowers   To whisk leaves and debris off your vegetable beds without scouring the surface, get a gas- or electric-powered leaf blower. Energy flow is maximized by means of tube extensions to produce cleansing gusts of air. Big, high-output blowers resemble vacuum cleaners and can be wheeled around the garden, but handheld or backpack models are more convenient. Portable blowers commonly have air-speed controls; vacuum or mulching options are also available.

Boots, Wellington   Commonly nicknamed "Wellies," these rubber boots are easy to slip on and off. The boots come in high- or low-cut styles. They are invaluable when working in saturated soil or standing water. The soles are thick and reinforced, providing foot protection and grip. High Wellies come up to the calf, where they can be drawn tight to keep out water.

C

Cage, Tomato   This galvanized, 32-inch (82-cm) high steel cage supports fully grown tomato plants and the heaviest of fruit. The cage openings are 8-inches (20-cm) wide, allowing easy access to your crop. The standard model can be stacked one on top of the other for efficient storage; others are hinged to fold flat for even tighter storage space.

Cart, Garden   A 2-wheeled garden cart is less tippy than the wheelbarrow and has more interior space. The bottom is flat, which makes it useful for hauling potted plants or planked wood. Garden-cart wheels resemble fat-tire bike wheels and are very maneuverable. A galvanized steel frame wrapped around thick plywood indicates a well-constructed cart.

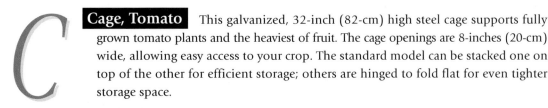

"The green metal chair is an indispensable piece of equipment. As Farmer Bagley said, "How can you grow anything without a chair? How else you going to see what's going on?"."

William Longgood

Cell Packs   These plastic trays filled with seedling "cells" are rooted in soil and divided into little sod units. Cell packs usually come in counts of 6, 36, 48, and 72. Pop out the cells when the plants have grown and transplant them into the garden or a container.

Claw —See Cultivator, 3-pronged

Cloche A cloche is most classically shaped like a bell jar and functions like a cold frame [see Cold Frame]. It is designed to protect the plants you may have set out in your garden in advance of ideal weather. Unlike a cold frame, which is constructed in the garden and then receives the plants, you bring the cloche to the plantings and place it over them like a hat. It also protects from wind, bugs, and birds. Cloches come in glass or plastic and in varying shapes and sizes.

Clogs A pair of garden clogs will spare your vegetable garden the heavy tread of a rubber boot. This footwear has an enclosed heel and is made of rubberlike plastic; cork insoles cushion the feet. Dirt and mud rinses easily off these shoes, which come in an array of bright colors.

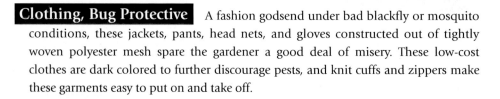

Clothing, Bug Protective A fashion godsend under bad blackfly or mosquito conditions, these jackets, pants, head nets, and gloves constructed out of tightly woven polyester mesh spare the gardener a good deal of misery. These low-cost clothes are dark colored to further discourage pests, and knit cuffs and zippers make these garments easy to put on and take off.

Cold Frame A cold frame allows plants access to sunlight in the cool of winter while protecting them from the elements. Its purpose is to promote early growth. Cold frames can be opened to help acclimate crops or flowers to the outside air. Most are of wood-frame construction with acrylic or plastic windows. They should be hinged to allow different degrees of air exposure [see step-by-step instructions, pg. 158].

Containers, Plant For creating a movable vegetable garden, either for decorative reasons or to protect plants during periods of inclement weather, plant containers are essential. They can be elaborate or simple, huge or tiny, hang from the rafters or tuck into a nook. Common container materials are terra cotta, cast stone concrete, glazed earthenware, woven twig or vine, cedar, redwood, and many, many forms of plastic. All containers should be washed thoroughly and sterilized before receiving any plantings.

"Other people's tools work only in other people's gardens."

Arthur Bloch

Crowbar When a mattock or pick won't do for major rock removal, consider the crowbar. This lean, long tool—the standard size is about 60 inches (1.5 m)—is perfect for manipulating a rock into another position or for pulling it out of the ground altogether. Do not consider anything but a high-quality steel model.

CULTIVATORS—Used to loosen soil for the optimal circulation of air and water through the soil, cultivators are also useful as weeders. The tools are pronged or tined and designed to stir up the first $1/2$ inch (12 mm) of topsoil. Most cultivators are about the length of a hoe, but there also are small handheld and wheeled models available. Hardwood grips and steel construction are the norm for quality tools.

Cultivator, Hoe Combination —See Hoe, Combination/Cultivator

Cultivator, 3-Pronged For cultivating the garden in a standing position, this cultivator is a comfortable choice and also works more ground than a small hand instrument can. It's especially good for loosening topsoil and stirring in compost or fertilizer. The tines and head should be forged from a single sheet of steel. Flexible tines are also desirable as they will give a bit when they hit a rock or other debris.

DIBBERS—A very simple garden tool, the dibber pokes holes in the ground so you can plant seeds or bulbs. The gardener's skill comes in determining how deep or wide to make the hole. There are fat and skinny dibbers in a number of styles. The best constructed generally have hardwood handles and carbon steel tips, but lighter weight materials will do fine for many jobs.

Dibber, Pencil-sized A very small but useful propagation tool, handy at the potting bench for poking seed holes into pots or flats of seedling trays, these small "pencils" are about 5–9-inches (12–25-cm) long with a tiny tip.

Dibber, Planting This dibber is constructed of polished aluminum and calibrated with grooves to help you determine the depth of the holes you want to make. A vinyl-covered T-grip tops this highly regarded dibber, which is designed to penetrate turf, sod, or tough soil.

Dibber, Straight or D-Grip The straight dibber is shaped like a carbon steel–tipped finger and performs just as one of your digits would if it were that sturdy. The D-grip dibber does the same thing, except it is heavier in weight—2 pounds (0.9 kg)—and sports a more secure grip. It's a better choice for stubborn soil.

Dusters   Constructed out of plastic and nylon, dusters deliver and apply dry forms of insecticide to the garden. Use them when winds are light or nonexistent and always wear a respirator. Hand-crank dusters are generously sized and have the capacity to cover large areas. Extension tubes at about 15 inches (38 cm) in length place the product where you want it.

Ear Protectors   When the quiet garden approaches rock-concert sound levels in the presence of blowers, rototillers, power mowers, and the like, the gardener is well advised to plug in some ear protection. Soft foam plugs are disposable and custom fit your ear canal. Preshaped foam plugs fit smoothly in the ear and often are attached to a cord for easy removal. Air-cushioned earplugs come with a light headband and relieve pressure on the ear canal. The most protective are earmuffs, with foam cushions surrounding the ear to shut out noise, and an adjustable headband.

Eye Protection   —See Goggles

Edgers   An edger allows the gardener to keep nice, clean lines at the vegetable bed or border, walkway or patio. Edgers are long-handled, half-moon-shaped blades that are very sharp. Carbon or forged steel heads are best. An edger should be kept well sharpened so the blade, not you, is doing most of the sod-cutting work.

Edgings, Lawn   Border markers that prevent lawn from creeping into the vegetable patch, lawn edgings come in plastic, terra cotta, concrete, wrought iron, aluminum, and wood. They are staked or pounded into the soil and are available in all sorts of configurations, styles, and lengths.

FORKS—They vary in shape, length, and number of tines, but forks all function as an extension of your hand. The fork scoops, lifts, and transports material as well as crumbling and turning soil. The best tools are constructed of forged steel and have long solid sockets that are riveted to the handle. The tines should be strong or they'll soon bend out of shape with heavy use. A fork should fit the individual, so test out the heft and size of several until you find one comfortable for you. Forks typically weigh from 2–5 pounds (0.9–2.3 kg) and are 3–4 feet (90–120 cm) in length. YD-grips lend additional control.

Fork, Bedding   Ten closely spaced tines make this fork a good choice for spreading around mulch and compost and for scooping it up. This fork is just under 6-feet (1.8-m) long, which lends it lots of reach. A forged steel head is best.

Fork, Broadfork   A specialty tool, the two-handled broadfork allows the gardener to use his or her body weight to work the fork into the soil for deep aeration, making it especially excellent for a vegetable garden. Ash handles and five forged-steel tines indicate high quality.

Fork, Compost   This specialty fork is constructed just for turning compost. The tines are thin and diamond pointed to allow it to penetrate the compost without destroying useful bugs and worms. The fork should have a forged carbon steel head and be securely joined to a high-quality hardwood handle. T-grips add power and control.

Fork, English Garden   A heavy, strong digging fork with four slender but chiseled tines, this fork penetrates deeply into tough rocky or clay soils without disturbing roots. It's long, at about 4 feet (1.2 m), making it better suited to a tall, strong gardener. Forged-steel construction and quality hardwood handles are a must.

Fork, Hand   This light, 3-tined, 15-inch (38-cm) long cultivator also is an efficient weeder in the vegetable garden. High-quality, enameled steel blades set in solid, hardwood ash are durable and rust resistant.

Fork, Hay or Pitch   The classic pitchfork of the old-fashioned farm is one of the most primitive "found" tools, descended from branches farmers simply picked up and put to use. The 3-tined pitch or hay fork is now constructed out of forged steel and secured by a bolt to a hardwood handle. Its function remains unchanged—to move hay, leaves, compost, and other lightweight matter from point A to point B.

Fork, Spading   A lightweight tool with 4 widely spaced tines that come to triangular points, the spading fork is good for tilling sandy and other light, crumbly soil. A light, stamped-metal head is adequate, but best durability is provided by a steel head.

> "Gloves…interfered with the tactile pleasure of gardening."
>
> *Gail Godwin*

GLOVES, GARDENING—Thorns, rocks, dirt, sticks, spiky leaves, and the human hand are not a good match. Gloved protection comes in the form of canvas, rubber, nylon, leather, and combinations of these materials. A glove with a grip on the palm is desirable when working with tools. Many gloves also feature gaiters or gauntlets constructed out of nylon, leather, or canvas to protect the forearm.

Gloves, Canvas Canvas gloves are best worn while working with dry materials since cotton can soak up water like a sponge. For standard gardening jobs such as weeding, digging, and pruning, the canvas glove is an inexpensive choice and provides adequate protection.

Gloves, Leather Offering more protection against thorns, rocks, and other sharp objects, leather gloves also repel water much better than does canvas. Good-quality leather is flexible and smooth against your hand. Pigskin is the toughest leather, followed by cowhide; goatskin is the most supple and makes for an elegant and very durable glove.

Goggles Eye protection is essential when working with axes or mallets, constructing a potting table or raised-bed supports, fertilizing or applying insecticides. Safety goggles wrap around the head and should fit snugly. Vent holes prevent the eyewear from steaming or fogging up. A lens made of polycarbonate material provides impact resistance.

Grass Trimmers Nylon-cord grass trimmers operate either by battery, electricity, or gas. The nylon filament whirls around at a very high speed, whipping through weeds and grass. It's most commonly used to trim spaces where lawn meets pavement, but with careful use at low speeds can keep lawn from encroaching on vegetable garden beds.

Handle Types In addition to the straightforward, rounded end of a shaft, there are several other hilt configurations—D, YD, and T. The D-grip is a strong snub grip that offers a firm hand rest for twisting motions; the best are made out of metal. The wooden or metal YD-grip resembles a D-grip but is more elongated; the sides of the grip are bridged with a metal reinforced crosspiece. The T-grip is a good hilt for pushing or tossing work and lends additional push power to smaller hand tools.

Hat, Cloth or Canvas Soft cotton hats can be crushed in your pocket or garden apron, dipped in water to cool your head, and used as a sweat rag if need be. Primarily, a hat keeps your head protected from the sun—and protects you when a 15-minute trip out to the garden turns into 2 hours. When it gets dirty or sweaty, just pop it into the washing machine. Look for a canvas hat with eyelets to provide air circulation.

Hat, Panama The true Panama hat is made in Ecuador and offers the widest-brimmed protection from a hot sun. Panamas are lightweight and woven in a way that allows air to circulate, keeping your head fairly cool. A model with a chin strap is useful to keep it from falling off your head when bending over.

Hilt —See Handle Types

HOES—A classic for the tilling and cultivation of vegetable and flower gardens, a hoe is used for weeding, and cutting or breaking ground. Blades come in different widths, made from stamped metal or steel, but the finest are forged out of one piece of steel. The best hardwood handles are made from ash or hickory. Because the cutting edge of the hoe is constantly smacking into dirt and rock, it's important to keep it oiled, clean, and sharp.

Hoe, Circle   A more recent garden innovation, the circle hoe has a fixed, hooplike carbon-steel blade that is sharp on the inner side and blunt on the outer. Instead of chopping the hoe into the soil, you pull it towards you to weed and aerate an area. Because the blunt end of the blade is on the outside, you can place it right up against a plant without cutting it.

Hoe, Combination/Cultivator   The small cultivator hoe has a 3-pronged cultivating fork on one side of the head and a sharp narrow hoe blade on the other. It's strong enough to cultivate heavy claylike soil and is useful for chopping up roots and digging holes for bulbs and seedlings. It can even take on small trenching jobs. Steel or wood handles are standard, and the head should be of high-quality steel.

Hoe, Draw   This classic hoe is fundamental for weed control, cultivation, and cutting and drawing trenches. The flat, forged steel blade is sharp and should be supported by a swan neck that allows leverage for cutting deep into the soil. A solid ash handle indicates a high-quality tool.

"Hoeing in the garden on a bright, soft May day, when you are not obliged to, is nearly equal to the delight of going trouting."
Charles Dudley Warner

Hoe, Grape   This tool came to the vineyards of the United States by way of Italy, which is why it also is known as the Italian Eye Hoe. The blade is scoop shaped and constructed of forged steel. It is somewhat short handled and heavy, which makes it a formidable chopping implement for tough vines.

Hoe, Hand   A light, short weeder, the hand hoe slices through roots, which makes it ideal for removing weeds from vegetable rows and flower beds. The hand hoe is 15-inches (38-cm) long and requires the gardener to kneel or sit when working. A good-quality hand hoe with a sharp steel blade is just as efficient as its larger cousins and can work in more delicate spaces.

Hoe, Narrow Field This lightweight, narrow-bladed hoe with a goose or swan-like neck has a 4-inch (10-cm) wide blade that makes it a good choice for small areas, sandy soils, beds, and borders. Hardwood handles, steel blades and necks indicate a quality field hoe.

Hoe, Onion Think of the draw hoe, then think of it in miniature. The swan neck and flat steel blade are the same in configuration, only smaller, for accessing hard-to-reach garden spaces or the diminutive needs of a container. A rust-resistant finish, hardwood handle, and leather hanging thong indicate a durable tool.

Hoe, Oscillating or Action A $1/2$-inch (12-mm) double stirrup-shaped blade distinguishes this tool from all others. The difference between this and a regular hoe is in the double-cutting push-pull motion that allows the gardener to destroy weeds at or below the soil surface without wasting energy with a chopping stroke. A good model should have a galvanized steel frame holding a tempered steel blade. Keep this tool well oiled.

Hoe, Stalham This heavy-duty dirt-pushing hoe has a broad 6-inch (15-cm) blade, thick handle, and goose neck. Comfortable and solid, the best versions are made of enameled steel, which helps the hoe slice through soil without sticking.

Holster A heavy-duty grain leather holster keeps pruners, saws, loppers, and shears safely enclosed by your side. The leather should be firmly riveted and sewn with waxed thread. Some models clip on; others fit just like a belt. Most holsters hold a single tool but there are double holsters that are just shy of a full-fledged tool belt.

HOSES—The 5-ply, PVC-tubed, vinyl-covered hose is a garden standard because it won't burst or crack in extreme cold or heat. At the same time, it is inexpensive enough to replace when the dog chews it or car tires mangle it. Hoses, the "long, thin buckets" of country lore, come in a range of lengths; the standard diameter is $5/8$ inch (16 mm). A good hose has brass couplings.

Hose, Soaker A soaker hose "leaks" water to a given area by means of a multitude of tiny holes. It waters slowly and evenly and is especially useful under drought conditions. High-quality soaker hoses are made of durable rubber, supplanting the canvas hoses that were prone to rot.

HOSE ACCESSORIES—Hose guides stake the hose above and away from walkways and toward vegetable beds. Pistol grip nozzles allow the gardener greater control over water pressure and direction. Rain wands and the smaller patio wand are rigid extensions that disperse water in a gentle, showering manner, making them perfect for container plantings and watering tender seedlings.

Hose, Guides These guides stake your hose above or around plants so the plants are not mangled by dragging the hose through the bed. There are three major types: Stakes, or steel rods coated with a smooth polyester that support the hose aboveground; plastic rotating guides that allow the hose to glide smoothly around them; and pop-up guides, which can be recessed into the ground when the hose is not in use.

Hose, Patio Wand A smaller version of the rain wand, the patio wand is perfect for watering container plants and hanging baskets. It's constructed out of aluminum and disperses water in a gentle shower.

Hose, Pistol Grip Nozzle This grip allows the gardener greater control over water pressure and the direction of the spray. Fancy nozzles allow you to jet- or flat-spray surfaces for cleanup or to lightly shower vegetable plants without disturbing the soil.

Hose, Rain Wands Lightweight aluminum makes this an easy-to-use tool for watering the back of the bed and other out of the way places. The rigid 40-inch (10-cm) extension attaches to a hose and gently waters seedlings and other delicate plants without drenching them.

"Garden tools have a special meaning. They represent one of the great milestones in human evolution, when man began to grow his own food. The first tool was probably a pointed stick to scratch the earth and plant a seed, a revolutionary act that may mark the real beginning of civilization, the transition from hunter to farmer and the first settled communities. Then he learned to attach a shell or sharp stone to the stick and he had a primitive hoe and progress was on its way."

William Longgood

K

KNIVES—Garden knives are specialized tools used for grafting, pruning, weeding, and cutting. These small instruments are designed for specific purposes and should not be interchanged. While all-purpose knives, or a pocket knife, can substitute for some tasks, the ease with which speciality knives perform their work makes them an ideal choice.

Knife, Budding   Very similar to the grafting knife, this tool features a small bump on the dull side of the blade to lift bark or hold a stock cut open so a bud can be inserted. Budding knives are useful for grafting rose, fruit, and small ornamental stock. These knives should be constructed from forged or stainless steel and feature a quality hardwood or horn handle.

Knife, Grafting   This small all-purpose knife is used for grafting, pruning, and cutting. The straight blade makes it a handy tool for the potting bench; many folding models are available to prevent accidents if children or pets are nearby. A quality knife has a forged steel blade and durable hardwood handle.

Knife, Grub   A flat, broad knife with one serrated and one smooth edge, this tool is used primarily to dig up bulbs and tubers. It also makes a good catch-all tool for some sawing or digging jobs. The blade typically is 6 inches (15 cm) in length.

Knife, Pruning   The blade of the pruning knife has a hooked, slightly curved end. Because of the curve it's not as handy for potting bench grafting or cutting jobs, but is a good tool for taking light cuttings from the garden. Hand-forged stainless steel will keep the sharpest edge and prevent "tearing" stems. Hardwood handles are best. Many folding models are available.

L

Labels/Markers, Plant   Unless you can remember what every little green sprig poking its way to the surface of your garden is, plant labels will help keep your crop tracked. Markers can be fancy, with verdigris finishes, or popsicle-stick plain. Popular materials include copper, zinc, wood, ceramic, and plastic. Seed packages can be placed over the labels, or they can be marked with a grease pencil. Many markers come pre-engraved with vegetable or flower names.

Loppers   One step up in power and size from the hand pruner and shears, loppers are designed to cut branches up to 3 inches (7.5 cm) in diameter. Loppers have a hooked nose to prevent branches from slipping out. Ratchet-action loppers make quick work of cutting by transferring the workload onto the tool from your wrist, which makes them a favorite of forestry workers. A good lopper is made of carbon steel with hardwood, aluminum, or steel handles. Cushioned grips are best.

Machete For chopping through brush and other clearing chores a 1 1/2–2-foot (30–45-cm) long machete is a handy item. Machetes are small enough to work with one hand but strong enough to hack through thorns and bramble. Rust-resistant carbon steel blades are first choice. Hardwood handles should fit your grip.

Mattock This digging and cutting tool with a pointed pick on one side and cutting blade on the other is useful for attacking tough shrubs and roots and for loosening rocks. Handle length is about 36 inches (90 cm) but smaller hand mattocks of a foot (30 cm) in length are available. Both versions should have solid forged carbon steel heads and high-quality hardwood handles. The head and handle should be securely fastened by an eye socket and bolt.

Meter, Moisture This simple tool has a graduated dial that indicates the humidity of your soil across a range of dry to wet. Insert the thin 3/4-inch (20-mm) probe deep into the soil and note the reading. However, readings mean nothing unless you know how much moisture a particular plant needs. Choose a meter that comes with a guide or booklet that addresses the particular needs of your plantings. Some models also come with light meters, which are particularly useful for indoor plants.

Misters These small, convenient watering devices that lightly humidify plants or seedling usually are made of plastic or glass. Larger models are available to cover vaster areas.

Netting A variety of sizes, weights, and shapes makes this accessory handy and adaptable to many garden situations. There are nets that can be used like trellises to help support pea, cucumber, and tomato plant growth. Other nets are designed to be draped over trees and vegetable patches to keep out pests and birds. Still others can be fashioned into hammocks to support heavy fruits such as melons and squashes. Most netting is made from nylon or polypropylene material and can be cut to fit the job.

Pants, Gardeners These sturdy cotton canvas pants offer lots of moving room, allowing you to bend or crawl in comfort. Reinforced knees or pockets for knee pads provide a welcome cushion for down-and-dirty jobs. Premium gardener's pants also feature loops and big side pockets to hold equipment.

Pad, Kneeling Soft, plastic-coated foam pads, usually with a carrying handle, protects knees from the hard ground surface when working in the garden. They are an inexpensive and convenient item that will greatly increase your enjoyment of gardening as a hobby by preventing injury and discomfort.

Pads, Knee Portable, lightweight knee pads can be strapped on and used for protection in small spaces where a kneeling bench won't fit. They should be made of closed-cell EVA foam, which is soft and water resistant. Some have hard shells of polyurethane that are ridged for a secure grip.

Pick A pick is pointed on one side and has a slightly narrow blade on the other. It is used like a chisel to break up tough clay or rocky soils and also makes a good prying tool. Don't use a pick to grub out roots as the pointed end can stick and wrench your back. A pick is swung like an ax and requires some strength and control. It typically weighs from 8–9 pounds (3.6–4 kg). A well-made model has a solid carbon steel head.

Pick-and-Hoe A miniature version of the mighty 8-pound (3.6-kg) standard pick, the pick-and-hoe weighs just 2 pounds (0.9 kg). The blade side of this tool can be used as a hoe to weed a small garden; the pick end breaks up soil and works well around trees and other areas a full-sized pick might mangle. Solid carbon steel heads and high-quality hardwood handles are the norm for the best models.

Planters, Bulb Depending on how many bulbs you are placing in the garden you can choose from two styles: short or long handled. If you don't mind kneeling for a bit to plant a small number of bulbs, a short-handled planter will suffice. For setting in hundreds of them a long-handled planter is a must to save your back. Both work the same way: Stamp the can-shaped device into the ground and pull up the dirt, leaving a hole fit for a bulb. Stamped-metal planters are inexpensive but will not hold up in the long term; the best models are made of stainless or carbon steel.

Planter, Bulb, Heavy-duty This is the tool for bulb planting in sod or grass. Push on the foot rest to work the planter in, then twist the handle to bring up the dirt. The T-shaped handle should have a rubber grip, and the tool should be forged of solid carbon steel.

Planter, Bulb, Quick-release A planter with a handle that squeezes the dirt together and then releases it easily, this tool saves strain on your wrist. It's also light-weight, at just under 1 pound (0.5 kg). The planter should be of high-quality steel.

Pots —See Containers, Plant

Pot, Peat Though peat pots are a little pricier than the average seedling-carrying plastic pot, their beauty is that they can be popped right into the soil, where the roots of the plant extend out of the peat and into the earth. Because the "pots" are made of organic material, they contribute nutrients to the soil as they decay. Easy as this sounds, peat pots must be kept moist until they are planted or the roots of the plant will harden and fail to take hold.

Presser board This stiff, flat, foot-long (30-cm) piece of hardwood with an attached handle presses the topsoil uniformly over new seed plantings. It not only keeps your hands clean but provides a more even tamping.

Sundial You promised yourself you were only going to check on the zucchini and pinch prune the tomatoes, and an hour later the sun sparkles off the beautiful bronze of the sundial, reminding you that the kids need to be picked up from soccer practice. The shadow falling across the calibrated face indicates it is time to get up and get going! Even if you can't make heads nor tails of sundial readings, a sundial, in many styles and forms, is a beautiful and historic accent for the garden.

Supports Twine, stakes, floral tape, and vine nails are the unheralded heroes of the garden. They hold up tender young plants, keep mature specimens from falling over in the wind and rain, train plants to grow in a desired direction, and keep fruits from direct contact with the soil. Supports come in many different forms and are made from rope, metal, bamboo, plastic, or wood.

T **Table, Potting** A work bench for the gardener, a potting bench traditionally is constructed of weather-resistant woods such as redwood or cedar [see Building a Potting Table, pg. 134]. Used primarily for propagation and storage, a potting bench offers a steady work surface for potting plants, setting seedlings, mixing materials, and making cuttings. A good bench should have decent storage for tools and equipment and ample workspace. Folding models are available if space is at a premium.

Tarps Made from burlap, canvas, polyester mesh, or polyethylene, tarps are as essential for piling and hauling clippings, cuttings, and weeds as the wheelbarrow is for transporting heavy objects. Some tarps have a built-in drawstring, which makes them extra secure and useful for gathering fruits and vegetables.

Thermometer, Compost This device will help you determine whether you need to turn or water the pile. The higher the temperature, the quicker material decomposes. A compost thermometer registers 0–220°F (-18–105°C), with an ideal cooking range of 95–131°F (35–55°C). The 20-inch (50-cm) temperature probe is constructed of stainless steel.

Ties Plant ties secure branches or stems around stakes and trellises. The best choices are foam-covered wire tires, which cushion and protect the plant; twine, which is sturdy and also biodegrades; and plant clips, which act like clothespins, for easy use and removal.

Tiller, Hand   This short-handled but strong 4-tined tool is designed to till and cultivate small areas of a vegetable or flower bed. The forged steel head works to loosen up the soil and also is useful for removing small rocks and roots. The standard size is 17-inches (43-cm) long with 5$\frac{1}{2}$-inch (14-cm) tines.

Timers   Automatic water timers can be set to cycle for dousing once a day, once a week, three times a day, or whatever your garden needs. Best of all, they supplant our own, sometimes unreliable, personal clocks, and just get the job done. Electronic timers, set to a start and duration time, are battery operated and hook on to the garden faucet. Non-electric timers are powered by the flow of the water and can be set to water once a day for a choice of length.

Tool Racks   Spare the tool shed or garage of clutter with a tool rack that allows you to hang shovels, hoes, rakes, loppers, and hats. Racks are made out of strong tubular steel, with a polyester or chrome finish. They also come in a more traditional pegged hardwood form.

Tote, Gardener's   If you don't feel like dragging around half the contents of your tool shed on your person, consider a garden tote. A good tote has a hard, flat bottom to keep items in place and offers lots of large side pockets. Best construction is of durable cotton canvas with a leather-reinforced handle.

Traps, Animal   Gophers, squirrels, raccoons, and opossums are just a few of the garden pests who can maim your fragile plants. To humanely trap these small creatures, a rust-resistant galvanized metal and wire mesh cage is best. No strong springs can hurt the animal or you. Bait it, trap your prey, and transport it to a shelter or natural woodland area. A variety of sizes exist to accommodate the size of your prey.

Traps, Insect   Mechanical bug traps prevent the use of chemical insecticides. One of the most popular traps is the lanternlike "bug zapper," which, when baited, attracts flies or wasps and kills them with electric current. At night, a light attracts even more specimens. Beetle and slug traps are also widely available.

Tray, Potting   If your potting bench is otherwise known as the breakfast nook or dining room table, a potting tray can help you plant your seeds *and* get a meal on the table. These sturdy polypropylene units hold small pots, trowels, and seeds, and have a raised back so that additional little buckets can be snapped on to hold extra items. Their compact dimensions—22 $\times$ 24 $\times$ 7$\frac{1}{2}$ inches (56 $\times$ 60 $\times$ 19 cm)—allow for easy cleanup and storage.

TROWELS—A small shovel for planting, weeding, mixing, and digging tasks, most trowels have round heads but some are pointed. Cheap trowels are constructed of stamped metal and are not well attached to their handles. As this tool will be with you for a long time, it's best to get one of forged carbon or stainless steel. The blade should be solidly riveted to a comfortable grip of high-quality polished hardwood. The standard trowel size is 12 1/2-inches (32-cm) long.

Trowel, Big American The "maxitruck" of trowels for major digging and transplant chores has a slightly pointed blade especially suitable for rocky soils. A solid socket should attach the carbon steel head to a hardwood handle. It weighs in at 1 pound (0.5 kg) and is 14-inches (35-cm) long. Use it for heavy chores that require moving lots of soil, and for larger plants.

Trowel, Long-Handled A good choice for hard to reach spaces in the vegetable garden, the long, narrow blade of this trowel makes it easy for the kneeling gardener to reach the back of a bed. Epoxy-covered carbon steel models cut through the soil with less effort.

Trowel, Transplanting This specialty planting/digging trowel has a long broad blade that digs deep into the soil. Excavate transplant holes and use it to blend potting mix with native soil. A rubber handle is a good grip choice and an epoxy-coated carbon steel blade makes this a tool that will last for years.

Trowel, Weeding The weeding trowel is distinguished by its long pointed blade. This is a tough trowel, designed to dig out difficult weeds. Your weeding work will be made easier if you pick an epoxy-coated steel model. The elongated shape and light weight of this trowel also make it useful for container gardening.

"There, with her baskets and spades and clippers, and wearing her funny boyish shoes and with the sunborn sweat soaking her eyes, she is part of the sky and earth, possibly a not too significant part, but a part."

Truman Capote

Trugs This traditional English flower carrier is made of light wood such as birch or is woven from rush. It is shallow, with a fairly flat, slatted bottom, making it ideal as a carrier for tender vegetables such as tomatoes, peppers, and eggplant. A newer version out of England is the tub trug, a flexible plastic bucket with handles that is ideal for transporting any harvest.

Twine   Made out of tightly woven jute or sisal threads for strength, twine primarily is used to tie seedlings to stake supports and direct the growth of more mature plants. Since twine is made out of natural material, it eventually biodegrades, which makes for a better garden aesthetic than do decaying pieces of plastic or metal.

Watering Can   The elegant copper watering can with a brass rose (the sprinkler nozzle at the end of the spout) has evolved from the primitive jugs and buckets our gardening ancestors used to haul water to the crops. Modern watering cans are made from galvanized steel, brass, copper, aluminum, or polyethylene. Usual capacity ranges from pints to gallons (0.5–2.8 l). Spouts are long or short, and the cans tall and oval or squat.

Watering Can, Conservatory   This style of can with a very long neck is useful for a collection of greenhouse plants, for the back of the vegetable bed, and for hanging baskets. The most durable cans are fashioned out of galvanized steel and have a brass rose (sprinkler head).

Weather Instruments   Rain gauges, outdoor thermometers, and humidity indicators are just some of the monitoring devices that give the gardener precise readings of the weather from inside the house. Gathering all of this information in a season's journal is a good way of keeping a history of your garden and noting the effects weather has on your plantings. The equipment is fairly inexpensive and available from garden supply stores, nurseries, and catalogs.

WEEDERS—There are many types of hand weeders to choose from, when your own well-gloved hand does not suffice. A good weeder should dig into the soil with little effort, slice out the weed and remove it, and have a slightly springy action to help cushion your hand if you strike a rock. Forged steel heads, no matter what the shape, are best, and a cushiony grip is also desirable.

Weeder, Cape Cod   This is a traditional weeder with a pointed, knifelike blade bent at a right angle to the handle, which makes it easy to maneuver around plantings. The narrowness of the blade and the pointed tip also make it a good tight-space tool. Best materials are high-carbon steel for the blade and a hardwood handle.

Weeder, Dandelion   Good for removing weeds with deep taproots, the 2 pronged mouth of this weeder is attached to a lever that locks the prongs around the root. The entire weed, root and all, is pulled out in one motion. This weeder is 4-feet (1.2-m) tall, which makes it more efficient for a large expanse of garden. Prong, lever, and socket should all be of cast steel with a rust-resistant finish.

Weeder, Fishtail or Asparagus   This weeder cuts off weeds at the root, and its narrow V-shaped blade makes it especially efficient for small or tight spaces. It's a good fit for a rock garden and around pavement. This short—15-inch (38-cm) long—but strong instrument should be constructed from forged carbon steel coated with enamel.

Weed Torch   You can dispense with the chemicals with this weed weapon. The 34-inch (86-cm) tube-torch runs on propane and the flame can be adjusted for intensity. One zap shrivels weeds in an instant, killing the root as well. It also comes in handy as a de-icer for walkways and porches.

"I've had enough of gardening—I'm just about ready to throw in the trowel."

Anonymous

Wheelbarrows   The "wooden ox," invented in China, is now constructed from solid galvanized steel. Then, as now, it is devoted to hauling rock, sand, dirt, compost, timber, and Halloween pumpkins. The beauty of the design is that the weight of all this matter rests on one pneumatic tire. Hardwood or steel tube handles make a wheelbarrow easy to lift and maneuver over all sorts of terrain.

Widgers   Made in England, with English precision, this shoehorn-shaped steel tool is 7-inches (18-cm) long and designed to carefully handle and place tiny seeds in soil. The miniature, concave end of the widger holds the seeds and rolls them out one at a time for the most precise planting control. This is a tool for the steady of hand.

Appendix

Plant Hardiness Throughout the World

Europe
Plant Hardiness Zones

4	-30 to -20°F (-34 to -29°C)
5	-20 to -10°F (-29 to -23°C)
6	-10 to 0°F (-23 to -18°C)
7	0–10°F (-18 to -12°C)
8	10–20°F (-12 to -6°C)
9	20–30°F (-6 to -1°C)
10	30–40°F (-1 to 4°C)

Australia
Plant Hardiness Zones

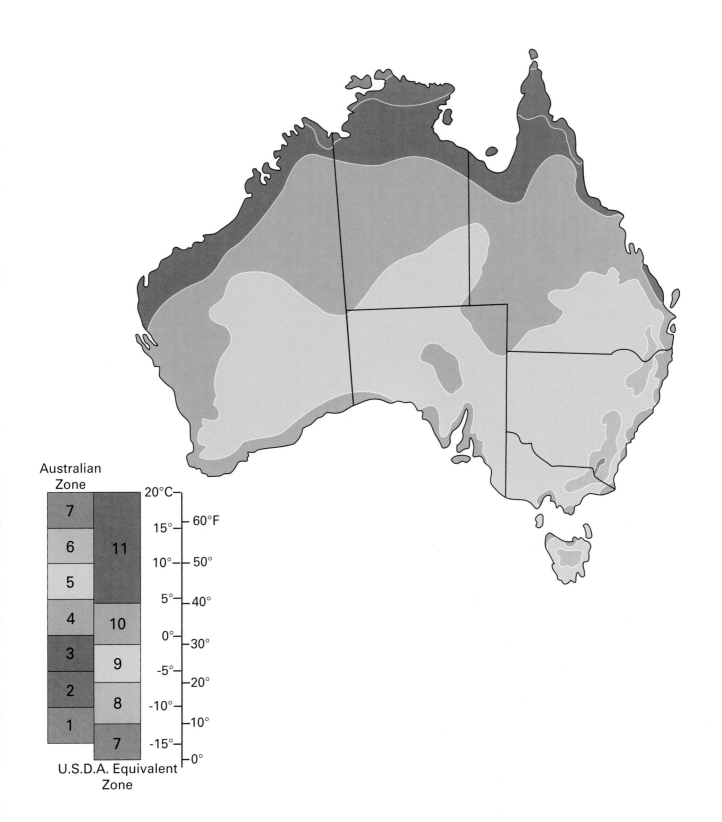

Australian Zone

7	11
6	
5	
4	10
3	9
2	8
1	7

20°C
15° — 60°F
10° — 50°
5° — 40°
0° — 30°
-5° — 20°
-10° — 10°
-15° — 0°

U.S.D.A. Equivalent Zone

VEGETABLE	MATURITY DAYS FROM SEED	FREEZING POTENTIAL	STORAGE TEMPERATURE	PERCENT HUMIDITY	LENGTH OF STORAGE
Amaranth	40–70	not recommended	45°F (7°C)	90	1–2 wks
Artichoke	perennial	not recommended	50°F (10°C)	80	1 wk
Asparagus	perennial	excellent	35°F (2°C)	90	2–3 wks
Bean, Asparagus	65–70	good	45°F (7°C)	90	1–2 wks
Bean, Broad	80-100	good	35°F (2°C)	90	1–2 wks
Bean, Lima	60–90	good	35°F (2°C)	90	1–2 wks
Bean, Runner	60–85	good	35°F (7°C)	90	1–2 wks
Bean, Snap	60–85	good	35°F (7°C)	90	1–2 wks
Beet	45–60	fair	35°F (2°C)	95	12–20 wks
Broccoli	55–85	excellent	35°F (2°C)	90	1–2 wks
Brussels Sprouts	80–90	excellent	35°F (2°C)	90	3–5 wks
Cabbage	50–100	not recommended	35°F (2°C)	90	3–5 wks
Cabbage, Chinese	50–85	not recommended	35°F (2°C)	90	4–8 wks
Cantaloupe	70–100	not recommended	40°F (4°C)	80	2–3 wks
Cardoon	160–180	not recommended	35°F (2°C)	90	1–2 wks
Carrot	40–60	excellent	35°F (2°C)	90	12–16 wks
Cauliflower	55–80	good	35°F (2°C)	85	2–4 wks
Celery	90–120	not recommended	35°F (2°C)	90	4–6 wks
Collards	60–90	fair	35°F (2°C)	90	1–2 wks
Corn, Ornamental	60–100	good	35°F (2°C)	90	less than 1 wk
Corn, Popcorn	60–100	good	35°F (2°C)	90	2–4 wks
Corn, Sweet	60–100	good	35°F (2°C)	90	less than 1 wk
Cress, Garden	40–70	not recommended	40°F (4°C)	90	1–2 wks
Cress, Water	55–70	not recommended	40°F (4°C)	90	1 wk
Cucumber	55–65	not recommended	40°F (4°C)	85	1–2 wks
Eggplant	100–140	not recommended	40°F (4°C)	90	1 wk
Endive	85–100	not recommended	35°F (2°C)	90	2–3 wks
Garlic	90+	excellent	35°F (2°C)	60	12–16 wks
Gourd	85–100	not recommended	55°F (13°C)	40	12–20 wks
Greens, Various	NA	not recommended	35°F (2°C)	90	1–3 wks
Herb, WS	NA	excellent	40°F (4°C)	80	3–4 wks
Herb, CS	NA	excellent	35°F (2°C)	90	2–3 wks
Kale	55–75	excellent	35°F (2°C)	90	1–2 wks
Kohlrabi	45–60	fair	35°F (2°C)	90	2–4 wks
Leek	120–170	excellent	35°F (2°C)	90	4–12 wks
Lettuce	65–80	not recommended	35°F (2°C)	90	2–3 wks

VEGETABLE	MATURITY DAYS FROM SEED	FREEZING POTENTIAL	STORAGE TEMPERATURE	HUMIDITY	LENGTH OF STORAGE
Melon	70–100	not recommended	45°F (7°C)	80	2–3 wks
Mustard	30–40	not recommended	35°F (2°C)	90	1–2 wks
Mustard-Spinach	40–60	good	35°F (2°C)	90	2–3 wks
Mustard, India	30–40	not recommended	35°F (2°C)	90	1–2 wks
Okra	55–65	good	45°F (7°C)	90	1 wk
Onion, Drying	80–150	excellent	35°F (2°C)	65	4–12 wks
Onion, Green	50–75	not recommended	35°F (2°C)	90	2–3 wks
Parsnip	100–130	fair	35°F (2°C)	90	8–12 wks
Pea, English	55–70	excellent	35°F (2°C)	90	1–3 wks
Pea, Snap	55–70	good	35°F (2°C)	90	1–2 wks
Pea, Southern	60–90	excellent	35°F (2°C)	50	8–12 wks
Pepper, Hot	60–95	fair	50°F (10°C)	90	2–3 wks
Pepper, Sweet	60–95	fair	50°F (10°C)	90	2–3 wks
Potato	90–110	not recommended	40°F (4°C)	80	12–16 wks
Potato, Sweet	110–150	fair	60°F (16°C)	75	12–16 wks
Pumpkin	90–120	fair	60°F (16°C)	60	8–16 wks
Radish	22–70	not recommended	35°F (2°C)	90	3–4 wks
Rhubarb	perennial	excellent	35°F (2°C)	90	2–4 wks
Roquette	90–100	not recommended	35°F (2°C)	90	1–2 wks
Rutabaga	60–90	fair	35°F (2°C)	90	8–16 wks
Salsify	120–150	fair	40°F (4°C)	90	8–12 wks
Shallot	60–120	excellent	35°F (2°C)	65	4–12 wks
Sorrel	perennial	not recommended	35°F (2°C)	90	1 wk
Soybean	45–100	good	35°F (2°C)	90	2–3 wks
Spinach	40–50	good	35°F (2°C)	90	1–2 wks
Spinach, N. Z.	50–75	not recommended	50°F (10°C)	90	1 wk
Squash, Summer	50–65	fair	45°F (7°C)	75	1–2 wks
Squash, Winter	60–110	good	55°F (13°C)	50	12–20 wks
Sunflower	70–80	good	40°F (4°C)	50	15–30 wks
Swiss Chard	45-55	good	35°F (2°C)	90	2–3 wks
Tomatillo	120	good	40°F (4°C)	75	4–6 wks
Tomato	50–90	good	40°F (4°C	80	1 wk
Tomato, Husk	120	good	40°F (4°C)	75	4–6 wks
Turnip	30–60	fair	35°F (2°C)	90	12–16 wks
Watermelon	90–110	not recommended	40°F (4°C)	80	2–3 wks

Resources

GARDENING ON-LINE

General Gardening Websites:

(www.botany.com) Botany.Com. Excellent plant encyclopedia. Lists by common and botanical names.

(www.gardenweb.com) GardenWeb. Extensive forums, links, seed plant exchange, site search, glossary.

(www.garden-gate.prairienet.org) The Garden Gate. Online books, magazines, catalogs, glossaries, shopping. Special Midwest oriented resources.

(www.horticulture.com) The Horticulture Web. Site search, business updates in agriculture.

(www.almanac.com/garden) The Old Farmer's Almanac. Gardener's companion, tips, charts, seed and watering information.

(www.sierra.com/sierrahome/gardening) SierraHome.Com. Extensive gardening links, product, gardening softwear, free downloads, how-to guides, plant encyclopedia.

(www.plants.usda.gov/plantproj/plants) United States Dept. of Agriculture Natural Resources Conservation Service. This is the site for the national plant database.

(www.reeusda.gov) Cooperative state and research education service of the USDA. Lists all state partners.

(www.homearts.com) HomeArts: Gardening. Excellent plant encyclopedia, discussion forums, seed swaps, link to Country Living Gardener.

(www.rebeccasgarden.com) Rebecca's Garden. Garden crafts, weather, tips, how-tos, message board, link to the television show.

(www.gardenguides.com) Garden Guides. Flower, vegetable and herb information site, search, links, forums, order catalogs.

(www.backyardgardener.com) Backyard Gardener. Information on various types of gardening: alpine, perennial, annual, vegetable. Valuable seed germination data base, (under propagation), and forums.

(www.vg.com) Virtual Garden: Where Gardens Grow. One of the best, most comprehensive sites. Time-Life plant encyclopedia, zone locator, search, gardening basics, library, landscaping tips, many links.

(www.gardennet.com) GardenNet. Plant information by type and group, links, catalog requests, shopping, discussion, travel information.

(www.gardentown.com) GardenTown. Major message board and chat room, lots of Canadian input.

(www.ortho.com) Ortho Online. Tips, ideas, books, search, flower and vegetable garden information, product list.

(www.nws.noaa.gov) National Weather Service home page. Radar, NWS regional reports, current conditions, forecasts.

(www.pp.clinet.fi/%7emygarden/frameone.htm) FlowerGarden. Good links, flower dictionary, gardening news, encyclopedia.

(www.plantamerica.com) PlantAmerica: Multimedia Tools for Horticulture and Design. Excellent directory; Nursery search, and state by state arboretum and garden search.

(www.tpoint.net/neighbor) or (www.io.com/neighbor) The Gardening Launch Pad. Many links, mostly non-commercial. Information, tips, categories of interest, zone finder.

(www.mastercomposter.com) Master Composter. Local, national and international programs, composting products, message board, how-to advice.

(www.garden.com) Garden.Com. Shopping, magazines, tips, chat, seeds, tools, accessories, books, zones.

Seed and gardening catalog companies:

(www.desertplants.com) American Desert Plants, Inc.

(www.arborandbloom.com) Arbor and Bloom

(www.burpee.com) Burpee Seed Company

(www.gardeners.com) Gardener's Supply Company

(www.heirloomseeds.com) Heirloom Seeds

(www.johnnyseeds.com) Johnny's Selected Seeds

(www.parkseed.com) Park Seed Company

(www.smithhawken.com) Smith & Hawken

(www.monticello.org) Thomas Jefferson Center for Historic Plants

(www.thompson-morgan.com) Thompson & Morgan Ltd.

(www.whiteflowerfarm.com) White Flower Farms

University horticultural sites:

(www.aggie-horticulture.tamu.edu) Texas A&M University, Aggie horticulture. Good southwest guide to wildflowers, extensive links, classes.

(www.hcs.ohio-state.edu) Ohio State University, horticulture and crop science. Covers trees, shrubs, groundcover, flowers, fruit, vegetables, landscaping. Search and links.

(www.uwex.edu/ces/ag) University of Wisconsin Extension - agriculture and natural resources. Newsletter, links, education.

(www.cce.cornell.edu/topics/agriculture.html) Cornell University Cooperative Extension. Agriculture site, topics in urban horticulture, sustainable agriculture, consumer horticulture; links to other resources.

(www.msue.msu.edu) Michigan State University Extension. Home horticulture and topics specific to various states; publications.

(www.gnv.ifas.ufl.edu/) University of Florida Institute of Food and Agriculture Sciences. Organic production, master gardener, extension agent resources, library.

(www.ou.edu/cas/botany-micro/www-vl/) University of Oklahoma - Virtual Library of Botany. Extensive links to university and research botanical sites; many links of use to home gardener.

Botanical Associations:

(www.aabga.org) American Association of Botanical Gardens and Arboreta. Supports North American botanical gardens. Newsletter, program and meeting information, links, internship listings.

(www.calhortsociety.org) California Horticultural Society. Education, links, programs.

(www.ars.org) American Rose Society. Reviews of rose varieties, show results.

(www.nargs.org) North American Rock Garden Society. Wildflowers, alpine flora, rock garden planting, seed exchange, construction advice, library, search.

(www.masshort.org) Massachusets Horticultural Society, founded 1829. Library, regional gardening information.

(www.bulbsociety.com) International Bulb Society. Forums, search, free downloads, bulb publications.

(www.cactus-mall.com/cssa) Cactus and Succulent Society of America, Inc. International organization dedicated to preservation of cactus and succulents. Mail order seed available.

(www.rhs.org.uk) Royal Horticultural Society. RHS flower trials and research, plant breeding, articles, plant collection database.

Botanical Gardens:

(www.nybg.org) New York Botanical Garden. Plant information, shopping, search, library.

(www.bbg.org) Brooklyn Botanical Gardens. Ideas for the garden, shopping, search.

(www.mobot.org) Missouri Botanical Garden. Education, horticulture, links, library, research.

(www.chicago-botanic.org) Chicago Botanic Garden. Reference, tour, database for regional plants, book reviews, plant information.

(www.butchartgardens.com) The Butchart Gardens, Vancouver Island. Visitor guide, history, images.

(www.rbgkew.org.uk) The Royal Botanic Gardens, Kew. Information on what's new, collections, history, databases, can order publications online.

Online Gardening Magazines:

(www2.garden.org/nga) National Gardening Magazine, published by National Gardening Association. Gardening articles, tips, article search, email queries.

(www.chestnut-sw.com) Weekend Gardener. Advice, links, weather guide.

(www.gardenweb.com/cyberplt) The Cyber-Plantsman. Online magazine of GardenWeb: events, book reviews, glossary, people in gardening.

(www.digmagazine.com) Dig Magazine: Home and Garden Diversions. Articles, forums, plant maintenance.

(www.taunton.com/fg) Fine Gardening Online. Articles, index, current issue.

(www.hortmag.com) Horticulture Magazine Online. Current articles, shopping, back issues.

(www.hortuswest.com) Hortus West: A Western North America Native Plant Directory and Journal. Order article reprints, preview current articles, seed search, message board.

SEED CATALOGS

Abundant Life Catalog
P.O. Box 772
Port Townsend, WA 98368

Agway Inc
Box 4933
Syracuse, NY 13221-4933

Bountiful Gardens
18001 Shafer Road
Willits, CA 95490

Burgess Seed & Plant
1700 Morrissey Dr
Bloomington, IL 61704-7100

Comstock Ferre & Co
263 Main St or 236 Main St (?)
Wethersfield, CT 06109-1822

Cooks Garden
P.O. Box 535
Londonderry, VT 05148

Cruickshank's
1015 Mount Pleasant Road
Toronto, Ontario M4P 2M1

D V Burrell Seed Growers Co
P.O. Box 150
Rocky Ford, CO 81067-0150

De Giorgi Seed Co
6011 N St
Omaha, NE 68117-1634

Ed Hume Seeds
P.O. Box 1450
Kent, WA 98035

Fedco Seeds Inc
P.O Box 520
Waterville, ME, 04903

Garden City Seeds
778 Highway 93 North
Hamilton, MT 59840

Garden of Delights
14560 SW 14th St
Fort Lauderdale, FL 33325-4217

Gardens Alive
5100 Schenley Pl
Lawrenceburg, IN 47025-2181

Geo. W. Park Seed Co. Inc.
1 Parkton Ave.
Greenwood, SC 29647-0001

Gurney Seed & Nursery Corp
110 Capital St
Yankton, SD 57079

Harris Seeds
P.O. Box 22960
Rochester, NY 14692-2960

Jackson & Perkins Company
P.O. Box 1028
Medford. OR 97501-0198

Johnnys Selected Seeds
Foss Hill Rd
Albion, ME 04910

Liberty Seed Company
P.O. Box 806
New Philadelphia, OH 44663-0806

Otis Twilley Seed Co Inc
121 Gary Road
Hodges, SC 29653

Peaceful Valley Farm Supply
P.O. Box 2209
Grass Valley, CA 95945-2209

Redwood City Seed Company
Box 361
Redwood City, CA 94064-0361

Shepherds Garden Seeds
30 Irene Street
Torrington, CT 06790

Southern Exposure Seed Exchange
P.O. Box 170
Earlysville, VA 22936

Stark Brothers
P.O. Box 10
Louisiana, MO 63353

Stokes Seeds Inc
183185 W Blvd
Fredonia, NY 14063

Territorial Seed Company
20 Palmer Ave
Cottage Grove, OR 97424-951

The Gourmet Gardener
8650 College Blvd
Overland Park, Kansas 66210

Tomato Growers Supply Co Inc
P.O. Box 2237
Fort Myers, FL 33902

Tripple Brook Farm
37 Middle Rd
Southampton, MA 01073-9584

Vesey's Seeds for Short Seasons
P.O. Box 9000
Calais Me 04619

W. Atlee Burpee CO
300 Park Ave
Warminster, PA 18991-0001

Index

A

Access paths, 127, 149
Advice, 100, 138, 174
Amaranth, 33, 168, 308
  soil temperature, 162
  spacing, 176 (table) (see also Spacing)
American Horticultural Society, 97
Ants, 266
Artichokes, 28, 128, 277–278, 287, 308
  soil temperature, 162
  spacing, 176 (table) (see also Spacing)
Asparagus, 309
  companion planting, 117–118 (see also Planting)
  harvesting, 28, 32, 128, 277, 279 (see also Harvest)
  mulching, 34 (see also Mulch)
  seeds, 168
  soil temperature, 162
  spacing, 176 (table) (see also Spacing)
  storage, 292 (see also Storage)
Asparagus, beans, 162
Autumn
  cool-season vegetables, 36
  harvesting, 286 (see also Harvest)
  planning, 33–37 (see also Planning)
  storage, 289 (see also Storage)

B

Bacillus thuringensis (BT), 240–241, 251
Bacteria. (see Disease; Fungus)
Bats, 265
Beans
  asparagus, 162
  broad, 162, 168
  butter, 313
  chickpeas, 312
  dried, 310–311
  fava, 311–312
  garbanzo, 312
  gram, 312
  green, 291
  harvesting, 28, 33, 277, 282–284 (see also Harvest)
  horse, 311–312
  lima, 162, 168, 176, 313
  planting, 32, 166–168 (see also Planting)
  pole, 33, 199, 229
  preserving, 33, 294, 303 (see also Preserving)
  romano, 314
  runner, 162, 168, 176

  snap, 162, 168, 176, 314
  soy, 163, 169, 177, 315
  storage, 291 (see also Storage)
  supports, 33, 231 (see also Supports)
  wax, 314
  windsor, 311–312
  yam, 339–340
Bees, 149
Beets, 162, 168, 315
  harvesting, 33, 273 (see also Harvest)
  planting, 34 (see also Planting)
  preserving, 301–304 (see also Preserving)
  spacing, 176 (table) (see also Spacing)
  storage, 292 (see also Storage)
Belgian endive, 328–329
Berries
  blackberry, 316
  blueberry, 317–318
  currant, 318–319
  elderberry, 319
  gooseberry, 318–319
  harvesting, 28, 32–33 (see also Harvest)
  mulching, 34 (see also Mulch)
  preserving, 295 (see also Preserving)
  raspberry, 319–320
  strawberry, 320–321
Bibb, lettuce, 343–344
Bin, compost, 210–211
Birds, 186–187, 239, 258, 265
Blackberries, 316
Blanching, 295 (see also Preserving)
Blueberries, 317–318
Bok choy, 278, 329
Bolting, 32–33, 115, 277
  care, 191 (see also Care)
  planning, 33, 110 (see also Planning)
  timing, 108
Bone meal, 207
Borders, 4–5
  fences, 43
  terraces, 2–3, 94
  trellises, 233
Boring pests, 251 (see also Pest control)
Brining, 293 (see also Preserving)
Broad, beans, 162, 168
Broccoli, 162, 168, 321–322
  harvesting, 283–284 (see also Harvest)
  planting, 32 (see also Planting)

preserving, 301–304 (see also Preserving)

spacing, 176 (table) (see also Spacing)

storage, 292 (see also Storage)

watering, 199 (see also Watering)

Brussels sprouts, 162, 168, 176, 277–278, 322

Buds, 224

Bugs (see Insect damage; Pest control; Pests)

Burn, chemical, 182

Butter, beans, 313

Butterhead, lettuce, 343–344

C

Cabbage, 162, 168, 278, 323–324, 329

Chinese, 278, 329

harvesting, 28, 278, 283–284 (see also Harvest)

preserving, 292–293 (see also Preserving)

spacing, 176 (table) (see also Spacing)

watering, 199 (see also Watering)

Cabbage, Chinese, 162, 176

Cages, 33 (see also Supports)

Calendar, 30, 162–163 (see also Seasons)

Canning, 28, 293, 300 (see also Preserving)

Cantaloupes, 114–115, 162, 168, 176

Captan, 268

Cardoon, 162, 168, 176

Care, 27, 29, 65–68

bolting, 191 (see also Bolting)

cultivation, 56–57, 65, 189, 190 (see also Cultivation)

disease, 56–57 (see also Disease)

fertilizer, 65, 189–190 (see also Fertilizer)

fungus, 185 (see also Fungus)

mulching, 56–57, 65, 189, 191 (see also Mulch)

nutrients, 48

pests, 56, 58 (see also Insect damage; Pest control; Pests)

planning, 101–102, 125 (see also Planning)

plant loss, 102

pruning, 189, 191 (see also Pruning)

rewards of, 121

seedlings, 178 (see also Seedlings)

shaping, 189, 191

sunlight, 65 (see also Sunlight)

supports, 189, 191 (see also Supports)

thinning, 189, 191

transplants (see Transplants)

watering, 65, 189–190 (see also Watering)

Carrots, 162, 168, 324–325

harvesting, 28, 33, 109, 273, 287 (see also Harvest)

planting, 32, 110 (see also Planting)

preserving, 295, 301–304 (see also Preserving)

seed leaves, 179–180

spacing, 176 (table) (see also Spacing)

thinning, 226–227

Catalogs, 25, 130, 133, 141, 147, 153

Cauliflower, 162, 168

broccoflower, 325

harvesting, 28, 283–284 (see also Harvest)

planting, 32 (see also Planting)

preserving, 301–304 (see also Preserving)

spacing, 176 (table) (see also Spacing)

watering, 199 (see also Watering)

Cayenne pepper spray, 261–263

Celeriac, 287–288, 326–327

Celery, 168

celeriac, 287–288, 326–327

harvesting, 283, 285 (see also Harvest)

planting, 114–115 (see also Planting)

preserving, 301–304 (see also Preserving)

spacing, 176 (table) (see also Spacing)

Celery, cabbage, 329

Celtuce, lettuce, 344–355

Chard, 163, 277–278, 303, 373–374

Chayote, 327

Chemical burn, 182, 212, 214

Chemical control (see also Insect damage; Pest control)

agents, 246

beneficial insects, 264–265

benlate, 270

boring pests, 251

captan, 268

fertilizer, 207 (see also Fertilizer)

fungus, 270 (see also Fungus)

herbicides, 217

maneb, 268

pesticides, 182, 207, 214, 217, 238, 242, 246

results, 270–271

rodents, 260

slugs, 255

spraying, 238 (see also Spraying)

terraclor, 270

when to use, 242

whiteflies, 256–257

Cherries, ground, 338

Cherry, tomatoes, 374–375

Chickpeas, 312

Chili, peppers, 358–359

Chinese, cabbage, 162, 168, 176, 278, 329

Chives, 282, 329–330

harvesting, 277 (see also Harvest)

storage, 291 (see also Storage)

Chloropyrifos, 251

Choy, 278, 329, 351–352

Chutneys, 298–299

Climate, 69–70, 99–100 (see also Microclimates; Temperature; Weather)

average growing temperature, 86–87

cold-winter, 78
Gulf Stream, 79
information, 80
location, 33, 69–70, 85 (see also Location)
man-made structures, 90–91
microclimates (see Microclimates)
mild-winter, 79
planning, 69 (see also Planning)
radiated heat, 88–89
reflected light, 89–90
seasonal changes, 80–83
sunlight angle, 80–82 (see also Sunlight)
temperature, 75, 78, 85, 87 (see also Temperature)
timing, 87
zones, 71–74 (see also Zones)
Cloche, 165
Club root, 270
Cold frames, 53
    construction of, 158–160, 164
    germination, 157, 164–165 (see also Germination)
    hardening, 164, 180
    transplants, 151 (see also Transplants)
Collards, 162, 168, 176, 330–331
Companion planting, 116–118, 242 (see also Planting)
Compost, 19 (see also Mulch)
    adding, 51
    disease, 35 (see also Disease)
    making, 208
    nutrients, 215
    organic, 212 (see also Organic)
    peppers, 212
    pH, 212
    soil preparation, 40, 49, 140 (see also Preparing; Soil)
    spring, 31
    sterilization, 166, 212
    tomatoes, 212
Compost bin, 210–211
Conservation, water, 94
Containers
    decorative, 149
    drainage, 174 (see also Drainage)
    gardening in, 2, 6, 9, 122, 172
    peat pots, 172
    plant quality, 175
    sterilization, 167
    transplants, 173–175, 178 (see also Transplants)
    watering, 174 (see also Watering)
Control (see Chemical control; Pest control)
Cooking, 115, 291, 298–299, 375–376
Cool-season vegetables, 43, 85, 155 (see also Vegetables)
Corn, 30
    harvesting, 28, 33, 277, 281 (see also Harvest)

hybrid, 103
ornamental, 162, 168, 176, 331–332
peas use for support, 117 (see also Supports)
planting, 32 (see also Planting)
pollination, 105
popcorn, 162, 168, 176, 331–332
preserving, 33, 294, 301–304 (see also Preserving)
storage, 291 (see also Storage)
sweet, 162, 168, 176
watering, 199 (see also Watering)
Cos, lettuce, 346–347
Cress, 162, 168, 176
Crisphead, lettuce, 345–346
Cucumbers, 162, 168, 332–333
    companion planting, 117 (see also Planting)
    frost, 33 (see also Frost)
    harvesting, 28, 34, 109, 277 (see also Harvest)
    preserving, 301–304 (see also Preserving)
    spacing, 176 (table) (see also Spacing)
    storage, 291 (see also Storage)
Cultivation, 216–219 (see also Tilling)
    care, 56–57, 65, 189, 190 (see also Care)
    raised beds, 218 (see also Raised beds)
    roots, 216–217 (see also Roots)
    row gardens, 4
    soil texture improved by, 219 (see also Soil)
    supports, 231 (see also Supports)
    transplants, 183 (see also Transplants)
Currants, 318–319

D
Damping off, 186, 268
Decorative, containers, 149
Decorative, corn, 281, 331–332
Deer, 58, 261
Dehydration, 33, 84, 291, 294–295 (see also Drying)
Dehydrator, 33, 84, 291, 294–295
Depth, planting, 168–169 (table) (see also Planting)
Determinate, tomatoes, 105
Diazinon, 251
Dirt (see Soil)
Disease, 267–271 (see also Fungus)
    care, 56–57, 185 (see also Care)
    cold and damp weather, 154
    compost, 35, 166 (see also Compost)
    conditions, 57
    damage, 185–186
    damping off, 186
    fungal, 267
    humidity, 84
    inspecting for, 56
    pests, 239 (see also Pest control; Pests)
    pH, 140–141

planting, 27 (see also Planting)
preventing, 268
prions, 207
pruning, 228 (see also Pruning)
resistant plants, 267
rodents transmit, 260
row gardens, 5
signs, 178
sterilization, 172
summer, 33
variety, 138
viral, 57, 186, 267
watering, 185 (see also Watering)
Double digging, 47, 51, 102, 139, 142–143, 213
roots, 50–51
Downy mildew, 268 (see also Disease; Fungus)
Drainage, 52, 59, 63–64, 93, 95
containers, 174
planning, 93, 95 (see also Planning)
Dried, beans, 310–311
Drying, 33, 282, 291, 294 (see also Preserving)
onions, 163, 169, 177

E

Eggplant, 162, 168, 273, 333–334
harvesting, 277, 280 (see also Harvest)
preserving, 294–295 (see also Preserving)
spacing, 176 (table) (see also Spacing)
storage, 291 (see also Storage)
supports, 231–232 (see also Supports)
Elderberries, 319
Endive, 162, 168
curly, 334–335
escarole, 334–335
harvesting, 277–278 (see also Harvest)
spacing, 176 (table) (see also Spacing)
English, peas, 163, 169, 177, 355–356
Erosion, 95, 222

F

Fall (see Autumn)
Fava, beans, 311–312
Fencing, 43 (see also Borders)
Fennel, 287–288
Fertility test, 141–142 (see also Testing)
Fertilizer, 207
applying, 182, 214
bone meal, 207
care, 65, 189, 190 (see also Care)
chemical, 207
chemical burn, 182, 212, 214
compost, 208 (see also Compost)
foliar, 213

fungus, 185 (see also Fungus)
liquid, 208
manure, 208
mulch, 222 (see also Mulch)
nutrients, 185
organic, 182, 207, 265 (see also Organic)
problems, 215
root zone, 213
seeds, 182 (see also Seeds)
selection, 206–208
soil preparation, 26, 140 (see also Preparing; Soil)
solid, 208
specialty, 214
spring, 32
teas, 208
Flowers, 106, 233
Foliage, 27, 32, 185
Foliar, fertilizer, 213
Freezing, 28, 103, 292–293, 301–302 (see also Preserving)
French intensive gardening, 6, 47, 102, 122
Frogs, 265
Frost
cold and damp weather, 154–155
cucumbers, 33
harvesting, 288 (see also Harvest)
mild-winter, 79
mulch, 35 (see also Mulch)
seasons, 75, 78, 85
spring, 31
tomatoes, 33
zones (see Zones)
Fruit, 232
Fungus (see also Disease; Mildew)
care, 185 (see also Care)
club root, 270
cold and damp weather, 154
compost, 166 (see also Compost)
controlling, 57, 268
damping off, 186
downy mildew, 268
fertilizer, 185 (see also Fertilizer)
humidity, 84
mulch, 222 (see also Mulch)
oxygen, 195
powdery mildew, 270
preventing, 268, 270
pruning, 228 (see also Pruning)
row gardens, 5
soil temperature, 31 (see also Soil; Temperature)
sterilization, 172
storage, 290, 292 (see also Storage)
types of, 267–268

G

Garbanzo, beans, 312
Garlic, 162, 168, 329–330, 335–336
  harvesting, 33, 283–284 (see also Harvest)
  preserving, 294–295, 302 (see also Preserving)
  rotation and variation, 119
  spacing, 176 (table) (see also Spacing)
  storage, 291 (see also Storage)
Germination, 168–169 (table)
  microclimates, 156 (see also Microclimates)
  mulch, 173 (see also Mulch)
  planting depth, 166–169 (table) (see also Planting)
  seeds, 172 (see also Seeds)
  soil, 166 (see also Soil)
  soil temperature, 154
  sprouting, 179
  temperature, 157, 164 (see also Temperature)
  transplants, 151 (see also Transplants)
Giardiniera, 295–297
Gooseberries, 318–319
Gophers, 58, 259
Gourds, 34, 162, 168, 176, 336–337
Gram, beans, 312
Grapes, 295
Green, beans, 291
Green, onions, 177
Greenhouse
  germination, 157, 165 (see also Germination)
  mini, 9
  seedlings, 9, 151–152 (see also Seedlings; Transplants)
Ground, cherries, 338
Growing seasons (see also Seasons)
  frost, 85 (see also Frost)
  sunlight, 83 (see also Sunlight)
  zones (see Zones)
Growth cycle, 87
Gulf Stream, 79
Gypsum, 63

H

Hardening, 54
  cold frames, 164, 180 (see also Cold frames)
  transplants, 178–181 (see also Transplants)
Harvest, 28, 168–169 (table), 273–275
  amaranth, 33
  artichokes, 28
  asparagus, 28, 32, 277, 279
  beans, 28, 33, 277, 282–284
  beets, 33–34, 273, 292, 301–304
  berries, 28, 32–33
  cabbage, 28
  carrots, 28, 33, 109, 273

  cauliflower, 28
  continuous, 277–282
  corn, 28, 33
  cucumbers, 28, 34, 109
  flavor, 1, 17, 274, 280, 286, 293, 302
  garlic, 33
  gourds, 34
  lettuce, 28, 32, 109
  mature, 283–286
  melons, 33–34
  mulch, 273, 287 (see also Mulch)
  onions, 32–33, 109
  parsnips, 33
  peanuts, 33
  peas, 28, 32–33
  peppers, 33, 109
  planning, 108, 127 (see also Planning)
  popcorn, 33
  potatoes, 33–34, 273
  pumpkins, 28, 34
  radishes, 28, 32
  rhubarb, 32
  root crops, 28, 273
  salsify, 33
  shallots, 33
  spinach, 32
  squash, 28, 33–34
  storage, 274 (see also Storage)
  summer, 33
  supports, 231 (see also Supports)
  sustained, 102, 105
  sweet potatoes, 33, 287–288
  timing, 108
  tomatillos, 33
  tomatoes, 28, 33, 109
Heat zones, 97
Heirloom vegetables, 20–23 (see also Vegetables)
Herb garden, 6
Herbicides, 217
Herbs, 162, 168, 291
Hills, 64, 170–171, 196
Hobby, gardens, 17–19, 20, 37
Horse, beans, 311–312
Horseradish, 277–278, 287, 337
Hoses, soaker, 52, 102
Hot, peppers, 163, 169, 358–359
Hot frames, 133
Humidity, 84, 88–91, 194, 292 (see also Moisture; Watering)
Husk, tomatoes, 163, 299, 338
Hybrid, corn, 103
Hydroponics, 199
Hylemya antiqua, 119

I

Iceberg, lettuce, 345–346
Indeterminate, tomatoes, 105
India, mustard, 169, 177
Indian, corn, 331–332
Insect damage
  chewing, 239–243
  controlling (see Pest control)
  scoring and rasping, 248–251
  sucking, 244–248
  transplants, 178 (see also Transplants)
Insecticidal soaps, 251
Insecticides, 246 (see also Pesticides)
Insects, 186–187 (see also Insect damage; Pests)
  beneficial, 264–265
  controlling (see Pest control)
  spraying for (see Chemical control)
Integrated Pest Management, 238
Intensive, 6, 47, 102, 122 (see also Raised beds)
Irrigation (see also Watering)
  adjusting, 201
  drip, 202
  hoses, 201
  in-ground, 198–200
  mounds, 171
  pipe, 52
  planning, 101 (see also Planning)
  row, 196
  row gardens, 4–5
  watering cans, 201

J

Jams, 298–299
Jerusalem artichokes, 287, 338–339
Jicama, 287–288, 339–340

K

Kale, 162, 168, 340–341
  harvesting, 288 (see also Harvest)
  planting, 34 (see also Planting)
  preserving, 303 (see also Preserving)
  spacing, 176 (table) (see also Spacing)
Kohlrabi, 162, 168, 341–342
  harvesting, 283, 285 (see also Harvest)
  preserving, 295 (see also Preserving)
  spacing, 176 (table) (see also Spacing)

L

Landscaping
  access paths, 127
  leveling, 94
  microclimates, 88, 90, 156 (see also Microclimates)
  trees, 91

Leaf, lettuce, 346
Leeks, 162, 168, 287–288, 302, 342–343
  preserving, 294–295 (see also Preserving)
  spacing, 176 (table) (see also Spacing)
  storage, 291 (see also Storage)
Legumes, 294
Lettuce, 162, 169, 343–347
  bibb, 343–344
  butterhead, 343–344
  harvesting, 28, 32, 109, 277–278, 283–284 (see also Harvest)
  spacing, 177 (table) (see also Spacing)
  storage, 292 (see also Storage)
  thinning, 226
  watering, 199 (see also Watering)
Leveling, 94
Lima, beans, 162, 168, 176, 313
Lizards, 265
Loam, 45 (see also Soil)
Location, 42–43, 93, 187 (see also Planning; Preparing; Spacing)
  climate, 69–70 (see also Climate)
  direction, 95
  landscaping (see Landscaping)
  microclimates, 88–91 (see also Microclimates)
  rotation and variation, 119
  seeds or transplants, 149 (see also Seeds; Transplants)
  shaping, 189, 191
  size, 103–107, 120
  slope, 93–94
  temperature, 85 (see also Temperature)
  terrain, 95
  water, 94–95 (see also Watering)
  wind, 150
  zones, 71–74 (see also Zones)
Looseleaf, lettuce, 346

M

Mammals, 186–187
  controlling, 258, 259–263
  deer, 58, 261
  gophers, 58, 259
  moles, 58, 259
  opossums, 261
  rabbits, 261
  rats, 260
Maneb, 268
Man-made structures, 88–91 (see also Microclimates)
Melons, 163, 169, 273, 347–350
  harvesting, 33–34, 283–284 (see also Harvest)
  irrigation, 198 (see also Irrigation)
  mulching, 222 (see also Mulch)

preserving, 301–304 (see also Preserving)

spacing, 177 (table) (see also Spacing)

storage, 290–291 (see also Storage)

summer, 291

supports, 33, 230–232 (see also Supports)

winter, 290

Meter, pH, 140–141

Mexican, potatoes, 339–340

Microclimates (see also Climate; Weather)

germination, 156 (see also Germination)

  landscaping, 88, 90, 156 (see also Landscaping)

  man-made structures, 88, 90, 156

  radiated heat, 88–89

  reflected light, 89–90

  soil temperature, 156 (see also Soil; Temperature)

  wind, 90

Microgardening, 6–7, 9 (see also French intensive gardening; Raised beds)

Mildew (see also Fungus)

  downy, 268

  powdery, 270

  row gardens, 5

Mild-winter, 79

Miniature, tomatoes, 374–375

Mini-greenhouse, 9

Moisture, 84 (see also Watering)

  humidity, 84, 88, 91, 194, 292

  mulch, 173 (see also Mulch)

Moles, 58, 259

Mollusks, 186–187, 239, 252–255

Mounds, 64, 171, 196

  irrigation, 171 (see also Irrigation)

Mulch, 18, 220–223

  asparagus, 34

  berries, 34

  boring pests, 251

  care, 56–57, 65, 189, 191 (see also Care)

  compost (see Compost)

  erosion, 222

  fertilizer, 222 (see also Fertilizer)

  frost, 35 (see also Frost)

  fungus, 222 (see also Fungus)

  germination, 173

  harvesting, 273, 287 (see also Harvest)

  low-growing crops, 33

  moisture, 173 (see also Humidity)

  nitrogen, 66

  nutrients, 215

  organic, 222 (see also Organic)

  pest control, 257–258 (see also Pest control)

  plastic sheeting, 220–222, 251–253, 287

  postseason care, 29

  spring, 31

  straw, 66, 155, 222–223

  temperature, 173

  transplants, 180 (see also Transplants)

  watering, 173 (see also Watering)

Mustard, 163, 169, 350

  harvesting, 277–278 (see also Harvest)

  preserving, 303 (see also Preserving)

  spacing, 177 (table) (see also Spacing)

N

Natural fertilizer, 182 (see also Compost; Fertilizer; Mulch)

Nematodes, 252–253

Nitrogen, 44, 48, 182, 204, 206

  lacking, 185

  mulch, 66 (see also Mulch)

  salts, 141

  soil preparation, 139 (see also Preparing; Soil)

Nutrients, 48, 185, 215 (see also Compost; Fertilizer; Mulch)

O

Okra, 163, 169, 177, 291, 351

Onions, 163, 169, 351–352

  harvesting, 32–33, 109, 277, 282–284 (see also Harvest)

  planting, 110 (see also Planting)

  preserving, 294–295, 302 (see also Preserving)

  rotation and variation, 119

  spacing, 177 (table) (see also Spacing)

  storage, 291 (see also Storage)

Opossums, 261

Organic

  chemical analysis, 48

  compost, 208, 212 (see also Compost)

  fertilizer, 207 (see also Fertilizer)

  garden, 264–265

  mulch, 222 (see also Mulch)

  pest control, 237–238, 246 (see also Pest control)

  pesticides, 242–243, 246–247

Ornamental, corn, 162, 168, 176

P

Pak choy, 329, 351–352

Parsnips, 33, 163, 169, 353–354

  harvesting, 287 (see also Harvest)

  preserving, 295 (see also Preserving)

  spacing, 177 (table) (see also Spacing)

Paths, 127

Peanuts, 354

  harvesting, 33, 283, 285 (see also Harvest)

  planting, 114–115 (see also Planting)

  preserving, 33 (see also Preserving)

Peas, 277, 355–357
  drying, 282
  English, 169, 177, 355–356
  harvesting, 28, 32–33, 282–284 (see also Harvest)
  planting, 32 (see also Planting)
  planting depth, 166–167, 169 (table)
  preserving, 33, 294, 303 (see also Preserving)
  snap, 169, 177
  southern, 163, 169, 177
  storage, 291 (see also Storage)
  supports, 117, 231 (see also Supports)
Peas, English, 163
Peas, snap, 163
Peat pots, 172, 179
Peppers, 357–360
  cayenne, 261–263
  chili, 358–359
  composting, 212 (see also Compost)
  harvesting, 33, 109, 277, 280 (see also Harvest)
  hot, 163, 169
  preserving, 294–295, 299, 302 (see also Preserving)
  spacing, 177 (see also Spacing)
  storage, 291 (see also Storage)
  sweet, 163, 169
Perennials, 117, 287
Pest control, 14 (see also Pests)
  Bacillus thuringensis (BT), 240–241
  beneficial insects, 264–265
  beneficial plants, 266
  birds, 258
  chemical, 237–238, 242, 248–249 (see also Chemical control)
  compost, 265 (see also Compost)
  deer, 58, 261
  gophers, 58, 259
  hand control, 248, 255
  insecticidal soap, 242–245, 248
  Integrated Pest Management, 238
  moles, 259
  mulch, 257–258, 265 (see also Mulch)
  natural, 252
  opossums, 261
  organic, 237–238, 242, 246 (see also Organic)
  organic gardening, 264–265
  pillbugs, 257
  rabbits, 261
  rodents, 260
  sowbugs, 257
  whiteflies, 256–257
Pesticides, 182, 207, 214, 217, 238, 242, 246, 249
  chemical, 182, 207, 214, 217, 238, 242, 246 (see also Chemical control)
  organic, 242–243, 246–247, 251 (see also Organic)

Pests, 186–187 (see also Insect damage; Pest control)
  ants, 244–245
  birds, 258
  boring, 250–251
  care, 56, 58 (see also Care)
  chewing, 239–243
  companion planting, 116 (see also Planting)
  deer, 58, 261
  detection of, 58
  gophers, 58, 259
  Hylemya antiqua, 119
  infestations, 58
  inspecting for, 56, 102
  moles, 58, 259
  mollusks, 252–255
  nematodes, 252–253
  pillbugs, 257
  rabbits, 58, 261
  rodents, 260
  scoring and rasping, 248–251
  slugs, 58, 252, 254–255
  snails, 58, 252, 254–255
  sowbugs, 257
  sucking, 244–248
  whiteflies, 256–257
pH, 139-142
  compost, 212 (see also Compost)
  testing, 139–142 (see also Testing)
Phosphorus, 44, 48, 182, 204, 206
  lacking, 185
  man-made, 207
  plant quality, 175
  soil preparation, 139 (see also Preparing; Soil)
  testing, 141 (see also Testing)
Pickling, 295–297
Pillbugs, 257
Pinching, 224–226 (see also Pruning)
Planning, 17–19, 25–26, 99–100 (see also Preparing)
  autumn, 33–37 (see also Autumn)
  calendar, 30, 162–163
  care, 101–102 (see also Care)
  climate, 69 (see also Climate)
  drainage, 93, 95 (see also Drainage)
  drawing garden plans, 125–126
  harvesting, 108–110, 127 (see also Harvest)
  irrigation, 101 (see also Irrigation)
  landscaping (see Landscaping)
  location (see Location)
  overproduction, 106
  postseason care, 29
  preserving, 133, 138 (see also Preserving)
  raised beds, 131 (see also Raised beds)
  size, 103–107, 120

soil preparation, 102 (see also Soil)

spring, 30–32

summer, 32–33

sunlight, 125–127, 131 (see also Sunlight)

variety, 133–138

Plans, 125–126

Planter boxes, 8

Plant hardiness zones (see Zones)

Planting

beans, 32

beets, 34

broccoli, 32

calendar, 162–163

carrots, 32, 110

cauliflower, 32

celery, 114–115

companion planting, 116–118, 242

corn, 32

depth, 166–169 (table)

disease, 27 (see also Disease)

kale, 34

onions, 110

peanuts, 114–115

peas, 32

preparing for, 99–100 (see also Preparing)

pumpkins, 32, 171

radishes, 32

roots, 166

rutabagas, 34

salsify, 34

seasons, 75, 78 (see also Seasons)

seedlings, 53–54 (see also Seedlings)

seeds, 53, 166–167, 170 (see also Seeds)

spinach, 114–115

squash, 32, 171

succession, 114–116

sunlight, 155 (see also Sunlight)

sweet, potatoes, 32

tomatoes, 32

transplants, 53–54, 181 (see also Transplants)

turnips, 34

watering, 170–171 (see also Watering)

Planting depth, 166–168 (table)

Plants, 27 (see also Vegetables)

beans (see Beans)

beets, 33–34, 273, 292, 301–304

beneficial, 266

broccoli, 32, 199, 283–284, 292, 301–302

cantaloup, 114–115

carrots, 110 (see also Carrots)

cauliflower (see Cauliflower)

celery (see Celery)

chickpeas, 312

companion planting, 116–118

corn (see Corn)

cultivation, 216–219 (see also Cultivation)

decorative, 149

decorative containers for, 149

disease, 185–186, 267–271 (see also Disease)

enjoyment, 147

fertilizer (see Fertilizer)

hardiness zones, 71–74 (see also Zones)

harvesting (see Harvest)

kale, 34, 288, 303, 340–341

nourishment, 204–205

onions (see Onions)

options, 53–55

peanuts, 33, 114–115, 283, 285, 354

peas, 355–357 (see also Peas)

pests (see Pest control; Pests)

planting depth, 166–169 (table) (see also Planting)

problems, 184–187

pumpkins (see Pumpkins)

quality, 175

radishes (see Radishes)

rotation and variation, 119

rutabagas, 34, 287, 295, 301–304, 365

salsify, 33–34, 336

seasons, 75, 78 (see also Seasons)

seeds, 166–167 (see also Seeds)

selecting, 173–175, 178

simple needs of, 2, 39, 66, 101, 132

soil temperature, 162–163 (table) (see also Soil; Temperature)

spacing, 176–177 (table) (see also Spacing)

spinach (see Spinach)

squash (see Squash)

stress, 59

succession planting, 87, 114–116

supports, 229–234 (see also Supports)

Swedish turnips, 365

sweet potatoes (see Sweet, potatoes)

tomatoes (see Tomatoes)

turnips, 34, 287, 295, 301–304, 378

variety, 133–138

warm-season, 155

watermelons, 114–115

zones (see Zones)

Plastic sheeting, 220–222, 251–253, 287

Plowing (see Tilling)

Pole, beans, 33, 199, 229

Pollination, 105

Popcorn, 162, 168, 331–332

harvesting, 33, 281 (see also Harvest)

preserving, 33, 294 (see also Preserving)

spacing, 176 (table) (see also Spacing)

Postseason care, 29 (see also Care)
Potassium, 44, 48, 182, 204, 206
  man-made, 207
  preparing soil, 139 (see also Preparing; Soil)
  testing, 141 (see also Testing)
Potatoes, 163, 169, 285, 360–362
  harvesting, 33–34, 273, 283 (see also Harvest)
  Mexican, 339–340, 349–350
  new, 285, 291
  preserving, 301–304 (see also Preserving)
  spacing, 177 (table) (see also Spacing)
  storage, 289, 291 (see also Storage)
  sweet, 163, 169, 177 (see also Sweet, potatoes)
Pots, peat, 172
Potting soil, 152, 166 (see also Soil)
Potting table, 134–137
Powdery mildew, 270 (see also Fungus)
Precipitation, 84, 88 (see also Humidity; Moisture;
  Watering)
Preparing, 17–19, 26, 42–43 (see also Location;
  Planning)
  compost, 140 (see also Compost)
  fertilizer, 140 (see also Fertilizer)
  garden care, 101–102 (see also Care)
  landscaping (see Landscaping)
  planning plantings, 99–100 (see also Planting)
  row gardens, 5
  soil, 139–144, 170 (see also Soil)
  tilling, 52–51, 139, 142–144
Preserving (see also Storage)
  beans, 33, 294, 303
  berries, 295
  blanching, 295
  brining, 293
  cabbage, 293
  canning, 28, 293, 300
  cold and moist, 292
  cool and dry, 285, 291
  corn, 33
  drying, 282–283, 293, 295–297 (see also Drying)
  flavor, 1, 17, 274, 293, 302–303
  freezing, 28, 103, 292–293, 301–302
  fungus, 292 (see also Fungus)
  giardiniera, 295–297
  jams, jellies, and preserves, 298–299
  nutrition, 293
  peanuts, 33
  peas, 33, 282
  pickling, 293, 295–297
  planning, 133, 138 (see also Planning)
  popcorn, 33
  preparing vegetables for, 302 (see also Preparing)
  processing, 28, 292

  refrigeration, 282, 291
  relishes, 295–297
  salt, 293, 295–297
  spinach, 293
  storage, 289–292 (see also Storage)
  texture, 1, 293
  tomatoes, 105, 294–295, 299, 301–304
  vinegar, 295–297
  warm and dry, 290
Processing, 28, 292 (see also Preserving)
Pruning, 224, 226–228
  care, 189, 191 (see also Care)
  compound, 228
  fungus, 228 (see also Fungus)
  pinching, 224–226
  shaping, 228
  thinning, 224, 226–227
  tools, 26, 29, 35, 228
Pumpkins, 163, 169, 362–363
  harvesting, 28, 34, 283 (see also Harvest)
  irrigation, 198 (see also Irrigation)
  mulching, 222 (see also Mulch)
  planting, 32, 171 (see also Planting)
  preserving, 301–304 (see also Preserving)
  spacing, 177 (table) (see also Spacing)
  storage, 289–290 (see also Storage)
  supports, 33, 230, 232 (see also Supports)
  winter, 289

R

Rabbits, 58, 261
Radiated heat, 88–90
Radicchio, 328–329
Radishes, 163, 169, 363–364
  harvesting, 28, 32, 287 (see also Harvest)
  planting, 32 (see also Planting)
  preserving, 301–304 (see also Preserving)
  spacing, 177 (table) (see also Spacing)
  thinning, 226
Rain, 84, 88 (see also Watering)
Raised beds, 8–9
  cultivating, 218 (see also Cultivation)
  location, 93 (see also Location)
  planning, 26, 131 (see also Planning)
  soil, 6, 47 (see also Soil)
  temperature, 86 (see also Temperature)
Raspberries, 319–320
Rats, 260
Reflected light, 89–90
Refrigeration, 282 (see also Preserving)
Regions, 36, 71–74 (see also Zones)
Relishes, 295–297
Reverse-season, 80

Rhubarb, 163, 169, 364–365
  harvesting, 32, 277–278 (see also Harvest)
  preserving, 299, 301–304 (see also Preserving)
Rodents, 58, 259–260
Romaine, lettuce, 346–347
Romano, beans, 314
Rootbound, 179
Root line, 219
Roots
  asparagus (see Asparagus)
  crops, 273
  cultivation, 216–217 (see also Cultivation)
  depth, 142
  development, 179
  double digging, 50–51 (see also Double digging)
  fertilizer, 182 (see also Fertilizer)
  fungus, 270 (see also Fungus)
  planting, 166 (see also Planting)
  soil, 166 (see also Soil)
  transplants, 174, 180 (see also Transplants)
  watering, 193 (see also Watering)
Root zone, 213
Roquette, 163, 169, 177
Rotation, 119
Rotenone, 242
Row gardens, 4–5, 122
Runner, beans, 162, 168
Rutabagas, 163, 169, 365
  harvesting, 287 (see also Harvest)
  planting, 34 (see also Planting)
  preserving, 295, 301–304 (see also Preserving)
  spacing, 177 (table) (see also Spacing)

S

Salsify, 163, 169, 366
  harvesting, 33 (see also Harvest)
  planting, 34 (see also Planting)
  spacing, 177 (table) (see also Spacing)
Sauerkraut, 293
Scaled-down, gardens, 6–7 (see also Raised beds)
Seasons
  autumn (see Autumn)
  calendar, 30, 162–163
  changes, 80–83
  growing, 83, 85
  planting, 75, 78 (see also Planting)
  reverse-season, 80
  sunlight, 155 (see also Sunlight)
  winter, 36, 78, 349–350
  zones (see Zones)
Seed catalogs, 25, 130, 133, 141, 147, 153
Seed leaves, 179
Seedlings, 108–109 (see also Transplants)

  care, 178 (see also Care)
  choosing, 147–153
  cold frames, 152 (see also Cold frames)
  fertilizer, 182–183 (see also Fertilizer)
  greenhouse, 9, 151, 152
  insect damage, 178 (see also Insect damage; Pest control)
  long-harvesting, 153
  options for planting, 53–54 (see also Planting)
  planning, 108–109 (see also Planning)
  selecting, 152–153, 173–175, 178
  soil, 139–144 (see also Soil)
  storing, 178
  temperature, 151 (see also Temperature)
  thinning, 226–227
  transplants, 138 (see also Transplants)
  vegetables (see Vegetables)
  watering, 175, 185 (see also Watering)
Seeds
  asparagus, 168
  catalogs, 25, 130, 133, 141, 147, 153
  choosing, 40, 147–153
  containers, 172 (see also Containers)
  fertilizer, 182 (see also Fertilizer)
  germination, 172 (see also Germination)
  planting, 53, 166–167, 170 (see also Planting)
  planting depth, 167–169 (table)
  selecting, 152–153
  soil, 139–144 (see also Soil)
  spacing, 170 (see also Spacing)
  watering, 167, 170 (see also Watering)
Sets, 150–151
Shallots, 163, 169, 366–367
  harvesting, 33, 283–84, 288 (see also Harvest)
  preserving, 302 (see also Preserving)
  spacing, 177 (table) (see also Spacing)
  storage, 291 (see also Storage)
Shaping, 189, 191, 228 (see also Location; Planning)
Size, 103–106 (see also Location; Planning)
  sustained harvesting, 102, 105 (see also Harvest)
  yield, 102, 120
Slugs, 58, 186–187, 239, 252, 254–255
Small-space gardens, 6–7, 9 (see also French intensive gardening; Raised beds)
Snails, 58, 239, 252, 254–255
Snakes, 265
Snap, beans, 162, 168, 314
Snap, peas, 163, 169, 177, 355–356
Soaker hoses, 52, 102
Soap, insecticidal, 242–245, 248, 251
Soil, 187
  amendments, 50, 52
  cultivation, 219 (see also Cultivation)

erosion, 95, 222
fertility testing, 141–142
final preparation, 52, 180
germination, 166 (see also Germination)
improving, 47, 49–52
loam, 45
location, 40 (see also Location)
lure of, 20–23, 132
microclimates, 156 (see also Microclimates)
moisture testing, 199, 201 (see also Moisture)
mulch (see Mulch)
pH, 139–142
potting, 152, 166
preparation, 49–50, 139–144, 170 (see also Preparing)
raised bed gardens, 6 (see also Raised beds)
roots, 166 (see also Roots)
samples, 140
solarization, 252–253
temperature, 27, 31, 86, 154–155, 162–163 (table)
    (see also Temperature)
testing, 45–47, 51, 61, 139–142 (see also Testing)
texture, 44–47, 49–50, 139, 219
Soker hoses, 197–198
Solarization, 252–253
Solstice, 82
Sorrel, 163, 169, 177, 273, 277–278
Southern, peas, 163, 169, 177, 356
Sowbugs, 257
Soybeans, 163, 169, 177, 315
Spacing, 125, 127, 176–177 (table) (see also Location)
    recommend, 138, 167
    thinning, 226–227 (see also Cultivation)
    transplants, 181 (see also Transplants)
Spinach, 163, 169, 273, 367–368
    harvesting, 32, 277–278 (see also Harvest)
    planting, 53, 114–115, 166–167 (see also Planting)
    preserving, 293, 303 (see also Preserving)
    spacing, 177 (table) (see also Spacing)
    thinning, 226
Spraying, 238
    cayenne pepper, 261–263
    organic pesticides, 247 (see also Organic; Pest control)
Sprouts, 368
Squash, 273, 291, 369–371
    harvesting, 28, 33–34, 283 (see also Harvest)
    irrigating, 198 (see also Irrigation)
    mulching, 222 (see also Mulch)
    planting, 32, 53, 166–167, 171 (see also Planting)
    preserving, 301–304 (see also Preserving)
    seed leaves, 179–180
    storage, 289 (see also Storage)
    summer, 163
    supports, 33, 230 (see also Supports)

Squash, summer, 169, 177
Squash, winter, 163, 169, 177
Staking, 33, 189, 191, 229–234 (see also Supports)
Sterilization, 166–167, 172, 212
Storage, 289–292 (see also Preserving)
    beans, 291
    cold and moist, 292
    cool and dry, 291
    dehydrated vegetables, 33, 84, 291, 294–295
    fungus, 290, 292 (see also Fungus)
    humidity, 84, 292
    preserving, 292 (see also Preserving)
    refrigerator, 291
    warm and dry, 290
Storing, 28, 178 (see also Preserving)
Strawberries, 320–321
Structures, 88–91, 156
Succession planting, 53, 114–116, 166–167 (see also Planting)
Sugar, peas, 357
Summer, melons, 348–349
Summer, squash, 163, 169, 369–370
    harvesting, 28, 277, 280 (see also Harvest)
    spacing, 177 (table) (see also Spacing)
    storage, 291 (see also Storage)
    supports, 231–232 (see also Supports)
Sunchokes, 338–339
Sunflowers, 163, 169, 177, 371–372
Sunlight, 83
    angle, 80–82
    care, 65 (see also Care)
    direction, 95
    location, 40, 43 (see also Location)
    man-made structures, 90
    planning, 125–127, 130, 150 (see also Planning)
    planting, 155 (see also Planting)
    plant quality, 175
    seasons, 83, 155 (see also Seasons)
    shade, 87
    solarization, 252–253
    temperature, 165 (see also Temperature)
    trees, 69–70
    weeds, 220
Supports, 27, 189, 191, 229–234
    beans, 33, 231
    cages, 33
    decorative, 233
    fruit, 232
    melons, 33
    pumpkins, 33
    row gardens, 5
    squash, 33
    stakes, 33

transplants, 185 (see also Transplants)

trellises, 233

Swedish, turnips, 365

Sweet, corn, 162, 168, 176

Sweet, peppers, 163, 169, 359–360

Sweet, potatoes, 163, 169, 301–304, 372–373

  harvesting, 33, 287–288 (see also Harvest)

  planting, 32, 53, 166–167 (see also Planting)

  spacing, 177 (table) (see also Spacing)

  storage, 289–290 (see also Storage)

Swiss, chard, 163, 169, 373–374

  harvesting, 278 (see also Harvest)

  preserving, 303 (see also Preserving)

  spacing, 177 (table) (see also Spacing)

T

Table, potting, 134–137

Temperature, 71–74, 162–163 (table) (see also Climate)

  amaranth, 162

  artichokes, 162

  asparagus, 162

  average growing, 86–87

  cool and damp, 284

  effects of, 85–87

  flowering, 85

  germination, 154, 157 (see also Germination)

  harvesting, 284, 288 (see also Harvest)

  highs, 80

  ideal, 87

  location, 85 (see also Location)

  maximum, 87

  microclimates, 88–91 (see also Microclimates)

  minimum, 74–75, 78, 85

  mulch, 173 (see also Mulch)

  protection, 33

  radiated heat, 88–89

  raised beds, 86 (see also Raised beds)

  reflected light, 89–90

  soil, 31, 86, 155 (see also Soil)

  storage, 289 (see also Storage)

  sunlight, 165 (see also Sunlight)

  timing, 87

  transplants, 151 (see also Transplants)

  vegetables, 154 (see also Vegetables)

  winter, 78

Terraces, 2–3, 94

Terraclor, 270

Terrain (see Location)

Testing, 139–142

  fertility, 141–142

  moisture, 61–62 (see also Moisture)

  soil, 45–47, 51–52, 61–62 (see also Soil)

  watering, 62 (see also Watering)

Texture, 63

  improving, 219

  preserving, 1, 293

  soil, 44–47, 49–50, 139, 219

Thinning, 27, 189, 191, 224, 226–227

Tilling, 52–51, 139, 142–144 (see also Cultivation; Weeds)

Toads, 265

Tobacco, 267

Tomatillos, 163, 169, 338

  harvesting, 33, 277, 280 (see also Harvest)

  preserving, 299 (see also Preserving)

  spacing, 177 (table) (see also Spacing)

Tomatoes, 163, 169, 374–377

  cherry, 374–375

  compost, 212 (see also Compost)

  cooking, 115, 375–376

  determinate, 105

  frost, 33 (see also Frost)

  harvesting, 28, 33, 109, 277, 283, 286 (see also Harvest)

  husk, 163, 299

  indeterminate, 105

  miniature, 374–375

  planting, 32, 53, 166–167 (see also Planting)

  preserving, 105, 294–295, 299, 301–304 (see also Preserving)

  pruning, 224–226 (see also Pruning)

  slicing and eating, 377

  spacing, 177 (table) (see also Spacing)

  storage, 290–291 (see also Storage)

  supports, 231–232 (see also Supports)

  thinning, 228

  tobacco, 267

Tools, 26, 29, 35, 166, 170, 228

Transplants, 54, 108–109 (see also Seedlings)

  care, 178 (see also Care)

  choosing, 147–153

  cold frames, 152 (see also Cold frames)

  containers, 173–175, 178 (see also Containers)

  cultivation, 183, 219 (see also Cultivation)

  fertilizer, 182–183 (see also Fertilizer)

  greenhouse, 151–152

  hardening, 178–181 (see also Hardening)

  insect damage, 178 (see also Insect damage; Pest control)

  long-harvesting vegetables, 153

  mulching, 180 (see also Mulch)

  planting, 53–54, 181 (see also Planting)

  roots, 174, 179

  selecting, 152–153, 173–175, 178

  soil preparation, 139–144 (see also Preparing; Soil)

  spacing, 181 (see also Spacing)

storing, 178
supports, 185 (see also Supports)
temperature, 151 (see also Temperature)
vegetables (see Vegetables)
watering, 175, 181 (see also Watering)
weather, 185
Trees, 90–91
  sunlight, 69–70 (see also Sunlight)
  wind, 90–91
Trellises, 233 (see also Supports)
Turnips, 163, 169, 378
  harvesting, 287 (see also Harvest)
  planting, 34 (see also Planting)
  preserving, 295, 301–304 (see also Preserving)
  spacing, 177 (table) (see also Spacing)

U

U.S. Department of Agriculture, 100

V

Variety, 133–138
Vegetables, 54, 108–109 (see also Plants; Seedlings)
  average growing temperature, 86–87 (see also
    Temperature)
  beans (see Beans)
  beets, 33–34, 273, 292, 301–304
  bolting, 115 (see also Bolting)
  broccoli, 32, 199, 283–284, 292, 301–302
  cantaloup, 114–115
  carrots, 110 (see also Carrots)
  cauliflower (see Cauliflower)
  celery (see Celery)
  chickpeas, 312
  companion planting, 116–118
  cooking with, 115, 291, 298–299, 375–376
  cool-season, 36, 80, 85, 91, 154–155, 199
  corn (see Corn)
  cultivating, 216–219 (see also Cultivation)
  dehydrated, 33, 84, 291, 294–295 (see also Drying)
  disease, 185–186, 267–271 (see also Disease)
  fertilizer (see Fertilizer)
  flavor, 1, 17, 274, 286, 293, 302
  hardiness zones, 71–74 (see also Zones)
  harvesting (see Harvest)
  heirloom, 20–23
  kale, 34, 288, 303, 340–341
  loss, 102
  nourishment, 204–205
  onions (see Onions)
  organic, 264–265 (see also Organic)
  peanuts, 33, 114–115, 283, 285, 354
  peas, 355–357 (see also Peas)

pests (see Pest control; Pests)
planning (see Planning)
planting depth, 166–169 (table) (see also Planting)
problems, 184–187
pumpkins (see Pumpkins)
quality, 120
radishes (see Radishes)
roots, 28, 287 (see also Roots)
rotation and variation, 119
rutabagas, 34, 287, 295, 301–304, 365
salsify, 33–34, 336
seasons, 75, 78 (see also Seasons)
seeds, 166–167 (see also Seeds)
selecting, 173–175, 178
simple needs of, 2, 39, 66, 101, 132
soil temperature, 162–163 (table) (see also Soil;
  Temperature)
spacing, 125, 127, 176–177 (table) (see also Spacing)
spinach (see Spinach)
squash (see Squash)
storage, 289–292 (see also Storage)
stress, 59
succession planting, 87, 114–116
sunlight (see Sunlight)
supports, 229–234 (see also Supports)
Swedish turnips, 365
sweet potatoes (see Sweet, potatoes)
tomatoes (see Tomatoes)
turnips, 34, 287, 295, 301–304, 378
variety, 116, 133–138
warm-season, 35, 85, 91, 154–155
watering, 170 (see also Watering)
watermelons, 114–115
zones (see Zones)
Vinegar, 295–297 (see also Preserving)
Vines, 191

W

Watercress, 378–379
Watering, 59–64, 192 (see also Irrigation)
  acid rain, 59
  cans, 197
  care, 65, 189, 190 (see also Care)
  conservation, 94
  containers, 172, 174
  cool-season vegetables, 199
  correct way, 184, 199–202
  disease, 185 (see also Disease)
  drainage, 52, 59, 63–64, 93, 95 (see also Drainage)
  harvest, 284 (see also Harvest)
  hills, 64, 171, 196
  humidity, 84, 88–91, 194, 292

hydroponics, 199
location, 40, 95 (see also Location)
mulch, 173 (see also Mulch)
osmosis, 193–194, 204
overhead, 196
over watering, 195
planting, 170–171 (see also Planting)
plant quality, 175
problems, 184, 194–195
roots, 217
row irrigation, 196
seedlings, 185 (see also Seedlings)
seeds, 167, 170 (see also Seeds)
soker hoses, 197
spring, 32
summer, 33
supports, 231 (see also Supports)
testing, 61–62 (see also Testing)
texture, 45–47, 59, 63
transpiration, 193
transplants, 175, 181 (see also Transplants)
water stress, 59–60
Watermelons, 114–115, 163, 169, 177
Wax, beans, 314
Weather (see also Climate; Microclimates)
cold and damp, 155
hardening (see Hardening)
man-made structures, 90–91, 156
mulch, 155 (see also Mulch)
transplants, 185 (see also Transplants)
Weeds, 65, 217 (see also Cultivation; Tilling)
care, 56 (see also Care)
mulch (see Mulch)
sunlight, 220 (see also Sunlight)
Whiteflies, 256–257
Wind, 88–91
location, 150 (see also Location)
microclimates, 90 (see also Microclimates)
pollination, 105
trees, 90–91
Windowsill germination, 165
Windsor, beans, 311–312
Winter
cool-season vegetables, 36
melons, 349–350
temperature, 78 (see also Temperature)
Winter, squash, 163, 169, 283, 370–371

Y

Yam, beans, 339–340
Yams, 372–373
Yield, 120

garden size, 103–107, 120
raised bed gardens, 8 (see also Raised beds)

Z

Zones, 70–74
cold-winter, 78
frost, 79 (see also Frost)
Gulf Stream, 79
location, 71–74 (see also Location)
mild-winter, 79
reverse-season, 80
seeds or transplants, 149–150 (see also Seeds;
Transplants)
storage, 289 (see also Storage)
sunlight angle, 80–82 (see also Sunlight)
year-round gardening, 79
Zucchini, 369–370